Studies in International Relations

Edited by

Charles MacDonald
Florida International University

A Routledge Series

Studies in International Relations

Charles MacDonald, *General Editor*

Promoting Women's Rights
The Politics of Gender in the European Union
Chrystalla A. Ellina

Turkish Foreign Policy and Turkish Identity
A Constructivist Approach
Yücel Bozdağlioğlu

Organizing the World
The United States and Regional Cooperation in Asia and Europe
Galia Press-Barnathan

Human Rights in Cuba, El Salvador and Nicaragua
A Sociological Perspective on Human Rights Abuse
Mayra Gómez

Negotiating the Arctic
The Construction of an International Region
E. C. H. Keskitalo

The Common Fisheries Policy in the European Union
A Study in Integrative and Distributive Bargaining
Eugénia da Conceição-Heldt

Malaysia and the Development Process
Globalization, Knowledge Transfers and Postcolonial Dilemmas
Vanessa C. M. Chio

International Environmental Treaties and State Behavior
Factors Influencing Cooperation
Denise K. DeGarmo

Political Corruption in the Caribbean Basin
Constructing a Theory to Combat Corruption
Michael W. Collier

International Election Monitoring, Sovereignty, and the Western Hemisphere Idea
The Emergence of an International Norm
Arturo Santa-Cruz

International Election Monitoring, Sovereignty, and the Western Hemisphere Idea

The Emergence of an International Norm

Arturo Santa-Cruz

Routledge
New York & London

Published in 2005 by
Routledge
Taylor & Francis Group
270 Madison Ave,
New York NY 10016

Published in Great Britain by
Routledge
Taylor & Francis Group
2 Park Square,
Milton Park, Abingdon,
Oxon, OX14 4RN

Routledge is an imprint of Taylor & Francis Group.

Transferred to Digital Printing 2009

International Standard Book Number-10: 0-415-97443-7 (Hardcover)
International Standard Book Number-13: 978-0-415-97443-1 (Hardcover)
Library of Congress Card Number: 2005015187

Library of Congress Cataloging-In-Publication Data

Santa Cruz, Arturo.
International election monitoring, sovereignty, and the Western hemisphere idea : the emergence of an international norm / Arturo Santa-Cruz.
p. cm. -- (Studies in international relations)
Includes bibliographical references and index
ISBN10: 0-415-97443-7 (hbk)
ISBN10: 0-415-80335-7 (pbk)

ISBN13: 978-0-415-97443-1 (hbk)
ISBN13: 978-0-415-80335-9 (pbk)

1. Election monitoring. 2. Sovereignty. 3. Intervention (International law)--Political aspects. 4. Election monitoring--South America--Case studies. 5. South America--Politics and government. I. Title. II. Series: Studies in international relations (Routledge (Firm))

JF1001.S243 2005
320.1'5'098--dc22 2005015187

T&F informa
Taylor & Francis Group
is the Academic Division of T&F Informa plc.

Visit the Taylor & Francis Web site at
http://www.taylorandfrancis.com

and the Routledge Web site at
http://www.routledge-ny.com

Publisher's Note
The publisher has gone to great lengths to ensure the quality of this reprint but points out that some imperfections in the original may be apparent.

To Brigit, Hannah, and Diego

Contents

Preface

International election monitoring is an intriguing subject in part because it suggests a paradox: cross-boundary involvement in a domestic affair. It is intriguing of course only because of the assumption that state borders are sacrosanct. Scholarship, in contrast, attempts to be more of a commons or an agora, in which academics trade on a stock of knowledge and engage each other in an argumentative process. In putting a puzzle together, in this case, the effect of international election monitoring on state sovereignty, it is advisable to find partners and mentors. For as Keynes wrote, "It is astonishing what foolish things one can temporarily believe if one thinks too long alone." While writing this book, which comes out of my doctoral dissertation, I was lucky and found the right company. I thus incurred many intellectual and personal debts to a lot of people. I would like to thank them here for their time and support. First, I thank Peter J. Katzenstein for believing in this project and for his constant encouragement and enlightened suggestions, which were an exceptional stimulus for pursuing this work. I would also like to thank, Valerie Bunce, Mathew Evangelista, Kathleen O'Neill, and Hector Schamis for their valuable comments and suggestions while this work was a dissertation.

Without my interviewees' cooperation, I could have not carried out this research. I therefore thank Sergio Aguayo, Jorge Alcocer, Genaro Arriagada, Judy Butler, Thomas Carothers, Manuel Carrillo, father Miguel D'Escoto, Ramiro de Valdivia, Hernán Felipe Errázuriz, Melvin Estrada, Mariano Fiallos, Linda Frey, Larry Garber, Juan Ignacio García, Oscar Godoy, Carlos Huneeus, Mónica Jiménez, Matías Krüger, Antonio Lacayo, César Landa, Shelly McConell, Jennifer McCoy, Patrick Merloe, Santiago Murray, Nguyen Huu-Dong, Robert Pastor, Carlos Portales, Jeffrey Puryear, Rafael Roncagliolo, Elizabeth Spehar, Martín Tanaka, Manuel Tello, monsignor Sergio Valech, Allen Weinstein, José Woldenberg, Kenneth Wollack, Rosa Marina Zelaya, and those who asked to remain anonymous.

I also would like to acknowledge here the priceless contributions of hospitality, logistics, and locating documents always delivered with grace and without return, provided by friends and family: Peter Costantini, Bruce D'Arcus, Beth Fugget, Joel Migdal, Holly Ruthrauff, Rick Rice, Jacqueline Rioja, Laura Santa Cruz, Stella Villagrán, and Ana Laura Zapién. I would like to thank my colleagues at the Department of Pacific Studies at the University of Guadalajara for creating the friendly and collaborative intellectual environment in which the writing of this work took place. I am also indebted to Charles MacDonald for reading the entire manuscript and making useful suggestions to improve it, to Benjamin Holtzman, my editor at Routledge, for his patience and timely support, and to Michelle Merritt for her proofreading. Brigit and Hannah from the beginning, and Diego a few months after, provided the joy that has encouraged me to keep working on this project, and gave my work healthy perspective. This book is dedicated to them.

For funding this project and my studies at Cornell at different stages I thank the Latin American Studies Program and the Einaudi Center, at Cornell University; the MacArthur, Ford, and Hewlett Foundations (through the Institute of International Education); Mexico's Consejo Nacional de Ciencia y Tecnología (Conacyt), Programa de Mejoramiento del Profesorado (Promep), and the Fundación Magdalena O. vda. de Brockmann.

For permission to publish parts of work that I have previously published, I acknowledge:

Instituto de Ciencia Política, Pontificia Universidad Católica de Chile, for permission to use sections of "From Transition to Consolidation: Mexico's Long Road to Democracy," *Revista de Ciencia Política* 22 (1), and "Redefining Sovereignty, Consolidating a Network: Monitoring the 1990 Nicaraguan Elections," *Revista de Ciencia Política* 24 (1).

Cambridge University Press, for permission to use sections of "Monitoring Elections, Redefining Sovereignty: The 2000 Peruvian Elections as an International Affair," *Journal of Latin American Studies* 37 (4).

Cambridge University Press, for permission to use sections of "Constitutional Structures, Sovereignty, and the Emergence of International Norms: The Case of International Election Monitoring," *International Organization* 59 (3).

Colegio de México, for permission to use sections of "Creando una red y redefiniendo la soberanía: La observación del plebiscito chileno de 1988" *Foro Internacional* 45 (3).

Taylor & Francis Group, for permission to use sections of "From Santiago to Lima: The Organization of American States and Political Integration in the Americas after the Cold War," *Global Change, Peace & Security* 17 (2).

Center for the Pacific Rim, University of San Francisco, for permission to use sections of "Redefining Sovereignty, Monitoring the 1994 Mexican Elections," *Pacific Rim Report* 37.

Institute for International Studies, University of Technology, Sydney, for permission to use sections of "The Emergence of a Transnational Advocacy Network: International Election Monitoring in the Philippines, Chile, Nicaragua, and Mexico," *Portal: Journal of Multidisciplinary International Studies*, Vol. 1, No. 2.

Introduction

National elections are now international events—and international election monitoring (IEM) an institutionalized practice in world politics.[1] Thus, for instance, the United Nations (UN), the Organization of American States (OAS), the Commonwealth, and the Organization on Security and Cooperation of Europe all engage in it. However, election monitoring is not the monopoly of intergovernmental organizations (IGOs). There are many international nongovernmental organizations (INGOs) actively involved in this practice as well; the Carter Center, the International Human Rights Law Group, and the Washington Office on Latin America, are three well-known examples.

But the institutionalization of IEM is recent. Fifteen years ago, none of the IGOs mentioned above systematically observed electoral processes in sovereign states. Interestingly, though, INGOs have been monitoring elections regularly since the early 1980s. The emergence and subsequent normalization of IEM are puzzling. Why has international election watching come to figure so prominently in the international agenda in less than two decades? Furthermore, is it the case that IGOs followed INGOs in embarking in this practice?

These questions are relevant because they address the issue of the changing notion of state sovereignty. In the modern state system issues of domestic governance in sovereign states have traditionally been placed out of the realm of international action. Thus, in the postwar period national elections have been considered to fall within Article 2 (7) of the UN Charter, which establishes that the organization and its member states cannot intervene "in matters which are essentially within the domestic jurisdiction of any state." Hence, in 1988 UN Secretary-General Javier Pérez de Cuellar noted that the world organization "does not send observers to elections" in sovereign states.[2] It could be argued that since the UN becomes involved in domestic elections only if it has been asked to do so by the government of the state where the electoral process is to take place, the international legal sovereignty of that state is not compromised.[3] But this only begs the question of why these invitations have proliferated only in the last few years.

Moreover, stating that IEM has affected the notion of state sovereignty does not imply that sovereignty is conceived of as absolute in the first place. That is, it need not be assumed that state sovereignty used to be complete, or that it was uncontested before the practice of election monitoring began. It is a historical fact that state sovereignty has never meant absolute control within state borders.[4] Therefore it is still valid to argue that the greater prominence of international election watching entails a redefinition of what sovereignty means in international politics.

This work is about both reconstructing the factors that made IEM's emergence possible, and pondering the effects of this process on state sovereignty—one of the ordering principles of international relations. I thus show how elections have become international events. Contrary to conventional wisdom in International Relations (IR)—to judge by the neglect of this phenomenon in the literature—I argue that the study of IEM does not belong (only) in the field of Comparative Politics. As a system-wide phenomenon, IEM should not be restricted to the study of purely domestic politics or of foreign policy.[5] I argue that sovereignty has been partially transformed by the recent emergence of IEM. Furthermore, I locate the origins of this change in the Americas, claiming that the western hemisphere's normative structure was particularly conducive to this new understanding of state sovereignty. From a moderate constructivist standpoint, using a narrative explanatory protocol, I present an overview of IEM's development, distinguishing three phases.[6] The case I consider here should be of broader interest because similar processes of what is now called "constructive intervention" have taken place elsewhere, most notably in Europe, after the Cold War.

In this introductory chapter I first present a brief synopsis of what are usually considered the antecedents of modern election monitoring. Secondly, I introduce my general argument on the normative structure of the Americas, state sovereignty, and IEM. In the last section I briefly outline the organization of the book.

ANTECEDENTS OF IEM

International plebiscites have been a recurrent feature of the modern state system. Consonant with the concept of popular sovereignty advanced by its revolution, Republican France carried out several plebiscites. Thus, French annexation of Comtat-Venaissin and Avignon in 1791, and of Savoy, Mulhouse, Hainaut and Rhineland in 1792, was subjected to popular vote in those territories. Nevertheless, the practice of consulting the population to be incorporated vanished with the revolutionary fervor. By 1795 France was no longer using the plebiscite method, nor was it an issue at the 1815 Congress of Vienna.

But by the second half of the nineteenth century, plebiscites were back. They were used in the process of Italian unification, and in the annexation of Savoy and Nice to France. More significantly, in 1857 a European Commission composed of French, British, Prussian, Russian, Austrian, and Turkish representatives organized the general elections in Moldavia and Wallachia.[7] Nevertheless, the practice of international plebiscites was again ephemeral.

The plebiscite was to gain momentum again after the First War. The Treaty of Versailles established that the frontier between Germany and Denmark was to be determined using that method. This first plebiscite in this process was related to a territorial dispute in North Schleswig dating back to 1848. The 1866 Treaty of Prague called for a plebiscite, but it had never been carried out.[8] Thus, the Treaty of Versailles created an International Commission as the highest authority in the area, which organized the plebiscite.[9] Similarly, the German-Polish frontier was to be determined by three plebiscites, and the one between Germany and France in the region between Lorraine and Luxemburg by another one.[10] In contrast to these five plebiscites called for in the peace treaty with Germany, the one with Austria contained only one: that of the Kalgenfurt Basin.[11]

This is not to say that the plebiscite became the preferred mode to settle border disputes. It was rather a marginal practice in establishing state boundaries; in fact, of the twelve plebiscites contemplated by the treaties that ended the World War I, only half were carried out.[12] Nevertheless, its value as an element of international diplomacy was reaffirmed in this period. The plebiscite was accepted as a legitimate means to determine issues of sovereignty.

Hence, the end of World War II and the creation of the UN brought the issue of international plebiscites to the fore again. This time, though, they were of a different nature. On the one hand, the UN was asked to monitor electoral processes in divided countries, such as Germany and Korea. On the other, the UN was given the task of supervising elections in trust and non-self-governing territories.[13] The international organization had set as one of its objectives at its founding the achievement of "self-government" for colonial territories. Thus, in 1953 the General Assembly adopted a resolution outlining the criteria for the realization of that objective, and proposing several alternatives to colonial status—all of which were to be decided through democratic means by the people of the subjected territories. Thus, the UN became involved in organizing and carrying out plebiscites in several non-self-governing (e.g., Cook Islands in 1965, and West Irian in 1969) and trust territories (e.g., Togoland under British Administration in 1956, Togoland under French Administration in 1958, and Western Samoa in 1961).[14]

As in the interwar period, though, the use of plebiscites or referenda monitored by an international organization was not the general rule. In many cases the colonial powers themselves remained in control of the electoral processes leading to independence, without requesting UN involvement. Nevertheless, the UN supervised about 30 balloting processes in trust and self-governing territories.[15] But again, these were instances in which the issue at stake was the granting of sovereign status by the international community.

More relevant to my central concern in this book is an anomalous case that took place in 1977. In that year, General Omar Torrijos, President of Panama, requested the UN Secretary-General to send a mission in to observe the vote on the recently concluded Panama Canal treaties with the United States. Secretary-General Kurt Waldheim appointed a 7-member mission which observed the plebiscite and reported favorably on it. I consider this case an anomaly because this was the first time that the UN had observed an electoral process in a sovereign country, not in a territory in the process of becoming one. Interestingly, the Secretary-General did not ask the General Assembly (nor the Security Council) for approval. But, given the international dimension of the process he had been invited to witness (the plebiscite was, after all, about an international treaty), he consulted with the United States.[16]

The next year, by virtue of Security Council resolution 435, the UN became involved in a sui-generis and protracted process: creating the conditions that would allow the people of Namibia to freely elect a Constituent Assembly, which in turn would write the Constitution under which Namibia would become a sovereign state. The situation was sui-generis because this was not a case of UN involvement in a self-determination process since the issue of independence had been settled years before. In any case, although the UN created the United Nations Transition Assistance Group (UNTAG) in 1978 in order to carry out the mission established in the above mentioned resolution, it was not applied until 1989, when more than 97% of the registered voters participated in the electoral process.[17] In order to avoid the inauguration of yet another one-party state in Africa, the UN took special care in writing the electoral legislation and guaranteeing a peaceful and free electoral process in Namibia. The two decades that elapsed before Security Council resolution 435 was finally implemented testify both to the salience the Cold War had on regional conflicts,[18] and to the increasing importance the establishment of democratic regimes was acquiring in the international arena. The 1989 Namibia experience was the culmination of colonial-era UN monitoring.[19]

The historical sketch presented above is the general milieu in which IEM would eventually emerge. But there is an "ontological gap" between this historical background and IEM as we know it. Contrary to what some of the leading experts on "the right to democratic governance" maintain, from the fact that the UN had a legal right to intervene and sanction electoral processes in trust and colonial territories, does not follow that the practice would eventually extend to sovereign states.[20] That is why Pérez de Cuellar pointed out in the late 1980s, as noted above, that the UN did not engage in election monitoring in sovereign states. The Secretary-General was right on the mark. There was no logical or normative mechanism linking international plebiscites to modern IEM. It would take a denser normative complex, one where state sovereignty was framed as a composite construct which included representative government as an important if sometimes implicit element, for it to emerge. This normative complex, I maintain, first emerged in the Americas—and it is here where the mechanism connecting IEM to previous state practice can be found.

THE WESTERN HEMISPHERE'S NORMATIVE STRUCTURE, IEM, AND STATE SOVEREIGNTY

The Argument in Brief

I argue that it was the combination of a series of systemic and domestic factors in the Americas that made the environment in the hemisphere particularly conducive to the emergence of IEM. Significantly, though, it arose in a delimited part of the Americas: Latin America. This is not to suggest that the region was self-contained in this respect. North America, and specifically the United States, played a key role in the emergence of IEM in Latin America. Hence, my inquiry considers the interaction between these two main regions of the hemisphere. I am not saying that these subcontinents are two naturally independent regions. In fact, during the nineteenth century the United States often served as a "role model" for the nascent Latin American states, which were frequently ready to follow the republican institutions of their northern neighbor.[21] The point is to look into the factors that might have made of the Americas a unique international (sub)system, and into the interaction that created two distinguishable regions within the hemisphere. These two issues, the *Americas* as a region, and *Latin America* within the Americas, constitute the *historical structure* that made the emergence of IEM possible.

The first of the two issues, the *Americas* as a region, is closely related to what has come to be known as the "Western Hemisphere Idea" (WHI). As early as 1813, Thomas Jefferson wrote that the governments to be formed in the nascent states, "will be *American* governments, no longer to be involved in the never-ceasing broils of Europe. The European nations constitute a *separate* division of the globe; their localities make them a part of a *distinct system*. . . . America has a hemisphere to itself. It must have a separate *system of interest* which must not be subordinated to those of Europe."[22] According to Arthur P. Whitaker, Jefferson's statement was "the first flowering" of the WHI.[23]

By WHI Whitaker refers to "the proposition that the peoples of this Hemisphere stand in a special relationship to one another which sets them apart from the rest of the world."[24] Interestingly, the perception of being "apart from the rest of the world" does not necessarily imply the existence of a community of interests among the states of the Americas. In effect, implicit in this "special relationship" is the interplay not only of the new world states, but also of its two main sub regions—a relationship that most of the time has been a contentious one. It is important to note this because it is common to equate western hemispherism with regional cooperation. For instance, Javier Corrales and Richard Feinberg define "Hemispherism" as "the active attempt by nations in the hemisphere to redirect their foreign policies in favor of a closer and coordinated cooperation with one another."[25] The focus is then often shifted to what are defined as formal institutions of cooperation, such as the Inter-American Development Bank or the Pan American Health Organization. But as Whitaker himself made clear in his seminal text, "the distinction between the idea and its various political expressions . . . should be constantly kept in mind."[26] The precision is significant because it makes clear that the "Idea" refers to patterned interaction *per se,* not to cooperation. It is the "Idea" as a normative structure producing order in the sociological sense, more than as its institutional manifestations producing cooperation, that interests me.[27]

Whitaker's work is important because it highlights the distinctiveness of the collective representation that emerged in the Americas. Nevertheless, it emphasizes the separateness of the "new world" from the "old," as well as the new system's cohesiveness, at the expense of the interaction of its two constitutive regions. However, their interplay was a fundamental element in the construction of the new hemispheric ethos; I would argue that the tension-ridden subregional interaction was part and parcel of the WHI. Using Whitaker's work as a theoretical foil, I take the WHI to be the normative structure of the Americas as a separate system of interests—with the caveat that it is one made of two sharply contrasting regions (more on this below). By producing and reproducing the fundamental values and social order among the member states of the hemisphere, the WHI enabled a distinctive idea of state sovereignty.

And it was this idea of sovereignty, I maintain, that allowed IEM to emerge in the Americas before anywhere else. This is so because the composite understanding of sovereignty in the Americas had two constitutive elements: representative government (and later human rights broadly speaking) and non-intervention. Thus, for instance, Article 5 of the 1948 OAS Charter noted, "The solidarity of the American States and the high aims which are sought through it require the political organization of those States on the basis of the effective exercise of representative democracy," while also stating that "International order consists essentially of respect for the personality, sovereignty and independence of States." It was the ever-present tension between these two components of the regional understanding of sovereignty, an understanding that evolved for over a century, that allowed the states in the hemisphere to embark in IEM as early as 1962 (even if the monitoring carried out back then was more symbolic than real). Ultimately, then, IEM is about state sovereignty.[28]

I conceive of sovereignty as a structural component of the international system, one that has been produced and reproduced in tandem by the practice of state and nonstate actors.[29] Being a structural element, sovereignty does not dictate behavior, but rather shapes the identity and interests of the actors; that is, it produces behavioral dispositions, not particular actions.[30] Furthermore, sovereignty has no grounding in itself. It is what the normative structure underpinning the existence of the states makes of it; without this grounding, sovereignty is an empty vessel, incapable of providing a basis for state interaction.

At bottom, sovereignty is about legitimacy—legitimacy understood as "the normative belief by an actor that a rule or institution ought to be obeyed."[31] But sovereignty is also partially malleable. I say partially because, being a structural element, it is by definition not completely malleable—at least within certain periods.[32] Being a social construct, though, it remains plastic by definition. Thus, as Cynthia Weber has put it, "The legitimate privileges and competencies of states are markedly different in the eighteenth, nineteenth, and twentieth centuries."[33]

IEM is one way through which the meaning of sovereignty has gradually changed. Its effect on the construction of sovereignty, and therefore on the identity and interests of states, is indeed straightforward: the recognized rights of states are now explicitly delimited by an international element. As UN Secretary-General Boutros Boutros-Ghali put it in 1992: "The sovereignty of states must be considered under the sovereignty of human rights."[34] And thanks to the work of several monitoring organizations, the right to free and fair elections was widely recognized by the early 1990s as a human right. Interestingly, though, this change in the system-wide understanding of human rights and sovereignty had its origins in the Americas, where IEM resonated with the normative structure of the continent, the WHI.

It was in the Americas, after all, where INGOs started to systematically monitor elections. Their pioneering work was partly made possible by the continental discourse on human rights and democracy. And it was only after the entrance of INGOs into IEM, often interacting with IGOs, that this practice became "real" (in the sense of being performed thoroughly). That is why by the late 1980s and early 1990s, when a state accepted monitors, it was engaging in a partial redefinition of both its sovereignty and interests. The composite, implicit understanding of state sovereignty enshrined in the WHI had thus become explicit. At the dusk of the twentieth century, state sovereignty in the Americas unequivocally included what used to be considered an essentially domestic affair: the right to democratic governance.

PLAN OF THE BOOK

I develop the argument summarized above in the following manner. In Chapter One I elaborate my theoretical approach around the meaning and construction of sovereignty in international politics, and assess two alternative explanations: neoliberal institutionalism and neoclassical realism. There I argue that these two approaches' individualist and materialist bent (respectively) prevent them from satisfactorily accounting for the puzzle posed by IEM. In the second chapter I present in more detail the normative structure of the Americas, offer a preview of the development of IEM in the hemisphere, and introduce some methodological considerations for the study of IEM. Furthermore, I argue that the advent of the Cold War did not displace the WHI as the fundamental normative structure of the Americas. The emphasis in Chapter Two is on the analytical links between the historical narrative, and the early instances of IEM, such as the 1962 missions to Costa Rica and the Dominican Republic, and the 1963 mission to Honduras.

In each of the ensuing four chapters (three-six) I consider in more detail four landmark cases that allow me to trace the evolution of modern IEM: Chile 1988, Nicaragua 1990, Mexico 1994, and Peru 2000. The

Chilean case illustrates the importance of INGOs in the (re)launching of IEM in the Americas, in what can be considered the birth of the IEM network. Chapter Four on the Nicaraguan elections shows how the IEM network was consolidated at the dawn of the 1990s—as state sovereignty was being redefined.

The following chapter deals with what could be considered a critical case in the development of IEM: the Mexican 1994 elections. Mexico was critical in the institutionalization of this practice because it had been staunchly opposed to it on sovereignty grounds. The Mexican case thus epitomizes in a straightforward manner the way IEM came to redefine state sovereignty. In Chapter Six I deal with the 2000 Peruvian elections, which evidenced perhaps more than any other, how democracy and national elections more specifically had become an international affair by the end of the twentieth century. By this time, INGOs and IGOs were acting coordinately observing elections—with the full complacency of state authorities. In the concluding chapter I first sketch out the normalization of IEM worldwide, viewing it as a case of "constructive intervention;" secondly, I revisit my theoretical argument; I then briefly bring in the discussion on democratic peace, and consider some recent approaches to the related issue of "democracy promotion." I end by discussing the place of IEM in IR theory.

Chapter One

On the Meaning of Sovereignty

What effect has IEM had on the construction of state sovereignty? Put differently, has the emergence of IEM significantly impacted the meaning of sovereignty? Or has it just been a minor compromise with inconsequential effects? The answer, of course, depends on how one looks at, or constructs, the "facts" since, as Goethe once observed, "Every fact is already a theory."[1] Stephen Krasner's 1999 book on sovereignty, for instance, clearly points to the latter option: IEM's impact on sovereignty has been inconsequential;[2] a constructivist approach, to the former: IEM has had a significant impact on the changing meaning of sovereignty. I begin this chapter by considering Krasner's argument in some detail, both because it addresses the sovereignty problematique directly, and because his approach is a well-articulated composite of the individualist and materialist perspectives I take issue with (more on this later). His outlook, in one manner or another, is indeed pervasive in IR. Moreover, Krasner's work is a good starting point because it reproduces and magnifies an epistemological dichotomy espoused both by individualist and materialist approaches: that between the "logic of appropriateness" and the "logic of consequences."

Thus, after considering Krasner's take on sovereignty in the first section of this chapter, in the second I develop my approach to the meaning of sovereignty. I take a moderate constructivist stand, drawing especially on the work of Thomas Risse-Kappen, and Christian Reus-Smit. From the first one I take his introduction into the IR literature of Jürgen Habermas' theory of communicative action, and, more precisely, of the logic of argumentative rationality. The latter represents a third mode of social action that breaks the alleged dichotomy between the logic of appropriateness and the logic of consequences. From Reus-Smit I draw on his work on constitutional structures, in order to present the WHI as the fundamental constitutional structure of the region.

In order to trace how changes in the meaning of sovereignty might take place, in the third section I look at Margaret Keck and Kathryn Sikkink's work on Transnational Advocacy Networks. In addition to linking structural and agent-level matters, bringing these organizations into the picture serves to highlight the utility of the logic of argumentative rationality for moving our theoretical understanding on the meaning of sovereignty forward. At the end of this section, I briefly recap my approach. Finally, in section four I introduce two alternative explanations representing, respectively, the individualist and materialist perspectives: neoliberal institutionalism and neoclassical realism.

SOVEREIGNTY AS INDIVIDUAL RATIONALITY AND MATERIAL INTERESTS

In the last few years, Krasner has taken on a subject-matter that is of special interest to constructivist approaches: sovereignty. Beyond thematic convergence, though, his work is important for the current IR debate not only because it addresses the sovereignty problematique from his own approach, which he terms "organized hypocrisy," but also because it engages alternative explanations, mainly sociologically-oriented ones.[3] In order to contrast the two approaches, Krasner, following James March and Johan Olsen, grounds them in the logic of consequences, and in the logic of appropriateness, respectively. Whereas in the logic of consequences actions are seen as a "negotiation among rational actors pursuing personal preferences or interests,"[4] in the logic of appropriateness "actions are seen as rule-based. . . . evoking an identity or role and matching the obligations of that identity or role to a specific situation."[5] Krasner asserts at the outset of his 1999 book: "The basic contention of this study is that the international system is an environment in which the logics of consequences dominate the logics of appropriateness. . . . International rules can be contradictory . . . and there is no authority structure to adjudicate such controversies (6)." Thus, he claims that "The logic of appropriateness of Westphalian sovereignty, the exclusion of external actors from internal authority arrangements, has been widely recognized but also frequently violated (8)."

Krasner is thus building on the opposition between the logic of appropriateness and the logic of consequences to erect a second-order dichotomy between anarchy and hierarchy (i.e., between international and domestic politics).[6] For him, "Rulers are likely to be more responsive to domestic material and ideational incentives than international ones (42)." But this sharp divide is directly related to his individualist ontology. As Krasner notes, "The starting point for this study, the ontological givens, are rulers

. . . The assumption of this study is that rulers want to stay in power and, being in power, they want to promote the security, prosperity, and values of their constituents (7)." Furthermore, he notes that in actor-oriented perspectives like his, "the actors and their preferences are exogenous; actor-oriented perspectives do not attempt to explain them (43)."

In Krasner's approach, international institutions are viewed in merely instrumental terms by state actors. As he puts it, "For rulers making choices . . . adhering to Westphalian sovereignty might, or might not, maximize their utility (9)."[7] Furthermore, Krasner claims that "Outcomes in the international system are determined by rulers whose violation of, or adherence to, international principles or rules is based on calculations of material and ideational interests, not taken-for-granted practices derived from some overarching institutional structures or deeply embedded generative grammars. Organized hypocrisy is the normal state of affairs (9)."

As the quoted passages show, the self-interested rational actor and the inside/outside dichotomy are at the core of Krasner's "organized hypocrisy" approach. But there is a third element that is also central to his perspective, one which, although not occupying a privileged ontological position, serves as its baseline: a materialist understanding of power. Krasner's approach has a tendency to equate brute facts with power. For him, power is practically coterminous with material resources; interests, on the other hand, might be material or ideational. That is why he states that "The modality through which norms might be violated depends on the configuration of power and interest (27)." And referring specifically to US influence on the Latin American countries, Krasner notes that "Only after the United States became powerful enough to assert its own sphere of influence at the turn of the [twentieth] century were the constitutional structures of some Caribbean and Central American republics influenced, sometimes dictated, by American Rulers (154)." Along the same lines, when discussing conventions, one modality through which he asserts sovereignty might be violated (more on this below), he contends that they "only involve interests, usually ideational rather than material. Power is irrelevant (28)."

In this manner, harnessing the tools of mainstream approaches, to wit: an individualist ontology and a materialist understanding of power, and erecting the logic of appropriateness/ logic of consequences divide as the fundamental one within IR, Krasner elaborates a rather sophisticated model that seeks to explain the persistence of sovereignty in international relations. He distinguishes four meanings of sovereignty: domestic, interdependence, international legal, and Westphalian. Of these four meanings, he is mainly concerned with the last one, which he defines as "an institutional arrangement for organizing political life that is based on two principles:

territoriality and the exclusion of external actors from domestic authority structures (20)." Thus, Krasner identifies "the exclusion of external actors from internal authority arrangements" as *the* "logic of appropriateness of Westphalian sovereignty (8)."

In order to account for the persistence and importance of sovereignty as an institution, Krasner distinguishes two dimensions: institutionalization and durability. Institutionalization refers to "the extent to which actual behavior conforms with principles and norms," and can be high or low, whereas durability refers to "the extent to which principles and norms endure in the face of changing circumstances (44)," and can also be high or low. He finds sovereignty as an institution puzzling, because although it has a low level of institutionalization, it has shown a high degree of durability.

Krasner claims that the Westphalian sovereignty model, in which "institutional norms are enduring but frequently ignored," has received the least attention by students of international relations, despite the fact that it "characterizes many aspects of the international system (66)." This contradictory state of affairs (i.e., sovereignty's low institutionalization and high durability) he calls "organized hypocrisy." For Krasner, organized hypocrisy "occurs when the logic of appropriateness and the logic of consequences are in conflict (66)," which, as noted above, he claims is the usual situation in international politics. Furthermore, Krasner distinguishes four modes through which sovereignty can be compromised: conventions, contracts, coercion, and imposition. He maintains that "The Westphalian model has been violated through all four of these modalities (26)."

Equipped with this individualist *cum* materialist framework, Krasner takes on sociologically-oriented approaches, and especially constructivism. Beyond the problematic outcome of theoretical debate he engages in, of particular interest for my purposes here is Krasner's treatment of human rights and their relationship to sovereignty.[8] For him, they stand in an antinomic position. As he puts it, "The norm of autonomy, the core of Westphalian sovereignty, has been challenged by alternatives including human rights (8)." Nevertheless, he sees the human rights regime as fundamentally inconsequential, either because it is empty rhetoric, or because states enter into them by way of conventions (which are voluntary and noncontingent) for purely instrumental reasons. Thus, Krasner holds that "General statements of principle like the Universal Declaration of Human Rights can only affect Westphalian sovereignty indirectly if they in some way mobilize domestic groups that then influence authority structures (32)." Alternatively, Krasner maintains that "When enforcement and monitoring provisions have been weak, as has generally been the case for human rights regimes, rulers might sign because, even though they are indifferent or antipathetic to human rights within their own state, they might believe that signing would make their regime more palatable to external and internal actors (32)."

The European Human Rights Convention is for Krasner an instance of the instrumental use of norms. He writes: "After the Second World War, it was preferable for the rulers of western Europe to sign the European Human Rights Convention, which compromised their Westphalian sovereignty, than to insist that the domestic autonomy of their polities be unconstrained (24)." Even conceding that European rulers signed into this agreement by merely instrumental reasons, the question of why human rights would constitute useful means to their ends still remains. As Robert B. Edgerton noted, "Unless rules were considered important and were taken seriously and followed, it would make no sense to manipulate them for personal benefit."[9] The logic of argumentative rationality and the concept of constitutional structure, to which I now turn, shed some light on that matter, and provide a way out of the *cul de sac* created by the deceiving opposition between the logic of appropriateness and the logic of consequences.

SOVEREIGNTY AS ARGUMENTATIVE RATIONALITY AND CONSTITUTIONAL STRUCTURES

Constructivism, like other sociologically-oriented approaches, is about rule-guided behavior. Rule-guided behavior, though, is not at odds with strategic interaction. To suggest so would reduce sociological perspectives to a gross structural determinism most of them have nothing to do with. Perhaps this problematic rendering of approaches concerned with norms has to do with the tendency to deduce that simply because individualist approaches are based on the atomist, rational, self-interested actor, sociologically-oriented ones are based on a determinist conception of the social structure. But the structurationist flavor of at least moderate constructivism makes clear that even when actors conform to social norms in their behavior (and these norms need not be "good"), they do have choice among the many, often conflicting norms structuring their actions. As Ludwig Wittgenstein pointed out a long time ago, the grammar of "following a rule" comprises that of "making a mistake."[10]

Or as Thomas Risse-Kappen, following Jürgen Habermas, noted more recently, "rule-guided behavior [should also be seen] as a conscious process."[11] He calls the process by means of which actors adjudicate what norm to apply to a specific situation "logic of truth seeking or arguing."[12] This logic does not stand in an oppositional relationship to the previous two (logic of appropriateness and logic of consequences); it shares elements from both. But neither does it stand halfway between them, as Risse-Kappen seems to suggest.[13] Although the deliberative behavior characteristic of the logic of arguing, as he notes, "is as goal oriented as strategic interaction,"[14] the fact that actors are not taken to have pre-social, fixed preferences, as the logic of consequences does, puts the logic of arguing closer to the logic of appropriateness. But in any case, by emphasizing more forcefully the strategic component of the interaction, the logic of arguing constitutes a useful bridge between the logic of appropriateness and the logic of consequences.

The key to the logic of arguing is rational action. But Habermas proposes a deeper understanding of rationality than that common among IR scholars.[15] He privileges a stage that antecedes that of strategic interaction as usually understood. Habermas is concerned with the tasks actors carry out in order to define the context in which their interaction will take place. Thus, for instance, as Friedrich Kratochwil has noted, when US Secretary of the Navy James Forrestal complained in a 1946 letter to Walter Lippmann that the US government did not yet know whether in its relations with the Soviet Union it was dealing "with a nation or a religion," he was addressing the issue of whether there was an intersubjective knowledge "concerning legitimate aims and methods of foreign policy that would allow for the adjustment of differences."[16]

Habermas distinguishes between narrow, instrumental rationality, and communicative rationality. Expressions of the latter kind are "susceptible of criticism and grounding."[17] And the proper paradigm to explain rationality claims is the theory of communicative action, not those limited to the common notion of instrumental action.[18] Furthermore, communicative rationality "implies that the participants in a discourse are open to be persuaded by the better argument and that relationships of power and social hierarchies recede in the background."[19] The goal of the interaction is not to attain one's fixed preferences, but to achieve a reasoned consensus.

But communicative behavior is a continuum. In one extreme, it can be only about bargaining along the lines of the logic of consequences, that is, about fixed preferences. At the other extreme, communicative behavior can be about the pursuit of a reasoned consensus. It is in this case that actors try to convince others of the validity claims of their own arguments. This implies that the actors involved have not made their mind once and for all, that persuasion can go either way. In between these two extremes, communicative behavior can also be about what Risse-Kappen calls "rhetorical action," in which not all actors are prepared to be persuaded, but at least one is.[20] The existence of a common "lifeworld" is what makes the existence of communicative action possible in the first place. By lifeworld Habermas means "a culturally transmitted and linguistically organized stock of interpretive patterns."[21]

The lifeworld has three structural components. The first one, culture, is for Habermas "the stock of knowledge from which participants in communication supply themselves with interpretations as they come to an understanding about something in the world."[22] Society, the second element, has to do with "the legitimate orders through which participants regulate their membership in social groups and thereby secure solidarity." Personality, the third structural component of the lifeworld, refers to "the competences that make a subject capable of speaking and acting, that put him in a position to take part in processes of reaching understanding and thereby to assert his own identity."[23] Thus, for instance, when the Tokugawa leaders of Japan insisted to their Western counterparts that trade should be excluded from their intercourse, and later accepted the inclusion of the "most favored nation" clause in the treaties they signed, without understanding what it meant, they were evincing a lack of the "stock of knowledge" that modern states possessed in the late nineteenth century.[24] In contrast, the states of the Americas were born not only with a shared stock of knowledge and distinct and recognized personalities, but also with a sense of belonging to a distinct society, the one demarcated by the WHI.

Communicative action is thus possible because the existence of a "background consensus" means that it is possible to reach an agreement on the validity of intersubjective claims.[25] Although similar in some ways to the "common knowledge" of rational choice, the Habermasian lifeworld is of a different nature, if only because being intersubjectively constructed, it is not the mere aggregation of subjective beliefs. One implication of the "intersubjectiveness" of the lifeworld is that the boundaries of the self are at stake in social interaction (whereas they are not at issue in the interaction of autonomous actors merely sharing common knowledge).[26]

The question that arises is then: to what extent can we say that the international system possesses a lifeworld? This brings me back to Krasner's assertion that "International institutions are never embedded."[27] If this is the case, it would seem that the existence of a lifeworld in the international realm is equally unlikely. But again: constructivists do not argue that the international system is a community in the same sense (or to the same degree) as most nation-states are. As Kratochwil has put it, "the international arena is still but a negative community. In other words, it is a community which is, at best, based on a mutual recognition of rights and united by common practices."[28] Nevertheless, as Hedley Bull cogently argued, there are enough elements in the international environment to warrant viewing it as an "international society."[29] Furthermore, considering specific regions of the world and particular issue areas, posing the existence of a (continuously in the making) common lifeworld seems even more justified.[30] The WHI, I argue, has functioned as a lifeworld in the Americas, serving as the core of its sovereignty regime.

Alternatively, the WHI can be conceived of as a "constitutional structure."[31] Constitutional structures are created by the practice of the relevant actors, whose interaction is guided by intersubjective understandings, for the purpose of solving the basic problem of international politics: coexistence in an anarchical system. Christian Reus-Smit defines constitutional structures as "ensembles of three deep constitutive values: a shared belief about the moral purpose of centralized political organization; an organizing principle of sovereignty, and a norm of pure procedural justice."[32] The moral purpose of the state lies at the core of the constitutional structures, as it "provides the foundations for both the principle of sovereignty and the norm of procedural justice, thus determining the standards of legitimate statehood and rightful state action."[33] It is in this sense that sovereignty both as a concept and as an organizing principle mediates, as Kratochwil has suggested, "between the realm of the 'is' and the realm of 'ought.'"[34] That is why, at bottom, sovereignty is about legitimacy.[35]

The basic tenets of the constitutional structures, in my case the WHI, set the guidelines for state interaction, determining not only who is a legitimate actor, and what constitutes appropriate behavior, but also what counts as a valid argument. Accordingly, individuals draw upon linguistic and argumentative resources according to the structure in which their action takes place.[36] Constitutional structures can thus be thought of as communicative structures. Like the latter, the former are not permanent, establishing once and for all what is allowed and what is not. As *communicative* structures, they are constituted and enacted by reasons. Not all reasons, though, have the same validity; some are more fundamental than others. Those that are more closely related to the fundamental values of the constitutional structure resonate louder. Only actors that conform to the discourse of the constitutional structure are deemed legitimate. Actors are thus constructed with a discursively-bound identity, an identity that implies the recognition of others, provides a relatively stable understanding of self and, therefore, constitutes actors as social objects.

States as social objects are thus the crystallization of discursive patterns at both the domestic and the international domains. But each of these patterns has different levels, or layers. As John Gerard Ruggie has pointed out, the sovereign character of states, as far as their international interaction is concerned, belongs to the structure of the international system itself, since it is about the *terms* of differentiation of the units, not about the units themselves. It is an intrinsically social feature of the state system. For sovereignty, as Janice Thomson has written, "is not an attribute of the state but is attributed to the state by other states or state rulers."[37] The nonhierarchical nature of sovereignty, or rather the *terms* of differentiation of the modern state system, can then be considered analogous to the equality of citizens in ancient Greece. As Hannah Arendt put it, "The equality of the Greek *polis* . . . was an attribute of the *polis* and not of men, who received their equality by virtue of citizenship, not by virtue of birth."[38] Likewise, sovereign states might be conceived of as the "citizens" of modern international society.

But the terms of differentiation that distinguish state sovereignty are just one "layer" in the discursive pattern that forms the international system. Sovereignty is not self-referential. As Reus-Smit puts it, "Unless embedded within a larger complex of values, the principle of sovereignty cannot alone provide that state with a coherent social identity . . . sovereignty has no purposive content. . . . Furthermore, it provides an inadequate justificatory basis for action."[39] In the case of Latin America at least, the idea of human rights goes back to the colonial period.[40] Hence, human rights and representative government have been fundamental in validating the claim to sovereign statehood; they have been the "nodal points" around which the discourse on state sovereignty in the Americas has coalesced.[41] The WHI has thus infused the states of the continent with a social collective identity that made the emergence of IEM logically possible.[42]

By bringing constitutional structures in, I am making a methodological move away from the Habermasian framework. That is, whereas in communicative structures power recedes to the background, it has a more prominent role in constitutional structures. As Reus-Smit has noted, "the values that constitutional structures comprise originate within the domestic political cultures of dominant states. . . . Once embedded in the practices of states, however, the values that make up constitutional structures condition the behavior of strong and weak states alike, facilitating both domination and resistance."[43] I thus move back in the direction of the logic of appropriateness, and the more conventional norms literature. Norms, it should be remembered, do not exclude power as a pervasive element in social interaction.

But in any case, both conventional constructivism and communicative action theory in IR share as their objective "the interrogation of the *discourses* themselves, within which the notions of identity and change, sovereignty, community, and internal and external order function."[44] Furthermore, and in a vein closer to classical approaches, both perspectives agree with Francis Hinsley in that the task of the IR scholar is to show "how and why interests themselves change."[45] What the logic of arguing adds to the usual constructivist work is a compatible framework for following the process of norm-creation and/or enactment. It covers an area of social interaction where the two other logics overlap. Thus, in times of flux, when actors might be uncertain about their interests, or when their identities might be undergoing change, the logic of argumentative rationality kicks in. As Risse-Kappen notes, "Argumentative processes are particularly crucial (1) when mobilizing international public opinion. . . . (2) when the oppressive state starts 'talking the talk.' . . . and (3) in some rare cases, when the transnational and domestic advocacy coalition actually manages to convince rather than force leaders to change course and remedy the human rights situation for good."[46]

A further benefit of bringing in the logic of arguing is that since any communicative process needs actors to do the arguing, this framework brings to the forefront the choice element that sometimes recedes to the background in conventional constructivist approaches.[47] Thus, showing how the engagement of domestic nongovernmental organizations (NGOs) and INGOs with state actors has partially modified both the meaning of sovereignty and the state interests that go with it should drive home not only the point that sovereignty is not a self-referential concept, but also that it is continually negotiated between state and non-state actors. This is relevant for my research since, as Ian Hurd has suggested, "How things are 'made to happen' in international affairs is an important inquiry that points to the need to look further into the stability of the institution of sovereignty."[48] Transnational Advocacy Networks are an instance of a kind of actor that has become particularly relevant for understanding precisely how the partial redefinition of sovereignty has been 'made to happen' in the last decades. I consider them in more detail next.

TRANSNATIONAL ADVOCACY NETWORKS AS INTERLOCUTORS AND SOVEREIGNTY BUILDERS

The concept of Transnational Advocacy Networks (TANs) is particularly germane for arguments involving norms and argumentative processes. In their path-breaking book on the subject, Keck and Sikkink note that "A transnational advocacy network includes those relevant actors working internationally on an issue, who are bound together by shared values, a common discourse, and dense exchanges of information and services. Such networks are more prevalent in issue areas characterized by high value content and information uncertainty. At the core of the relationship is information exchange."[49] Arguing is thus vital to TANs' internal performance. But it is also fundamental for their interaction with other actors. As Risse-Kappen notes, since TANs do not usually have at their disposal substantial material resources, "they have to rely on the 'power of the better argument.'"[50]

Furthermore, considering how TANs affect what is generally considered a *states-only* matter (sovereignty), serves as a reminder that the state-centrism of IR approaches—constructivism included—should be considered more as a methodological convenience than as a clear-cut ontology. True: the state as a corporate actor might be self-organizing and thus "pre-social" at the international level.[51] But such a hypothetical primigenious condition would probably not be the most salient feature of a state after it acquires the attributes, such as external sovereignty, that only social interaction can endow it with. Moreover, just as Alexander Wendt argues that "Marxism's 'material base' actually is shot through and through with ideas,"[52] I would argue that state sovereignty, at least as articulated in the WHI, is actually shot through and through with societal elements. After all, human rights and representative government—what might be considered a liberal element—make up the societal core of states. Without its societal grounding, state sovereignty becomes an empty vessel, an idea in search of a purpose.[53]

TANs might then be conceived of as bridges between state and society. As Keck and Sikkink's definition suggests, TANs are not formed exclusively by non-state actors, such as NGOs, some religious groups, or a purported "global civil society." They might also include some state agencies, and even IGOs. This means that TANs are not necessarily in an external position vis-à-vis the state (or the state system). As Keck and Sikkink put it, "Because part of states and international organizations also participate in these networks, the process of negotiation within the emergent cosmopolitan community is not 'outside' the state."[54]

TANs can also be thought of as "communicative structures."[55] As such, they create discourses which sometimes frame issues in novel ways, thus bringing them to the international agenda. Take the case of "female circumcision." It was only after a network of women activists framed the issue in terms of "genital mutilation," that it acquired new salience, thus making it into the international agenda (with the UN, for instance, emitting a series of recommendations).[56] Similarly, by engaging in IEM since the early 1980s, an emergent TAN not only gave this practice a new impetus, but also redefined its constitutive rules. From then on, IEM was no longer the monopoly of states and IGOs.

Alternatively, from a moderate constructivist perspective, TANs can be considered both as a structure and as an agent. As the former, it patterns the interaction of its members, and infuses them with identity; as the latter, it puts forward specific policy proposals in the international arena. The key to its dual character lies both in its decentralized and horizontal organizational arrangement, and in the kind of strategies it employs. The core of the network is not a bureaucratic apparatus or a continuously mobilized membership, but a small group of political entrepreneurs who focus on specific events (such as electoral processes) and, more fundamentally, the information its members exchange. The social nature of the information gathered (and constructed) becomes the raw material for a new discourse.

This social structure is then enacted by concrete actors who employ a strategy Keck and Sikkink call the "boomerang pattern." As they put it, "When channels between the state and its domestic actors are blocked, the boomerang pattern of influence characteristic of transnational networks may occur: domestic NGOs bypass their state and directly search out international allies to try to bring pressure on their states from outside."[57] Thus, for instance, the mothers of the *Plaza de Mayo* in Argentina enhanced their cause and put pressure on the Argentinean state by resorting to human rights activists outside their county. Similarly, the Chilean opponents to the Pinochet regime formed alliances with foreign actors in order to put the dictator in the international spotlight, and thus get leverage in their negotiations with the regime.

By "throwing" the boomerang, network activists thus become players on the international scene. The practice of TANs as agents helps redefine not only the role of nonstate actors in the international arena, but also the structure of the interstate system. As authors from the English School noted decades ago, and constructivists more recently, the interstate system is not solely characterized by a Hobessian state of nature in which only material capabilities, as such, matter. At bottom, the modern state system is constituted by institutions and norms which infuse both anarchy and material factors with meaning. That is, a normative structure underlies the basic components of the state system.

Although TANs are not state actors, their action affects interstate politics. As I noted, states are shot through and through with societal elements. The evolution of sovereignty is clear in this respect: from being a "principle" for appropriate behavior among states in the eighteen century, by the twentieth century it had become a "territorial ideal," in which the focus is on the relationship between territory, power, and accepted forms of *political organization*.[58] This transformation had profound consequences both for the way states related to one another, and for the way states related to their population. In a similar vein, as Sikkink has noted regarding the effects of TANs activity in the human rights realm, "When the state recognizes the legitimacy of international interventions on the topic of human rights and changes its domestic human rights in response to these international pressures, it reconstitutes the relationship between the states, its citizens, and international actors."[59] It is then through the practice of state and nonstate actors that the state system is reproduced and transformed—and that both "do state sovereignty."[60]

That is why it is important to trace the "life history" of international norms, and not just to postulate their existence. The work by Risse-Kappen and Sikkink (1999) is particularly illuminating in tracing norms from the international to the domestic level. They conceive of the process by which international norms are internalized by states as a process of socialization. But not socialization à la Kenneth Waltz, which is limited to change of behavior;[61] for Risse-Kappen and Sikkink, in contrast, socialization includes change in behavior but is not coterminous with it. For them, the most interesting feature of the socialization process has to do with changes in actors' attributes. Thus, Risse-Kappen and Sikkink distinguish three types of causal mechanisms, or ideal types of social action, in this process: 1) instrumental adaptation and strategic bargaining; 2) moral consciousness-raising, argumentation, dialogue, and persuasion; and 3) institutionalization and habitualization.[62] Each of them roughly corresponds, in the sense of being the prevalent mechanism, to the sequential stages in the socialization process. Thus, for instance, leaders of authoritarian states embarked on a liberalization process usually begin by "talking the talk" of their (domestic and foreign) opponents, and then start making tactical concessions. If the process evolves into a transition to democracy, the concessions made for instrumental reasons become internalized and thus part of the identity of the state.[63]

The process of norm socialization can be explained only to a point by individualist approaches; the road beyond that point can only be traversed with the help of sociologically-oriented ones. It is for this reason that the two approaches, or the two logics (appropriateness and consequences), cannot always be conceived of as alternative explanations, standing alongside. Oftentimes the issue of causal depth gets in the way. Methodologically, Risse-Kappen and Sikkink's approach is thus valuable because it evinces the different layers of the socialization process. Empirically, their model is useful in tracing the process by which international institutions encourage the spread of norms around the world. Furthermore, since their model conceives of the socialization process as a sort of two-level game, it leaves room for accommodating international variation in the spread of norms.[64] The explicit point of Risse-Kappen and Sikkink's approach, on the other hand, is to account "for the variation in the domestic effects of international norms."[65] The norm-diffusion process is seen as acting outside-in.

Another piece by Sikkink, this one co-authored with Martha Finnemore, however, deals with the mirror-image of this process, shedding some light on the early phases of arguing, norm-creation, and institutionalization. In this work, Finnemore and Sikkink (1998) develop the norm "life cycle" model. The cycle has three phases: emergence, cascade, and internalization. In the first phase, norm entrepreneurs "create" issues by "framing" them. That is, activists try to use language that both dramatizes the issue at stake and makes it resonate with the general public's discourse. This process might take place at the domestic level, as happened with the anti-slave trade in nineteenth century Britain.[66] It is during the first phase that the inside-out element of the life-cycle model is clearer.

The crucial link comes in the second phase, "norm cascade," for it is necessary for the emergent norm to reach a threshold, and then "become institutionalized in specific sets of international rules and organizations."[67] Without institutionalization, norm diffusion from the bottom-up becomes more difficult. Finnemore and Sikkink pose two ways norms might reach a tipping point. The first is when the emergent norm reaches a critical mass. That is, as more states adopt the norm, there comes a moment when "norm cascade" begins (they suggest this usually happens only after one-third of the total states have adopted the norm). The second way an emergent norm can reach a tipping point is when critical states (i.e., "those without which the achievement of the substantive norm goal is compromised") adopt it.[68] At this point, the rate of adoption of the new norm increases—even without domestic pressure.

Finally, in the third, "internalization" phase, norms work down from the international to the domestic level. Finnemore and Sikkink point out that international norms are more likely to be adopted "during periods of domestic turmoil in which the legitimacy of elites is threatened."[69] An instance of norm diffusion in the midst of domestic turmoil took place in the countries of Eastern Europe in the late 1980s as they rushed, virtually en masse, to embrace Western democratic principles.

Finnemore and Sikkink's approach moves us forward by effectively tracing the origins of international norms. Their focus on norms entrepreneurs, and the idea of a tipping point being necessary for norm cascade are particularly germane to my argument, since the emergence of norms does not just happen, and it takes something more than good luck for them to spread internationally. This is not to suggest that focusing on norm entrepreneurs or inflection points settles the issue of norm diffusion.[70] But as long as the activities of those agents are framed in the context of the discourse in which they operate, this model serves to emphasize the mutual constitution of agents and structures in a normatively-bounded communicative action process.

I would only add an alternative way in which norms might reach a tipping point—a way I consider more suitable to the problematique I deal with. This alternative way is a constitutive one, in which neither sheer numbers or the consent of "critical" states is essential. In this path, norms cascade simply by "expressing" a foundational element of the international *cum* domestic system. Since the element in question, for instance, popular sovereignty, is so deeply embedded in our understanding (from both the domestic and the international points of view) of what a polity ought to be, it is very difficult for state leaders to ignore it. As R. B. J. Walker has observed, "sovereignty expresses and works to reproduce a specific relation between claims to difference and claims about the forms of commonality and structure that permit claims to monopoly [to legitimate authority] to have any meaning at all."[71] Alternatively, it can be argued that the liberal element contained in the WHI "carries within it not the seeds of its own destruction, but the seeds of its own expansion. Liberalism, with all its historical shortcomings, contains a subversive element that plays into the hands of activists."[72]

Hence, for instance, state leaders in the Western hemisphere, willingly or not, began talking-the-talk of the norm of free elections as defined by IEM practice. It was then possible for a few, not necessarily "critical" states to instantiate and thus catapult the emergent norm—making it reach a tipping point. In a sense, therefore, it can be said that the emergent norm was already there: both outside (the international system) and inside (the domestic structure) in a latent state. It is the *nature* of the emergent norm, more than the number or the type of states which adopt it, that is critical in this path. The constitutive way does not negate the other ones—it subsumes them. Once a norm is realized in this path, it spreads out quickly. Had the popular *cum* territorial notion of sovereignty been absent from the WHI, the IEM TAN would not have thrived the way it did.

In short, the WHI as the constitutional structure of the Americas has grounded the hemispheric understanding of sovereignty, an understanding that has been produced and reproduced both by state and nonstate actors. I claim that without the WHI, IEM would not have emerged in the Americas in the early 1960s. Moreover, had token monitoring not existed, "real" (or at least nonstate-lead) IEM would not have emerged. The unintended consequence—reminiscent of the principle of sensitive dependence on initial conditions of the *butterfly effect*—of this protracted process, has been that states have partially redefined their identity and national interests.[73]

ALTERNATIVE EXPLANATIONS

The issue of the emergence and consolidation of IEM seems amenable to at least two other approaches besides the one I outlined above: neoliberal institutionalism (NLI), and neoclassical realism (NCR).[74] Neither of them, however, is meant to explain the kind of problematique I am dealing with. Although my analysis of IEM is problem—not approach—driven, my understanding of the nature of the issue to be explained favors the choice of a normative, systemic approach.[75] My interest has to do with the system-wide *normative* structure, with the way this framework produced an inter-subjective hemispheric understanding of sovereignty that made specific foreign policy decisions possible in the first place. But I am also concerned with the way the discourse that evolved produced a patterned interaction that went beyond pre-social, instrumental self-interest, and material calculation. That is, states have adopted specific identities and played certain roles to advance their interests. But these roles and identities are not merely idiosyncratic, nor do they correspond to completely discrete agents. They are part of a structure and therefore should be considered as a manifestation of structural determinants.[76] In my view, in so far as the states' foreign policies regarding IEM are part and parcel of the systemic distribution of interests, they acquire a structural component.[77] They cease being mere process, as in most systemic IR theories. The state, or more concretely, its domestic structure, becomes process, a process in which both state and non-state actors relate mutually in constructing the state's foreign policy as structure.[78]

In contrast, NCR is a theory of foreign policy which aims to explain either purely domestic decisions, or how the state structure reacts to material changes in the international system.[79] The domestic structure of states is the focus of analysis. NLI, on the other hand, although focusing on the international system, aims to explain the provision of public goods by an aggregate of rational, self-interested actors. The logics of appropriateness and arguing are superfluous to both approaches.

I mention these caveats in order to make clear that the insufficiencies I will point to in the alternative approaches are not entirely their fault: to a large extent they have to do with the fact that I am using them to explain something that these approaches were not meant to explain in the first place.[80] In a sense, then, the deck is stacked in my favor. But as Alexander Wendt and James Fearon have argued, the question of which theoretical approach to use for a specific puzzle should be a pragmatic one.[81] Furthermore, neoliberal institutionalism and neoclassical realism do have something to say about the problematique I am dealing with. IEM should not be totally out of their theoretical radar—even if they start from a different conception of it.[82] This is one reason why it is important to consider them in some detail. These two approaches plus the constructivist one I put forward, thus, could be seen as complementary. But another reason to bring the other two perspectives in is to make explicit the points at which different theoretical approaches part company. This should be a useful exercise: the unveiling of real fault lines among different perspectives should depict an ontological and methodological section of the theoretical crust of IR.

Neoliberal Institutionalism

NLI intends to explain cooperation among egotists from a systemic perspective. It focuses on the structure of incentives in which self-interested actors interact. The central variable of NLI is interest.[83] It is interested in explaining the possibility of cooperation among self-interested actors by means of institutional arrangements. The publication in 1984 of Robert Keohane's *After Hegemony: Cooperation and Discord in the World Political Economy* marks the turning point in the mainstream scholarship on international institutions.[84] In that volume, Keohane defines "cooperation as mutual adjustment. . . . because discord sometimes prevails even when common interests exist."[85] He does not consider cooperation among democracies to be automatic.[86] For him, deception and not violence is the most salient consequence of the anarchical environment.[87] Keohane first assumes that mutual interests among states exist, and then analyzes the conditions under which they will lead to international cooperation. International cooperation is thus akin to public goods.

Keohane argues that institutions make a difference in world politics. He defines institutions as a "persistent and connected set of rules (formal and informal) that prescribe behavioral roles, constrain activity, and shape expectations."[88] He argues that international institutions are important because they affect the incentives states face. Consequently, "variations in the institutionalization of world politics exert significant impacts on the behavior of governments."[89] This is why his perspective is systemic.

In order to show how cooperation can materialize, and how institutional variation matters, Keohane focused his attention on international regimes.[90] These he defines as "institutions with explicit rules, agreed upon by governments, that pertain to particular sets of issues in international relations."[91] International regimes in this perspective are important because, by disseminating information, they lower the transaction costs associated with cooperation. For him, regimes are "information providing institutions,"[92] and as such can contribute to ameliorating the chronic suboptimal provision of common goods in the anarchic international system.

The emphasis is thus placed on how regimes, by lowering transaction costs, make it cheaper for governments to negotiate agreements.[93]

In NLI regimes may acquire a life of their own. Since the costs of regime creation exceed the costs of regime maintenance, international regimes may continue to exist even after the hegemon that created them has declined, or after their originally intended purposes have been met. That is why for Keohane it is possible to have cooperation after hegemony.

Drawing on Antonio Gramsci, Keohane understands hegemony as resting "on the subjective awareness by elites in secondary states that they are benefiting, as well as on the willingness of the hegemon itself to sacrifice tangible short-term benefits for intangible long-term gains."[94] It is this more interpretive, less conventional notion of hegemony that opens the possibility for decoupling the hegemon's egoistic interest from the existence of international regimes. That is, regimes are in this conception no longer epiphenomenal; they might become intervening or even autonomous variables.[95]

By embedding its members' interests, international regimes acquire certain autonomy from the hegemon. Nevertheless, the decision to join or remain in a regime is still taken by state actors in purely rational, cost-benefit terms. Moreover, although "common interests" are assumed by NLI, for them to be consistent with the more fundamental concept of self-interest, those common interests are by necessity no more than focal points. That is, if the concept of self-interest is to play the central role assigned to it by this approach, it has to refer to something more than the mere arrangement of means toward an end. If this was all that was meant, it would be no different from realist and constructivist approaches. Self-interest in NLI should then refer to the utilitarian regard for the utility of others, where "Nothing is taken for granted or valued for its own sake, only for the payoff it brings to the self."[96]

Keohane has argued that an actor's utility function can incorporate the preferences of others, and thus altruistic behavior should also be seen as rational behavior.[97] But as Stefano Guzzini notes, "if behavior can be either driven by egoism or altruism, by one thing and its opposite, then human action becomes indeterminate."[98] In any case, the self-interest assumption is pervasive in the actual practice of rational-choice inspired approaches, including NLI.[99] Thus, there is no reverberation of normative factors built into the theory: the utility functions of the states involved remain independent from one another throughout the analysis.[100] This is why Keohane recognizes that "regimes can be used to pursue particularistic and parochial interests."[101] NLI thus simply focuses on constraints and incentives; it "takes states' conceptions of their interests as exogenous: unexplained within the terms of the theory."[102]

By identifying the areas where self-interest might actually lead to international cooperation, this approach has more to say about when a regime will be needed than how it will emerge.[103] Institutions are seen as mere enablers: they make cooperation possible.[104] In this approach, they are simply instrumental and epiphenomenal; they do no more than facilitate the exchange of information. Society is the mere aggregation of individuals.[105] Consequently, from this perspective actors, at most, submit to social pressure—they do not internalize social norms.[106]

Neoclassical Realism

In NCR, as in any version of realism, material capabilities are the starting point. "Realist core assumptions," Gideon Rose has written, "tell scholars what to expect in broad terms: International outcomes will match the relative distribution of material capabilities."[107] Or as William Wohlforth has put it, "The ABC of realism is that relative gains and losses are what matters."[108] Nevertheless, three features distinguish this approach from the dominant structural realism. One is that neoclassical realists endow power with purpose. For Randall Schweller, "Because power is useful for achieving any national goal, we cannot make accurate foreign policy predictions without specifying the *purposes* of power."[109] For neoclassical realism, as Stephen Brook and William Wohlforth point out, the neorealist take on material capabilities as "it is actually far too narrow to provide a productive background for developing and evaluating models of how ideas affect strategic behavior."[110] State purpose is required to obtain a more accurate picture of state action.

Interestingly though, in neoclassical realism purpose ends at the state's borders. There is no point in talking about purposeful power at the systemic level. For Schweller, "theories of international politics do not require specification of the purposes of power."[111] This is then the second difference between neoclassical realism and neorealism: the former is "a body of realist foreign policy theory."[112] For this kind of theories, the key dependent variable is not patterned state interaction, but the behavior of specific states.[113] Thus domestic factors play an important role in this approach. Neoclassical realism explicitly incorporates domestic preferences and domestic structure into the analysis.[114]

The third difference with structural realism has to do with the way material capabilities, "the basic parameters," get translated into actual foreign policy behavior. [115] Perceptions is the key mechanism through which this happens. In neoclassical realism, perceptions work as intervening variables between power and state policy.[116] According to Jeffrey Talaferro, "perceptions serve as a conduit through which structural variables translate into foreign policy."[117] Thus, it is not enough for the analyst to track the changes in relative capabilities of a state in order to infer the change in policy. As Ethan Kapstein has observed, "changes in capabilities do cause changes in behavior, but the direction of that behavioral change is indeterminate."[118] This is because the proximate causes of state behavior are perceptions: "*decision-makers' assessments of power are what matters.*"[119]

The relative capabilities of the state are thus the beacon of statesmen. But in this approach this structural feature acts simply as a constraint on state policy. For in NCR the system has no effect other than to mark the limits to state behavior by configuring a positional whole. It does not generate identities or interests.[120] That is why talk about the purpose of power stops at the state's boundaries. As Peter Feaver puts it, "the theoretical purchase and empirical scope of realism's key causal mechanism [is] system constraint."[121] From this vantage point, the limits to the promotion of democratic regimes in the Americas are set by the distribution of material capabilities. As Rose explains,

> From the Founding onward. . . . Americans [i.e., U.S. citizens] have generally agreed that their domestic institutions should be disseminated to others but have disagreed over the form this ideological transmission should take ['exemplars' vs. 'crusaders' with the latter winning in Woodrow Wilson's times]. . . . From a neoclassical realist perspective, the first place to look in explaining such a shift would not be the intellectual history or presidential psychology, but the massive increase in relative power the country had experimented between Adams and Wilson.[122]

Hence, neoclassical realism puts a premium on clearly delineating where material incentives end, and where ideational elements begin. If the demarcation line is not clearly established (as this approach assumes is legitimate, feasible, and commendable to do), the analyst soon runs into the endogeneity problem, with ideational factors being just a reflection of the deeper structure of material incentives.[123]

SUMMARY

I have presented in this Chapter Three plausible kinds of explanations for the emergence and normalization of IEM. NLI rests on self-interest; it relies fundamentally on the actors' instrumentalist conception of each other. NCR relies also on an instrumentalist logic, but the emphasis is placed on coercion: power defined in material terms can always be used by a state with superior capabilities to compel other states to orient their behavior in a certain direction.

The constructivist approach, as previously discussed, rests on a mechanism that, although subsuming the other two, is not a mere restatement of them: legitimacy. The richness of legitimacy lies in the fact that it does not preclude either action based on self-interest nor that based on coercion; instead, it adds an important ideational element that is absent in the other two approaches: an intersubjective structure. For the normative belief is not reducible to private preferences nor to mere superstructure.

The starting point in the legitimacy-based approach is thus neither presocial utilitarianism or self-interest, nor capabilities as material "base." The starting point is the shared understandings that give self-interest and material facts meaning. As Aaron Wildavsky put it, "no interests without selves to have them, and no selves without cultures to generate them. In short, no cultures, no interests."[124] But also, as Janos Kornai noted in his comprehensive study of the socialist system, what is usually thought of as "superstructure" can actually reshape its "base"—thus reversing the usual arrow of causality.[125] That is why I maintain that it is within the basic parameters of the normative structure that states define their interests, and that material capabilities acquire a life of their own, confronting them *as* external structure.[126]

Thus, going back to Krasner, to argue that "In the international system norms, including those associated with Westphalian sovereignty and international legal sovereignty, have always been characterized by organized hypocrisy," and that "Norms and actions have been decoupled. Logics of consequences have trumped logics of appropriateness (220)," is to misconstrue IR's subject matter. Sovereignty is *not* organized hypocrisy—such a term suggests that it is just a virtuous facade behind which hides the true evil core of international politics. Sovereignty is instead disciplined order, an order that is produced by the patterned interaction of the component units of the international system. If we accept that states are socially constituted (both at the international and the domestic level), the fact that something more than the pursuit of "self-interest" is involved in international politics becomes evident.[127] Furthermore, in a norm-free international environment (or in one in which norms were truly superfluous) even the pursuit of self-interest would be nonsensical.[128] The "logic of appropriateness" is thus not opposed to the "logic of consequences;" the former simply subsumes the latter. The challenge is to grasp the concrete effects of the seemingly etheric normative element.

It is precisely the belittling (or misunderstanding) of normative factors that leads Krasner to assert, as noted, that it was only in the twentieth century, after the United States had amassed considerable material capabilities, that its influence on the "constitutional structures" of some Latin American countries was felt—thus ignoring the profound and pervasive normative impact of the domestic structure of the United States in the Americas since the early nineteenth century. As I suggested in the introduction, sovereignty as enshrined in the WHI precisely implied this permeation.

The problem illustrated by Krasner's work is indeed pervasive in the discipline. Thus, for instance, Kenneth Waltz has stated that "American behavior over the past century in Central America provides little evidence of norm-guided self-restraint in the absence of countervailing power."[129] Even conceding for the sake of the argument what Waltz leaves implicit (that only the pro-social self-restraint attitude, but not the nasty one of intervention, can be explained by normative approaches), wouldn't one expect actually even less "self-restraint" on the part of the United States in Central America during the twentieth century (i.e., even before the onset of the Cold War) if we were to limit ourselves either to the self-interest of the hegemon, or to the abysmally skewed distribution of capabilities in the Americas, as the only explanatory factors of U.S. behavior?

But if we look at the construction of the national interest of the United States in terms of the normative structure in which its conduct has been embedded, we can better understand both the realpolitik nature of its interventionism and its "self-restraint." The strategic conduct of the United States, like that of any other state for that matter, is embedded into a wider social structure.[130] To put it another way: if we think about the history of the sovereignty regime in the western hemisphere say, in the last 100 years, stripped from all normative (i.e., legitimacy-based) elements, would it resemble in any way what has actually happened? Could we expect a practice like IEM to have emerged and normalized in that scenario? This work aims to shed light on that broad issue. I take on this task in the next chapter by considering in more detail the normative structure of the Americas which made IEM's emergence possible, reviewing some early monitoring instances, providing a preview of the development of IEM in the Americas, and discussing some methodological issues involved in reconstructive accounts like this.

Chapter Two

The Western Hemisphere Idea and the Emergence of IEM

IEM in the Americas did not appear out of thin air in the early 1960s. It was the result of a thick normative structure underpinning state interaction in the new world, a social tapestry that had been over a hundred years in the making. This chapter is devoted to analyzing the relationship between the WHI as the continent's normative structure and IEM, and to considering some methodological issues. In the first section I show how the hemispheric understanding was constructed. I maintain that the WHI functioned as the constitutional structure of the hemisphere, and that it continued to do so even after the advent of the Cold War—which I consider in the second section. In section three I briefly review the emergence of IEM, looking at some of the world-wide pioneering, OAS-led instances of election monitoring, such as the 1962 missions to Costa Rica and the Dominican Republic. In the fourth section I review the subsequent appearance of IEM outside the regional organization. The convergence of IGOs and INGOs in the business of election monitoring is then considered in section five. Finally, in the sixth section I offer some methodological considerations about inquiring into IEM, emphasizing the pertinence of using a reconstructive or particularizing strategy.

The presentation of the historical framework in which IEM emerged takes the bulk of the space in this chapter. By presenting a thick chronological narrative, I intend to contextualize the appearance of IEM in the Americas; but I also use history for analytics in making the case that the emergence of IEM in the continent was neither mere coincidence nor sheer voluntarism. There existed already in the early 1960s something deeper than a mere elective affinity, an adequate cause, between this practice and the constitutional structure of the western hemisphere. I show why the emergence of IEM was not all that extraordinary in this normative setting—one could even say that it was something to be expected.[1] That is why, following Max Weber's dictum that "In the cultural sciences, the knowledge of the universal or the general is never valuable in itself," I advocate a particularizing approach to IEM.[2] Nonetheless, this chapter also makes the methodological claim that it is possible to inquire into eminently social and nonmaterial issues of the international scene, such as IEM, in a manner that engages both mainstream and radical perspectives.

THE WESTERN HEMISPHERE IDEA

As I pointed out in the introduction, by the early nineteenth century Latin America and the United States had constituted themselves into the two main regions of the western hemisphere, even as the latter was emerging as a separate subsystem in world politics. The separateness of the new world made it possible for it to become a self-contained "system of interests," as Jefferson pointed out in the quoted passage above. The constitutional structure underlying both the "system of interests" and the concomitant patterned interaction among its constitutive members created the conception of state sovereignty which would eventually lead to the emergence of IEM in the Americas before any other region of the world. Let's look at this long-term process in more detail.

By the third decade of the nineteenth century the interaction of the nascent Latin American states amongst themselves and with the United States was producing a *regional subsystem,* in the sense that a regional identity was being experienced not only by its members but also by external actors.[3] In this context, Europe was the relevant other for the American states. Hence, despite its unilateral nature, the Monroe Doctrine, which claimed that the system still emerging in the Americas was "essentially different" from that of Europe, was mostly welcomed by the Latin American states.[4] But this regional identity did not go much further that demarcating a territory from which the Europeans were to be excluded. During most of the nineteenth century the United States and Latin America were to remain distant neighbors.

It was not until the 1880s, after most Latin American states had been consolidated and the United States had endured the Civil War, that Pan Americanism gained momentum.[5] At the time when Latin American statesmen were increasingly concerned with U.S. intervention in the internal affairs of their states, and a strong anti-Yankee feeling was becoming widespread in some intellectual circles in the subcontinent, the United States started a rapprochement with its southern (and Caribbean) neighbors. It was in this context that the 1889 Washington conference of American States, which is widely considered as the inauguration of the modern Inter-American System, took place.[6] It was then that the Commercial Bureau of the American Republics (later known as the Pan-American Union) was established. Hemispheric conferences, at which important regional matters such as nonintervention and the treatment of foreigners were discussed, became a feature of state practice in the Americas: during the first half of the twentieth century, there were 15 such meetings.[7]

But the mere existence of these fora did not imply a convergence of interests among the participating states. On the contrary, there were deep disagreements among the statesmen of the hemisphere. Perhaps the most salient dispute related to the tutelary aims of the rising hegemon. By the turn of the twentieth century, not only had the United States become a continental power at the expense of its southern neighbor, it was also involved in imperial pursuit in other states in the region. Thus, according to the 1905 Roosevelt Corollary to the Monroe Doctrine, "the United States would become the policeman of the western hemisphere. It would interfere in the affairs of any nations unable to handle their own affairs—intervene for the purpose of eliminating conditions which might encourage European intervention"[8] The subordinated states of the hemisphere resented this position, but there was not much they could do. The Inter-American subsystem was unquestionably unipolar: no other state in the hemisphere was able to challenge the United States.

Thus, at the third Pan-American Congress in Rio de Janeiro in 1906 the Latin American states and the new dominant power clashed over issues such as the principle of nonintervention, which the latter resisted.[9] Hence, for instance, under the Platt Amendment, the United States "legally" intervened in Cuba from 1906 to 1909. By the 1920s, as Yankee phobia was gaining a second air in Latin America, the United States began to play a less ostensibly dominant role in the inter-American system.[10] The Hoover administration took the first steps of what under the next administration would come to be known as the "Good Neighbor" policy. But this did not mean yet a fundamental change toward its hemispheric neighbors: still at the 1928 Havana Pan American Conference the United States opposed the doctrine of nonintervention, so dear to the Latin Americans.[11]

A few years later, though, with the arrival of Franklin D. Roosevelt to power, the United States did make a veritable about-face in its policy toward Latin America. At the 1936 Inter-American Conference for the Maintenance of Peace, held in Buenos Aires, in the context of the by then widely proclaimed "Good Neighbor Policy," the United States accepted without reservations the doctrine of nonintervention. Thus, the Declaration of Principles of Inter-American Solidarity and Cooperation that came out of the Buenos Aires Conference stated that "Intervention by one State in the internal or external affairs of another State is condemned." Significantly, the Declaration also noted that the American states "have a common likeness in their democratic form of government and their common ideals of peace and justice, manifested in the several Treaties and Conventions which they have signed for the purpose of constituting a purely American system."[12] Thus, the hemispheric discourse on solidarity based on democratic values, and not only on its severance from the old world, acquired new salience.[13]

The vitality of the regional compact was confirmed at the 1945 Inter-American Conference on the Problems of War at Peace, held in Mexico City. By the Act of Chapultepec, the signatories decided to augment the scope of the hemispheric understanding. Accordingly, the participating states agreed to establish an inter-American collective security system once the war was over. More telling, though, was the zeal with which, a month after the Chapultepec meeting, Latin American states defended the recognition of regional systems at the United Nations Conference on International Organization, held in San Francisco. Thus, for instance, using Pan-Americanism as an example of what a regional system can accomplish, the Colombian delegate argued for the right of regional systems to deal with security problems without having to be authorized first by the United Nations Security Council. The Latin American effort, supported by the United States, was successful, as reflected in articles 52–54 of the UN Charter.[14]

Thus, the "separate system" Jefferson had envisioned for the Americas would materialize 135 years later, with the promulgation of the Bogotá Charter and the establishment of the OAS in 1948. In addition to the sense of separation from the European system, I would argue that the idea that ran through this period and made the crystallization of hemispheric institutions possible, although apparently of domestic character, was in fact infused with the systemic "American 'spirit'": republicanism.[15] As Nicholas Onuf has put it, "The legacy of republicanism tells us that independent states are connected, and not just by circumstance."[16]

Nineteenth-century republicanism was certainly not the same as classical republicanism. The classical, formal conception of republicanism as rule by the few, had already given way to an understanding of republicanism as a type of government.[17] The importance of representative government had been the leit-motif of the inter-American system—even before the principle of nonintervention became prevalent. Thus, the Treaty of Perpetual Union, League, and Confederation adopted at the 1826 Panama Congress called for the suspension or even expulsion of undemocratic governments from the organization.[18] Similarly, by the 1907 Central American Treaty of Peace, sponsored by Mexican President Porfirio Díaz and US President William Taft, the five signatories committed their countries not to recognize "any other Government which may come into power in any of the five Republics as a consequence of a *coup d'etat,* or of a revolution against the recognized Government, so long as the freely elected representatives of the people thereof have not constitutionally reorganized the country."[19]

Although Roosevelt had warned against basing US policy "not on the firm ground of national interest but on the treacherous sands of international democratic propagandism,"[20] in 1914 President Woodrow Wilson proposed a Pan-American Pact by which, among other things, the signatories would mutually guarantee their republican forms of government.[21] Fittingly, when Wilson took office he refused to recognize the government of Victoriano Huerta in Mexico, who had overthrown the democratically elected government of Francisco Madero in 1913. In order to grant its recognition, his administration demanded that a popularly elected government be installed, and that Huerta not be a candidate in the electoral process.[22] In the next decade, at the above-mentioned Havana convention, the Cuban representative warned that "[if] we declare in absolute terms that intervention is under no circumstance possible, we will be sanctioning all the inhuman acts committed within determined frontiers."[23] In a similar vein, Uruguayan Foreign Minister Alberto Rodríguez Larreta wrote in his famous 1945 note that "The purest respect for the principle of non-intervention of one state in the affairs of another . . . does not protect unlimitedly the notorious and repeated violation by any republic of elementary rights of man." And that in the relations among the states of the western hemisphere "the parallelism between peace and democracy" should be "an indeclinable norm of action."[24]

It is thus not surprising to find several references to representative democracy as the only legitimate form of government in the 1948 OAS Charter. Its preamble, for instance, states that the "true significance of American solidarity and good neighborliness can only mean the consolidation on this continent, within the framework of democratic institutions, of a system of individual liberty and social justice based on respect for the essential rights of man." More explicitly, as noted in the introduction, Article 5 (now Article 3) maintains that "The solidarity of the American States and the high aims which are sought through it require the political organization of those States on the basis of the effective exercise of representative democracy," while at the same time equating international order with respect for the independence and sovereignty of states.

As the article just quoted makes clear, there has been an inherent tension in the inter-American system: the tension between representative government as a common discourse that unites the states of the Americas, and nonintervention as a principle intended to keep the United States out of Latin America. The nonintervention principle is just the obverse, usually neglected side of the WHI's most conspicuous one: the idea of a compact of republican states separated from Europe. That is, by virtue of the fault line dividing the United States from its southern neighbors, the latter made nonintervention an integral part of the WHI. Thus, while representative government was to be closely associated with the "compact" component of the WHI, more forcefully pushed by the United States,[25] nonintervention would come to be associated with the fault line separating the two regions, with Latin America being its main proponent. This is the second issue of the historical structure I am concerned with: *Latin America* within the Americas.

To claim that Latin American states had common interests vis-à-vis the United States is not to suggest that the relations among themselves were immaculate. Their all-too-frequent political disputes in the nineteenth century, for instance, make clear that their intercourse has been imbued with conflict practically from the onset. Yet, Latin American states came to develop a common identity vis-à-vis the dominant power. In the same way that Europe was the relevant other for the hemisphere, as the Monroe Doctrine made clear early in the post-independence period, the United States was the relevant other for Latin America, as its demand for the recognition of the nonintervention principle evidenced. Thus, not only did the Latin American states come to consider themselves as constituting a regional subsystem, but they were also perceived that way by the United States and other external actors.[26] After all, "geography," as Tom Farer has noted, "is a perception, not a fact."[27]

And the perception of a different identity was already present by the time of the 1826 Congress, to which, tellingly, the United States had not been originally invited.[28] Thus, during the nineteenth century Latin America developed political programs and ideologies that, while heavily influenced both by European and North American thinkers, were "distinctive and authentically 'Latin American.'"[29] Sometimes imbued with racist elements, as in José E. Rodó's claim that Latin America, as opposed to "the mighty confederation," had "an inheritance of race, a great ethnic tradition to maintain,"[30] this common ideology cemented a Latin American identity. Thus, at the 1906 third Pan-American Congress, the Latin American states vehemently argued, against the United States, in favor of both the Calvo Doctrine, regarding the principle of nonintervention, and the Drago Doctrine, concerning the principle of equal treatment to foreigners.[31] By the time of World War I, the policies of Latin American states made clear that there was "little in the way of a community of *hemispheric* interests."[32]

The rise, after World War II, of the United States as one of the two world superpowers only reinforced in the Latin American states the need to obtain a guarantee from their northern neighbor. It was in this context that the above-mentioned article 5 stating the importance of both representative democracy and the respect for the sovereignty and independence of member states was included in the OAS Charter. But Article 15 of the same document states still more forcefully that "No State or group of States has the right to intervene, directly or indirectly, for any reason whatever, in the internal or external affairs of any other State. The foregoing principle prohibits not only armed force but also any other form of interference or attempted threat against the personality of the State or against its political, economic and cultural elements."

Significantly, though, by the mid-twentieth century representative government in particular, and human rights more broadly, had become an integral part of Latin American diplomatic discourse, not only in the hemisphere but in world politics. Thus, for instance, Brazil and Uruguay wanted to include some sort of democratic clause in the OAS Charter.[33] Moreover, Latin American diplomats were instrumental in the drafting and passing of the American Declaration on the Rights and Duties of Man, before the United Nations passed the Universal Declaration—in whose manufacturing, not accidentally, they played a very active role.[34] In what now seems a prophetic statement, the Chilean representative told the General Assembly that "no one could infringe upon the rights proclaimed in it [the Universal Declaration] without becoming an outcast of the community of states."[35] Furthermore, Latin American diplomats were instrumental in the drafting and passing of the American Declaration on the Rights and Duties of Man *before* the United Nations passed the Universal Declaration. Actually, human rights would become, according to David Forsythe, "the bright spot on OAS history."[36]

Thus, at the hemispheric level, Latin American states, along with the United States, came to develop a complex institutional set that would enshrine not only the by then traditional discourses on representative government and nonintervention, but also the already alluded to Inter-American Treaty of Reciprocal Assistance. By means of these institutional arrangements, Latin American states aimed not only at cooperating with, but also at containing, US power. Put differently: Latin American states wanted to contain the region's hegemon by institutionalizing their cooperation with it. Furthermore, Latin American states were successful in creating a much more democratic organization than the UN, as manifested in the

OAS Charter's recognition of formal equality for all member states.[37] The emerging Cold War as normative (and material) structure undoubtedly contributed to make this arrangement acceptable to the United States. As Farer has noted,

> the democratic forms of the OAS system appealed both to the self-consciously idealistic strain in U.S. foreign policy and to the natural inclination of a status quo power—necessarily delighted with the postwar dispensation—to consolidate and legitimate its position in terms of prevailing values. And the values that prevailed, in the aftermath of a war against their antithesis, were respect for the independence of small states and rejection of force as a tool of diplomacy.[38]

Hence, in spite of all the importance they had traditionally attached to representative government and human rights, nonintervention came to be the paramount principle for Latin American states—in accordance with the wider international practice. As Larman Wilson and David Dent have put it, "The principle of nonintervention is the most important law duty in the [OAS] charter, and it *transcends* all the other duties, including that of promoting representative democracy and the protection of human rights."[39] The advent of the Cold War led Latin American states to an increasingly maximalist interpretation of the nonintervention principle. With the still incipient human rights policy of the United States being subsumed under its anticommunist crusade, Latin American diplomats were wary that the colossus of the north could use the hemispheric consensus on human rights and representative government as a tool for intervention. As a Mexican diplomat and scholar on foreign relations put it 10 years after the OAS had come into existence, "[w]hile this fear exists, while the present situation does not change, the *cornerstone* of the [I]nter-American system, its guiding principle, will not be democracy, but intransigent non-intervention."[40]

The fact that the nonintervention principle came to have such legal prominence in the inter-American system was of course not reflected in actual practice. Blatant intervention by the United States in Guatemala in the 1950s, in Cuba and the Dominican Republic in the 1960s, in Chile in the 1970s, and in Grenada and Panama in the 1980s are just a few instances of the lip service the regional hegemon often paid to its hemispheric commitments. That is why for many Latin American scholars the inter-American principle of nonintervention was simply a "myth," and for some US scholars—notably Krasner—an instance of "organized hypocrisy." Similarly, it is commonly argued that the traditional Latin American discourse on human rights and representative government has been nothing more than empty rhetoric, given the dismal record of most Latin American states on these issues.[41]

While both remarks are correct insofar as they point to an actual gap between lofty statements and practice, they incorrectly dismiss such normative components as epiphenomenal. In this logic, normative elements could at most supplement interest-based explanations of state behavior. My argument, though, is different: it is not that the constitutional structure can supplement mainstream (i.e. rationalist and material) approaches, explaining the residual variance that is not accounted for by "real" state interests. The argument I make is that the "real" interests of states were partly constituted by these principles.[42] That is why, one the one hand, US intervention in the continent has not been more frequent, and, on the other, even the maximalist interpretation of the nonintervention principle made by Latin American governments allowed for external intervention (e.g., via foreign observers) in what would otherwise be considered a domestic affair: national elections.

This is not to say that the United States suddenly converted to the *principle* of nonintervention at the 1936 Buenos Aires Conference (the historical record promptly contradicts this assertion). It is not to say, either, that Latin American statesmen have always been concerned about human rights and democracy (the historical record is again awfully clear in this respect). What I am suggesting is that once the discourse on nonintervention and human rights and representative government was adopted, it was bound to have real effects—intended or otherwise. Thus, since different states in Latin America behaved similarly in response to similar phenomena, talk about an underlying (if unobservable) structure at work is warranted.[43] Furthermore, this discourse came to shape state identity and state interests. More concretely, it produced a particular understanding of sovereignty in the western hemisphere, or, more specifically, in Latin America. It was a conception of sovereignty informed by the tension enshrined in the WHI, and grounded on higher order principles such as human rights and representative government. Hence, the unobservable constitutional structure at work not only shaped state behavior, but it also created states interests. Its effects were not only regulative but also generative.

In this underlying hemispheric understanding, sovereignty was conceived of as a discursive bundle, containing "clauses" on both nonintervention and representative government. Thus, in the same way that the nonintervention principle constrained and came to inform US behavior and interests in the hemisphere, the emphasis on human rights and representative government affected the identity and foreign relations of Latin American states.[44] This is why, as noted above, Latin American states recognized that human rights principles were above an absolute interpretation of nonintervention. Not surprisingly, then, at the Eight Meeting of consultation the Venezuelan Foreign Minister stated that although the four principles of nonintervention, human rights, representative democracy, and self-determination have equal legal standing in the OAS Charter, the second one, human rights, would be at the top of the hierarchy.[45] It was precisely this broad understanding of sovereignty that allowed the western hemisphere to become the forerunner in IEM.

By agreeing to the creation of the OAS as the forum where nonintervention and representative government issues were to be sorted out, Latin American states were enacting their understanding of sovereignty. This understanding was shot through and through with the (institutional) fact of US hegemony, a hegemony that implied not only its material superiority (and the usual concessions hegemons are willing to make to subordinated states), but also a set of common norms and thinking about order in the hemisphere.[46] That is why the OAS, as a manifestation of the WHI, should not be seen simply as a regime of cooperation, but rather as a specific arrangement of patterned interaction.

As Alberto Lleras Camargo, the first secretary general of the OAS put it, "The Organization in itself is neither good nor bad . . . it is what the member governments want it to be and nothing else."[47] It was thus the OAS as a concrete institutional arrangement that allowed the states of the Americas to become pioneers in the field of IEM. Not incidentally, Whitaker noted that the WHI was "a laboratory and proving ground for policies, institutions, and experiences that were *later* applied with advantage in the broader field of world affairs."[48]

THE ADVENT OF THE COLD WAR

Although nonintervention was the cornerstone of the OAS, the principles on human rights and representative government were not simply shelved by the Latin American states with the emergence of the Cold War. Rather, these principles were read off the constitutional structure according to which Latin American states had internalized a complex understanding of their sovereignty, an understanding that involved the airing at the hemispheric level of what could otherwise be considered domestic affairs. If the previous understanding on representative government had not existed, or if it had just been put on hold by the emergence of the Cold War, IEM would not have emerged in Latin American in the early 1960s. This is not to deny that the Cold War as global normative structure both constrained and shaped the emergence of IEM. But I claim that it did so only to point out that there was, at the regional level, a more fundamental structure at work, one that made IEM possible even after the onset of what I conceive of as a structural intervening variable: the Cold War (more on this in the methodological section).

The deeper structure was the WHI, out of which came a distinctively regional understanding of sovereignty, an understanding that made the emergence of IEM in the Americas—but nowhere else—possible. The irreducible common denominator that republicanism represented in the hemisphere implied the extrapolation, to the continental level, of the principle according to which in any republic "coercion and concern for the common good dance on together."[49] That is, there was an implicit understanding regarding not only the ubiquitous presence of coercion in the relations among the states of the hemisphere (despite their formal equality),[50] but also regarding the latent existence of common interests. These common interests were, of course, peace and security.

But in the Cold War context, the easiest means to achieve these ends came to be for Latin American states to insist on *what appeared to be* absolute nonintervention, and for the United States to try to subsume the institutional arrangements created after the war under its anticommunist crusade. The WHI came thus to be apparently encapsulated within the Cold War. It nevertheless served as an ideational *constant* that, in so far as it gave *content* to the practice of both state and non-state actors during the Cold War, helps to account for their differentiated strategies in this period.[51] That is, the WHI permeated the Cold War as normative structure in the western hemisphere, serving as a script for both statesmen and activists. Had the bipolar structure (in terms of both ideologies and material capabilities) not emerged, there would probably have been a deeper convergence on issues of democracy in the hemisphere following World War II. Alternatively, had the WHI not existed, the discourse on representative government and human rights would have been by and large absent in the Americas during the Cold War.

However, Latin American states were marginal in the inception and development of the Cold War. The latter was primarily an ideological battle between two superpowers: the United States and the Union of Soviet Socialist Republics. In forging a worldwide coalition, the United States sought to export its domestic values. It was a strategy that, as John Gerard Ruggie has put it, "linked the pursuit of American interests to a transformative vision of the world order that appealed to the American public."[52] This John Ikenberry calls "America's Liberal Grand Strategy." Ikenberry argues that it had been "built around a wide-ranging set of claims and assumptions about how democratic politics, economic interdependence, international institutions, and political identity contribute independently and together to encourage stable and mutually acceptable political order."[53] Nevertheless, the US strategy had two scripts: containment of Communism, and the establishment of a liberal-democratic order.[54] Within this global strategy, the input of the Latin American states was bound to be peripheral. As a matter of fact, the OAS largely became a tool of the dominant power.[55] Its role in ostracizing Cuba in 1962, and in approving US interventionism in the Dominican Republic in 1965 are just two examples of this.

The United States was fighting a war on many fronts, and the ideological one became paramount. As former Secretary of State Dean Rusk put it during the Vietnam War: "The United States cannot be secure until the total international environment is ideologically safe."[56] And at least within the western hemisphere, sometimes rabid anticommunism became the dominant strategy. Thus, for instance, United States tried to overthrow democratically elected governments it perceived as going against its interests in Guatemala (1954), British Guiana (1953–64), Ecuador (1960–63), Brazil (1964), the Dominican Republic (1965), Costa Rica (in the mid-1950s) and Chile (1970–73).[57] As Secretary of State Henry Kissinger would candidly put it, "I don't see why we need to stand by and watch a country go Communist due to the irresponsibility of its own people."[58]

Before 1973, as Sikkink has noted, "human rights were rarely explicitly considered in the US foreign policy calculus."[59] It was only after 1976, when human rights legislation was passed in the Congress, and mainly during the Carter administration (1977–1980) that human rights issues figured prominently.[60] This prominence was going to be short-lived, though. Reagan's first Secretary of State, Alexander Haig, declared that the previous administration's preference for human rights had been substituted for the East-West competition.[61] But past governmental commitments are sticky. As Thomas Carothers has noted, "The prodemocracy influence of the congressional Democrats on the Reagan administration's Latin America policy can be understood as the extension into the 1980s of the human rights consciousness that gained a place in U.S. foreign policy in the 1970s."[62]

Hence, by choice or by inertia, but more likely as a rhetorical strategy intended to further its own policy goals, the Reagan administration began to make of "democracy promotion" a central part of its foreign policy toward the hemisphere—thus adhering to the WHI. The kind of democracy to be promoted, of course, was to be one modeled after that existing in the United States. As Carothers has noted, "Supporting democracy too often resembles the application of a preprinted checklist in which the institutional forms of U.S.-style democracy are financed and praised while the more complex and more important realities of political life are ignored."[63] In the opinion of many observers, what the US government has actually been promoting is "low intensity democracy," that is, "a form of democracy whereby the focus is on formal electoral rights, with little consideration paid to the wider socio-economic power structure, and with the military often remaining in the wings should reform go too far."[64]

But the characterization of the regime type promoted by the United States is not central to my main argument (since, as noted in the introduction, this work is *not* about democracy). What matters here is to trace the trajectory of the normalization of IEM—which was closely linked to "democracy promotion" programs. Thus, a year after Reagan's 1982 speech before the British Parliament, in which he stated his objective "to foster the infrastructure of democracy," the National Endowment for Democracy (NED) was created. It was established by the US Congress in order to "promote United States nongovernmental participation. . . . in democratic training programs and democratic institution building abroad" and "to strengthen democratic electoral processes abroad through timely measures in cooperation with indigenous democratic forces."[65]

Initially, the Reagan administration put the democratic seal on regimes that hardly qualified as democratic, such as the Salvadorian one. Nevertheless, having entered the democracy discourse, the Reagan administration had to make its rhetoric more consistent with its deeds. Thus, in 1986 the administration issued a "major policy statement" indicating that it "opposed tyranny in whatever form, whether of the left or of the right."[66] As Carothers put it, "Having made democracy the stated goal of its policy . . . the Reagan administration soon found that its policy was evaluated in those terms. . . . This opened the way for an evolution toward policies with real prodemocratic substance."[67]

With the double impetus of the Latin American transitions to democracy, and the born-again taste for democracy promotion on the part of the regional hegemon, the OAS updated its basic documents.[68] Thus, in 1985 in Cartagena de Indias, Colombia, it amended its Charter, endowing the organization with a new mission, the promotion of democracy. The 1985 Protocol of Amendment, as the OAS Unit for the Promotion of Democracy document setting the standards for its observers notes, "provides the general principle for the new kind of election monitoring by the Organization."[69] But despite this attuning between the stated goals of the Latin American countries and the United States,[70] the organization itself was largely marginalized in hemispheric affairs. As will become clear in the next two chapters, the major initiatives during the second half of the 1980s circumvented the hemispheric grouping.[71]

Nevertheless, the endurance *after* the onset of the Cold War of practices reflecting the composite understanding of sovereignty that the states of the hemisphere had constructed (what appeared to be a sort of schizophrenic discourse, including both absolute nonintervention and hemispheric cooperation) poses a puzzle for mainstream IR. More sociologically-oriented approaches, on the other hand, would relate this patterned behavior to the logic of appropriateness, in which action is seen as the product of rules and identities that indicate appropriate behavior in given situations, or to the logic of arguing, in which actors seek to reach a reasoned consensus, as argued in the previous chapter.[72] For these approaches, patterned behavior is more than the mere aggregation of strategic choices. For as Wildavsky put it, "Every choice is not only intended to be decision rational, it must also be culturally rational."[73]

THE EMERGENCE OF IEM

It was the historical background, or more precisely the WHI as constitutional structure outlined in the previous sections, which enabled IEM to emerge in the hemisphere in the early 1960s. Its origins, however, go back to the late 1950s. A speech given by Venezuelan President Arnoldo Betancourt in 1958 serves as an illustration of the mood that transpired in the hemisphere at the time. In his inaugural address he suggested that "Regimes which do not respect human rights, which violate the liberties of their citizens and tyrannize them with political police ought to be subjected to a rigorous cordon sanitarie and eradicated by the collective peaceful action of the Inter-American juridical community."[74] The next year, Betancourt suggested that the OAS recognize only "regimes born of free elections and respecting human rights."[75]

Along the same lines, at the 1959 Fifth Meeting of Consultation, the *Declaration of Santiago* stated that "The governments of the American republics should result of free elections."[76] Suitably, in that meeting Nicaragua presented a project on the use of international electoral observers. Also at the 1959 meeting, the Council of Jurists of the organization was asked to study the "possible juridical relationship between respect for human rights and the effective exercise of representative democracy, and the right to set in motion the machinery of American international law in force."[77] The Council in turn asked the Inter-American Judicial Committee to consider the matter, which ruled by majority that the Bogotá Charter did not allow collective action to take place in support of democracy.[78]

But the issue of democracy as a legitimate concern for the organization did not vanish from the agenda after the 1959 Santiago meeting. The next year, at the Seventh Meeting in San José, Costa Rica, an Argentine draft called for the creation of an OAS Council committee "to consider the request of any government that, with a view to fitting its political life into the active operation of American democratic principles, may for that purpose wish to be advised, or *to demonstrate to international public opinion* that those principles are effective within its jurisdiction."[79] Along the same lines, the United States submitted at the meeting a draft calling for the introduction of international observers. Thus, considering the 1959 Nicaraguan initiative, there were three proposals on the subject of international election monitoring by 1960 in the OAS' agenda.

The first instance of IEM carried out by the regional organization crystallized in Costa Rica. In January 1962 the Costa Rican government requested the Secretary General to send observers to the 4 February presidential elections. A three-member mission was then put together. The team produced a report in which it considered the "previous conditions," "concurrent conditions" and "subsequent conditions" for a democratic election. It noted that "the Constitution, the legislation, and the current electoral practices in Costa Rica meet all the requirements of a democratic electoral regime."[80]

The observers visited several polling places in the country's capital, San José, and in several other towns. The report mentions the consensus among all contending political parties in that the government was acting impartially in the electoral process.[81] The observers concluded that "the electoral act that took place on Sunday 4 February 1962 was carried out with the utmost order and without any incident worth mentioning in all the territory of the republic."[82] The day after the elections, the members of the OAS team met with President Mario Echandi in order to thank him for "the trust deposited by the Government of Costa Rica in the OAS, as shown by its request for an electoral observation mission."[83]

The mission acknowledges the opportunity it was given "to penetrate into the heart of such a transcendental election."[84] In its conclusions, the observers' report notes that "it would be convenient to suggest to extend to other countries that request it, the endeavor of technical assistance by OAS observers that has been put in practice in this opportunity."[85] Perhaps because the request of the Costa Rican government was sent directly to the Secretary General, and because Costa Rica's political regime was widely recognized as democratic, this foundational IEM experience passed practically unnoticed in the hemisphere.

The regional organization's second venture into IEM, though, was rather different. The same year the Costa Rican monitoring took place came a second request, this one from the government of the Dominican

Republic. In contrast to the previous case, the issue of sending observers to the Antillean country was more contentious. At the 1960 San José Conference OAS foreign ministers had rejected an offer by the Dominican Republic to accept electoral observers, on the basis that "this would constitute OAS intervention in the internal affairs of a member state."[86] Nevertheless, following President Trujillo's assassination in May 1961, President Balaguer, the new head of State, started introducing democratic reforms and appealed to the OAS for assistance on electoral matters once again.

The OAS responded positively to this second request and sent a three-member technical assistance mission. After the Dominican government asked for further services, the mission suggested that foreign observers attend the December elections, to which the government agreed. On this occasion, the OAS mission was composed of almost fifty "distinguished individuals" from throughout the Americas.[87] As Jerome Slater has observed, "In view of the long tradition of non-intervention, the deep involvement of the OAS in Dominican internal matters was remarkable."[88]

Concurrently with the December elections, the First Symposium on Representative Democracy took place in Santo Domingo within the OAS framework. Two of the topics on which the event focused were self-determination and nonintervention. It was concluded that: "self-determination does not mean the violent destruction of the principles and standards that constitute the basis of the regional organization, instead of adherence to established procedures," and that "the idea of nonintervention is a projection into the sphere of international relations of the ideas of freedom and equality in relations between individuals in a given state." Furthermore, the Symposium cited among the actions that "cannot be described as intervention. . . . [those taken] by the authorities of the regional organization in fulfillment of international standards freely consented to by the state towards which they are directed."[89] Nonintervention was not considered a self-referential value, but rather part and parcel of the hemispheric constitutional structure.

The next year (1963), the OAS sent two electoral assistance missions to Central America: one to Nicaragua to observe the 3 February presidential elections, and another one to Honduras to provide technical assistance for the 13 October general elections. The former endeavor was composed of three observers, and it produced no final report. The latter, while also consisting of only three members, delivered a comprehensive report—over sixty pages-long—of the Honduran electoral system, which included suggestions for the then forthcoming elections. In preparing the report, the mission visited the Central American country for an unusually long period—sixty days.[90]

In presenting their observations to the Honduran government, the members of the mission noted that their suggestions "would imply comprehensive reforms that impact beyond the sphere of the vote."[91] Thus, for instance, the OAS envoys suggested changes in the relationship between the Army and the Civil Guard, and in the voting method.[92] The observers, tellingly, praised the Honduran government for "voluntarily putting at the consideration of the American commonwealth its political performance," and remarked that the Honduran electoral process was "a common cause of the continental democracy."[93]

IEM was thus not just a practice imposed by the United States on its weak neighbors. Furthermore, it is important to note that although by the late 1960s the hegemon had for all practical purposes lost effective control of the regional organization,[94] IEM continued at about the same pace during the following years, with 11 missions between 1965 and 1978.[95] Thus, for instance, the report from the Preparatory Commission for the Consultative Meeting of Ministers of Foreign Affairs on Representative Democracy, submitted to the OAS Council in February 1965 stated that "the existence of antidemocratic regimes constitutes a violation of the founding principles of the Organization of American States, and a danger for the solidary and peaceful interaction in the Hemisphere," reaffirming that the "governments of the American Republics should emanate from free elections."[96] Seven years later, in 1972, Secretary General Galo Plaza addressed a note to the Chairman of the Permanent Council on the advisability of standards being established by the Council for the appointment of election observers.[97] Although the OAS was not to specify those standards for a long time (until the late 1990s), it continued to send observers to member states on an ad hoc basis through the 1970 and 1980s. Being a bona fide member of the inter-American community continued to be a relevant matter for member states.

Hence, in 1980 the Guatemalan government requested the regional organization to observe its municipal elections as a "demonstration to the international community" of the democratic nature of its political regime.[98] Four years later, another Guatemalan request mentions that the government "has committed itself, both domestically and internationally, to hold a pure and honest election."[99] Similarly, that same year the Salvadoran government requested observers to the regional body so that they could be "eyewitnesses to the progress El Salvador has made along the paths of the democratic system of government."[100] With missions also to Bolivia, Ecuador, and Grenada, among others, by 1984 the OAS had observed 22 elections in member states. It was in this context that the OAS made the above-mentioned amendments to its Charter in Cartagena.

THE APPEARANCE OF NON-OAS IEM

Just as state-sponsored IEM in the Americas was becoming more systematic in the late 1970s and early 1980s, INGOs entered the scene, often interacting with domestic monitoring groups. But the arrival of INGOs to this arena was not *deus ex machina*-like. It was an intrinsic component of the development of the democratic discourse in the hemisphere. Those states of the hemisphere with the strongest civil societies were, not surprisingly, the ones with more active NGOs. Here again, the fault line between the United States and the rest of the hemisphere was pronounced. The United States has historically had the most articulated and independent civil society in the Americas, of which Alexis de Tocqueville's *Democracy in America* is early evidence. In addition, the hegemonic position of the United States in the hemisphere put the INGOs of this country in a privileged position vis-à-vis its counterparts in the hemisphere.

As INGOs from the United States began to broaden their scope of activities, which had traditionally been centered on traditional human rights issues, the convergence with domestic groups in Latin America working on political rights issues came readily.[101] Thus, the Washington Office on Latin America (WOLA) started monitoring elections in 1978, sending observers to Bolivia. Two years later it observed the Guyana elections; in 1981 the electoral process in Honduras, and in 1983 WOLA observers monitored the 1983 elections in Argentina. That same year the International Human Rights Law Group (henceforth the Law Group) established its Election Observer Project, working with activists of the target states. In 1984, the Law Group published *Guidelines for International Election Observing*, by its then Project Director Larry Garber, which would become the standard for election observing both for INGOs and IGOs.[102] In 1984 WOLA and the Law Group jointly observed the elections in Nicaragua and Uruguay.[103] The Law Group also observed the elections in Grenada that year, and in 1985 the ones that took place in El Salvador and Guatemala. By 1990, the Law Group had organized 25 election monitoring missions, mostly in Latin America, but also in Asia and Africa.

Also in 1983, as noted, the NED was born. Despite its links to the US government, the NED was established as a private nonprofit, bipartisan organization. It is primarily a grant-making institution, and the majority of the programs on democracy promotion funded by it are carried out by the National Democratic Institute for International Affairs (NDI), and the International Republican Institute (IRI), both established as offshoots of the NED in 1983, and affiliated with the Democratic and Republican parties, respectively. These institutes, but NDI more aggressively, have been very active in monitoring elections worldwide.

Likewise nongovernmental, and also with manifest links to the US government, is the Carter Center, established in 1982. Headed by former President Jimmy Carter, in 1986 it hosted a conference on democracy in the Americas, which renown politicians from around the continent attended. As a result of the conference, 12 former and current heads of government from the Americas established the Council of Freely Elected Heads of Government, which was to be based at the Carter Center.[104] The Center's staff, and President Carter in particular, became the core of the Council. Among the Council's founding goals was "to promote multilateral democratic transitions and to reinforce the consolidation of new and re-emerging democracies in the region."[105] Its first election monitoring mission was to Haiti in 1987, at the request of the transitional government. Earlier that year, NDI-NRI had sent a joint mission, of which Larry Garber of the Law Group was a member, to observe the constitutional referendum.

INGOs have been instrumental in the success of cases that proved crucial to the institutionalization of electoral observation. Thus, for instance, the Carter Center played a crucial role in the 1990 Nicaraguan election. Former President Carter acted as a mediator between the Sandinista government and the opposition in order to solve some problems that arose in the electoral process, and he pushed for the organization of quick counts.[106] Moreover, prominent INGO members, such as Garber, joined the OAS team in Nicaragua. Garber, who as I noted before wrote the Law Group's *Guidelines,* also drafted the OAS Observers Guide used by the regional organization in Nicaragua.[107] INGOs contributed to create the synergy that made the initial informal involvement of IGOs in electoral observation possible. It is thus not surprising that when the issue of creating a specialized electoral unit emerged at the UN, it was welcomed by INGOs.[108]

INGOs have also been instrumental in the emergence and consolidation of an international network of electoral observation.[109] Thus, for instance, the example set by US and US-supported networks of NGOs in the field of election monitoring greatly contributed to the emergence of a strong network of this kind in Mexico.[110] But again: U.S. NGOs are not all-powerful entities that by their mere presence in the target state make the emergence of a robust observation network possible. It takes two well-developed civil societies to create an effective network in a country. In this sense, the interaction that took place between domestic and foreign observers in Haiti in 1987, is very different from that of Chile in 1988, or in Mexico in 1994, since the former country lacks the more consolidated civil society the other two possess.[111]

It was thus the constitutional structure created by state practice that made the emergence of this network of INGOs possible. Since INGOs have very different interests and identities from states or IGOs, the emergence of an INGO-based IEM TAN in the hemisphere in the 1980s gave rise to a very interesting dynamic in this arena. Thus, there have been occasions in which IGOs have not been present at some electoral processes (either because they declined to send a mission, or because they were not invited by the national government), but INGOs have observed them. In the Americas, this happened in Haiti in 1987, in Chile 1988, and in Panama in 1989.[112] The work of INGOs during the 1980s can thus be considered a second phase in the history of IEM in the continent, a phase in which the monitoring of elections became much more substantial, as the teams sent by INGO tended to do a much more exhaustive job than the token delegations traditionally sent by the OAS. The INGOs, however, were building on the state discourse and practice that preceded them within the OAS—and more generally, on the WHI as constitutional structure.

THE CONVERGENCE OF IGOS AND INGOS: THE IEM TAN CONSOLIDATES

The third phase started in 1989–1990, when INGOs, the OAS, and the UN, converged in their IEM activity—and thus consolidated the IEM TAN—in the Nicaraguan electoral process of that year. Over two thousand accredited foreign observers of more than two hundred organizations were present in Nicaragua on election day. The UN and the OAS established the largest and most comprehensive electoral observation missions ever in a sovereign country. The OAS team alone consisted of 433 observers. The end of the Cold War, and the continued wave of democratic transitions in Latin America, reinvigorated the OAS, as noted before. In this new context, the promotion of democracy became a central objective of the organization, both declaratively *and* in practice.

Thus, in November 1989, before the electoral process in Nicaragua was over, the OAS General Assembly recommended sending observation missions to member states that requested it.[113] Seven months later, at the Eight Plenary Session, the OAS General Assembly passed a resolution calling for the creation of the "Unit for Democratic Development," in order to "respond promptly and effectively to member states which, in the full exercise of their sovereignty, request advice or assistance to preserve or strengthen their political institutions and democratic procedures."[114] Significantly, the resolution notes "with appreciation" the role the OAS played in the still recent Nicaraguan experience. The Unit for the Promotion of Democracy (UPD), as it was finally called, was established in October 1990.

In addition, on June 4, 1991, at the 21st regular session of the OAS General Assembly, the foreign ministers of the regional body issued a declaration entitled the *Santiago Commitment to Democracy and the Renewal of the Interamerican System.* Noting that the end of the Cold War had brought "new opportunities and responsibilities," the member states declared their renewed and expanded commitment to the promotion and defense of representative democracy and human rights. Going further, the next day the organization passed Resolution 1080, which creates a mechanism to react to "the sudden or irregular interruption of the democratic political institutional process" in any member state.[115] With the 1991 *Santiago Commitment* and Resolution 1080, as Domingo Acevedo has noted, "For the first time, an international organization has explicitly ruled that governments should be held internationally accountable to the regional community for the means by which they have taken and secure power."[116]

The same year it was created, the ground-breaking mechanism was triggered by the military forces that ousted Haitian President Jean-Bertrand Aristide on 30 September. The OAS stepped in and took several ostracizing measures against the junta. Subsequently, when on 5 April 1992 Peruvian President Alberto Fujimori perpetrated what amounted to a self-coup, the mechanism established in Resolution 1080 was activated for the second time. International pressure forced Fujimori to attend the Organization's meeting in Barbados the following month, and to accept specific steps to restore democracy in his country.[117] From that moment on, the OAS would become a permanent fixture in the Peruvian electoral processes, deploying an unprecedented activist mission in 2000—while the president would praise the regional body for "respecting the principle of nonintervention."[118]

The transit from the first to the third phase was neither linear nor smooth; there were no pre-established "stages" nor a unidirectional sense of progress leading to a "definitive" condition. The fact that some countries within the hemisphere began to call for international observers did not mean that there was a consensus around this issue. Mexico, for instance, consistently opposed international observers, until it finally accepted them in 1994. Furthermore, the emergence of INGOs participation in the early 1980s was no fortuitous coincidence. The OAS' reluctance to take any meaningful action in defense of democracy in the 1970s and early 1980s was "not the result of an absence of legal authority to act," as former Costa Rican foreign affairs minister Carlos Facio has noted.[119]

INGOs then became involved in IEM in order to fill a vacuum. Moreover, the entrance of IEM INGOs into the scene roughly corresponds to the wave of democratic transitions that began in the late 1970s in Latin America. Thus, in 1978 the opposition took over peacefully in the Dominican Republic; the next year an elected leader was inaugurated in Ecuador; in 1980 Fernando Belaúnde came back to power by popular vote in Peru; Argentina ended eight years of military rule in 1984, and Brazil inaugurated its first civilian administration in two decades in January 1985. Something more than mere elective affinity between the wave of democratic transitions and the emergence of INGOs devoted to IEM seems to have been going on.

Hemispheric interaction had indeed created the normative setting that made some sort of real intervention to defend democracy possible. Previous OAS practice might thus have been a *necessary* but not sufficient condition for the emergence of IEM INGOs.[120] This emergence took place in an environment in which the decaying authoritarian governments of many Latin American states were openly hostile to these INGOs, not only because they regarded their activities an undue interference in their domestic affairs, but also because their practice was not sanctioned by an IGO. As Michel Foucault once noted: "People know what they do; they frequently know why they do what they do; but what they don't know is what what they do does."[121] The unintended appearance, from the point of view of the states, of a network of INGOs involved in IEM thus contributed to the partial redefinition of these states' national interests. A redefinition that finally led to the convergence of the third phase.

Hence, in addition to the emergence of IEM in the Americas, which is my starting point, there have been two important innovations to the constitutional structure represented by the WHI. The first one came with the involvement of NGOs, and more fundamentally, of INGOs. This innovation does not refer to state behavior per se, but to the mere set of actors involved in IEM. For the states of the Americas this development meant two things: the unexpected arrival of a new player, and that the nature of IEM was going to change—it was bound to cease being a symbolic practice.

The second innovation to the constitutional structure was the internalization, by the states of the hemisphere, of this renewed, reinvigorated conception of IEM. At this point, the name of the game changed, and states became INGOs' partners. IEM was not only becoming "the only game in the hemisphere," but states had stopped being the only legitimate players. The normalization of IEM in this third phase brought with it a veritable change in state identity and interests—and a concomitant redefinition of sovereignty (see table 2.1).

Table 2.1: Evolution of IEM in the Americas

Phase	Actors	Countries
First	OAS	Bolivia, Costa Rica, Dominican Republic, Ecuador, Guatemala, Honduras, Nicaragua . . .
Second	OAS, NGOs, INGOs	Argentina, Bolivia, Costa Rica, El Salvador, Chile, Grenada, Haiti, Uruguay
Third	OAS, UN, NGOs, INGOs	Colombia, Haiti, Nicaragua, Mexico, Peru, United States, Venezuela. . .

INQUIRING INTO IEM: METHODOLOGICAL CONSIDERATIONS

As I mentioned in the introductory chapter, I focus on four instances of IEM as my in-depth cases: Chile 1988, Nicaragua 1990, Mexico 1994, and Peru 2000. The first one was a milestone in INGO-led IEM, in which non-state actors were openly defying an authoritarian regime. The second case represents the transition to the phase in which INGOs, states and IGOs began to act concurrently. The third case, Mexico 1994, is important in that it shows how one of the most important and nationalist states in the hemisphere, one that had traditionally been opposed to IEM, finally came to accept this practice in its own territory. Finally, the Peruvian case illustrates, as I suggested before, the normalization of IEM—and of the new understanding of sovereignty and state interests.

During the period my four cases took place, the Cold War went from being a pervasive element to a mere historical fact.[122] It must therefore occupy a prominent place in my narrative. Drawing on the work of Alastair Johnston, I conceive of the Cold War—as I noted before—as a structural intervening variable. Following John Hobson, by intervening variable I mean "a 'contingency,' which is added on to the basic causal variable"—in my case the WHI.[123] In other words, given the existence of WHI in the Americas, the Cold War was possible but not necessary for the emergence of IEM.[124] In Johnston's work, strategic culture is a deeply embedded normative structure operating at the level of the units (i.e., states) that serves as an ideational constant. In order to link his second-image concept to the international system, Johnston posits the existence of an intervening structural variable: the material environment. Since the ideational constant, in his case strategic culture, imbues the structural intervening variable with meaning, the latter serves only as a proximate cause to the changes, but not as the ultimate explanatory factor. That work is done by cultural factors. In my case, since changes in material capabilities were marginal in explaining the emergence of IEM, I replace the material structure as an intervening variable with what I consider a second-order normative structure: the Cold War. Thus, changes in the WHI as constitutional structure (or ideational constant) are given by changes in the Cold War as a second order normative structural intervening variable.[125] Contra Waltz, though, the WHI as an ideational constant that created a particular kind of anarchy in the western hemisphere does not drop from the analysis, since it imbued the intervening variable with meaning.

But both the WHI and the Cold War were enacted by, and adapted to, specific domestic structures. Domestic structure plays at the unit level an analogous role to that of the WHI at the hemispheric one: it patterns and gives meaning to state-society relations. There are of course a variety of domestic structures, each patterning social interaction at the domestic level in a particular way. Thus, drawing on a rich two-decade-long domestic structural research agenda within the International Relations literature, Thomas Risse-Kappen distinguishes six ideal types of domestic structures, such as state-controlled, corporatist, and society-dominated ones.[126] Since each type of domestic structure expresses the idiosyncrasy of the nation-state in question, it conditions the peculiarities IEM acquires in it. An exhaustive analysis of this process would be the subject matter of a work on area studies or comparative politics, not on IR, like this one.[127] But considered from the perspective of IR theory, domestic structure and the specificities IEM might adopt in it look different. From this vantage point, domestic structure might be considered a second image intervening variable, linking domestic and international politics.[128] Intervening because, from a systemic perspective, the type of domestic structure is contingent. For instance, for IEM to emerge, it was possible (but not necessary) that it was instantiated in state-controlled and corporatist structures, as will become clear in the following chapters. But since I go case by case in four countries looking at how actually existing IEM came into being, I have to look closely at their domestic structures. It is here, after all, that the hydra-headed IEM battle was fought for the most part—even if it was not always related directly to its subtext: state sovereignty.[129] Domestic structure is therefore a fundamental category for my analysis. Furthermore, careful consideration of domestic structures should be useful in shedding some light on an aspect constructivist projects like mine often fall short of: showing "how international practices actually shape state interests and identities."[130]

Accordingly, the nature of this study is genealogical. I proceed by means of a "narrative explanatory protocol," linking the events I analyze to concrete precursors "that most plausibly had causal relevance within the social collectivity" epitomized by the WHI.[131] My starting point is the present, in which IEM has become commonplace but, like in any genealogy, my objective is to "explain the formation of this present in terms of its past. . . . to describe how the present became logically possible."[132] Furthermore, like genealogical narratives, mine is episodical, focusing "only on those aspects of the past which are crucial to our understanding of what was singled out as problematic in the present."[133]

Although I consider the four episodes, or cases, separately, I am looking at a large case, or process, which I divide into several cases. So I have several linked observations, not just one. In this sense, I am working with a case, but I am also making a comparative study. Mine is then a "heuristic" case study, since I am trying to discern new general problems; I want to find out what changes in the international normative structure made the emergence of this practice possible.[134] Although my dependent variable is "international election monitoring" (and its concomitant redefinition of sovereignty), its manifestation varies in each specific case. In order to link my four cases, I ask the same general questions—informed by my theoretical approach—in each of them. I am interested both in the differences and in the similarities among the four cases. That is why I use both the comparative method and the method of structured, focused comparison.[135]

Each case can be considered an "observational unit," that is, a data category which I use for data collection and analysis. On the other hand, the WHI as constitutional structure is my "explanatory unit," that is, the theoretical category I use to account for the *pattern* observed: the emergence and normalization of IEM.[136] The general pattern emerging through IEM in the Americas should then be consistent with the constitutional structure of the WHI as mediated by the Cold War (that is why I conceive of the Cold War as a contingency). Thus, although my observational units are specific countries, my explanatory unit is systemic.

I intend to develop a constitutive theory of international election monitoring. That is why I inquire into the normative structure that has made this practice possible, and into the process by which it became generalized in the 1990s. But the relationship between the normative structure and the actual practice is conceptual, not causal in the covering-law sense of it. That is, I do not conceive of the constitutional structure of the international system and of international election monitoring as existing independently of each other, as most positivist theorists do when they speak of "dependent" and "independent" variables. The practice of international election monitoring is not previous to or independent of the normative structure; their relationship is internal. When we are dealing with constitutive inquiries like mine, in which we try "to account for the properties of things by reference to the structures in virtue of which they exist," the independent/dependent variable distinction is not very useful.[137]

This does not mean that I am not doing "normal" science. Working within the positivist framework, I follow a "particularizing" (as opposed to a "generalizing") strategy; that is, I attempt to explain an outcome (international election monitoring) by giving a detailed account of the events that led up to it. Following Richard Miller and John Searle, I conceive of a cause as the condition or background necessary for the triggering of an event, not as the trigger itself.[138] There is of course some overlap between this approach and the more conventional causal ones. Nevertheless, I rely not on covering laws (like mainstream positivists do), but on component laws, which do not claim to immediately connect the final outcome to the initial conditions. As David Dessler has put it, "Like any sound positivist explanation, reconstructive accounts explain by showing that the event in question was to be expected in the circumstances in which it occurred."[139] This is the case with my subject matter. That is why I said there was something deeper than a mere elective affinity between the WHI and IEM. What existed was an adequacy on the level of meaning.[140] Following Weber, I conceive of the relationship between the practice and the normative structure as one of "adequate causation;" this term, unlike elective affinity, does imply causality, although in a socio-historical context. The reconstructive account I present is intended precisely to elucidate from what concrete historical pathway IEM emerged.

I recognize that talking about doing constitutive theory while identifying dependent and independent variables might seem contradictory, but I want to be able to address both sides of the theoretical debate (i.e. rationalists and post-positivists).[141] In order to do this, I make compromises on both fronts, such as talking about "variables" while working with a minimalist definition of them.[142] It is thus clear that my stance within the constructivist camp is, as I noted earlier, closer to the "modernist" or moderate stream represented by the work of authors such as Peter Katzenstein, Friedrich Kratochwil, John Ruggie, and Alexander Wendt, than to the post-structuralist one of Richard Ashley, James Der Derian, R. B. J. Walker, and Cynthia Weber.[143] I do not mean to deny the important contributions made by the latter scholars to the current debate in IR, even less to simply write them off by suggesting that their work is not social science. Far from that—their relativist position might even be considered "social science *par excellence.*"[144] But only this positioning within the constructivist approach allows me to do "normal" science while at the same time challenging some of the assumptions that have pervaded much of IR. Therefore, the familiar causal elements in my narrative do not do most of the explanatory work, since they are in fact subsumed by my deeper constitutive argument. I do not believe in causality (as usually understood) all the way down.[145]

I argue that the change observed during the four decades of IEM practice in the hemisphere is best seen as a process of structuration, in which agents and structure interacted and reconstituted each other. Thus, I maintain, by the end of the twentieth century, neither agents nor structure were the same as they had been at mid-century. The constitutional structure had changed insofar as it now more explicitly incorporated a component on representative government attached to the notion of state sovereignty, whereas the actors, particularly states, were different insofar as they had come to redefine both their identity and their interests. An indicator of this change is that at the turn of the century state and non-state actors were constantly and comfortably engaged in a discussion of issues concerning domestic governance within the framework of international norms. INGOs devoted to IEM were perhaps more drastically affected by this process, since their very existence was a product of it.

Thus, the enduring effects of this gradual process for international politics were the result of 1) a structure in which changes in material capabilities in the region were far from being a meaningful explanatory factor, and 2) a process of state interaction that produced cooperation but was *not* predicated upon actors with completely formed pre-social interests. Hence, it is an ideationist and social structure, not a material and individualist one, that explains the emergence and consolidation of IEM.

CONCLUSIONS

The fact that IEM appeared first in the Americas was no accident. As I have shown above, the continent's constitutional structure was conducive to it. Absent this hemispheric understanding, IEM would most likely have not emerged in the western hemisphere earlier than anywhere else. This is not to suggest that without the WHI IEM would never have taken place in the Americas. After all, activists, states, and IGOs in other latitudes also got in the habit of monitoring elections in the 1980s. In the same way that IEM became an export commodity of the new "system of interests" (i.e., the Americas), it could have been imported by this region as well had it emerged somewhere else.

But it did not—and that's my point: the particular constitutional structure that is capable of accounting for the emergence of IEM is the WHI and none other. Only in the western hemisphere was there not an "ontological gap" between this practice and the wider normative structure. Once it emerged and became normalized there, IEM began its world-wide diffusion as an international norm. The early cases reviewed in this chapter thus constitute the prolegomena of modern IEM.

I have argued that an approach that is sensitive both to the historical and normative structure of the international (sub)system is best suited for tracing the development of IEM. That is why I put forward a genealogical, constructivist explanation. Nevertheless, I have also contended that it is important to frame the issue in a manner that is amenable to other approaches. Otherwise we are heading to theoretical closure on issues that have just begun to be explored. I contrast the three approaches reviewed in the previous chapter in the concluding chapter. Thus, in the rest of this work I elaborate a narrative explanatory protocol of modern IEM. I start in the following chapter by looking at a foundational case: the 1988 Chilean plebiscite.

Chapter Three

Chile's 1988 Plebiscite: The Birth of the IEM Network

There were about 400 international observers in Chile's 5 October 1988 plebiscite. The event was held in accordance with the 1980 Constitution created by the junta (whose members had overthrown the democratically elected government of Salvador Allende in 1973). According to the new legislation, General Augusto Pinochet was named President of the Republic for an eight-year term, but sometime before the end of that term, the government was required to conduct a plebiscite in which the electorate would be asked to accept or reject the government's presidential candidate. A "Yes" victory would then mean the government candidate's serving another eight-year term, after which multi-candidate elections would be held. A "No" victory, on the other hand, would mean that Pinochet would remain in office for one more year, and would be required to hold multi-candidate elections ninety days before his term came to an end. After 15 years of military rule, it was obvious that, as the regime's Interior Minister would put it, "the great world political forces were interested in the Chilean process."[1] But it was more than that. Juan Ignacio García, head of the autonomous Electoral Service Office at the time of the plebiscite, is more precise in his judgment: "the Chilean case is emblematic in the sense that it was the first case with so much support from international observers."[2]

The widespread international interest in what could otherwise be considered a domestic affair contrasts with the isolation of the military regime—Chile was a pariah on the international community. Thus, for instance, soon after the coup a myriad of states broke diplomatic relations with Chile.[3] A few years later, the Philippine dictator Ferdinand Marcos, one of the few state leaders who was in good terms with the military regime (outside those of the military leaders of the Southern Cone), canceled a visit of the Chilean president to Manila—when Pinochet was already on the plane.[4] Likewise, when cabinet members traveled abroad, they had to do it with the utmost discretion.[5]

The junta, of course, resented this treatment. Thus, for instance, after the UN condemned in 1977—for fourth year in a row—human rights violations in Chile, Pinochet organized a "national consultation" asking the voters whether or not, "In the face of the international aggression unleashed against the government of our fatherland, I back President Pinochet in his defense of the dignity of Chile and reaffirm the legitimacy of the government of the Republic to head sovereignly the process of institutionalization of the country."[6] Thus, whereas the Chilean government felt threatened by the outside world and resorted to the sovereignty artifice recurrently, its political opposition saw in the international community an ally to restore democracy and human rights in their country. For the opposition, human rights and democracy transcended sovereignty, at least as interpreted by the regime. As Carlos Huneeus, an academic and former member of the *Technical Committee for the No* in the 1988 plebiscite campaign, observed, "the internationalization of the struggle against the dictatorship" had taken place long before. Furthermore, and in a more pragmatic tone, he noted that "we [in the opposition] had assumed that without international support we would not get anywhere."[7]

But the Pinochet regime did care about its international standing and, accordingly, it did not deny the legitimacy of the human rights discourse.[8] As Forsythe has noted, "Latin elites no less than North American elites accepted in the abstract the validity of democratic and human rights principles."[9] That is why right after the September 1973 coup, the military regime allowed a visit by the president of the Inter-American Commission on Human Rights, and later on, in the mid 1980s, it agreed to the UN sending a special rapporteur on human rights.[10] There was a kind of "schizophrenia" in the way the Chilean government recognized the legitimacy of human rights while constantly violating them.[11] Thus, the regime began playing the sovereignty card in relation precisely to human rights issues, stating that anyone who denounced the human rights situation in Chile was a traitor.[12] That is why by the time the issue of foreign observers came in 1988, the sovereignty issue was passé. As Genaro Arriagada, speaker of the Executive Secretariat of the *Command for the No* put it, "the sovereignty issue was already solved, because that had been dealt with in the context of human rights. Consequently the point, the discussion in Chile, when it [IEM] comes, is sort of out of date."[13]

In order to understand the meaning of IEM in Chile, one therefore has to refer to the salience of the WHI in the early 1980s. This is because the discourse on representative government and human rights characteristic of the WHI was specially relevant in Chile. Thus, for instance, when in 1985 Fernando Volio, the former Foreign Minister of Costa Rica, was sent by the UN as human rights rapporteur to Chile, he established a direct connection between the improvement of human rights and the necessary steps for the restoration of democracy.[14] As Kathryn Sikkink and Stephen Ropp have noted, "International network pressures and other attendant socialization processes were more comprehensive and forceful toward Chile than toward any other Latin American country."[15]

But the investigation into the international monitoring of the 1988 plebiscite also has to deal with the thawing of the Cold War by the time the electoral process took place, since the fading of the Soviet "threat" had a definitive impact on the policy of the regional hegemon toward Chile. The vanishing of the Cold War acted as an intervening variable insofar as it made the costs of a relatively free and fair plebiscite more acceptable both to Washington and to the hard-liners within the Chilean regime.

Thirdly, of necessity, the inquiry also needs to address the Chilean domestic structure, since it filtered the systemic pressures exercised by the WHI and the Cold War. The Chilean democratic tradition is of paramount importance in this respect. As Darren Hawkins has put it,

> In countries where human rights norms are more firmly established, either by historical precedent or by a growing diffusion throughout civil society, authoritarian elites have greater difficulty evading international pressures. To demonstrate their legitimacy, they must adopt the language of human rights and claim some adherence to human rights standards rather than simply arguing, as do many Asian regimes, that Westernized international norms do not apply.[16]

Consequently, before delving into the issue of the international monitoring of Chile's 1988 plebiscite, in the first half of this chapter I briefly touch on the contextual elements just mentioned: the WHI, sketching the state of inter-American relations and its associated principles by the mid 1980s; the Cold War, considering it only insofar as it impinged on the inter-American system, the activities of INGOs, and Chilean politics more particularly; and Chile's domestic structure, highlighting its more salient features and their development before and after the 1973 coup.

Having done this, in the second half of this chapter I trace the process that culminated in the massive foreign observation of the 1988 Chilean plebiscite. Here I first introduce the political context leading to the plebiscite, highlighting the contribution of foreign actors, as well as the government's response to the presence of foreign observers. Secondly, I consider in more detail the work of the two most influential delegations of foreign observers to Chile: the ones sent by the Law Group and NDI.

This chapter serves to bring home three theoretical claims advanced in the previous two chapters: that the WHI as constitutional structure was the adequate cause of the emergence of modern IEM; that human rights activists cooperating internationally were instrumental in the launching of IEM in the late 1980s; and that domestic structure in which the monitoring takes place serves as a second image intervening variable, linking domestic and international politics. Thus, this chapter traces part of the process by means of which international practices have shaped state interests and identities.

ON THE WHI, THE COLD WAR, AND CHILE'S DOMESTIC STRUCTURE

As noted in the second chapter, there was a double movement in the 1980s. Pushing in one direction was the wave of democratic transitions in Latin America, and the greater emphasis on democracy in the OAS Charter, along with the move of "democracy promotion" to center stage in US foreign policy; the undertow was the increasing deterioration of the relationship between the United States and most Latin American countries, with the consequent marginalization of the regional organization. There were many reasons for the increasing rift between the United States and its Latin American neighbors, but chief among them was the unilateral impulses of the Reagan administration. There was, indeed, a sort of correlation between good inter-American relations and OAS-activism.[17]

The 1982 Falklands/Malvinas war, and the 1983 US invasion of Grenada are just two instances of regional developments that made clear to Latin American leaders both the dispensability of the regional organization to the regional hegemon, as well as the US renewed unilateral bent.[18] Thus, the emergence in the early 1980s of the Contadora Group, and later of the Support Group, and eventually of the Rio Group, all explicitly excluding the United States and proposing ideas to solve the Central American imbroglio which were at odds with those emanating from Washington, was further evidence of the increasing futility of the OAS (more on Contadora and the Central American crisis in the next chapter). As it happened, by the mid-1980s the mere existence of the OAS seemed to be at stake.[19]

In this context, it is not surprising that the already mentioned democratic enthusiasm of the Reagan administration seemed of a highly dubious nature to Latin Americans. Furthermore, Reagan's flaunting of "democracy promotion" as one of his central foreign policy tools made it appear suspicious not only to the hemisphere statesmen, but also to US human rights activists—and even to the Carter administration holdouts at the State Department.[20] Thus, the new US Ambassador to the UN, Jeane Kirkpatrick, criticized the "goals" of the previous administration, such as the promotion of human rights, for being "abstract,"[21] and a few years later a State Department document boasted that, under President Reagan, "the emphasis [had] shifted [from human rights] toward a policy championing the broader values of democracy."[22] For the Reagan administration, democracy indeed became "the principal stated goal of its Latin America policy."[23] The declared single-mindedness of the new discourse of course only served to increase the widespread suspicion that Washington held a purely instrumentalist view of "democracy promotion."

Regardless of the true motives of the Reagan administration's avowedly preferred foreign policy instrument, and of whether its was bound to bring positive or negative consequences to Latin America, the fact remained that there was a new impetus for democracy in the subcontinent. One of the historically most troubled regions of the hemisphere, Central America, was a vivid sign that things were in fact changing. As Brian Loveman has noted, "1986 was the first time in Central American history that Costa Rica, Nicaragua, Honduras, El Salvador, and Guatemala all had elected civilian governments at the same time."[24] In this context, Chile became a crucial test for the "democracy promotion" policy of the Reagan administration. In 1986 it issued a statement noting that it opposed all forms of dictatorship, of left or right. The previous year, Ambassador Harry Barnes had arrived to Santiago, making clear his sympathies to the Chilean democratic forces. If the United States wanted to defeat the Sandinistas in Nicaragua waving the banner of democracy, it could not support a non-democratic regime in the Southern Cone. Barnes' tenure in Chile was going to prove decisive for effectively bringing US pressure in favor of the democratic transition—to the point that the Pinochet regime even considered the possibility of declaring him *persona non grata.*[25] The Reagan administration appeared to be showing, at least in some fronts, consistency with its pro-democratic rhetoric, thus attuning to the democratic trend in the region.

Furthermore, along with the wave of democratic transitions came a greater emphasis, both by state and non-state actors, on human rights. Human rights activists in the United States at first didn't want to get involved in democracy promotion activities, such as IEM. For them, "there was this sense of original sin in the election observing business," as carried out by the Reagan administration.[26] Nevertheless, as noted in the previous chapter, at about the same time organizations such as the Law Group began observing elections. There where then two kinds of groups involved in IEM: "democracy" organizations (such as the Carter Center, the Center for Democracy, NDI and NRI), and human rights groups. The pressure on the remaining dictators, and on the leaders of the incipient democracies on the part of INGOs was thus increasing. This external, non-state pressure was undoubtedly a contributing factor to the human rights norm cascade that took place in the hemisphere in the mid 1980s.[27] As Ellen Lutz and Kathryn Sikkink have noted, "Leaders of authoritarian governments sometimes responded to these pressures because as members of an international or regional society of states they had been 'socialized' to care about what other states think about them."[28]

Chile being a paragon of a democratic and well-institutionalized state in the Americas (more on this below), foreign criticism of its political system was bound to be especially damaging for the Pinochet regime. But the fact remained that the Chilean government was, to a large extent, a product of the Cold War. The United States oftentimes put the ostensibly more ideological component of its containment policy over the geopolitical one—as the covert operations it undertook to bring the Allende government down in 1973 illustrate.[29] The anti-Communist discourse of the Pinochet regime thus served the purpose of legitimating itself in the eyes of Washington and its staunchest supporters. Hence, winning the tacit approval of the Nixon and Ford administrations at first served to ameliorate the ostracism the Chilean government was otherwise subjected to by most members of the international community.

Furthermore, by the early 1980s, when it was becoming increasingly clear that the Soviet Union was losing its cast as a geopolitical threat, the ideological component of the Cold War became more salient.[30] That is, the usual *Cold War = bipolarity* equation usually put forward by realists (and many US policy makers) was becoming increasingly untenable (just at it had been in its origins, since the ideological confrontation between the two superpowers predated the bipolar distribution of capabilities).[31] President Reagan's metaphysical portrayal of the Soviet Union as the "evil empire" only served to highlight the ideational bedrock of the Cold War.

In the western hemisphere, the postulated struggle between "good" and "evil" was taking place at the isthmus. Thus, as Robert Pastor has noted, the new Republican administration "chose to send the Soviets the first signal by drawing a line in Central America."[32] The Report of the President's National Bipartisan Commission on Central America states that the country's involvement in the region was justified in order "to preserve the moral authority of the United States."[33] Reagan himself warned at the time that if his country ignored "the malignancy in Nicaragua," it would "spread and become a mortal threat to the entire New World."[34]

The OAS was to become one of the most conspicuous victims of the messianic unilateralism of the Reagan administration. Latin American states began to meet in smaller fora to deal with the region's problems. The most noticeable and influential was the above-mentioned Contadora Group. Formed in 1983 by Colombia, Mexico, Panama, and Venezuela, the Contadora Group (named after the Panamanian island in which its members first met) set out to launch concrete proposals to deal with the Central American crisis that were openly at odds with those of the United States. With the addition of the Lima "Support Group," and the ensuing constitution of the Group of Eight (or Group of Rio de Janeiro, for the Brazilian city where it was formed), it became clear that the rift between the United States and Latin America was only widening. The political will that coalesced around the Contadora Initiative became a bulwark for Latin American states in their struggle against Washington's unilateralism (more on Contadora in the next chapter).[35]

But if Central America became the US- designated battlefield for the Cold War in the continent, South America evolved into an area of détente as the military dictatorships began falling in the early 1980s. Thus, although the Reagan administration originally embraced the dictatorships of the Southern Cone, by the late 1980s it was increasingly distancing itself from the few remaining ones—including the one headed by Gen. Pinochet. This distancing did not mean, though, that Washington was going to recur to the regional organization to actively promote democratic transitions. Not in the slightest. In the democratic wave of the Southern hemisphere, the OAS remained at the margins. With the partial exception of some Central American countries, political transitions were mostly home-grown affairs in the hemisphere; similarly, disputes between the states, such as the one involving Argentina and Chile over the Beagle Channel, were left to the parties involved. As Larman Wilson has noted "the previous inter-American practice 'to try the OAS first' in conflict resolution from the 1950s through the 1970s has run its course."[36] That is why by the late 1980s many in the hemisphere were writing requiems for the organization.[37]

The diminished stature of the regional body was a mixed-blessing for the Chilean regime. On the one hand, it meant that the criticisms coming from the organization would not carry as much weight as they used to. But on the other, it increased Chile's seclusion since it did not have many alternative fora where it could make its voice heard in the international arena. Furthermore, diplomatic isolation was particularly damaging domestically because Chile had traditionally prided itself on being a model state in the hemisphere.

The exemplariness of Chile is important. As former Chilean President Patricio Aylwin has written, his country's democratic tradition had been a "just motive of national pride."[38] As a matter of fact, Chile's stable and democratic life had been exceptional in Latin America. Since 1932, and until the 1973 military coup, Chile was one of the few states in the region which managed to have democratically elected leaders. Hence, with the advent of a dictatorial regime, Chile lost not only international prestige, but also external power.[39] The enduring democratic condition of the austral country rested on the three pillars of its domestic structure: an active civil society, a well-defined party system, and a strong state. I now briefly consider each of them in turn.

Chile has historically had a large and active civil society, even if not of the traditional sort.[40] That is, during most of the democratic life of the country, civil society organizations have been linked, if not subordinated, to political parties. Civil society has thus suffered from "insufficient autonomy."[41] Paradoxically, once the military regime was installed in 1973, and political parties were banned, autonomous organizations flourished. As Philip Oxhorn has put it, "Prior to the military coup, political parties dominated all forms of social mobilization in Chile. For the urban poor, this generally prevented the emergence of any autonomous forms of organization, as popular organizations quickly became overwhelmed by narrow partisan interests. The military regime changed all of that."[42]

Interestingly, what the military regime was not able to change was the deeply-rooted "tripolarity" of the party system—the second pillar of Chile's domestic structure.[43] The political cleavages that made the consolidation of a conservative party, a leftist party, and a centrist party remained during the dictatorship of Pinochet. Thus, at the organizational and elective levels at least, the political parties in Chile simply went into a 15-year-long latent state. The three-thirds party system thus reemerged strong—even if tactically reconfigured—for the 1988 plebiscite campaign.[44]

At the basis of both the tripartite party system and the energetic civil society lied the third pillar of Chile's democratic tradition: a strong state. For most of its history since gaining independence from Spain in 1818, Chile has had a strong and centralist state, one that has been at the center of social and political life. As Manuel Garretón has put it, "All social organizations had to operate through the party system in order to gain access to the instrument of ordering and redistribution—the state."[45] The strength of its state was indeed a source of the "high status and prestige" of Chile in the hemisphere.[46] But the strength of the Chilean state has not customarily lied on sheer or arbitrary force. On the contrary. In Chile state strength has historically been premised on the rule of law. The characteristically Latin

American "politicized state," in which "political institutions are considered tentative and are reviewed instrumentally, not as permanent fixtures," did not materialize in the austral country.[47] In Chile there was a profound legalistic culture, and therefore a state with strong constitutional and republican foundations emerged.[48] Furthermore, unlike most other Latin American countries, the military in Chile was not decisive in resolving power struggles.[49]

The "democratic compromise" that emerged in the 1930s, however, was bound to fall victim to its own limitations in the early 1970s.[50] Increasing political and economic demands gave rise to an "overload" the system was unable to process.[51] Thus, by the late 1960s, the domestic structure of Chile could be characterized, in Risse-Kappen's terminology, as one of stalemate. Whereas its political institutions remained centralized and its society strong, the policy networks, that is, the links "between state and society and the norms regulating the coalition building processes,"[52] had become highly polarized.[53]

"Stalemate" domestic structures, as Risse-Kappen defines them, "are characterized by comparatively strong states facing social organizations in a highly polarized polity and political culture emphasizing distributional bargaining. Social and political conflicts among the major players are unlikely to be resolved in this type of system; decision blockades are expected to occur frequently."[54] This actually describes Chile's situation at the dusk of the democratic compromise. Thus, for instance, the government of Salvador Allende, elected in 1970 with 36.2 percent of the popular vote, lacked a majority in Congress. In his 1973 presidential address, Allende complained that the scrutiny his government was being subjected to by the legislative power was of an "unprecedented intensity."[55] Not surprisingly, his administration resorted to a myriad of legal sleights of hand in order to bypass Congress. Three months before the coup, the House of Representatives, controlled by the opposition, passed a resolution calling the Allende government unconstitutional.[56]

It was in this context that the military coup took place on 11 September 1973. The Chilean ousting, however, wasn't just a coup like those common in the rest of Latin America. It was a symbol of the state of affairs of the Chilean domestic structure. As Arriagada has put it, "Chilean democracy was not broken by a complot of the men in military fatigues . . . Democracy [in Chile] was wounded from before."[57] Similarly, Oscar Godoy has noted that "it was the maladies of the democratic political institutions that led us to the break up of the democratic regime [in 1973]."[58]

The military regime marked an unprecedented era in Chile's history. Although at first it seemed to be merely reactive, starting its fourth year it began to evince a long-term transformative project.[59] Thus, in his famous "Chacarillas discourse" of 9 July 1977, Pinochet set as a national objective the construction of a new political regime. The "new democracy" Pinochet promised ought to be, in his words, "authoritarian, protected, integrative, technified, and of authentic social participation [sic]."[60]

The political route announced in Chacarillas culminated in 1980–1981. On 11 September 1980, to commemorate the seventh anniversary of its inauguration, the military regime organized a plebiscite on a new constitution. The plebiscite was a mock—as the fact that no electoral registry existed suggests.[61] Nevertheless, six months later, in March 1981, the new Constitution was ratified. These two events, the plebiscite and the promulgation of the constitution, as Garretón has noted, "marked a high point in the Pinochet regime's political institutionalization."[62]

The 1980 constitution was, not surprisingly, anything but liberal and democratic. It was instead the consummation of Pinochet's "protected democracy" project.[63] Thus, for instance, the armed forces were given a tutelary role in the political affairs of the country, Parliamentary powers were curtailed, and ideological pluralism was denied.[64] Pinochet was also given the right to remain as Army Commander for eight years after his first term ended. Moreover, the new Constitution was accompanied by 29 transitory articles which made the situation established in the fundamental law even worse. Hence, for instance, transitory article 14 assigned the presidency of the country *ad hominem,* since it established that until 1989, "General Augusto Pinochet Ugarte shall continue as president of the Republic."[65] Additionally, General Pinochet was given the right, during the next eight years, "to freely designate and remove the mayors of all the country."[66] The new constitution did not make of the military regime a legitimate one.[67]

What the 1980 constitution did, though, was set a timetable that would eventually lead to a democratic regime (although the end point of course was not guaranteed by the constitution). Thus, as noted, the new legislation deeded the presidency to Pinochet for an eight-year term. But within ninety-days of the end of his mandate, the general was required to call for a plebiscite in which voters would be asked to accept or reject a government candidate (who turned out to be Pinochet himself). If the regime's candidate won, he would be president for an eight-year term; if he lost, then Pinochet would remain in office for one more year and multiparty elections would be held within a year.

By the time the plebiscite took place, Chile's domestic structure could be characterized, again following Risse-Kappen, as close to state-controlled ones. In them, the political structure is highly centralized and the executive power strong, whereas society is relatively weak due to "the absence of strong intermediate organizations in the policy networks."[68] I say that Chile's domestic structure unfolded into something close to a state-controlled one because it does not completely fit the ideal type. One key difference in this respect is that state-controlled structures generally possess a weaker society than that of Chile where, as noted, societal organization remained strong but moved from the political to the social arena. Furthermore, the political institutions in Chile were more responsive, in their own way, to a legalistic order than is the case in state-controlled domestic structures.

In addition to setting a timetable for the military regime, the new constitution also established new foundational principles. The 1980 constitution became one of the four distinguishing features of the Chilean military regime. The new constitution came to symbolize the legacy of the military.[69] That is perhaps the reason why the military regime would follow it so religiously in the decade ahead. As Eugenio Tironi, an academic and political activist who opposed the military regime and later became part of the Aylwin administration has noted, "In every moment, and even when it was unpopular or it had adverse effects on its own interests, general Pinochet followed the institutional steps to which his regime was obliged, following in this manner both the Chilean legalist culture and the sense of honor that goes with the military preparation."[70] Similarly, Patricio Aylwin, speaker of the *Command for the No* and Pinochet's successor as president of Chile, has noted that "the fact that the military government decided to endow itself with a juridical institutionality which would regulate its exercise was a transcendental fact. This is a very Chilean characteristic."[71]

But the normative aspect was just one of the central defining characteristics of the military regime. A second one was its distinctive economic ideology. The new constitution's purpose was, in fact, to emphasize the differentiation between economic, political and social life.[72] The military regime was a precursor of a neoconservative ideology that had as one of its basic components the most radical vein of economic liberalism.[73] The "Chicago boys," a team of technocrats who carried out the structural reforms of the Chilean economy, became an icon of what came to be popularly known as "neoliberalism." They were indeed the architects of the "Chilean miracle." The individualist and conservative economic tenets of the Pinochet regime became a central legitimization feature of the new legal order. As the Chilean daily *El Mercurio* approvingly put it a few days after the 1980 plebiscite, "The politicians that allowed or created the state of affairs that led to the failure of Chilean democracy were defeated by the alliance between the military and economists."[74] The economic ideology of the Chilean military regime made it especially dear to two of the most outspoken, conservative, and influential politicians in the world at the time: Ronald Reagan and Margaret Thatcher.

In addition to the legal arrangement and the economic doctrine, a third defining element of the military regime in Chile was the unprecedented levels of concentration of power in one person. In effect, after being formally declared president of the Republic in 1974, Pinochet kept the title of commander-in-chief of the Army. This was highly unusual not only for a country with a strong democratic tradition like Chile, but also for other military dictatorships in South America, where the head of state was not also the head of the military forces. Pinochet's dictatorship was no sultanism, though. As Huneeus has noted, "In Chile there was a pronounced centralization of authority and power, but this happened within an institutional order with an important decision-making center, the Government Junta, which remained the highest authority of the regime, and was able to limit Pinochet's ambitions at times."[75]

The fourth and last distinguishing feature of the military regime in Chile was the pervasive use of coercion.[76] Not that other Latin American dictatorships had not resorted to brute force widely, but the Pinochet one excelled at it. Furthermore, as Tironi has noted, "for Chileans, the merciless repression on the part of the state was a completely novel experience."[77] But widespread repression there was in the military era. At least 3000 people died, victims of state violence.[78] The security forces routinely resorted to the use of torture. Thus, for instance, a 1985 OAS report noted that torture had been "a deliberate policy of the Government of Chile carried out throughout the period that began on 11 September 1973."[79] Or as a 1988 Americas Watch Report put it, "The government of Augusto Pinochet has practiced an encyclopedic range of human rights violations during the past fifteen years."[80]

Furthermore, assassination and torture weren't the only favored ways through which the military regime consistently violated human rights. Another one was through the exile of dissidents—more than 10,000 Chileans were sent abroad by the Pinochet regime.[81] Illustrative in this respect was the 1976 exiling of two prominent opposition leaders, on the grounds that they "constituted a threat for the internal security of the State," after they sent a letter denouncing the human rights situation in Chile to an OAS meeting taking place in Santiago.[82]

But the exiling of political opponents was a tool that would eventually backfire on the military regime. As Carlos Portales has noted, "One of the byproducts of Chilean exile was the diverse and fluid quality of the personal contacts that opposition leaders made with other Latin American and

European elites."[83] The internationalization of the cause of the Chilean political opposition contrasted from early on with the isolation of the military regime.[84] It was the work the exiles started abroad, practically upon arrival to their new countries, and in conjunction with local NGOs, that determined the expedited construction of an international network to support human rights in Chile. Thus, as Ropp and Sikkink have claimed, "one can argue that Chilean networks almost 'invented' the boomerang [effect]" characteristic of TANs.[85]

Also instrumental in the development of the Chilean human rights network was the Chilean Catholic church. Immediately after the 1973 overthrow, the Catholic church became involved in the Pro-Peace Committee, a human rights organization that functioned until 1975. Thereafter, the church established the *Vicaría de Solidaridad* (Vicariate of Solidarity), which became a focal point for human rights activists.[86] The church thus became a "protective umbrella" for human rights activists of various political persuasions.[87] Interior Minister Sergio Fernández once referred to the church as "one of the greatest obstacles facing the government."[88] Furthermore, as Garretón has noted, "the Catholic church emerged as a substitute for the political arena and as an actor that performed additional oppositional functions."[89]

In this manner, the church also became involved with grassroots organizations.[90] The bulk of these organizations, however, were territorially based, that is, they were organizations centered on specific *poblaciones* (shantytowns). And it was in the *poblaciones* where the intense social mobilization that took place in the 1983–1985 period was organized. In the context of a severe economic crisis, as reflected, for instance, in the fall of the gross domestic product by 13.4 percent in 1982, public protest intensified. During the next three years, social mobilization became a fixture of Chilean life. This forced the regime to make some concessions, such as the appointment as Interior Minister, in August 1983, of Sergio Onofre Jarpa, a veteran party leader, thus breaking with the profile of the rest of the ministers in Pinochet's cabinet.[91]

Jarpa implemented a policy of *apertura* (opening), starting with a "National Dialogue" (mediated by Santiago's Archbishop Juan Franciso Fresno) with the opposition. Nevertheless, the dialogue led nowhere, and Jarpa ended up quitting in February 1985. Later, around the time an arsenal linked to the Communist Party was discovered, in August 1986, and that an attempt was made on the life of General Pinochet the following month, the cycle of protests practically ended. Subsequently, the regime hardened its position, and it eventually recovered the political initiative.[92] However, the protests initiated in 1983 had set in motion a modest liberalization period which would culminate in the 5 October 1988 plebiscite.[93] Having briefly sketched the state of the WHI, of the Cold War, and of Chile's domestic structure, which together interweave the normative milieu in which the 1988 plebiscite took place, I now turn to it.

THE 1988 PLEBISCITE AS AN INTERNATIONAL EVENT

The campaign for the 1988 plebiscite started on August 30th. On that day, the commanders-in-chief of the armed forces met to nominate the government's candidate for the next eight-year presidential period. Not surprisingly, the chosen one was Gen. Augusto Pinochet. This was the third occasion in which the military regime had resorted to the polls.[94] This time, however, the nature of the voting process was substantially different.[95]

To begin with, on this occasion the legal framework of the electoral process was established well in advance. Thus, when the commanders met to designate the government's candidate, they were acting in accordance with transitory article 27 of the 1980 constitution. This article established that the commanders of the armed forces should meet at least 90 days prior to the end of Pinochet's term (March 1989) in order to propose to the country the person who would hold the office of the presidency for the next constitutional period, whom citizens could then, in a plebiscite to be held no earlier than 30 days, and no later than 60 days after the candidate's name was proposed, accept or reject. More fundamentally, the 1988 plebiscite was different from the previous two voting exercises in that it had the support of an electoral register.

Appearances to the contrary, the opening of the register, on 25 February 1987, would prove to be fundamental for the development of the plebiscite. I say appearances to the contrary because the conditions did not look very promising when the register was reopened. Thus, for instance, it didn't seem very encouraging that Pinochet headed the electoral lists, receiving electoral registration number one, as he was the first Chilean to go to the registering tables.[96] As Arriagada has noted, "That symbol made the regime opponents uncomfortable: that day, the electoral history of the country would restart with the registration of the person whom had ordered to burn the electoral records in 1974."[97] Furthermore, in early 1987 opposition parties did not favor taking part in the plebiscite. Instead, they were calling for free elections. But it wasn't only the political opposition which rejected the plebiscite. Large sectors of civil society also favored multi-candidate elections. Thus, for instance, in March 1987, a group of well-known personalities established the Committee for Free Elections (CEL). However, both the opposition and civil society groups began to call on the citizenry to register—regardless of the nature of the voting act that would eventually take place. The opposition forces set themselves a goal of six-million registered voters for election day.[98]

The most conspicuous effort in the registration drive was the one carried out by the Crusade for Civic Participation (CIVITAS). Formed in March 1988 under the leadership of CEL-member Mónica Jiménez, CIVITAS was a private, nonpartisan foundation of the laity affiliated with the Catholic church. Its focus was twofold: voter registration, and civic education. It did not advocate a "Yes" or "No" position, limiting itself to inculcate civic duties. Although in the months immediately following the opening of the electoral registry citizens did not go massively to enroll, things began to change by mid-1987. On June 10, the Chilean Catholic Bishops' Conference issued a pronouncement calling on all Chileans to register as voters so that "there shall not be one single Chilean not registered in the Electoral Register and not one who does not vote when the time comes."[99] With the launching of the Crusade, the registration process acquired momentum.

Foreign donors such as USAID played an important role in supporting the activities of CIVITAS and other civic organizations. Thus, for instance, USAID gave a $1.2 million grant to the Inter-American Center for Electoral Assistance and Promotion, of the Inter-American Institute for Human Rights, which funded some of CIVITAS' civic education programs."[100] Similarly, after the government refused to make the *carnets* (which were required for citizens to be able to register to vote) available for free to those who could not afford them, NED provided funds so that no citizen would be left without a *carnet* for lack of money.[101] The Ford Foundation also funded a voter registration program in 1988.[102] The Crusade was involved in these and many other tasks intended to encourage massive attendance to the polls.

In this manner, citizen participation centered on electoral aspects, not on social demands anymore, remained active during 1987–88. Traditional social movements entered the civic and political effort late.[103] It was going to be the interaction between civic organizations such as CIVITAS and CEL, with the opposition parties, that constituted the most efficacious response to the regime.[104] Thus, for instance, CIVITAS helped CEL conduct an independent "quick-count" which would prove crucial on plebiscite day,[105] and both organizations worked with international observers.[106] But the outstanding results of this joint effort were already evident on the date Pinochet was nominated, and the electoral registry was closed. On 30 August 1988, 7,435,913 people had registered to vote—more than 90 percent of all Chileans over 18 years of age. The initial goal of six million registered voters had been amply exceeded.[107]

Furthermore, by August 30th the opposition had decided to participate in the plebiscite. It was in January 1988 that opposition groups dropped their demands for free elections, and accepted to take part in the plebiscite. The campaign for the "No" started in early February, after the majority of the opposition parties constituted the *Command for the No,* and decided to use the electoral laws in order to be able to count with *apoderados* (poll observers) at the polling places on 5 October.[108]

Deciding to participate in the plebiscite had not been an easy decision for the democratic forces. For them, accepting the steps set forward by the military regime was tantamount to recognizing the legitimacy of the 1980 constitution. That is why achieving the holding of free elections was considered by the opposition an important political victory. But it had become evident that after 1986 the military regime had recovered the political initiative—helped in no small measure by the perceived success of its economic model.[109] The opposition forces retook a proposal made back in 1984 by Patricio Aylwin, of the Christian Democratic Party (PDC), which postulated that the opposition should simply ignore the legitimacy issue in its struggle for democracy. As Aylwin declared in August 1984: "I am willing to use the existing institutionality with the sole objective of changing it."[110] Although this proposal was still premised on the opposition's struggle for free elections, its bottom line was also applicable to the dilemma the opposition faced three years later. The bottom line, of course, was that the opposition should take advantage of any space opened by the regime. Thus, in November 1987, the PDC announced that it would take part in the plebiscite if there were no free elections, and on January 1988 it called on citizens to vote for the "No" option.[111] 14 political parties, recognizing that the political movement favored the regime's timetable and design, soon agreed to join forces and face the regime in the plebiscite as the *Command for the No.*[112]

As Ricardo Lagos, now Chile's president and then a prominent Socialist leader of the Command, has noted, "the Command for the "No" was different from a conventional electoral coalition in that it was united against the "Yes" and in favor of democracy."[113] That is, the 16 parties that came to form the Command were able to agree only on a basic demand: people should be given the choice to democratically elect their president in a multi-candidate election in 1989.

With the opposition forces formally opposing the regime, Gen. Pinochet initiated a metamorphosis in early 1988. He stopped being the iron-fisted general, and started acting like a regular politician. Pinochet began appearing in rallies, wearing civilian clothes, and projecting a grandfatherly image. Concurrently, poor neighborhoods were showered with public works and other kinds of patronage.[114] Previously, in the second semester of 1987,

Pinochet had rearranged his cabinet, installing what a Junta-member called "the cabinet of the projection." Its purpose was to guarantee the continuation of the regime at least until 1997, when, according to the 1980 constitution, multi-candidate elections would be held.[115] Accordingly, in May 1988 Interior Minister Sergio Fernández reaffirmed "the commitment of the Government, and of the Armed Forces, with the triumph of the 'Yes.'"[116]

But there were also encouraging signs for the opposition. Starting in 1986, the regime had started to promulgate the "political" or "organic" laws that would constitute the legal framework for the plebiscite. These laws included, among others, the Organic Law on the Registration System and the Election Service; the Constitutional Organic Law Concerning Political Parties, and the Constitutional Organic Law on Popular Voting and Scrutiny.[117] Thus, for instance, the new legislation established that there would be an electoral registry, that the Electoral Service would be in charge of the enrollment, and that political parties would be allowed to take place in the electoral campaign and the scrutiny of the ballots.[118] Although the *Tribunal Calificador de Elecciones* (TRICEL, the special electoral court), another creation of the 1980 Constitution, was not supposed to be established until the 1989 elections, the recently instituted Constitutional Tribunal ruled that it should also function for the plebiscite. The military regime adhered to the ruling, and constituted the TRICEL. This decision was of great importance, since it contributed to somehow leveling the playing field for the contending forces.[119] The Constitutional Tribunal, as Tironi has noted, "watched over the celebration of a plebiscite that conformed to basic democratic rules."[120] Significantly, the electoral legislation passed in 1986–87 was, as Election Service's Director Juan Ignacio García has noted, "a copy of the one that was valid since 1925," and that was suspended after the 1973 coup.[121] The return to the normative order of the democratic period thus constituted a guarantee for the opposition.

By mid-1988, with the registration drive in full swing and the unity of the opposition forces growing stronger, the *Command for the No* had become a solid organization, staffed by some of the brightest politicians and academics of Chile (more on this below). The Command gave itself a complex and well articulated structure, consisting of a six-member Directive Committee, with Patricio Aylwin, as its speaker, and an Executive Secretariat, headed by Genaro Arriagada. Within the Secretariat there were, among other instances, a Technical Committee, in charge of opinion surveys and campaign strategy, and a Creative Committee, devoted to the planning of the image and slogans of the "No" campaign; it was within this last Committee that the "No" campaign's clever and successful slogan, "Happiness is coming!," was coined.[122]

As Aylwin has pointed out, in order to prevent a fraud from happening, the *Command for the No* took three kinds of safeguards: "a) poll watcher teams at the polling tables; b) general systems of scrutiny, parallel to the official ones, and c) important and representative presence of international observers."[123] When plebiscite day came, the Command was able to have *apoderados* at practically all polling tables—over 22,000. This was not a minor achievement. When the campaign started, many ordinary citizens didn't want to be identified with the opposition forces.[124] That is why for Carlos Portales, then member of the International Commission of the Technical Secretariat, having covered almost all polling places with *apoderados* "was the best thing" the Command did.[125]

The Command was also able to install a Central Computing Center, in which it undertook a parallel count, whereas CEL carried out a quick count. Interestingly, foreign actors played an important role in this task too. The idea of having poll results disaggregated by polling table, instead of consolidated results, came from a specialist brought to Chile by NDI, Glenn Cowan. As Arriagada recalls, "Cowan made some presentations here that were decisive for us. He came and told us: 'look, you shouldn't focus on the final count [. . .] because what happens then is that there is a power shutdown, the computer system breaks down, and you're left with nothing. Consequently, the only way you can do it is to have completely disaggregated information down to the lowest level, which is the voting table.' So we organized that."[126] In deciding to carry out a parallel count, the opposition wanted to prevent happening to them what had recently happened to the opposition in Mexico's presidential elections, where the computer system "broke down" on election night.[127]

But for the Command leadership the "best guarantee" against the risk of fraud or the non-recognition of the results by the regime was the presence of international observers.[128] That is why there was an International Commission working within the Technical Committee. The Commission, as Aylwin has noted, "realized important contacts at the international level, and thanks to them the Chilean democratic opposition was accepted as a valid interlocutor not only in friendly countries, but also in international organisms such as the OAS, the UN, and the European Parliament."[129] International solidarity with the opposition's cause was crucial. As Arriagada has put it, "a fundamental factor of the opposition's power was the backing and the solidarity of international public opinion, and of the majority of governments from Europe, Latin America, and North America, which contrasted with the isolation of the military regime."[130]

The burgeoning international solidarity with Chile's opposition forces was accompanied by a noticeable deepening in the change of US policy toward Chile initiated in 1985, with the arrival of Ambassador Barnes. Thus, for instance, Congress approved a $1 million appropriation for NED, earmarked for the *Command for the No,* and in December 1987 the US government imposed economic sanctions on Chile.[131] As the plebiscite approached, it was evident that even one of his staunchest supporters, Ronald Reagan, was deserting Pinochet. In this context, the *New York Times* reported that "The Chilean leader [Pinochet] avoids all but the most passing contact with Harry G. Barnes Jr., the U.S. Ambassador and a vocal advocate of the Reagan Administration's policy of promoting a return to democracy here."[132] Accordingly, human rights organizations such as Americas Watch and WOLA reported approvingly on the harder US stance toward Chile—and Interior Minister Fernández would later complain that "there was no doubt about where Washington's sympathies lay."[133]

This more pro-democracy Washington policy continued until the day of the plebiscite. Thus, probably feeling the heat from abroad, but also the increasing pressure at home, the military regime lifted the state of emergency a week before Pinochet was nominated; and the day after his nomination, it declared the end of exile—thus allowing 430 Chileans to return to their country and join the forces working for the "No" option.[134] The environment in which the opposition would begin the formal—and short—campaign for the plebiscite seemed auspicious.

The "No" campaign was certainly a success. Just a couple of months before it formally started, the Command confidentially got the results of a voter survey made by research center FLACSO with the advise of US poll specialist Peter Hart. The results indicated that 27.6 percent of the voters favored the "No" option; 25.8 the "Yes" option;" and 33.3 had not made up their mind yet.[135] The design and development of the campaign thus proved crucial for convincing the undecided third. And in this task, Arriagada has noted the "fundamental role that intellectuals of the social sciences area played."[136] This wasn't, though, a novelty in Chilean politics. It had begun since the late 1970s, and had led, according to Edgardo Boeninger, himself an intellectual and central political actor in the Chilean transition, to "the modernization of politics" in the mid-1980s.[137] In the context of the plebiscite campaign, Chilean intellectuals "provided new ideas, information, techniques, and advice. And they persuaded politicians to listen to them."[138]

The role intellectuals played in restoring democracy in Chile is germane here because it throws light on the indirect influence foreign actors had in this realm as well. As Jeffrey Puryear, who was sent to Chile shortly after the military coup by the Ford Foundation, and has studied the role Chilean intellectuals played in their country's transition has noted, foreign donors made it possible for many Chilean social scientists to keep working during the military regime.[139] Thus, for instance, the average annual support from Ford Foundation to Chile between 1980 and 1988 was about $800,000.[140] Moreover, "Most of the intellectuals who played important roles in Chile's transition to democracy operated exclusively on foreign funds for a decade or more. They were crucially empowered by foreign donors."[141]

A conspicuous example of the indirect way through which foreign donors contributed to the Chilean transition in general, and to the "No" campaign in particular, were the Center for Development Studies (CED), and the CIS consortium. The former was directed by Boeninger, and was completely funded by foreign donors.[142] CED played an important role in achieving the convergence of opposition forces. As Garretón observed, CED "made the Christian Democrats realize that the socialists, at least at the technical level, weren't brutes; and made the left realize that the Christian Democrats weren't fascists."[143] CED joined with two other research centers, the Latin American Institute of Transnational Studies (ILET), and SUR, to form the CIS consortium. CIS was created in order "to bring modern political campaigning techniques and political consulting more generally to Chile's political opposition."[144] CIS received training on focus groups from the New York-based Sawyer/Miller Group. Staff from the consulting firm went to the austral country to train Chilean academics, and suggested that CIS request funds from (magnate and philanthropist) George Soros. Having obtained those funds (some $30,000), "CIS and Sawyer/Miller organized, in August 1987, the first focus group ever carried out for political purposes in Chile."[145] It was with information obtained through this novel technique, that the "No" campaign was designed and ran.

TV was also a key element in the success of the opposition's campaign—and one in which foreign funded and/or trained intellectuals played an important role as well. The "political laws" passed during 1986–87 established the existence of a daily, free 30-minute "franja" (strip) on TV for both options so that they could reach the voters (15 minutes each). Conveniently, though, the regime chose a broadcast time that it assumed would minimize its audience: 11: 15 at night. But as Tironi has noted, "Unexpectedly . . . *the franja* became a rating success, and a political factor that would have enormous consequences for the result of the plebiscite."[146] A poll taken after it took place found that around 93 percent of the registered voters had watched the spots of the "No" campaign.[147] According to Kenneth Wollack, now NDI's Executive President and a member of the observer mission to Chile, "the television adds that the 'No' campaign ran was a demonstration to the Chilean people that the 16 parties were competent, that they had a platform, that they had an ideology, that they were future-oriented, that they could work together, and I think that image that they projected . . . that ultimately made a huge difference."[148] Even Sergio Onofre Jarpa, Pinochet's former Interior Minister, would later recognize that "the 'No' option's advertisement campaign was appropriate for the moment," and that "'Happiness is coming!' was a well chosen slogan."[149]

As with the campaign in general, Chilean intellectuals working within the Technical Committee, most of whom had solid foreign contacts, played an instrumental role in the opposition's franja.[150] Thus, the international support foreign foundations provided to Chilean intellectuals, plus the more explicitly political assistance civic groups and opposition forces received from abroad, became an important (not decisive) contributing factor for the success of the "No" campaign. As Allan Angell has noted, "international support for Chile was arguably more important than support for the democratic transition in other Latin American countries."[151]

And in this regard foreign observers were particularly relevant. Not that they were major players in the Chilean transition (only Chileans were), but their role was significant—and manifest. Juan Ignacio García, head of the Electoral Service, has noted that in the months leading to the plebiscite, he met with about 1500 persons related to monitoring missions. For him, the international dimension was "absolutely fundamental" in the Chilean 1988 electoral process.[152] International pressure began to mount in 1988. Thus, for instance, on 4 August, US Senators Edward M. Kennedy and Richard Lugar formed the "Committee to Support Free Elections in Chile." The Committee worked "with and through" the Law Group, and was co-chaired by former Presidents Jimmy Carter and Gerald Ford.[153] Similarly, around the same time 110 US Representatives sent a letter to Pinochet asking him that his government "cooperate with international observers."[154] Along the same lines, the International Parliamentarian Association for Democracy organized the largest contingent of international observers: it had more than 300 members.[155]

But unlike the work of foreign foundations supporting Chilean research institutions, the actions of INGOs involved in IEM were more openly political and, therefore, sometimes hostile to the military regime. The activities of international observers became manifest on several realms of life, something the government probably did not particularly appreciate. Thus, for instance, the *Vicaría* became a focal point for foreign observers. As *Vicaría*'s Monsignor Sergio Valech recalls: "international observers came constantly to the *Vicaría* . . . not only for the plebiscite itself, but also in order to know the situation the country was living . . . it was always a constant flow of people."[156] Similarly, as suggested above, there was a steady dropping of observers by the Electoral Service's office. In fact, the affability of the Service's head with foreign observers turned him into a "not totally acceptable person to the government."[157]

Not without basis, indeed, the government perceived foreign observers as allies of the opposition forces. WOLA's delegation is a case in point. It strived to maintain its impartiality, and called on all foreign observers to "maintain their credibility as detached witnesses by refraining from siding with one side or another and from intervening in a process in which only Chileans have the right to participate."[158] Nevertheless, it was not totally welcome by the government because it openly stated its disagreement with the holding of a plebiscite, instead of free elections. NDI's case is similar. As Wollack, NDI's Executive Vice-President at the time, noted: "we felt that we could legitimately support a 'No' vote because it was a democracy vote, it wasn't a vote for one candidate. So, we supported the 'No' campaign."[159] Not surprisingly, a 1988 *Chilean Political Background Document,* prepared by the Embassy of Chile in Washington, claimed that the foreign funds flowing to the opposition for civic education and election monitoring, among other activities, was tantamount to "foreign intervention."[160]

But the fact remained that, for the opposition, foreign support was crucial. More than a year before the plebiscite took place, Patricio Aylwin declared that "if there is an electoral register, an organized people, and *if poll watchers from around the world come to witness the electoral act,* it is not going to be possible [for the regime] to carry out a gross fraud, as the one which took place in 1980."[161] Aylwin's feeling was shared by many. Thus, for instance, CIVITAS' Mónica Jiménez recalls that "for us, international observers were a protection and guardianship."[162] For Carlos Portales, now at the Ministry of Foreign Affairs and then member of the International Commission of the Technical Secretariat, "foreign observers were like a guarantee that . . . there would be no tricks."[163] Genaro Arriagada, then Speaker of the Technical Secretariat, explains the function of foreign observers with more detail:

> the most important function [of the international observer] is one that is almost unconfessable, which is the following: if one has an apparatus, as we did, at the level of the voting table, the only way to break this scheme is [for the government] to break by force into the voting places, because our objective was the voting act. Therefore the only way was to shoot . . . disappear everything, and that's it. But that is very difficult to do when one has foreign observers. . . . therefore it is not the administrative problem of good votes, bad votes, but the fact that there is a guy there who stands there and says, and what is worst, a lot of those people are very courageous politicians, and consequently a dictator

> would have to put them in a charter, in a plane, get rid of them in the midst of a world scandal. So that their mere presence in the country is a guarantee . . . an insurance. That function is invaluable.[164]

Foreign observers were perfectly aware of their role and, furthermore, did not consider their presence in Chile as an intervention of any sort. For them, the right to free and fair elections was a basic human right that transcended borders. As Adolfo Suárez, co-leader of NDI's delegation, clearly stated in the mission's report: "The recent Chilean plebiscite, although formally an internal matter falling within the sovereign rights of Chile, also had an international dimension of major relevance. The old principle of classical international law regarding nonintervention in the internal affairs of other states is gradually receding in importance; consequently, the international community cannot be indifferent to the fight for freedom, human rights, and the rule of law."[165]

The Chilean government recognized the validity of the human rights argument; it thus did not simply reject the IEM activities of the many INGOs present in the country. Arriagada recognized that the regime possessed "some sensibility in regards to the international situation;"[166] and Monsignor Valech also noted that partially "because of the United Nations" and its previous work in Chile in the area of human rights, the Chilean government let the observers in.[167] The military regime thus developed what Larry Garber calls a "schizophrenic attitude." As he put it, "The government there [in Chile] refused to recognize 'observers' instead using the term 'testigos' [witnesses] to describe our presence. At the same time, the government did not prevent us from carrying out our job, and as was typical of the 1980s era, it actually had a schizophrenic attitude toward observers: on the one hand they often provided facilitation of the observers efforts, but were quite weary of the assumed sympathy that observers would have with the opposition parties."[168]

The Chilean government certainly did not put obstacles to foreign observers. Thus, for instance, both the Law Group and NDI acknowledged the cooperation of government officials.[169] Similarly, CIVITAS' Jiménez does not recall international delegations having any problems with the government.[170] This is not to suggest that the regime was fond of foreign observers, but it seemed to see them as something it had to live with. For Puryear, the government allowed foreign observers because it felt that "there [were] a set of rules you play by, and you don't generally violate those rules."[171] CEL's Godoy argues that the Foreign Minister of the time, Ricardo García, "had an open attitude, he wanted that [the plebiscite] be as transparent as possible." And he recalls that the day before the plebiscite, when García went to his house (they had been classmates in college), where "a group of people from the United States plus other politicians and people from the Center of Public Studies [a think tank with which Godoy was affiliated] analyzed a voter survey, he [García] was very happy to be in touch with the political observers."[172] Similarly, the Chilean embassy in Washington, beyond some early rhetorical skirmishes with the Law Group (see below), also cooperated with the observers.[173] Former ambassador Hernán Felipe Errázuriz, as a matter of fact, recalls not only not having any problem with the presence of US observers in his country, but also providing them with the necessary information.[174]

As noted, the Chilean government allowed the presence of foreign observers as tourists (i.e., it did not grant them observer status). Nevertheless, the governmental guidelines for these "tourists" explicitly allowed them to engage in election monitoring.[175] This ambiguous situation was a reflection of the predicaments the government faced regarding the monitoring of the plebiscite. At one level, the democratic tradition of the Chilean domestic structure, along with the normative environment of the Americas (the WHI), made it difficult for the military regime to simply reject IEM. Nevertheless, many within the military regime did not like having foreign observers at all. Junta member José Toribio Merino, for instance, flatly rejected the presence of foreign observers in Chile.[176] But then there were those who, putting the transparency of the plebiscite above any other consideration, preferred having foreign observers. They considered that tying the regime's hands was the best strategy—both for principled and instrumental reasons. As Arriagada pointed out, those within the regime who believed they were going to win supported having observers for strategic reasons, "and those [supporters of the regime] who believed that they were going to loose, thought that it was better that foreigners tell it to the military regime, instead of them telling it."[177]

There was of course some public posturing about the presence of foreign observers. Thus, for instance, Foreign Minister García once blasted against foreign observers. As the daily *El Mercurio* put it, "The government official emphasized that the intervention of foreign citizens in a process that belongs to Chileans 'constituted a form of intrusion in the internal affairs of our Republic.' He explained that 'we have opened the doors so that foreigners can come to Chile, to watch and witness the electoral act . . . But between this and meddling into what is a Chilean decision there is a large and deep difference.'" However, when a reporter asked García if the government hadn't considered that situation when it let them enter the country as tourists, García replied: "No, for a very simple principle: We in Chile have nothing to hide regarding our [electoral] process."[178] This kind of government statements were widely covered by the press.[179] But the fact was that, as Paul Drake has observed, "In 1988, it was futile to invoke nationalism to prohibit the arrival of foreign observers to verify the cleanliness of the plebiscite."[180]

Thus, most likely García's speech was for internal consumption. As CEL's Godoy noted, it was meant "to please the military men." Godoy recalls García having a very honest and open attitude toward the foreign observers, giving him guarantees that the observers from the International Republican Institute Godoy's Center of Public Studies (CEP) was hosting would be able to work tranquilly. According to Godoy, García was "with the doves, not with the hawks, he had a very open attitude."[181]

The highest spheres within the regime probably privileged the acceptance of foreign observers for strategic reasons. Disregarding the possibility of defeat—their polls consistently showed the "Yes" option ahead—they thought having foreigners validate their victory would increase the regime's legitimacy, both domestically and internationally. The presence of foreign observers could prove crucial if, as the regime feared, the opposition rejected the results in case of a "Yes" victory.[182] Godoy recalls that when he showed García the results of the CEP's poll at a gathering, which predicted a "No" victory, the Foreign Minister got very upset, made some phone calls, and left. Later, García told Godoy that "either Pinochet is a great actor [pretending that he thought he was going to win], or he was really surprised by the results."[183] The Foreign Minister told Godoy he believed the polls made by Gallup at the request of the government had been manipulated, although he also accepted that people within the regime, including himself, were influenced by the way the military operates (according to him, reporting not facts but targets).[184]

This was then the general environment in which the activities of foreign observers to the Chilean 1988 plebiscite transpired. In the next two sections I look with more detail at the work in Chile of the two organizations that carried out the most consistent work toward the plebiscite: the Law Group and NDI.

The Law Group

The Law Group is a nonpartisan organization established in 1978, based in Washington, D.C. Its mission is "to promote and protect human rights around the world through the application of international human rights law."[185] As noted in ChapterTwo, the Law Group started monitoring elections in 1983, and the following year it published the *Guidelines for International Election Observing*. Written by Larry Garber, who at the time was the Law Group's Election Observer Project Director, the *Guidelines* set forth the rationale for the human rights organization involvement in election monitoring. It notes that "Since the second [sic] World War, the right to political participation in one's government has been recognized as a fundamental human right."[186]

Similarly, a later Law Group report notes that "When the right to political participation is denied, other basic rights are in jeopardy," and states that "The Law Group believes that the right to genuine and periodic elections should be monitored to the same extent as other basic rights monitored by international organizations."[187] Making explicit the relationship between human rights and electoral matters was a major breakthrough for the emergence of IEM among INGOs. As noted, most human rights groups in the early 1980s were not in the business of observing elections.

I asked Garber about where the idea of framing election monitoring in terms of human rights came from. He replied: "At the time, I think that we believed that presenting election monitoring as a human rights task would provide some additional legitimacy to the venture. However, events quickly overtook this consideration, and before too long, i.e., within a couple of years of the publication of the guidelines, the two were well interwoven in the sense that everyone understood that election monitoring had a 'political' context."[188] For Thomas Carothers, an expert on "democracy promotion" at the Carnegie Endowment for International Peace formerly at the State Department, Garber was one of the "few key people" who moved election monitoring forward in the early 1980s, with the work he did at the Law Group. Indeed, Garber later distanced himself from the traditional human rights community and became more involved in "democracy promotion" in general and election observing in particular.[189] Thus, by the time of the Chilean plebiscite, Garber was NDI Senior Consultant for Electoral Process, and the person who wrote NDI's final report.

The Law Group's work in Chile started in August 1987, when it sent a fact-finding mission "to observe and examine the conditions affecting the fairness of the plebiscite and the degree to which it [could] be expected to reflect the free and informed will of the Chilean people."[190] The Law Group considered that "The international community has a role to play in encouraging the occurrence of an election consistent with international standards."[191] And in the specific case of Chile, "The role of observers is to report the consensus of the Chilean people as they assess the plebiscite process, to bear witness to the process of restoring democracy, and to inform the international community regarding Chile's attempt to realize the right of political participation."[192] Furthermore, by being present in an authoritarian country at a transitional period, Law Group observers also aimed at "provid[ing] moral support to those who fear participating in an electoral exercise may bring untoward consequences."[193]

In November 1987, the Law Group put out its *Report on the Chilean Electoral Process,* which contained the analysis and recommendations made by the first mission. In April 1988 it sent a second fact-finding mission; and in September-October it deployed its eight-person international delegation in and around Santiago.[194] Given the Law Group's expertise in election monitoring in general, and in the Chilean case in particular, it is thus not surprising that the Bi-Partisan Committee to Support Free Elections in Chile asked it to serve as counsel.[195]

In a preliminary report, the Law Group noted that while the Chilean Government justified holding a plebiscite instead of an open multi-candidate election because of the alleged dangers the country faced, "The Inter-American System. . . . does not recognize such a defense. . . . The clear practice in the Americas has been to forbid virtually all restrictions on the right to participate in a genuine election, particularly restrictions as broad in scope as those in effect in Chile."[196] In a subsequent preparatory report, the Law Group argued that "In accordance to contemporary practice, particularly in Latin America, the government should permit international observation of the upcoming electoral exercise and of the environment in which the process occurs." But it also noted that, "While the Chilean opposition has enthusiastically welcomed the presence of international observers for the plebiscite, the Chilean government has adopted a more ambivalent attitude."[197]

The government's "ambivalent attitude" had to do with a letter sent by the Chilean Ambassador in Washington to the Law Group in response to its August 1987 report. The Law Group had sent the Chilean Government a preliminary version of the report, and had asked it if it wished to make any comments. In reply, Ambassador Hernán Felipe Errázuriz stated: "Any official response would only lend undeserved legitimacy to a document which prejudges, and attempts to create doubt about, an electoral event which has not yet occurred."[198]

The relations between the Law Group and the Embassy would later become smoother, though. Hence, in a subsequent report the Law Group noted both that the Chilean government had "continued a dialogue with the Law Group during all stages of the project," and that Chile's Embassy in Washington had been "quite cooperative."[199] Furthermore, the publication also acknowledged that the military regime had "placed no restraints on delegation members regarding where they could travel or with whom they could speak"[200] The government was thus abiding both by Chile's long democratic tradition and the hemisphere's principles. But instrumental reasons were also at play in its allowing the presence of foreign observers at the electoral process. As a post-plebiscite Law Group report notes, "government officials and pro-government party leaders candidly acknowledged to the Law Group's delegation in September that the presence of foreign observers would lend credibility to the plebiscite result if there were a narrow 'Yes' victory."[201]

The National Democratic Institute for International Affairs

NDI started its work on Chile in 1985. In May of that year, it sponsored a conference on "Democracy in South America," in Washington, D. C.; political party leaders from Chile and other Latin American countries attended. A year later NDI, along with two Venezuelan political parties, organized another conference. This time it was held in Caracas, and the topic was Chile's transition to democracy.[202] Importantly, the parties attending the Caracas conference came from the broad political spectrum, from left to right. The ideological diversity of the conference, Kenneth Wollack, NDI's Executive Vice-President at the time noted later, was meant to be "a signal to the Chilean government that there was a sort of wall-to-wall conservative to socialist support for democratic transition in Chile."[203]

The following year, in April, NDI President Brian Atwood and Curtis Cutter, a consultant, visited Chile, and in May NDI invited four Chileans to participate in NDI's mission to the Philippine legislative elections. But the formalization of NDI's work in Chile with regards to the plebiscite started in July 1987, when it sent a mission to help out civil society and opposition groups working on a voter registration drive. Thus, in November, NDI helped organize a seminar attended not only by Chilean political and grassroots leaders, also by political consultants from Canada, the Philippines, Spain, the United States, Venezuela and West Germany.[204]

As Wollack recalls, "after the voter registration drive, the effort was turned into the *Command for the No,* and NDI worked very, very closely with the Command, on polling, on media advice, on organizational advice, providing some financial support to the Command."[205] Arriagada, of the Command's Executive Secretariat, points out that the Command asked NDI "for help in giving us advice on how to run a campaign, because in this country we hadn't had any for 17 years."[206] But in addition to its more political participation in the plebiscite campaign, during 1988 NDI also remained engaged in other "democracy promotion" activities, such as provision of grants for civic education and election monitoring, and the administration of most of the $1 million U.S. Congress appropriation for Chile.[207]

As the plebiscite approached, NDI sent a team to Chile in August to prepare for the impending plebiscite (although the exact date was not yet known, since the 1980 constitution mandated that the candidate be known at least 90 days before the end of Pinochet's presidential term in March 1989, everybody knew that the plebiscite was close). During the August preparatory trip, NDI *informed* the Chilean government of its upcoming observer mission.[208] The official response was positive. As Wollack declared to *El Mercurio:* "Even though we have not been invited by the government, we have been informed that if we want to come to see how the next election develops, we are welcome."[209] But the government's response was more than just distant hospitality. There was some sort of permissive, almost playful ambivalence to it. As Wollack recalls:

> They [at the government] said: 'you are welcome to come here as tourists,' but they, it was a game that they were playing, they accepted us, they said 'if you want to come,' and we made our own badges, we made our own badges at the time, just to make us look official. And there were times when we would go up to polling sites and the military would say, 'why are you here?' And we would say, 'we are observing the elections.' They would say, 'there are no observers here, so if you want to come back as tourists that is fine.' So you leave, you go a block away, you come back and they say, 'why are you here?' 'We are tourists,' 'ah OK you can go.' So there was a little bit of a game.[210]

In contrast, the regime's opposition was more forthcoming. During the same August visit, NDI received a letter from Sergio Molina, which stated: "The Committee for Free Elections (CEL) welcomes the NDI delegation which we believe demonstrates international support for a free and fair plebiscite."[211] The political opposition was interested as well in having a free and fair plebiscite, but it was also concerned about the legitimacy of the results. That is, the Command was interested too in the credibility of the outcome—even if the "No" option lost. And in this respect, international observer missions such as NDI had an important role to play. Wollack remembers Arriagada telling him that if Pinochet won cleanly, the opposition wanted NDI to state just that, that the government had won without stealing the election, in order to avoid violence in the streets.[212] Wollack says NDI observers would have done it: "we were prepared to say: 'this election wasn't stolen,' although we would still criticize the whole concept of a plebiscite. So that was a possibility, not a possibility we were looking forward to." Thus, the main role of the NDI's delegation, as Wollack saw it, was "to demonstrate to the Chilean authorities that we were going to be watching."[213] In its vigilant role, as in the one of technical assistance provider, NDI was quite successful.[214]

On plebiscite day, NDI's 55-member delegation divided into 13 teams and spread throughout Chile, performing their observing mission with enthusiasm. Some of its members might have indeed had too much enthusiasm.

Wollack recalls that when he and others in the delegation found out that in some polling places there were some very long lines, they thought that some people were not going to be able to vote,

> so we got hysterical, I will tell you, this was like the big thing in the morning [. . .] so we all charged, Suárez and myself, we all charged into the head of the election commission, Juan Ignacio García, who played a very decent role . . . but we went in, and we charged into the election commission, and then Larry Garber, Larry in our staff, Larry thought we were over-reacting, 'let's wait, let's wait,' no, we wanted to go in, we were concerned, so we charged into the election [commission], it was a learning experience, that since then we probably wouldn't do it, and we demanded that the election commission make an announcement that everybody in line would be allowed to vote. And Juan Ignacio said, 'well. . . . why don't we wait'. . . . he ended up making an announcement but, we went back to the polling sites three hours later, and there were no lines. Everything had worked.[215]

In its final report, NDI concluded that "The plebiscite was conducted in an orderly and fair manner."[216] It also recognized that although its delegation

> had to overcome the mixed signals sent by the Chilean government regarding their presence . . . Ultimately, no restrictions were placed on who could visit Chile as observers nor on where observers could go or with whom they could meet once they were in the country. Indeed, some senior government officials informally acknowledged the presence of the delegation, and assisted its activities by informing military and provincial officials outside the capital that observer teams would be visiting their regions. Although government representatives declined to meet formally with the delegation, the delegation leaders met privately with foreign ministry officials.[217]

On 5 October 1988, voter turnout was 97 percent. The "No" option obtained 54.7 percent of the votes, and the "Yes" option 43.0 percent. The day after the plebiscite, NDI's delegation co-leader Adolfo Suárez was asked what he would have said to Pinochet if they had met. Suárez responded: "I wouldn't dare to tell Mr. Pinochet anything. . . . Chile's people have already said it."[218] As witnesses to the Chileans' voice, though, the former Spanish President and other foreign observers had in actual fact sent a message to Pinochet and other state leaders. As Suárez himself wrote in the foreword to NDI's report: "the lack of freedom and systemic human rights violations have become transgression of international law that justify actions by the community of nations."[219] State elections were effectively in the process of becoming just "formally an internal matter falling within the sovereign rights" of states.

CONCLUSIONS

The 1988 Chilean plebiscite became a landmark in the history of IEM. It was the first electoral process in the Western hemisphere attended by so many international observers, thus marking the emergence of an IEM TAN—and the concurrent redefinition of state sovereignty. Furthermore, the absence of the OAS signaled the transfer of IEM's driving force, from an IGO to a multiplicity of INGOs. This shift is significant because, by giving IEM momentum, INGOs contributed to the eventual institutionalization of this practice in the realm of interstate relations. As Garber points out, the monitoring activities of NGOs since the early 1980s were "essential" in helping institutionalize IEM practice in IGOs.[220]

But this institutionalization would take place later, after the Nicaraguan elections. What had become evident by 1988, though, was that the Chilean case had become a focal point for the emergence of an IEM TAN—as the narrative above suggests. As a NDI's report noted, "there is now a cadre of political leaders from around the world who are committed to supporting the Chilean people as they continue their struggle for a democratic future."[221] Interestingly, though, an extra-hemispheric event served as a stepping stone both for the emergence of this "cadre," and for the success of the international monitoring of the Chilean plebiscite: the monitoring of the 1986 Philippine snap elections.[222]

The Philippine election monitoring effort was, in effect, an important referent for the Chilean plebiscite. Heraldo Muñoz, now a cabinet member in the Lagos administration, and a member of a later NDI mission to the archipelago, summarized the importance of the Philippine experience for his country in the title of a 1987 article: "Lesson From the Philippines: Organization and Participation in Free Elections."[223] In the time between the Philippine snap election and the Chilean plebiscite, NDI had been actively involved building bridges between civic organizations of the two countries, such as the above-mentioned November 1987 seminar in Santiago. As Garber argues, "The democratic activists participating in the elections, particularly in the Philippines and Chile, appreciated the different roles that the international community could play in supporting their efforts and encouraged the presence of international election monitors and the provision of other assistance from abroad."[224]

Garber also notes that "there was a good deal of communication from one region to another regarding organizing tactics, contributing to the rapid spread of both a democratization ethos and to an acceptance of international involvement, albeit by international NGOs and not until later by intergovernmental organizations, in the monitoring of elections."[225] During this early phase, the Law Group and other human rights groups opened the way for organizations like NDI.

Beyond the Philippine stimulus, though, the fact that in the Chilean plebiscite for the first time coalesced a myriad of nongovernmental (and semi-governmental) forces has to do with the normative structure of the Americas, the WHI. That is why after 1988 IEM became a common practice in the Americas—but not in Asia or Africa. Unquestionably, the thawing of the Cold War was an important contributing factor both to the success of the Chilean experience and to the eventual normalization of IEM in the Western hemisphere. But as I hope to have shown in this and the preceding chapters, absent the WHI, IEM could not have become institutionalized as rapidly as it did in the Americas. Thus, as I had ventured, if the state discourse that allowed for token IEM had not existed, "real" (or at least nonstate-lead) IEM would not have emerged. The existence of this discourse in turn validated and gave salience to the arguments put forward by human rights organizations as a rationale for their activities. The argumentative component was crucial in this landmark case.

Furthermore, the Chilean case shows that if a transitional state becomes the target of third phase-IEM, it partially redefines its identity and national interests. The regime that emerged from the 1988 plebiscite and the subsequent 1989 elections was much more cosmopolitan than the military one. Consequently, it had a substantially different conception both of its identity as a member of the international community, and of the protection of human and democratic rights as a constitutive part of its fundamental national interests. Accordingly, in 1990 Chile accepted the compulsory jurisdiction of the Inter-American Court of Human Rights.[226]

In summary, the international monitoring of the 1988 Chilean plebiscite illustrates the resilience of the WHI as constitutional structure, the receding importance of the Cold War as an intervening structural variable, the increasing salience of human rights activism in the Americas, and the emergent redefinition of state sovereignty. In this manner, I have traced part of the process by means of which international practices have shaped state interests and identities.

Chapter Four

Nicaragua's 1990 Elections: The Consolidation of the IEM Network

2,578 international observers were present on election day in the 1990 Nicaraguan elections—over six times as many as in the 1988 Chilean plebiscite.[1] The largest contingents came from the OAS and the UN—IGOs that were not present in the austral country. Also unlike Chile, the Nicaraguan elections were framed in terms of a regional peace process. That is, the timing and nature of elections was informed by the Contadora Initiative and the Esquipulas Agreements, both aimed at bringing peace to Central America. The international attention was focused by these regional efforts on peace making. Thus, the UN Secretary-General, when justifying his organization's presence in Nicaragua, noted that the elections had an indisputable international dimension: the regional peace process.

The 1990 Nicaraguan voting was hence a watershed—and not only because of the number of international observers and the presence of IGOs. It was a watershed also for the interaction of NGOs and IGOs, and foremost, for the redefinition of sovereignty it implied. As Robert Pastor has put it, by inviting international monitoring missions such as those of the OAS, the UN, and the Carter Center, the Nicaraguan government was "crossing [the] Rubicon of sovereignty. . . . Up until that moment, most governments . . . viewed elections as internal matters. . . . With the official invitations [to the above-mentioned organizations], the Nicaraguans transcended conventional definitions of sovereignty."[2]

Accordingly, in the analysis of the Nicaraguan case the issue that should figure most prominently is the state of the WHI as instantiated by the stances of the central actors in these developments, to wit, the United States and the countries involved in the peace process. The Cold War as intervening variable, on the other hand, had changed little since the Chilean plebiscite of 1988—indeed, much of the context in which the Nicaraguan elections were gestated overlaps (chronologically) with the Chilean electoral process. Therefore these larger contextual issues will receive less attention here than in the previous chapter. However, the domestic structure as intervening variable, through which the larger WHI and the Cold War were instantiated, remains a central focus of analysis. Thus, in the first section of this chapter I introduce Nicaragua's domestic structure. In the second I concentrate on the US—specially the two Reagan administrations'—policy toward Central America and its counterpart: the efforts of some Latin American states to limit US interventionism, and bring peace to the isthmus. In the third section I thus consider the 1990 elections, focusing on the work of three international actors: the Carter Center (CC), the OAS, and the UN.

This chapter shows how IEM contributed to make explicit the understanding of sovereignty enshrined in the WHI. After the Nicaraguan monitoring experience, it became clear that domestic elections were not only a domestic affair. Furthermore, this chapter also shows how the partial redefinition of state sovereignty was accomplished through the interaction of state and nonstate actors—just as the previous discussion of TANs suggests. Thus, the narrative in these pages drives home the twofold point that states should not be conceived of as totally self-organizing actors in the international arena, and that one of major principles of international politics—state sovereignty—has indeed been affected by IEM.

NICARAGUA'S DOMESTIC STRUCTURE

Writer and former Nicaraguan Vice-President Sergio Ramírez once referred to Central America as a "system of conducting vessels." The history of each of the five Central American states has, as a matter of fact, been intimately linked to one another since they became independent. The short-lived United Provinces of Central America is illustrative in this respect. Mexico annexed Central America in 1822, but the attempt lasted only one year. Shortly afterwards, the Central American states formed the United Provinces of Central America. Although the federation dissolved in 1839, the nascent states kept a close relationship.

But in the Nicaraguan case at least, the "conducting vessels" have led much farther than the isthmus—all the way to Washington. United States presence and influence has been a constant in Nicaraguan history. Indeed, Nicaragua even had a US citizen as president. In 1856 American filibuster William Walker became President of Nicaragua. As in the short-lived Mexican incorporation, the episode lasted only one year. In 1857, Walker was removed by the efforts of the five Central American republics—and the assistance of US magnate Cornelius Vanderbilt.

US intervention became a distinguishing feature of Nicaraguan politics in the twentieth century. Thus, for instance, in 1909 the United States helped overthrow the government of Liberal José Santos Zelaya, and three years later Conservative President Adolfo Díaz requested the continental hegemon to send troops to his country in order to prevent his government from falling. The marines ended up staying until 1933.[3] In the meantime, in 1923 a US political science professor wrote an electoral law passed by the Nicaraguan legislature.[4] Five years later, US President Calvin Coolidge nominated General Frank R. McCoy to supervise the 1928 elections. Interestingly, marines were not just election officials, but also representatives of President Coolidge, "who had promised Nicaragua an honest election."[5] Notably, all political parties in Nicaragua recognized the electoral results and deemed the process free and fair.[6] Only Liberal General César Augusto Sandino, an unbending opponent of US interference in Nicaraguan affairs, condemned the electoral process. Actually, Sandino had suggested that the 1928 elections be supervised "by representatives of Latin America instead of by [North] American marines."[7] However, the widespread legitimacy of the elections achieved what the marines had been unable to do—the downfall of Sandino. After the elections, Sandino's political support diminished drastically.[8]

The story would repeat itself two years later. In July 1930 US servicemen were sent to Nicaragua to aid "in the conduct of the elections by serving as chairmen of departmental election boards and as chairmen of the electoral boards in the various precincts for the counting of the ballots, and other similar electoral work."[9] Foreshadowing the opposition to the Sandinistas six decades later, leaders of the Conservative Party (then in the opposition) had warned that they would not participate in the November 1930 elections unless they were supervised by the United States. The results, again, were recognized by all parties.[10]

The Nicaraguan government even tried to bestow constitutional legitimacy upon US intervention by negotiating its version of the Platt Amendment, but Washington refused.[11] What the United States government didn't refuse to do, though, was to help the Nicaraguan government create a National Guard. Thus, in 1933, after consulting with the US Minister, Liberal President Juan Scasa appointed his nephew, Ansatasio Somoza García, as head of the new military establishment. Three years later, though, Somoza García used the Guard to overthrow his uncle.[12]

Somoza García set out then to establish a strong and effective government in Nicaragua—a novelty in the country's polarized and volatile political system. Somoza García's government (1937–1956) rested on four legs:

centralization of power, close association with the National Guard, the sidestepping of political parties, and the support of the United States.[13] Hence, for instance, in 1939 Somoza García suppressed municipal elections, thus avoiding party rivalry at the local level; he then distributed power according more to personal loyalties than to partisan identification.[14] A decade later, the founder of the Somoza dynasty culminated his efforts to bring stability to the country. In 1950 by means of what became known as the "General's Pact," subscribed by Somoza and his opponent Emiliano Chamorro, the Conservatives would formally recognize Somoza's rule. Even the Conservative daily *La Prensa,* owned by the Chamorro family, extolled the pact with a histrionic headline: "A political embrace changes all the country."[15]

The pact, though, would have unfortunate consequences for the Conservatives, causing internal strife. Pedro Joaquín Chamorro, nephew of General Chamorro, became the leader of the Conservatives who still opposed Somoza García, and skillfully used *La Prensa* as the permanent bastion to Somoza's rule. *La Prensa* would thus become a substitute for the domesticated political parties.[16] After Somoza García's politically motivated assassination in 1956, his place was occupied by his dauphin, Luis Somoza Debayle. Luis turned out to be a sort of enlightened despot—at least by Nicaraguan standards. Early on in his administration, he started a process of political liberalization, and his government presented the project mentioned in chapter two on the use of international electoral observers at the OAS 1959 Fifth Meeting of Consultation. More importantly, Luis Somoza promised not to seek reelection. He fulfilled his promise and in 1963 René Schick, a lawyer who had served Somoza senior as private secretary, and as Minister of Education under Luis's government, took office.[17] Significantly, an OAS observer mission was present at the electoral process, as noted.[18] Schick was able to stabilize the political environment, to improve the economic situation of the country, and even at times to take actions against the wishes of the National Guard. Along with his political patron, Schick opposed the nomination of the younger Somoza, Anastasio, for the next presidential term. But using the political and military clout of the National Guard, Luis's brother managed to be the Liberal Party's presidential candidate. In May 1967, a month after Luis' death, Anastasio took office.

Closer to the policies of his father than to those of his brother and Schick, Anastasio Jr., stalled the liberalization process started in the late 1950s. Furthermore, *Tachito*'s reign became synonymous with cronyism and corruption, building a personal empire. As the *Washington Post*'s Jack Anderson reported in August 1975, Somoza's businesses included shoe factories, banks, real state, coffee plantations, hotels, cabs, airlines, apparel, and brothels–among others.[19] Imitating his father's methods, he retained control of both the National Guard and the government; and also like the founder of the dynasty, Anastasio Jr. tried to buy the conservative opposition off. This time the pact was signed with conservative leader Fernando Agüero in March 1971. The terms of the pact included the dissolution of Parliament, its replacement by a constitutional assembly which would call for presidential elections in 1974, and the appointment of a three-member ruling junta—of which Agüero was part.[20] At a much more accelerated pace than the previous time, the most notorious effect of the pact was to unravel the anger of the by then legions of political opponents to the Somoza regime. Furthermore, the blatant corruption that characterized the governmental response to the devastating December 1972 Managua earthquake, and the political maneuvers that, as a consequence of the pact, culminated in the reelection of Somoza in 1974, only exacerbated the rarefaction of the political environment.[21]

Thus, Somoza's decision to start a new presidential term in December 1974 not only unified the small, fragmented, and rather isolated political parties that had inhabited the officially authorized political space, as well as some sectors of the press, but also the middle class. Furthermore, Somoza's ambition brought into the realm of the politically possible for some sectors of what had been his regime's loyal opposition the start of a dialogue with a group that until then had been beyond the pale: the Sandinista Front of National Liberation (FSLN). Founded in 1961 as a revolutionary organization, the FSLN had become a fixture of Nicaraguan politics, mainly in the mountains, but it had never represented a real threat to the regime (more on the FSLN below). In 1974, however, it reappeared with a highly visible urban attack in the house of a high official, moments after the US ambassador had departed. With Archbishop Miguel Obando y Bravo acting as a mediator in their negotiations with Somoza, the Sandinistas were able to obtain the release of 59 political prisoners (including FSLN's leader Tomás Borge), half a million dollars, the publication of an extensive communiqué on the press, as well as its broadcast over the radio, and safe exit. On planes provided by the Panamanian and Venezuelan governments, the Sandinistas flew to those countries.[22] From that moment on, the Sandinistas focused the attention of the Somoza regime.[23]

Time and potential allies were on the Sandinistas' side. Thus, for instance, the assassination in January 1978 of Pedro Joaquín Chamorro, *La Prensa*'s editor and one of the most respected political enemies of the regime, helped make the Sandinistas the opposition's focal point. Soon after the assassination, popular demonstrations broke out across the country, and a myriad of organizations declared a national strike. Somoza responded by declaring the state of emergency. In the meantime, the Catholic Church issued a statement openly supporting the strike, and calling on the regime's supporters not to collaborate "with sinful structures which not only prevent, but also hurt the common good."[24] Thus, a chief contributing factor to the eventual Sandinista triumph was the set of alliances the rebels made both with the Catholic Church and with some sections of the private sector.[25]

In September 1978, eight months after Chamorro's assassination, the Sandinistas launched a national offensive, and then rejected an OAS proposal for a national plebiscite in which Somoza's permanence in power was to be decided.[26] In June 1979, the Episcopal Conference headed by Cardinal Obando y Bravo issued a Pastoral Letter declaring that the political conditions in the country entitled the population to not recognize the authority of the government. The letter also justified popular insurrection.[27]

Concurrently, international factors played an important role during the last moments of *Somocismo*. Thus, for instance, at least since 1978 Mexico openly supported the Sandinistas, breaking diplomatic relations with Nicaragua in May 1979, and encouraging other countries in the region to follow suit.[28] But Mexican support was not only diplomatic—it was also financial and material. Furthermore, Mexican solidarity came from more than one front; thus the government's party, the Institutional Revolutionary Party, also contributed to the insurgents' cause.[29] Symbolically, *Quetzalcoatl II*, a Mexican presidential airplane, carried the governing Junta to power on 19 July 1979.[30]

Similarly, the United States drastically altered its policy toward Nicaragua around that time. Not that Nicaragua became an issue of central concern for the Carter administration, or that it even had an established policy toward the Central American country. But its principled, worldwide human rights policy dictated the stand to be taken toward Somoza. As Pastor, then director of Latin American and Caribbean Affairs on the National Security Council, has put it, "there was no specific policy toward Nicaragua in the Carter presidency; there were only human rights policies that applied to Nicaragua."[31] Thus, for instance, when a few months into the new administration the US government issued a human rights report condemning the Nicaraguan record, Somoza dismissed it saying it "constituted interference in the internal affairs of Nicaragua."[32] In February 1979, the Carter administration reduced its diplomatic relations with Somoza, and canceled military aid.

Similarly, as the 1970s wore down, the OAS began turning an increasing critical eye to the Somoza regime. Thus, for instance, a 1978 report on Nicaragua by the Inter-American Commission on Human Rights concluded that "The right to vote has been hindered by various obstructions of a practical and legal nature which limit its free exercise."[33] The following year, on 23 June, the OAS passed a resolution calling for the "immediate and definitive replacement of the Somoza regime," declaring the Nicaraguan government "the fundamental cause" of the critical situation the Central American country was going through. The resolution went further, requesting the "installation of a democratic government. . . . [and] the holding of free elections as soon as possible."[34] The significance of the resolution did not pass unnoticed to the Inter-American Human Rights Commission, which noted: "For the first time in the history of the OAS and perhaps for the first time in the history of any international organization, [the resolution] deprived an incumbent government of a member state of the Organization of legitimacy, based on the human rights violations committed by that government against its own population."[35]

By the late 1970s, Nicaragua's domestic structure could be characterized, again following Risse-Kappen, as state-controlled. In this type, as noted when discussing Chile's domestic structure by the time of the plebiscite, political institutions are highly centralized and the executive power is strong, whereas civil society is relatively weak.[36] In Somoza's Nicaragua, the authoritarian state, indeed, had become the dominant actor. By this time, though, it was clear that the Sandinistas had the upper hand, and that the Somoza regime was near its end. Within a month, the Sandinistas entered Managua among popular exultation.

Interestingly, the Sandinistas had achieved unity only three months before the path-breaking OAS resolution. Ever since its founding 28 years earlier, the FSLN had operated as a loose coalition of rebel groups. By the mid 1970s, there were three well-defined factions operating within the Front: "Prolonged Popular War," lead by FSLN founder Tomás Borge; "Proletarian Tendency," headed by Jaime Wheelock, and the "Insurrectional Tendency," better known as the *Tercerista* ("thirdist," because it was the third faction in discord), led by the brothers Daniel and Humberto Ortega. By the time the three factions signed their unity in Panama in March 1979, the *Terceristas* were hegemonic.[37] *Tercerista* hegemony rested on two unmistakable facts: its military effectiveness, which included the successful takeover of the National Palace with over a thousand people in it on 22 August 1978 and, more importantly, their more pragmatic bent. The *Terceristas* had been instrumental in forging a broad network of alliances that ultimately benefited the FSLN as a whole.

The Sandinistas were able to reach more mainstream sectors of the population basically by two means: first, through the close relationship they established with some progressive priests within the Catholic Church, and second, through the creation of a political front called the "Group of

Twelve." Regarding the former, although some clergy had begun collaborating with the FSLN since the late 1960s, it was not until the mid-1970s that the close links of some influential priests became public.[38] As for the latter, the Group of Twelve was formed in 1977 at the initiative of the Tercerista faction. It was born when people as diverse as a supermarket chain owner, a banker, a coffee exporter, and a writer, among others, met in San José, Costa Rica, to plot against the Somoza regime.[39] The strategic relationship of the FSLN with the Group of Twelve allowed the Sandinistas to present themselves as espousing fundamental liberal democratic values. Thus, for instance, Group of Twelve and Junta member Sergio Ramírez (whose membership in the FSLN was kept secret until after the fall of Somoza) declared a month before taking power that the new government "will take the route of representative democracy based on periodic elections, but with universal participation. . . . within a multi-party system, of course. We have had too much of a one party system."[40]

Certainly both the more moderate forces of the Nicaraguan opposition and the Carter administration did not place much trust in the democratic commitment of the rebels. This was especially true of the Carter administration, which, although certainly not supporting the Somoza regime, tried to prevent the Sandinistas from coming to power. The moderate allies of the Sandinistas, on the other hand, hoped to exert a more conservative influence on the rebels. Nevertheless, neither the US administration nor the Nicaraguans themselves were sure about what to expect of the Sandinistas. The FSLN as such was still in a stage of flux, and its doctrine and political agenda was therefore unknown—even to many of its members.

The FSLN was a traditional leftist party of sorts. It was a blend of Marxism, Sandino-inspired nationalism, third world internationalism and, to a lesser extent, Catholic liberation theology.[41] At the core of the FSLN, though, lied a Marxist conception of the political process. As Dennis Gilbert has noted, "Nothing is so central to the Sandinistas' conception of themselves and their place in history as their definition of the FSLN as a revolutionary vanguard."[42] Thus, for instance, "Prolonged Popular War" tendency leader Borge described it as "the vanguard of the workers and peasants . . . the living instrument of the revolutionary classes . . . the guide toward a new society."[43]

At a more practical level, though, the FSLN coalesced around three principles: nonalignment, political pluralism, and mixed economy.[44] Although the doctrinal base of the last principle was markedly leaning toward socialism, as the FSLN's economic policy would make clear later,[45] the Sandinistas understood that it was not possible to simply make private enterprise disappear in their country.[46] As a former Sandinista leader recognized later, there was always a contradiction between the FSLN's socialist aspirations and Nicaraguan reality.[47]

Similarly, the nonalignment principle was perhaps more an expression of anti-Yankee sentiment than of a desire for international neutrality. Thus, the help Nicaragua provided to other revolutionary movements in the region during the Sandinista years was partly due to the Sandinistas' faith in militant internationalism.[48] Nevertheless, recognizing the fact that the United States was an omnipresent political, military, and economic factor in the region, the FSLN leadership started toning down its anti-Washington rhetoric in its final years of clandestinity, and once in power it sought to accommodate US interests.[49]

But the key FSLN principle was the one that related to the organization of the Nicaraguan polity. To some extent, the Sandinistas seemed to be committed to a democratic system of government. Thus, in addition to the occasion referred to above in which Ramírez declared that the new government would adhere to representative democracy, the Sandinistas declared they would inaugurate an era of political pluralism. Thus, for instance, a week before their triumphant entrance into Managua, the Junta (in which the Sandinistas were a majority) sent a letter to the OAS Secretary General promising to respect human rights, and to hold "the first free elections that our country will have in this century."[50]

The discourse on representative democracy and free elections, though, was mostly intended to gain followers at home, and to placate adversaries abroad. For the Sandinistas, political pluralism was merely a "tactical" project; the strategic one was kept secret and was not based on liberal conceptions of democracy, but rather on Leninist notions of democratic centralism.[51] Thus, for instance, soon after Somoza fled the country and the plural Governing Junta that had been formed the previous month in Costa Rica was installed, it became clear that power lay elsewhere: in the FSLN's National Directorate.[52]

A few months later, in August 1980, the Council of State, a corporative legislative body inaugurated three months earlier, passed a decree postponing the holding of free elections until 1985. The FSLN's pronounced bias against political parties became manifest promptly: of the 47 seats in the Council, just 12 were assigned to political parties—only three of which went to parties not allied to the Sandinistas.[53] But as Valerie Bunce has put it, "democracy minus political parties is unthinkable."[54] In any case, although the decision to put off the elections caused deep dissatisfaction among the population, the Sandinistas justified it in terms of the calamitous state the country was left in after the revolution.[55] It was in that milieu that

Minister of Defense Humberto Ortega declared that "democracy neither begins nor ends with elections."[56] Similarly, as the promised elections approached, National Directorate member Bayardo Arce characterized them as a charade intended to gather international approval.[57] It was becoming increasingly clear that the Sandinistas were willing to severely compromise one of the three principles around which the FSLN coalesced: political pluralism.

The FSLN's practical disdain for representative democracy was no doubt linked both to the wider Nicaraguan state-controlled domestic structure and to its Marxist underground origins. To begin with, Nicaragua had never had a democratic system: it had rather had a sort of "sultanistic authoritarianism" which made the establishment of liberal democracy a daunting task for committed democrats, let alone for former guerrilla fighters.[58] By the Sandinista leadership's own admission, what they established after the revolution was a "different" kind of democracy, one with a dominant party system.[59] As the Law Group noted in the early 1980s, in Nicaragua a "very close association of the FSLN and the State" existed.[60]

If to the weight of the legacy left to the Sandinistas we add the particularities of the FSLN, an organization heavily influenced since its foundation by the Leninist idea of the political party, the unattractiveness of formal democratic procedures to the Sandinista leadership is not surprising. Undemocratic practices were common place both within the FSLN and its affiliated organizations. Thus, for instance, the mass organizations linked to the Front reproduced its vertical structure as soon as it came to power; furthermore, they were incorporated to it as mere appendices.[61] Not unexpectedly, since the FSLN considered itself the vanguard of the Nicaraguan people, once in power it felt justified to constrain the right of assembly of three social groups which it did not control: labor unions, opposition parties, and the Catholic Church.[62]

The case of the Church is particularly interesting. As in many other contexts in which political actors are restrained, the Catholic Church became an important political actor in Nicaragua (although it certainly also enjoyed a similar status during the Somoza regime).[63] Even though the Sandinista government made explicit attempts on several occasions to associate itself with the religious values of the population—as when President Ortega declared that "Christianity and Marxism are part of Sandinista democracy," or when the government decided to participate in the most important religious festivity in Nicaragua, or when it attempted to benefit politically from the 1983 papal visit—this kind of efforts mostly backfired.[64] The relationship between the Sandinista government and the Catholic hierarchy was one of continuous conflict.[65]

Nevertheless, the Sandinista government was far from being a totalitarian regime of the type seen in the former Soviet bloc. Unlike the parties that came to power in the aftermath of World War II in Eastern and Central Europe, the FSLN was not committed to an overarching ideology. Furthermore, it even lacked an agreed upon political program. That is why its different constituting factions did not merge when the FSLN seized power.[66] The crucial factor that prevented their differences from unraveling the Front was the constant state of siege the Reagan administration put their government through (more on this later). Another factor that prevented the Sandinistas from becoming diehards was the persistence of well delineated factions within the party, which meant that they had to constantly find accommodation with one another. As Gilbert has put it, "The Sandinistas are neither unbending ideologues nor pragmatists without principles."[67] Thus, real existing Sandinismo was much more moderate than what its radical discourse often suggested.

Interestingly, that was the case particularly in the electoral arena. For reasons that had more to do with the external environment than with domestic politics, the Sandinistas decided to hold the first elections a year in advance. The 4 November 1984 date was chosen for one reason: the Sandinistas wanted to have an impact on the US elections to be held two days later, in which Reagan was seeking reelection. More generally, the Sandinistas were concerned about their international legitimacy. As a high Foreign Ministry official put it, the 1984 elections were "a key element in our national defense strategy. Our internal legitimacy is not in question. What *is* in question is our international legitimacy."[68] The constitutive effects of the WHI as constitutional structure were clearly at work in Nicaragua's domestic structure.

Thus, the Nicaraguan government invited a myriad of (mostly sympathetic) organizations to monitor the elections.[69] As Miguel D'Escoto, Foreign Minister at the time, put it, the government decided to invite international observers as a "defensive" strategy, in order to show its legitimacy to the world.[70] Nevertheless, the electoral event did not achieve its objective—at least at the international level. Former Vice-President Ramírez would later recognize: "We only achieved halfway the legitimacy we were pursuing. The Latin American and European governments which had pressured or encouraged us to go to the elections, sent low level delegations to the swearing-in ceremony in January 1985. No Chief of State was willing to come. . . . our most important guest turned out to be Fidel Castro, who with his solidary gesture rather unbalanced the scenario."[71]

Not that the elections had been a sham—far from that. As a Latin American Studies Association report on the electoral process put it, "Without question, the November 4 [1984] elections were the cleanest held in Nicaragua since 1928, when U.S. marines were organizing and supervising the balloting."[72] Furthermore, for the Latin American practice of the time, they were fairly clean. Thus, for instance, the Electoral Law passed for the first post-Somoza elections faired well by international standards. Additionally, the autonomous Supreme Electoral Council (CSE) created by the Law, although dominated by pro-Sandinista members, proved an impartial and effective body.[73] With 75 percent of registered voters casting ballots on election day, the FSLN was the absolute winner, with 67.2 percent of the vote.[74] By committing the Sandinistas to holding periodic elections administered by an autonomous body, in accordance with established rules, the first post-Somoza electoral process did represent a "significant political opening."[75] As Philip Williams has noted, "The November 1984 elections signaled the formal adoption of liberal democratic institutions and an increased emphasis on political parties."[76]

Nevertheless, many factors coalesced to make the 1984 elections mostly inconsequential. Despite the mostly impartial legal framework in which the election took place, many other factors combined to undermine the holding of a free credible election. One of them was the lack of a leveled playing field. The FSLN exploited in a variety of ways the advantages of incumbency. As the WOLA's report put it, "The identification of the FSLN with the state made competition during the campaign difficult."[77] Additionally, the main opposition candidate, former Junta member Arturo Cruz of *Convergencia Democrática,* withdrew his candidacy after strong pressure from the Reagan administration to do so.[78] Thus, for many in the opposition the 1984 elections lacked legitimacy.[79] Similarly, by the mid-1980s even many European countries, which had traditionally supported the Sandinistas, began to express unease about what they perceived as increasing authoritarian tendencies of the Nicaraguan government.[80]

Soon after the elections, the National Assembly initiated the process of drafting a new constitution, which went into effect in January 1987. Nevertheless, the absence of an important sector of the opposition in the deliberation process, as well as the almost immediate suspension of constitutional guarantees due to the government's declaration of a State of Emergency, doomed the legitimacy of the new charter.[81] Thus, the political environment that transpired in Nicaragua eight years after the arrival of the Sandinistas to power was far from being one of democratic normalcy. Nicaragua's domestic structure, in fact, remained a state-controlled one: political institutions were centralized, the executive power dominated the others, and civil society remained weak. This is of course not to suggest that the Sandinista revolution did not bring about consequential changes to Nicaragua. It certainly did. But the broad contours of its domestic structure, following Risse-Kappen's classification, changed little.

The lack of democracy in Sandinista Nicaragua was of course not a entirely a homegrown product. The United States, and particularly the Reagan administration, were associates in it. The state of siege Washington put the Sandinistas in served to increase their authoritarian tendencies. The support provided by the United States to the "Nicaraguan Resistance," better known as *contras,* since 1981, was paradigmatic in this respect. As Andrés Pérez has noted, "The *contras* embodied one of the few points of FSLN ideology on which all could agree, e.g., that the United States and *Somocismo* were enemies of the revolution."[82] National Directorate member Bayardo Arce put it this way: "We are more centralist than democratic. . . . When there is war our centralism is strengthened."[83] The US invasion of Grenada in 1983 only came to confirm the Sandinistas' fear that the Reagan administration did not want anything short of their capitulation. President Reagan, after all, went on record to say that he would make them "say uncle."[84]

US POLICY TOWARD NICARAGUA AND THE LATIN AMERICAN RESPONSE

The same year Reagan came to power, there appeared an article by Jeane Kirkpatrick, his 1981–1985 United Nations Ambassador, in which she lambasted the Carter Administration's policy on human rights in general, and toward Latin America in particular. Regarding Nicaragua, Kirkpatrick asked rhetorically, "What did the Carter administration do in Nicaragua?," to reply: "*It brought down the Somoza regime.*"[85] Therefore, she argued, "The first step in the reconstruction of U.S. policy for Latin America is intellectual."[86] In a previous article, she had already articulated her classic distinction between good and bad dictators, an intellectualized variation of Roosevelt's dictum on the first Somoza.[87] Kirkpatrick alleged that "traditional authoritarian governments [like Somoza's] are less repressive than revolutionary autocracies [like the Sandinistas']. . . . they are more susceptible of liberalization, and. . . . they are more compatible with U.S. interests." Her reasoning became hegemonic within the Reagan team. Nicaragua certainly turned into their obsession. As Thomas Carothers has noted, "Nicaragua was the sole Latin American issue over which the hardliners in the administration maintained rigid control over the duration of the Reagan years."[88]

US officials were able to use the Sandinistas' pre-July 1979 discourse as ammunition. The Junta's pledge to respect human rights, remain neutral, and hold free elections after the departure of Somoza became the central point of contention. Washington argued that what it considered a breach of commitments of Nicaragua's government might entitle third parties, such as the United States or the OAS, to use coercion against the Sandinista government.[89] Nicaragua took the issue to the International Court of Justice (ICJ) in 1986. The Court accepted that, following the recommendation contained in the 23 June 1979 OAS resolution, the Nicaraguan Junta had indeed committed itself to holding free elections. Nevertheless, the ICJ considered that those issues were "questions of domestic policy." It ruled that the commitment to hold free elections was "an essentially political pledge."[90] National elections were, by the mid-1980s, still considered as falling outside the purview of the system-wide international community.

In any case, after the 1984 elections, which, as noted, were certainly no more deficient than many others in Latin America, the Reagan administration was pressed hard to find a rationale for its double standard. After all, only two years before it had inaugurated its "democracy promotion" program in neighboring El Salvador. The intention was to show that the electoral path was the only feasible, legitimate, and auspicious one, even for countries plagued by internal conflict like the Central American ones. It was in this context that the "demonstration elections" of El Salvador took place in 1982 (to elect a Constituent Assembly), and again in 1984 (to elect a President). Both electoral processes received not only Washington's blessing, but were largely engineered by it.[91] Notably, the US government spent more than $10 million for the 1984 elections—including, of course, expenses of election observers.[92] But although a State Department document later claimed that "a broad political spectrum" had contended for power in the presidential elections, left-leaning parties were excluded.[93] As Terry Karl has noted, the 1984 electoral process was a contest between El Salvador's center-right and ultra-right.[94]

In contrast, regarding Nicaragua, the Reagan administration engaged in a protracted effort to delegitimize its electoral process.[95] The strategy consisted basically in trying to use the Nicaraguan experience as a sort of "counter-demonstration" election. Thus, three months before the elections Reagan told the *New York Times* that "No person committed to democracy will be taken in by a Soviet-style sham elections."[96] On 5 November, the day after the elections, the State Department referred to them as an "electoral farce." Three months later, the Sandinista regime remained, according to Reagan, simply "a government that seized power out of the barrel of a gun—it's never been chosen by the people."[97] Similarly, Secretary of State George Shultz noted that "An election just as an election does not really mean anything. The important thing is that if there is to be an electoral process, it must be observed not only at the moment when people vote, but in all the preliminary aspects that make an election really mean something."[98]

The Reagan administration openly admitted that it was using a double standard. Echoing Kirkpatrick's argument on "authoritarian governments" and "revolutionary autocracies," a high US official involved in Central America policy put it this way: "The United States is not obliged to apply the same standard of judgment to a country whose government is avowedly hostile to the U.S. as for a country, like El Salvador, where it is not. These people [the Sandinistas] could bring about a situation in Central America which could pose a threat to U.S. security. That allows us to change our yardstick."[99]

But behind the effort to depict a political chiaroscuro in Central America, where in fact democratic development was still mostly gray, there was a sustained belligerent attempt to overthrow the Sandinista government. Since early 1982, the *Washington Post* had revealed that Reagan had approved a covert operations plan against Nicaragua. From that moment, and until 1988, as Pastor has noted, "the Reagan administration provided more military aid to the contras to overthrow the Nicaraguan government than the United States had provided to all five Central American countries from 1962 to 1980."[100]

In addition, the US government declared a trade embargo against Nicaragua in May 1985. The action was widely condemned by the international community. The UN Security Council demanded that the United States immediately lift the trade embargo, but it simply vetoed the resolution. The next year, the ICJ ruled on an accusation made by Nicaragua in 1984 against the United States for mining a harbor at Corinto. In its verdict, the Court condemned the US government to pay compensation to Nicaragua, but the former ignored the ruling. The Reagan administration was determined to prevail over the Sandinistas, regardless of the means it needed to employ.

But it soon began to pay a high price for such blatant unilateralism where it mattered the most: within its own country. By the mid-1980s, Congress started to restrain Reagan's aggressions against Nicaragua, particularly as they related to the contra war. The administration then found a covert (and illegal) way to keep the money flowing to those Reagan called "freedom fighters." But the operation was eventually discovered, and the "Iran-Contra" scandal exploded. In November 1986, Reagan was forced to dismiss National Security Council-member Vice-Admiral John Poindexter and his aide, Lieutenant-Colonel Oliver North—but not without telling Poindexter that his undertaking "will make a great movie one day."[101]

Reagan's interventionist policy also prompted a response from its southern neighbors. As mentioned in chapter three, in 1983 Colombia, Mexico, Panama, and Venezuela launched the Contadora Initiative in order to counteract Washington's interventionist policies and bring peace to the Central American region. But perhaps the most notable feature of this attempt was that it excluded the United States, a key player in the conflict. Furthermore, it is also telling that this effort was undertaken outside the OAS, even if the regional organization blessed the Contadora proposal.[102]

For the Contadora countries, at least initially, the objective was to bring to a halt the armed conflict in the region; internal democratization was secondary. In contrast, Washington insisted on bringing peace through what it considered to be a democratization process—particularly in Nicaragua.[103] In the initial phases, Mexico, with a new administration (Miguel de la Madrid's) that had abandoned the openly pro-Sandinista stand of its predecessor (José López Portillo's), played a key role as a mediator between the two key players in the Central American crisis: Nicaragua and the United States.[104] Thus, at Mexico's prodding, in June 1984 the two countries started talks in Manzanillo (Mexico). Nevertheless, Washington was determined not to make concessions of any sort to the Sandinistas, and it withdrew from the Mexican-sponsored talks in January 1985. Throughout this process, Mexico was able to continue to appear as a friend to the Sandinistas. As, former Foreign Minister Miguel D'Escoto put it, Mexico "was always the most important of all" of Nicaragua's friends.[105]

In the meantime, the Contadora initiative was kept at work with mixed results. Although the United States was able to increase the relative weight of democratization at the expense of regional security in the peace initiative, it was not willing to make meaningful concessions. Thus, in mid-1985 the Contadora's Support (or Lima) Group was created by the foreign ministers of Argentina, Brazil, Peru and Uruguay. The appearance of the new group strengthened the Contadora process not only by doubling the number of states explicitly concerned with bringing peace to the region, but also by involving in it countries which were not directly affected by the developments in the area. Furthermore, the fact that the total population of the countries in the two groups pursuing a peaceful settlement in Central America comprised over 90 percent of the subcontinent's population increased its legitimacy.[106]

Nevertheless, Contadora's record did not improve significantly. A year after the Support Group was created, the Contadora Initiative had put out four drafts of a treaty. The day after the deadline of the last draft submitted for signature to the Central American presidents had passed, the Contadora Group withdrew it. Two weeks later, on 20 June 1986, the

Sandinistas surprised the other governments by announcing that they would sign it—but by then the Contadora initiative was practically dead. A last effort to revive the peace process came six months later, with a meeting in Brazil of the foreign ministers of both the Contadora and Support groups, plus the Secretaries General of the OAS and the UN. At that meeting, the Rio de Janeiro Group, formed by the eight countries, was created, with the foreign ministers agreeing to visit all Central American countries in order to encourage them to renew peace negotiations.[107]

By that time, though, the Central American presidents, some of whom enjoyed widely recognized democratic credentials, such as Guatemala's Vinicio Cerezo and Costa Rica's Oscar Arias, had begun to take the peace process in their hands. With this move, not only the United States but also extra-regional Latin American countries were put on the margins of the peace process. President Cerezo invited the other Central American President to Esquipulas in May 1986 to discuss regional peace and the creation of a Central American Parliament. On that occasion (known as Esquipulas I), the participants referred to Contadora as Central America's "best political forum" to reach peace and democracy in the region.[108] Building on the Contadora initiative, in February 1987 President Arias presented a ten-point peace plan.[109] Six months later, at a second meeting in Esquipulas, the "Procedure for Establishing a Stable and Lasting Peace in Central America," also known as the Arias Plan, or Esquipulas II Agreement, was signed.[110]

The transition from Contadora to Esquipulas II was not an easy one. The fact that its chief architect, President Arias, was an interested party made things more complicated, at least initially. To begin with, Arias was openly hostile to the Sandinista government, and thus apparently very close to Reagan's position. For him, the emphasis should be put on democratization, not on regional security. Furthermore, for Arias the Sandinista regime was the main culprit. As he put it, "The Sandinista regime is the chief cause of the Central American crisis . . . The Sandinista regime is illegitimate."[111] Thus, during the Esquipulas I meetings, Arias told Nicaraguan President Ortega, "What you call democracy isn't called democracy here nor in any part of the world."[112] Not surprisingly, Nicaragua at first opposed Esquipulas II.

The central problem was that the Arias plan made domestic electoral processes the subject of international negotiations. For the Sandinistas, that was a violation of Nicaraguan sovereignty, and therefore "unacceptable."[113] Esquipulas II established that

> Elections . . . shall be subject to supervision by the corresponding electoral bodies, and the Governments concerned undertake to invite the Organization of American States, the United Nations, and the Governments of

> third states to send observers to verify that the electoral process has been governed by the strictest rules of equal access for all political parties to the communication media and by ample opportunities for organizing public demonstrations and any other type of political propaganda.[114]

On the other hand, the agreement also recognized the legitimacy of the Sandinista regime, while denying recognition to the insurgent groups of the region—the contras included.[115] For the Sandinistas, the most enticing part of the Arias Plan was that it actually opened a possibility for ending the contra war, which had been become an unbearable economic and political burden.

Thus, in the end President Ortega was persuaded to sign the agreement. Interestingly, the FSLN's National Directorate did not endorse the accord for three days after Ortega had signed it. Instead, as Borge noted, the leadership subjected it to "very deep and very serious questioning."[116] Interestingly, the Reagan administration was also opposed to the Arias Plan. In fact, it even tried to boycott it presenting an alternative, the Wright-Reagan plan, the same day the five presidents initiated their second meeting in Esquipulas. In the end, the presidents disregarded the emergent plan and focused on the one they had been working on.[117]

When it was announced that the Arias Plan had been accepted, the Reagan administration was largely disappointed—and divided. Thus, Secretary of State Shultz wanted to work with it, while Vice-President Bush found fault with it for giving Nicaragua "too much of what Communist leader Daniel Ortega wanted."[118] In the end, the Reagan administration pledged to work with Esquipulas II—although noting that it would keep its support to the contras, which went against the accord.

The Arias Plan was an original innovation with far-reaching consequences. As Jennifer McCoy, Larry Garber, and Robert Pastor have noted, it "represented a conceptual breakthrough in international relations."[119] At a practical level, the Arias Plan marked the comeback of the OAS, by making it part of the solution to the Central American imbroglio.[120] Furthermore, the Plan came to encompass issues that, although not formally part of it, were crucial for its success. One of them was negotiations between the Sandinistas and the Contras.[121] The Sandinistas had steadfastly opposed direct talks with the Contras, whom they considered US mercenaries. But by signing at Esquipulas, Ortega and the other participants had granted Arias the power to interpret their compliance with the agreement. And for the Sandinistas it was crucial, in order to avoid the resumption of US contra aid (which had not been renewed in 1987), to have Arias' seal of approval. For the Central American president, though, the building of a lasting peace in the isthmus passed through the holding of negotiations between the Sandinistas and the contras. Thus, when as an offshoot of Esquipulas II the Central American presidents met in Alajauela (Costa Rica) in January 1988, Ortega announced that his government was willing to open direct talks with the contras.[122]

Accordingly, the Sandinistas invited the contras to send a negotiating team to Nicaragua. The first direct meeting between the two parties initiated on 21 March 1988, at Sapoá. It was attended by Defense Minister Humberto Ortega, among other Sandinista officials; a couple of days later, the two parties signed an accord.[123] At a subsequent meeting of the five Central American presidents held in Costa del Sol, El Salvador, on 13–14 February 1989, the Sandinistas made several important announcements: that they would amend Nicaragua's constitution and several federal laws in order to comply with demands by the opposition; that they would advance the date of national elections from November to February 1990; and that the electoral process would be monitored exhaustively by international observers, especially from the UN and the OAS. The Costa del Sol forum was carefully chosen by the Sandinistas to make those announcements, particularly the one regarding the advancement of the elections. As Vice President Ramírez would later recall, that announcement was in large measure a response to the insistence of the other presidents.[124] In exchange for the Sandinistas' pledges, the other Central American leaders at Costa del Sol insisted on contra demobilization. More concretely, the Honduran president, from whose country the contras had been operating, promised to work in contra demobilization with the assistance of the UN and the OAS.[125]

The next Central American summit, in Tela, Honduras, in August 1989, focused mostly on the contras, with the Central American presidents agreeing that the irregular forces should be demobilized starting December.[126] It was not until this summit that the Nicaraguan opposition, after the government granted it further guarantees, agreed to participate in the 1990 elections.[127] But the Arias Plan was not limited to Nicaragua; it was meant to deal with the whole system of conducting vessels that is Central America. Thus, the peace agreements in El Salvador (1992) and in Guatemala (1996), as well as the creation of the Central American Parliament were also a product of the Esquipulas process.

Key to the eventual success of the peace agreements was the arrival of George Bush to the presidency of the United States in January 1989. Not that Bush was pro-Sandinista, but he had a less dogmatic position toward the Nicaraguan issue. Bush was not obsessed with Nicaragua, and he did not see it as a major threat to US interests. As Mariano Fiallos, President of Nicaragua's Supreme Electoral Council (CSE) at the time of the 1990 elections has noted, "the Bush administration had a more flexible and more efficient conception [of international politics], and less fundamentalist . . . so Bush changed the [US] position and accepted the multilateralism that Reagan refused to accept."[128]

Furthermore, the attention paid to the Central American country by the Reagan administration had blown the Nicaragua issue out of proportion in US politics. Thus, less than two months into the administration, the new Secretary of State, James Baker, met with Speaker Jim Wright and told him: "We want to wind this thing down . . . We are willing to substitute negotiations for military action."[129] Baker was determined, as he put it, "to remove the issue form the domestic political arena."[130] Thus, on 24 March 1989, the Bush administration and Congress reached the "Bipartisan Accord," by means of which the parties involved declared their support for the Arias Plan and rejected further military aid to the contras.[131]

But Bush and Baker felt comfortable putting the Nicaragua issue aside in part because they were confident that the new Soviet leadership, in the twilight of the Cold War, had changed its attitude toward Nicaragua. And undeniably, either because of "new thinking" or because of necessity, the Soviet Union had been changing its Nicaragua policy in the last years. Thus, around the time that Esquipulas was being negotiated, the diplomat in charge of Latin America at the Soviet Ministry of Foreign Relations told the Sandinistas that they should reach an agreement with the United States soon, put an end to the war, and get resources from Western countries, because the Soviet Union was no longer able to carry such a burden.[132] Washington was decided to make certain that the Soviet Union's Nicaragua policy had changed, and the same month that Baker approached Congress, Bush sent a letter to Soviet leader Mikhail Gorbachev in which he warned him that further Soviet aid to Nicaragua would damage the state of U.S.-U.S.S.R. relationships. In his reply, Gorbachev noted that his country had suspended military aid to the Sandinistas after 1988, in response to the US change of policy which favored the diplomatic course.[133]

Interestingly, the Bush administration seemed to be ready to live with a new Sandinista administration, as long as it won in a clean electoral process. Thus, in the days leading to the elections, Assistant Secretary of State Bernard Aronson met with Nicaraguan vice minister of foreign affairs Víctor Tinoco in order to set a plan to normalize relations after the expected Sandinista triumph.[134] The anticipated normalization of relations was no doubt a consequence of the Contadora process and the Arias Plan, which together contributed to delegitimize the militarist US policy in Central America. But the Arias Plan, by starting from a position that was closer to that of the United States, had a greater effect on the improved prospects for Nicaragua and, therefore, the region as a whole. As a State Department official put it, "Arias, more than any other Latin leader, single-handedly undid U.S. policy in Nicaragua."[135] The road to the Nicaraguan February 1990 elections indeed ran through an extensive and convoluted system of conducting vessels.

THE 1990 ELECTIONS

The 1990 Nicaraguan elections were seen both by Nicaraguans and by the international community more in terms of a regional security issue, than in terms of human rights, as had been the case with the 1988 Chilean plebiscite. The presence of international observers, as CSE's Fiallos has noted, was framed in terms "of contention of a regional war."[136] Similarly, for Antonio Lacayo, then at the National Opposition Union (UNO), "the 1990 elections in Nicaragua need to be seen within the context of a war, in which this country was immersed since the 1980s."[137] This framing is important because it led the Sandinista government to actively seek international observation of the electoral process. As CSE-member Rosa Marina Zelaya has noted, the international monitoring of the 1990 elections was important because "we were in war at that moment, and Nicaragua needed that those elections be credible."[138]

But unlike the previous electoral process, this time the elections needed to be credible on both fronts: the domestic and the external. The Achilles' tendon of the 1984 elections had been the domestic dimension, with the main opposition forces boycotting the elections. This time, the presence of the full political spectrum had been guaranteed in August 1989, and the next month the political parties that formed UNO announced the nomination of Violeta Chamorro as their presidential candidate, with Virgilio Godoy, a former cabinet member in the Sandinista government, as her running mate. On the international dimension, the participation of international observers, particularly of the OAS and the UN, agreed on in the context of the Arias Plan, assured third parties that the next Nicaraguan government would be a legitimate one.

The domestic and external dimensions of the electoral process, however, were mixed to an extent that made their consideration as two discrete realms illusory. The Nicaraguan 1990 elections were certainly an international event. For UNO, the absence of international observers would have meant its non-attendance to the electoral process. As Lacayo, chief advisor of Violeta Chamorro and Minister of the Presidency in her administration put it, "For us in the opposition . . . the international observation [of the 1990 electoral process] was an indispensable condition . . . if there had not been international observation, we wouldn't have gone to the elections."[139] Similarly, the OAS partly justified its presence in Nicaragua by noting that it was welcome by all the political forces.[140] In effect, as CES' Zelaya noted, "the perception of the citizenry, of the political parties was positive . . . the 21 political parties that participated [in the 1990 elections] agreed with the presence of electoral international observers . . . The presence of the UN and the OAS strengthened the validity of the results of the electoral body. Not because [the results] would or wouldn't have been false, but because there was a electoral-political support on the part of these missions."[141]

The consensus on the need for international observers is telling. There was of course some dissent inside the government and even within the CSE, which opposed the presence of international observers for sovereignty reasons. But as Fiallos has noted, "the situation was such that it was not possible to be toying with theories; something needed to be done to reestablish peace in Nicaragua, and [the presence of international observers in the elections] looked like a good opportunity."[142] Similarly, for Lacayo the issue of foreign monitors impinging upon Nicaragua's sovereignty was somewhat passé. For him,

> sovereignty had been lost long before, for us it had been lost since the moment that here many of the decisions were taken, along with government officials, by people from East Germany, Czechs, Bulgarian, Palestines, and people who were not Nicaraguan, and mainly the Soviets who came to give advise on all military aspects. That is to say that for us in the opposition sovereignty had been lost long ago, we rather had to rescue it by means of bringing democracy to Nicaragua, and by means of a government truly committed not only with rescuing our sovereignty but with an effective policy of non-alignment.[143]

Nicaraguans were indeed breaking new ground with their position regarding international observers. As Zelaya remembers,

> in 1990 there were governments that criticized Nicaragua for allowing electoral international observation, for being the cutting edge in this 'intrusion' . . . that allowing the presence of international observers was damaging to Nicaragua's sovereignty, among them [the critics] some Mexican leaders, and some Cuban leaders, sectors which were somewhat wary of the possibility that sovereignty could be hurt . . . And they were partially right, but the fact of the matter is that the electoral international observation [of the 1990 process] was a necessary evil.

Before this time, Zelaya notes, "the issue of sovereignty, the issue of independence, all that had always been above anybody wanting to put together such an important observation" effort.[144] The Nicaraguan Foreign Minister D'Escoto, in the meantime, did not have any qualms about the presence of international observers in the 1990 elections; for him, in any case, "the intervention was already there: it was US intervention, which we never ceased having."[145]

There were three kinds of international observers in the 1990 Nicaraguan elections, each subject to different regulations. The first and most important one was reserved for international organizations, which had special rights, immunities, and access to information. Although in theory only the OAS and the UN were in this category, in practice the CC/Council of Freely Elected Heads of Government (CFEHG) also belonged to it. The second category corresponded to "invited observers;" they were distinguished individuals or organizations such as Hemisphere Initiatives.[146] A subset of this category was the diplomatic body accredited in Managua who wanted to observe the process; they received a "courtesy pass" in order to make their monitoring activities easier. Finally, uninvited observers, who could monitor the process as tourists.[147] Thus, monitoring missions such as those of the Law Group or WOLA played an important but secondary role in the 1990 electoral process. As the Law Group put it in a pre-election report, "Three groups [of observers] in particular promise to be of key importance: the UN, the OAS, and former President Jimmy Carter's Council of Freely Elected Heads of Government."[148] There was, though, a common denominator in practically all observation efforts: US resources. As Rafael López Pintor has put it, "The importance of U.S. electoral assistance may be summarily assessed by stating that no relevant sector of Nicaraguan society was left without a share in this fund. . . . two of the three main observer missions (OAS and Carter) and some of the minor ones (Freedom House, the Costa Rica-based Center for Electoral Assistance and Promotion) were basically financed by direct U.S. aid."[149]

The main source of US funding was of course NED. In October 1989 Congress appropriated $9 million for the "promotion of democracy" in Nicaragua. Of this appropriation eight million went to NED, which in turn granted $4.12 million to NDI and NRI, in addition to $2.5 million for "noncampaign" activities of the opposition coalition UNO, with the rest going to a UNO-affiliated union group, to a civil education project, and to Nicaragua's SEC. Of the one million remaining from the appropriation that did not go to NED, $400,000 went to the CC, $250,000 to the Center for Democracy, and about $400,000 to the Inter-American Institute of Human Rights' Center for Electoral Assistance and Promotion (CAPEL).[150] As

William Leogrande has noted, NED's outlays for the Nicaraguan 1990 elections "dwarfed previous NED election support programs in Chile and the Philippines."[151]

In any case, the fact that an INGO such as the CC-CFEHG was granted a status similar to that of the two participating IGOs tells something not only about the nature of the INGO at issue, but also of the complexity IEM reached with the Nicaraguan elections. As McCoy has put it, this case "illustrated active coordination between IGOs and INGOs."[152] Nevertheless, the interaction of the three most important monitoring missions was not exempt from rivalry. It was no doubt benign rivalry, but rivalry nonetheless. As Pastor, a key member of the CC team put it, "Not only were Ortega and Chamorro competing for power, so too were Carter, Richardson, and Baena competing, although in a more subtle and perhaps subconscious way, for attention and credit."[153]

In the following sections, I deal in more detail with the work of each of the three main observer missions. I start with the CC because it represents the culmination of the NGOs drive to institutionalize IEM in the hemisphere; I then consider the OAS mission, in order to emphasize the continuity the Nicaraguan request represented for the regional organization; finally, I review the UN involvement in the Nicaraguan electoral process, which was an unprecedented experience for the international organization.

The Carter Center

As noted in chapter two, the CC is a sui-generis NGO. It could be considered a semi-governmental organization. This is so for several reasons. In the first place, the influence it is able to exert is due, to a large extent, to the fact that its leader is a former US president. In second place, at least occasionally, as was the case in the Nicaraguan elections, a large part of its funding comes from Washington; thirdly, sometimes it works in tandem with the State Department. During the Nicaraguan mission CC members oftentimes informed US officials of their activities in the Central American country. Thus, for instance, Pastor mentions several occasions in which he briefed and/or consulted with State Department officials.[154] Furthermore, when a special commission to observe the Nicaraguan elections named by President Bush was rejected by the Nicaraguan government, the CC's mission invited some of its members to join it.[155]

The CC actively sought an invitation to observe the 1990 elections.[156] When Daniel Ortega invited Carter to Nicaragua to attend the celebrations of the revolution's 10th anniversary, he sent Pastor in his place to get an invitation.[157] In Managua, Pastor met with President Ortega and Vice-President Ramírez. He used the CC's recent experience in the Panamanian 1989 elections to make his case. As Pastor recalls, he told Vice-President Ramírez: "Here is an idea: why don't you pick the person who denounced Noriega's election as a fraud, that would certainly put you in a strong position to convince because he's established his credibility and you know he can be trusted and we would be fair."[158]

Pastor proved to be a persuasive envoy, and Carter received the government's invitation on 3 August 1989; five days later, Carter officially accepted.[159] In his letter of acceptance, Carter promised Ortega that he would "work to ensure that the results of a free and fair election in Nicaragua will be respected in the United States and the rest of the world regardless of who wins or loses."[160] Thus, Carter set out to put together a 34-member "international and bipartisan" delegation."[161]

The "bipartisan" nature of the delegation clearly points to the semi-official nature of the delegation. But despite these two features, the relationship between the Carter delegation and the Bush administration was not always free of tension. As Pastor puts it:

> The relationship between the Carter mission and the Bush administration was a complicated one at several levels. The fact that Carter and Bush were of different parties and had contrary views of the contras strengthened Carter's negotiating hand in Nicaragua, although it also heightened suspicion among some in the Bush administration. . . . At a second level was the personal relationship . . . there was an unhappy chemistry [between Bush and Carter]. . . . Another important factor . . . was the Democratic control of Congress. Over the objections of the Bush administration, the Democrats inserted funds for the Carter Center observation into the AID budget, and when the Carter mission needed to confirm that the United States was not engaged in covert actions [for a mediation service related to the campaign], we approached the Democratic chairs of the Intelligence Committees directly.[162]

In designing its strategy for Nicaragua, the CC relied on the work done by NDI in Chile. The IEM TAN of INGOs that was born in Chile in the context of the 1988 plebiscite became a solid foundation for the work the CC did in Nicaragua in 1989–1990. In the final report, Pastor thanks Brian Atwood, Ken Wollack, Larry Garber, and Glenn Cowan, all of whom were actively involved in NDI's monitoring of the 1988 Chilean plebiscite, "for their advice and for the model they have developed for observing elections."[163] Nevertheless, the CC intended from the beginning to go much further than other monitoring groups had gone before. Being a high-profile organization, the CC mission was envisioned since August 1989 "*not [as] an observation mission; it would be a mediation project to define the terms that would allow all sides to accept the process and respect the election results.*"[164] Its role was, according to the CC's Managua office director Jennifer McCoy, to "actually influence the process, trying to improve, and help level the playing field."[165]

Thus, in 16–19 September co-chairs former Argentinean President Raúl Alfonsín, and Carter led the first pre-electoral visit to Nicaragua.[166] Delegation members met with government and electoral officials, and received assurances that their mission would have access, on par with the UN and OAS delegations, to the counting of the ballots, and would be given a copy of the vote tally sheet. The following month, from the 20th to the 23rd, former Venezuelan President Rafael Caldera and former Arizona Governor Bruce Babbit led a second visit.[167] The delegation observed the last Sunday of voter registration. Although the report on the registration process was positive, the mission also noted some problems, such as the insufficient number of polling places in areas where more than 400 voters had registered, and an unbalanced access to the media that negatively affected opposition forces.

In 13–16 December, former Presidents Carter and Daniel Oduber (Costa Rica), and former Washington state governor Daniel Evans led a third visit to Nicaragua in order to observe the formal start of the electoral campaign. During that visit, President Carter played an active role in bringing campaign violence under control. The most serious incident had occurred in the town of Masatepe, on 10 December, in which one person died and several resulted injured. According to Center for Democracy observers, stone throwing and fighting was initiated by Sandinista sympathizers; OAS observers, on the other hand, reported they were unable to determine which side started the violence.[168] Be that as it may, during his December visit Carter suggested the SEC spearhead negotiations leading to election guidelines among the parties. The Nicaraguan government agreed to his proposal, and asked him to help in the manufacturing of the proposed agreement.[169] On a fourth visit, on 5–6 January 1990, CC delegation-member Senator Christopher Dodd met with leaders of several political parties and witnessed political rallies.[170] On the fifth visit, 26–29 January, led by Carter and former Colombian President Alfonso López Michelse, Carter negotiated with Ortega the release of US funds destined for UNO and other non-Sandinista organizations. Along with UN and OAS observers, delegation members watched a trial of the electoral procedures to be followed on election day. The CC delegation concluded that "excellent technical preparations had been made for the voting." Among the main remaining problems it identified were ones that had to do with intimidation of opposition party candidates and *fiscales* (poll-watchers), media access, and FSLN use of state resources during the campaign.[171]

Right before the sixth and last pre-election visit, Carter and Pastor went to Washington and met with OAS Secretary General João Clemente Baena Soares and with Elliot Richardson, the UN Secretary-General personal representative. At that meeting, the two INGOs agreed to share the results of their respective quick counts with the CC—something they had been reluctant to do in previous negotiations.[172] This was a major achievement, given that as late as December, both organizations had been disinclined to even carry out a quick count, apparently fearful that this would somehow infringe on Nicaragua's sovereignty.

Previously, Carter had called Baena Soares and UN Secretary-General Javier Pérez de Cuellar, in order to finally sign an agreement (of which there had been almost 20 drafts) among the three organizations, but both had refused to sign the document.[173] But as Pastor recalls, in a December visit to Managua, "we sat down with the OAS and the UN representatives for two of the most difficult hours of negotiations during that trip . . . they surprised us by admitting that they were considering doing a quick count, but by themselves. Neither would cooperate with the other or with the Carter/Council."[174] Given that the CC had a much smaller mission than both INGOs, it could not undertake an exercise of this kind; having the information would be crucial for it to play a central role on election day.

The last pre-election visit took place February 8–11, and was led by Belize Prime Minister George Price.[175] The delegation visited several cities, where they attended rallies and noted that they were taking place in a peaceful manner. Delegation members also noted approvingly the extension of the deadline to name *fiscales*. However, they also heard about intimidation against UNO's *fiscales*, and about FSLN members being victims of *contra* violence. During this visit the CC's delegation was also able to obtain from the Nicaraguan government approval for an increase in the number of US legislators in its delegation, in order to include some members of the Presidential Commission that had been denied governmental approval to attend as observers in the February 1990 elections.[176]

Thus, the CC's 34-member delegation arrived in Managua on February 23. At a meeting that day with UNO candidate Violeta Chamorro, government officials Sergio Ramírez and Bayardo Arce, CSE's President Mariano Fiallos, and the heads of the UN and OAS delegations, Price elaborated on the international and bipartisan character of the group. Carter, for his part, explained how the CC/CFEHG mission would work in tandem with the two INGOs' delegations.[177] In a joint press conference held the next day—on the eve of the elections—Carter, OAS Secretary General Baena Soares, and UN

Special Representative Elliot Richardson, concluded that "conditions exist in Nicaragua in which the people may freely express their choices on the day of the election."[178] With 89 percent of eligible Nicaraguans registered to vote, this time there was more uncertainty about the outcome than in 1984.[179]

On election day, the CC's delegation covered all nine electoral regions, divided into 14 teams. The selection of polling places to be observed was made in coordination with the OAS, and when voting had concluded, CC's observers reported the results to the OAS in order to feed its quick count.[180] Most people, among them analysts, international observers, and even US officials, had been predicting a Sandinista victory.[181] The FSLN final campaign rally, held on February 21, gathered more than 600,000 people—outnumbering by far UNO's closing rally. Genaro Arriagada—the former speaker of the Executive Secretariat of the *Command for the No* in Chile's plebiscite—had been invited to Nicaragua by the CC; he recalls a delegation meeting on election day in which

> I made the case, in light of the Chilean experience, that the idea of losing didn't figure in the Sandinistas' minds . . . but that my hunch was that if in a given moment on election night, if the opposition's triumph actually happened . . . there was going to be a rupture within the regime, and the doves and the hawks were going to split apart . . . and that in that scenario there was going to be a fight among them, which necessarily needed to be solved in favor of the doves.[182]

Something along those lines did really happen. On election night, at 11:30, Ortega requested the presence of Baena Soares, Carter, and Richardson, along with their senior aids, at the FSLN headquarters for a meeting with him, Vice-President Ramírez, Foreign Minister D'Escoto, campaign manager Arce, and their American lawyer Paul Reichler. At that time, the OAS, the UN, the CSE, and the government all had preliminary figures showing a clear, irreversible lead of UNO's candidate Chamorro. At the meeting, the Nicaraguan President expressed his fear that violence could erupt among FSLN's and UNO's activists already celebrating in the streets if UNO prematurely declared victory. As Pastor recalls, President Carter then "urged President Ortega to make a statement before the morning news programs and to take credit for the democratic elections and the achievements of the revolution, while also acknowledging that he was losing and reaffirming his respects for the results."[183]

Leaving the FSLN's headquarters after 1:00 A.M., the three teams headed to the winning candidate's house. As Ramírez recalls, Carter "took on the function of mediator, which was crucial in order to achieve an understanding with the new government in moments of dangerous uncertainty."[184] Part of the problem was of course that the Sandinistas had not contemplated their defeat. As CSE's Fiallos put it, "The fact is that the Sandinista Front was not ready to lose."[185] In any case, once in Chamorro's house the three leaders helped negotiate an agreement by both sides to restrain the reaction of their respective followers. Furthermore, Chamorro requested from the three leaders the support of their respective organizations to achieve a smooth power transition. As Ramírez noted later, Carter's role as a mediator during the transitions period was "crucial for reaching an understanding with the new government in moments of dangerous uncertainty."[186] Similarly, Antonio Lacayo, Chamorro's campaign manager and later her Minister of the Presidency and chief advisor, recalls, "President Carter, his person, symbolized the issue of international observation, he gave international observation a face . . . he had a lot of authority over Mores and Christians."[187]

At six in the morning, Ortega went on national radio and TV and declared that he would abide by the results; two hours later, he conceded the election. Later on the 26th, Ortega invited Baena Soares, Carter, and Richardson to go with him to Chamorro's house to congratulate her on her victory.[188] UNO obtained 54.7 of the votes, versus 40.8 of the FSLN. In the National Assembly, UNO won 51 seats and the Sandinistas 39 (out of 92 seats). The day after the elections, speaking on behalf of the three major missions at a joint press conference, Carter declared that the electoral process just concluded "had been an impressive demonstration of freedom, democracy, and respect for human rights."[189]

The Organization of American States

The 1990 Nicaraguan elections were a turning point for the OAS' experience in IEM. As Elizabeth Spehar, head of the OAS' Unit for the Promotion of Democracy (UPD) notes, the organization's previous practice in this field was important because "the fact that . . . a country allowed that an outside organization came to witness the elections that were taking place, and to form an opinion and make it public at the international level" was significant in setting a precedent.[190] Furthermore, as UPD's Santiago Murray has noted, Nicaragua was one of the first countries, in the early 1960s, to request international observers to the OAS, which since then has contributed "in the promotion of the effective exercise [of representative democracy] by means of electoral technical assistance and observation."[191] Nevertheless, Spehar remarks that the pre-Nicaragua 1990 missions were "made within very clear parameters," and they were "limited in time, limited in objectives, limited in capacity, in technical terms."[192]

Having set a precedent, though, seems to have had an impact on the OAS response to the 1989 Nicaraguan request for electoral observation. As CSE's Fiallos recalls, unlike the UN, the OAS had "no problem" in accepting the Nicaraguan government's petition, because the hemispheric organization "was used to observing elections . . . it didn't seem to them to be something unusual."[193] Thus, a week after Nicaraguan Foreign Minister D'Escoto had sent the official request to the OAS, its Secretary General replied that he was "more than willing to provide all my support. . . . I am taking the measures necessary to establish the mechanism to put together the group of international observers."[194] Less than two weeks after the formal request, Baena Soares was in Nicaragua to observe the release of former members of the National Guard. He also met with President Ortega, members of the CSE, and with representatives of 14 opposition parties.[195]

As Baena Soares noted in a preliminary observation report, Nicaragua's request was based on the Esquipulas II framework, in which President Ortega stated his "intention . . . to develop a process of democratization and national reconciliation within his country."[196] For the regional organization, thus, the issue at stake was both regional security (Esquipulas II was after all a regional peace plan) and democratic transition in a member-state. Although the latter rationale for observing the electoral process would have lacked validity in other fora, such as the UN, in the OAS it seemed reasonable—the ideational underpinning of the WHI remained strong.

Thus, the agreement signed between the representative of the Nicaraguan government and the OAS on the privileges and immunities of the organization's observers, states in its preamble that "Article 138 of the Charter of the Organization of American States . . . provides that: 'The Organization of American States should enjoy in the territory of each Member such legal capacity, privileges, and immunities as are necessary for the exercise of its functions and the accomplishment of its purposes.'"[197] The observing of an electoral process was thus conceived of as being part of the "functions" assigned to the organization.

Unusual or not, the Nicaraguan request to the OAS was at least unprecedented. As OAS Secretary General Baena Soares noted, the organization experience in the Central American country in 1989–1990 "was not a passive observation."[198] The OAS endeavor was in fact more than observation—passive or otherwise. The task assigned to the regional organization was one of mediation, making it a central player in the electoral process. Thus, the OAS mission monitored legislative procedures for the reform of the laws on mass media and the electoral law, in compliance with the Costa del Sol agreements. Among other aspects the OAS mission was to cover were: voter registration, election campaign (monitoring of usage of election propaganda, use of radio and TV, access to the media, political rallies, use of resources), observation on election day, tallying process (opening of the ballot boxes, review of the ballots, counting of votes, review of the reports, review of the final results), and the development of a system for following up complaints.[199]

The mission was divided into several phases. In the preliminary one, in July-August 1989, the Secretary General signed two agreements, one with the Nicaraguan government, and one with the CSE, which laid the legal framework for the OAS activities in the Central American country. The first phase properly (i.e., after the preliminary one) covered the period 4 August-23 September, during which an initial group of 18 staff members established themselves in Nicaragua's nine voting districts. The second phase went from 24 September to 23 October, during which the number of observers was increased to 52. Their main task was to observe the voter registration process. The preliminary observation and coordination activities continued throughout November, and on 4 December the most intense phase started. It lasted until 20 February 1990, and covered the election campaign period. On election day, there were 433 OAS observers present throughout the country.[200]

As noted, a distinguishing feature of the IEM experience in Nicaragua was the coordination among different monitoring missions. Thus, for instance, the OAS Secretary General's second report notes that his delegation had been holding weekly "coordination meetings" with the UN mission, and that he had met with former President Carter and with Elliot Richardson, special representative of the United Nations Secretary-General for the Nicaragua mission, in order to coordinate their activities.[201] Beyond this apparently terse relationship, though, there was intense competition for public attention between the three organizations, and, at least between the two INGOs, sometimes there was open animosity. As Pastor observes, "The competition [among the three main observing missions] was most intense between the OAS, which regarded Latin America as its sphere of influence, and the UN, which happened to be led by a Latin American. The comments shared by officials from each organization with us about the other were almost as vitriolic as the ones exchanged between the FSLN and UNO."[202]

The sometimes problematic relationship between these last two organizations was partly structural, part of their own making. The structural part was that it was believed that the Sandinistas had invited the UN to check on the OAS, which they did not trust. As former Foreign Minister D'Escoto told me, "We never had very much confidence in the OAS . . . we felt more comfortable in the world-wide forum, the United Nations."[203] A UN mission member who asked his name not be used told me: "I believe the UN had been invited to counterweight the OAS, and the OAS knew that, so the rivalry was already in place." But the "non-structural" component was also important. As the same informant put it,

> the rivalry in Nicaragua [between the UN and the OAS in 1990] was intense, there were people at the UN who were actually persuaded that the OAS had infiltrated the UN offices and was privy to certain phone conversations and, put out a report a few days before we did that resembled in such detail the report that we had drafted that it was amazing, it was remarkable.

But beyond the antagonism between the two IGOs, and the competition between them and the CC, their interaction turned out to be positive. As CC's Pastor noted, "every mission that goes into a country, whether governmental or intergovernmental, is suddenly competing against each other, while they're trying to do their job, and their competition against each other is how do we do our job better, which is a good thing."[204] Similarly, CSE's Fiallos has noted the "appropriate equilibrium" achieved by the interaction of the CSE and the three main observer delegations.[205] In the OAS case, its mission covered all aspects of the electoral process, from voter registration and electoral laws, to voting procedures and the undertaking of a quick count. The last element, as Baena Soares put it in his final report, "was one of the most important items of our activities."[206] With a very large sample (4391 voting places), the OAS mission was able to independently have a very accurate projection of the final results by midnight on election day. Since the OAS numbers coincided with those of the CSE, the OAS contributed to ameliorate the state of uncertainty that prevailed among the Nicaraguans that night.

In his final report, the Secretary General concluded that the elections had been "free" and "honest," and praised both the Nicaraguan government and electoral authorities.[207] Based on the positive Nicaraguan experience, the Secretary General suggested that "a new perspective of performance [observing the whole electoral process] opens for this Organization," and concluded by stating that "in any future occasion in which this Organization is again asked to provide its collaboration. . . . we will be willing to respond" affirmatively.[208] The reaction of the member states' representatives was equally enthusiastic. Guatemala's ambassador Miriam Cabrera suggested: "We should find a mechanism so that you, Mr. Secretary General, and your collaborators, can always take part in our countries every time a party of this [electoral] kind takes place in one of them . . . since we are enthusiastic about the positive results that we ascertain today."[209] Similarly, US representative Luigi Einaudi said that "The delegation organized by the Secretary General is proving to the world that the OAS is very much relevant to the new democratic order that is emerging, not just in our hemisphere, but throughout the world."[210]

Edilberto Moreno, the Venezuelan ambassador, noted that the OAS was present in Nicaragua "without anybody, government nor opposition, thinking even remotely that we were in the threshold of an undue intervention."[211] Later Uruguayan representative Didier Opertti noted that "the OAS seeks a reasonable space of insertion in the issues of the region. This space brings with it a regulated insertion, an insertion that cannot obey either discretionality or free will, but the normative procedures of the system," and that the OAS had acted in Nicaragua "in conformity with the instruments that regulate its life, but also in favor of the international community's opinion."[212] But it fell upon Roger D. Wilson, Canada's Deputy Representative, to propose the creation of what would eventually become the UPD, by noting that his country favored "the development within the OAS of the capacity to observe elections."[213]

The United Nations

The monitoring of the 1990 Nicaraguan elections was an extraordinary experience for the UN. After receiving the request to observe the elections from the Nicaraguan Foreign Minister in March 1989, Secretary-General Pérez de Cuellar was rather hesitant. He noted that going to a sovereign country was "an exceptional undertaking which breaks new ground in our [the UN's] 44-year history."[214] In a letter he sent to the president of the General Assembly the following month, though, he noted that the Nicaraguan request was part of the Central American peace process, and announced that he was going to consider it.[215] As a UN document would later describe it, the Nicaraguan government's request to observe its 1990 elections "put the United Nations in a very particular situation. . . . there was no precedent for carrying out such observation in an independent country."[216]

Among the factors that the Secretary-General pondered for his eventual affirmative reply to the Nicaraguan request were the following: "First, it was not a request by a single Member State [but it is inscribed within] the context of the Esquipulas peace process; secondly, the General Assembly, in its resolution 34/24 of 15 November 1988 had requested the Secretary-General 'to afford the fullest possible support to the Central American Governments in their efforts to achieve peace.' . . . Finally, it was not simply a request for a token presence on election day."[217]

Thus, by 5 July the Secretary-General was ready to establish the United Nations Observer Mission to verify the electoral process in

Nicaragua (ONUVEN). Interestingly, almost two months before, on 8 May, he had sent a letter to the OAS Secretary General Baena Soares in which he proposed that the two IGOs observe the Nicaraguan elections jointly. In his reply more than a month later (22 June), Baena Soares noted that his organization had already started the monitoring process, but that he was interested in finding ways in which the two IGOs could collaborate.[218] In any case, when Pérez de Cuellar accepted to observe the Nicaraguan elections, he was careful to note that the undertaking would have "no effect on [the] established practice" of not observing elections in sovereign states.[219] Both the General Assembly and the Security Council subsequently expressed their support for the Secretary-General's decision. On 25 August ONUVEN became operational with a 17-member staff. Interestingly—because it was a sign of the enduring relevance of the Cold War—it was agreed that the observer mission should not include any citizen of either the United States or of the Soviet Union.[220] Eventually, ONUVEN would number over 250 members from 50 countries.[221] It was indeed an imposing delegation. As ONUVEN's final report notes,

> On 25 February, 207 ONUVEN observers travelled [sic] throughout Nicaragua, using 128 vehicles, two helicopters and four small boats. Assistance of various kinds was provided to the groups of observers by a team of 34 persons stationed at the Managua headquarters and at the regional offices. . . . the observers visited 2,155 JRVs [ballot receiving boards] located in 141 of the 143 municipalities in Nicaragua.[222]

Perhaps to a greater degree than both the CC and the OAS mission, the UN mission was active in a number of fields. As a UN document puts it, its tasks included

> verifying that political parties were equitable represented in the Nicaraguan Supreme Electoral Council and its subsidiary bodies; verifying that political parties enjoyed complete freedom of organization and mobilization, without hindrance or intimidation; verifying that all political parties had equitable access to State television and radio; verifying that the electoral rolls were properly drawn up; and informing the Supreme Electoral Council of any complaints received or any irregularities or interference detected in the electoral process.[223]

Shortly before the elections, ONUVEN issued a report in which it noted: "there can be no doubt that, compared with the elections of 1984, the current elections were characterized by greater pluralism, competitiveness and political openness." The pre-electoral report also concluded that "as . . . the people of Nicaragua go to the polls, they are in a position to decide between alternatives which have been given a reasonable chance to be aired. They will be able to freely determine their future government through the verdict of the ballot-boxes on 25 February 1990."[224] Publicly stating before the winner was determined that the elections complied with international standards was a calculated decision on the part of ONUVEN—and an important victory for the Sandinista regime. In this victory, though, the accompaniment of international monitoring missions, especially of the UN was particularly important. As the organization would later acknowledge it, its members acted "as conveners, conciliators and, where necessary, as gadflies."[225]

The UN's work was without a doubt wide and professional. Nicaragua-based journalist and Hemisphere Initiatives' observer Judy Butler concurs with the previously quoted nameless UN observer in that the world organization did a better job than the OAS in observing the elections. Butler says she "was aware of the level of professionalism far higher in the UN [mission] than in the OAS [mission]."[226] Similarly, CSE's Zelaya noted that "it was the United Nations, more than the OAS that played a crucial role" in the 1990 elections."[227]

UN activities were also far more comprehensive than those of the CC. CC-official McCoy recognized that unlike the two IGOs, which counted on large staffs who stayed in Nicaragua for a long time, "the Carter Center was there for a month, we just had one field officer which was me, I was the representative there, we didn't have people in all the cities, like the UN and the OAS."[228] Along the same lines, ONUVEN-member Shelly McConnell, now at the CC, noted that since the UN office was established in August 1989, the mission

> adopted a very complete mandate [in contrast with the CC's mission], I mean, it was wide. We had a technical team, for example, do nothing but examine the news on the media; we had people who examined all the complaints that were registered about things like candidates resigning multilateral organizations face a problem, of admitting the degree to which they may be treading on sovereignty. . . . it is true that they are unable to do certain things, and that they hesitate or they want to do it quietly. But in fact, they do quite a lot without taking credit for it because they dare not, so, for example, the UN was doing all those things, none of which the Carter Center did, the UN had many more people on the ground . . . who stayed for seven months, brought it up to 44 at one juncture . . . then to 250. . . . Carter would show up, and

> he would see a problem that had surfaced, and he would go solve it. The truth is, there had been six problems, but they had already been solved by the UN through much more systematic everyday work.[229]

UN Mission Chief Iqba Riza rightly described the UN verification process taking place in Nicaragua as "a step beyond observation," but "a step before administration."[230] CSE's Fiallos concurs: "In 1990 there was no observation [on the part of the UN], there was a verification."[231]

ONUVEN concluded that the electoral process "could be evaluated as free and fair."[232] The final report praises the job performed by the electoral authorities, emphasizing ONUVEN's "entirely positive assessment of the activities of CSE and of all levels of the electoral authority, which ensured that the electoral process was impartial and fair throughout."[233] According to the report, 94.3 of voting places functioned normally; 5.3 percent functioned with minor difficulties that did not affect the results, and 0.5 percent experienced serious problems.[234]

The mission carried out the already mentioned quick count which, according to a later UN document, "proved to be crucial in the overnight efforts by the Secretary-General's Personal Representative, Elliot Richardson, the Secretary General of the [OAS] and former United States President Jimmy Carter, involving the President of Nicaragua and the victorious opposition coalition."[235] The agreement reached that night between the Sandinistas and UNO on controlling each side's supporters, in which the international organization played a mediating role, "was a key factor in ensuring the successful initiation of the transitional efforts in which the United Nations played an important role."[236]

Tellingly, ONUVEN's final report recognized the precedent-setting effect of the endeavor just culminated. It rightly noted that the United Nations was "likely in the future to be called upon similar assignments."[237] Indeed. Four months later, Haiti officially requested the observation of its forthcoming Presidential elections. Unlike the Nicaraguan case, though, there was no international component to the Haitian request. Nonetheless, sign of the new times, the UN established the United Nations Observer Group for the Verification of Elections in Haiti.

CONCLUSIONS

The myriad of INGOs present in Nicaragua in 1990, many of which had also been active in Chile two years before, attest to the salience of the WHI as well as to the consolidation of the IEM network. Furthermore, the presence of IGOs in the region was no mere accident. INGOs and IGOs converged in

Nicaragua in large part due to the auspicious environment the WHI had created in the region. The contrast between the initial responses of the OAS and the UN to the Nicaraguan request is illustrative in this respect. Feeling at home with the Nicaraguan petition, the regional body had no problem responding affirmatively to it; the world organization, on the other hand, was much more wavering in its initial reaction. It knew it was venturing into unknown territory.

In this case, it was mainly the work of two IGOs, and one very particular INGO, that advanced the cause of IEM the most. Interestingly, the CC was not a traditional human rights organization; it was rather a "democracy" one, which had a broader understanding of human rights than traditional human rights groups. State officials, on the other hand, were certainly not operating under the conventional human rights discourse.

The 1990 electoral process in Nicaragua also drives home the point that if the interaction of domestic and systemic factors had not taken place, IEM would not have emerged. Absent either the international or the merely national dimension of the problematique at issue, this electoral process would not have meant what it has for the history of IEM. Furthermore, as suggested in the preceding pages, the Nicaraguan experience became crucial in the redefinition of state sovereignty. IEM has thus had real effects.

This groundbreaking international monitoring experience had thus little to do with merely rational or material factors; it was mainly the normative structure that held the Western Hemisphere together that made it possible.[238] In a recursive fashion, IEM then contributed to make explicit the understanding of sovereignty enshrined in the WHI. Furthermore, the fact that the partial redefinition of sovereignty this event implied was achieved in tandem by INGOs and IGOs demonstrates both the deeply social (i.e., not self-organizing) character of the state in the international system, and the malleability of one of the organizing principles of international politics. By means of the Sandinistas' assent of foreign actors getting actively involved in what used to be constructed as a purely domestic affair, the idea of what being a sovereign state means in international affairs was partially altered.

I am not suggesting that the Sandinistas agreed to the international monitoring of their elections merely for idealistic reasons. Rather, they accepted it on pragmatic grounds. They knew that they were being compelled to open up the electoral process to international scrutiny and, acting strategically, used the opportunity to attempt to save their revolutionary project. In this sense, the eventual seal of approval by the three main monitoring organizations would act as an insurance against continued aggression by the United States.

But beyond the issue of the extent to which IEM was forced on the Nicaraguans, there is a simple fact: IEM had become a modern "requirement." Like the one of colonial times, the modern requirement speaks of the importance of the normative element even in the intercourse among different social groupings—but with one crucial difference: the recent variety was part and parcel of a shared normative structure, the WHI. That is, in the Nicaraguan case, participants shared a lifeworld. Both foreign observers and Nicaraguans were acting within this common background. This is what is telling about the changes in sovereignty partially brought about by the Nicaraguan experience—the hemispheric normative structure that required and made them possible.

Chapter Five

Mexico's 1994 Elections: Sovereignty Redefined

There were 775 foreign and 81,620 national observers in Mexico's 1994 presidential elections.[1] In the Mexican case, though, more than the sheer number of monitors in the electoral process, what was significant was their mere presence. No observation effort at all had taken place in the previous 1988 presidential elections. Moreover, in 1990 President Carlos Salinas declared that Mexico's democracy was "not subject to external evaluation."[2] The following year, Mexico's representative at the OAS made clear that "The Mexican government considers a matter of national sovereignty the organization and vigilance of its electoral processes, and is opposed to the participation of foreign observers."[3] Consequently, when in 1992 the OAS General Assembly voted to amend the Charter so that a government which overthrows a democratic regime can be suspended from the organization, Mexico cast the only dissenting vote. As late as December 1993, Mexico expressed its opposition to foreign election monitors at the UN. For Mexico, therefore, accepting foreign observers in 1994 was a major breakthrough.

Likewise, for the history of IEM Mexico's case represented a litmus test: not only because of the size of the country, but precisely because it had been historically opposed to this practice. But Mexico's about-face on foreign observers, although fundamentally driven by domestic and even strategic considerations, was made possible by the normalization of IEM and the new international environment—both hemispherically and globally. Thus, in the Mexican case the issue of international monitoring was not framed in terms of human rights, as in Chile, nor in terms of a peace process, as in Nicaragua, but in terms of a two-fold problematique: a protracted transition to democracy *and* state sovereignty. That is, in Mexico 1994—sign of the times—these two usually separate issues converged. Furthermore, as I show below, the Mexican case epitomizes the complex interaction of state and non-state actors, both at the domestic and international level, characteristic of the emerging norm of election monitoring.

This chapter is divided into four sections. In the first one I consider Mexico's *longue durée* domestic structure, emphasizing both its nature and the long transition to democracy initiated during it.[4] In the second section I cover most of the Salinas administration (1988–1994), insofar as it constitutes the specific context in which the ground-breaking monitoring experience took place. In section three I look at the emergence of election monitoring in Mexico, and at the last electoral reform undertaken during the Salinas government. Finally, in the fourth section I consider in more detail the 1994 electoral process, and the three main actors involved in its monitoring: Alianza Cívica (Civic Alliance, henceforth AC), the UN, and the CC.

This chapter shows the extent to which the understanding of sovereignty enshrined in the WHI had permeated the international system in its entirety by the early 1990s. That is why the Mexican government was able to resort to the international institution par excellence when it needed to legitimize itself both domestically and internationally. Furthermore, this chapter sheds light on the importance of domestic structures in the differentiated instantiation of international norms. Had the ideology on nonintervention not been so pervasive in Mexico's domestic structure, IEM would not have figured so prominently in the 1994 electoral process. That is why the Mexican case illustrates so vividly what IEM has meant to the traditional understanding of sovereignty.

MEXICO'S DOMESTIC STRUCTURE

Unlike Chile, Mexico cannot claim a democratic tradition; still, it has never had a dictatorship of the kind of Pinochet's. Unlike Nicaragua, Mexico has not experienced the omnipresence of the United States, but like it Mexico lacks a democratic tradition to draw on. Mexico's domestic structure thus stands somewhere halfway between that of these two countries. If in the Chilean case the military dictatorship was an anomaly, and in the Nicaraguan the Sandinista regime ended up reproducing long established political patterns, in Mexico the administration that carried out the 1994 elections was the direct descendant, although much reformed, of the one established in the aftermath of the 1910 revolution. The authoritarian Mexican regime was by that time almost as old as the recently deceased Soviet one: 65 years old.

But unlike the Bolshevik party—and most political parties indeed—Mexico's PRI was not created in order to compete for power. It was established in 1929 as the National Revolutionary Party (PNR) by a group of victorious revolutionary leaders in order to maintain themselves in power by peaceful means. As Plutarco Elías Calles, the party's founder, put it in his 1928 state of the union address, the challenge for the "revolutionary family" was to "unite in order to nominate one candidate." But the requested unity was in fact more than to nominate, to rally behind the Great Elector: Calles himself.

Nevertheless, six years later, the fourth PNR member designated by Calles to occupy the presidency, Lázaro Cárdenas, rebelled against the "foremost leader" and forced him out of the country.[5] From then on, the "revolutionary family" agreed on an unwritten rule: the president in turn would have the right to choose his successor, by making him the party's candidate. In this way, in a somewhat dialectical process, the president reached the zenith of his power at the moment when he designated his heir.[6] This process, known as *dedazo,* would be religiously repeated every six years, in the fifth year of each administration.

The right to choose a successor, "the most important and most controversial unwritten rule of the Mexican system,"[7] was the most conspicuous symbol of one of the five key features of Mexico's post-revolutionary domestic structure: its presidentialism. Although the 1917 Constitution recognized the equality of the three branches of government and a federal pact, it established a strong executive branch. Furthermore, in practice the political system operated through the dominance of the executive and the centralization of power in Mexico City. Thus, for example, both Cárdenas (1934–1940) and Carlos Salinas tied in the record number of governors removed during their respective administrations: 17.[8]

Furthermore, the president in turn was also the leader of the party, which Cárdenas renamed Party of the Mexican Revolution (PRM) in 1938. The formal leadership of the party became a position analogous to cabinet membership, with the president removing party leaders as he pleased. As Lorenzo Meyer has observed, "the ample constitutional powers conferred to the president, together with the great meta-constitutional power given to him by the almost absolute control of the state party, inevitably lead to the emergence of what could be called the anti-constitutional power of the presidency."[9]

The blurred dividing line between the state and the party, whose name changed again in 1945 to Institutional Revolutionary Party (PRI), was the second distinguishing feature of the post revolutionary domestic structure. Thus, for instance, in the early 1930s President Emilio Portes Gil issued an executive order by means of which all federal employees were required to contribute financially to the party.[10] The party was actually another department of the public administration, with large budgets and staff. As Meyer and Héctor Aguilar Camín put it, "The iron-clad presidential control of the party in power—the PRI—and its extreme dependence on governmental resources were such that it was not really a political party but rather part of the structure of the federal government."[11]

A third pillar of the post revolutionary domestic structure was its corporatist arrangement. In the Mexican case, it was top-down, state corporatism.[12] Thus, for instance, entire industrial unions, peasant organizations, and small businesses associations were incorporated *en masse* into the different "sectors" of the party. This arrangement served not only to provide the party control of ample sectors of the population, but also to subordinate the legitimate interests of its constituencies through repression and concessions.[13] Large unions affiliated with the party were thus able to gain privileges other workers lacked, such as extended labor holiday periods and generous retirement programs, but at the same time were denied democratic and autonomous organization.

The specific practices and relative importance of the corporatist component of course changed over time.[14] Thus, for instance, under the Salinas administration there was a serious effort to marginalize corporatist organization in favor of a territorially-oriented structure. But even the Salinas regime resorted to the corporatist structure of its party to further its agenda.[15] Furthermore, Mexico's corporatism did not prevent the slow but sustained emergence of an independent civil society. Mexico was not, after all, a totalitarian state of the Soviet kind, nor a dictatorship similar to those of the Southern Cone. Independent associational life was an ever-present factor that only grew stronger with time. But still by the early 1990s, Mexico's domestic structure closely resembled the "corporatist" type, to use Risse-Kappen's terminology. As he notes, "*Corporatist* domestic structures are likely in cases in which powerful intermediate organizations such as political parties operate in a consensus-oriented political culture resulting in continuous bargaining processes geared toward political compromises."[16]

A fourth distinguishing feature of Mexico's domestic structure, and one that is crucial for understanding the monitoring experience of 1994, was the electoral component. I call it crucial because it became the privileged arena of Mexico's long transition to democracy, and therefore it was within its logic that the landmark monitoring experience was inscribed. Regular multi-party elections have been held in Mexico at least since the 1930s.[17] Nevertheless, until the 1994 ones, they were not competitive.

Thus, for instance, no opposition party ever held a state governorship before 1989, a senate seat before 1988, or the mayorship of a state capital before 1983. Instead, the electoral arena served to open a space of negotiation among the different factions of the governing coalition.

Although the president's decision was the determining factor in selecting his successor, the distribution of governorships and seats in Congress, among other positions, was left open for intra-party negotiation. Presidential elections thus became largely symbolic. As Aguilar Camín has noted, what was important in the transfer of power every six years was not who was elected in the elections, but who was going to be PRI's candidate.[18] Mexico thus had a hegemonic party system in which opposition parties were legal, but the electoral institutions prevented them from acceding to power. In hegemonic party systems, according to Giovanni Sartori, "Other parties are permitted to exist, but as second class, licensed parties; for they are not permitted to compete with the hegemonic party in antagonistic terms and on equal basis."[19]

The regime started to pay a heavy toll for its lack of political opening in the late 1960s. When confronted by a pro-democracy student movement in 1968, the government decided to repress it violently. This repression led to the emergence of guerrilla groups in the early 1970s. The undemocratic nature of the regime was further evinced when the conservative National Action Party (PAN), which had served as the regime's loyal opposition, decided not to nominate a presidential candidate for the 1976 elections, in protest for the unfair electoral system. Thus, after being the only official candidate, José López Portillo took office on 1 December 1976.[20]

Nevertheless, having kept the electoral avenue at least formally open turned out to be a fundamental factor both in the PRI being able to stay in power for still over two decades, and for Mexico's long transition to democracy. Thus, López Portillo decided to take action to improve the political environment soon after taking office. He decreed an amnesty law for political prisoners, and sent to Congress a sweeping electoral reform. The 1977 electoral reform is generally considered as the starting point of Mexico's long transition to democracy. Known as the Federal Law on Political Organizations and Electoral Processes, its most evident aim was to widen the political spectrum. Before it was passed, the party system was composed solely of the PRI, the PAN, and two small satellite parties. The 1977 reform changed the electoral landscape by making it legal for some political organizations, such as the Communist Party, to participate in elections; it also eased the requirements needed to qualify as a political party, thus creating an incentive for more political forces to join the electoral game. Furthermore, the reform also created 100 seats in the lower house to be allocated according to proportional representation (the other 300 seats were to be allocated by the traditional winner-take-all principle). In this way, opposition forces could have greater voice in the legislative process.[21]

The federal government remained in charge of organizing the elections, and the composition of the electoral body meant that the government and its party were still in control of the electoral processes.[22] But at least in one aspect, the 1977 electoral reform might be considered a success: by 1979 there were seven political parties. For the 1982 presidential elections, the dismal scene of a lonely candidate campaigning across the country did not take place again: there were seven presidential candidates, supported by nine political parties.

Nevertheless, by the end of the López Portillo administration, the PRI still enjoyed unfettered access to state resources, controlled mass organizations, and dominated the electoral machinery. It was thus clear that Mexico, as Aguilar Camín and Meyer put it, "had a party system on paper, but not in reality."[23] Irregular electoral practices were still common place by the mid 1980s. Thus, for instance, the 1986 electoral process to choose governor in the northern state of Chihuahua, which took place during Miguel de la Madrid's administration (1982–1988), was marred by fraud. Alleging to be the victim of an electoral assault, the PAN began a national protest movement and even took the issue to the Inter-American Human Rights Commission (more on this below).[24] Not surprisingly, the electoral legislation was amended again during de la Madrid's term.

But the 1987 reform did not rid the government and its party of controlling the electoral process. Thus, for instance, thanks to the principle of "proportionality" (of the share of votes in the previous election) the PRI had more votes than all other parties together in the Electoral Federal Commission, the body in charge of organizing the elections. Similarly, a "governability clause" was introduced, by means of which the party with the largest proportion of votes would automatically be granted 51 percent of the seats in the lower house. The reform's main advantage for the opposition forces was that proportional representation of the lower house was doubled (to 200 of its 500 seats), thus granting them greater voice in the legislative process.

But the same year this reform was passed, the worst political crisis within the "revolutionary family" took place. A faction headed by Cuauhtémoc Cárdenas, the son of former president Lázaro Cárdenas, split from the PRI after de la Madrid passed him, and chose Carlos Salinas de Gortari, as the party's candidate. Cárdenas then became the presidential candidate of several opposition parties, including the successor of the Communist Party, and the satellite parties that had traditionally supported the

PRI. Amidst widespread mobilization against what appeared to be a monumental electoral fraud, Cárdenas officially received 33.5 percent of the votes in the 1988 presidential elections. This was an unprecedented situation. Never had the government conceded that an opposition candidate had won such a high percentage of the popular suffrage—and never had a PRI candidate officially obtained such a low percentage of votes: 50.7. The day after the elections, Salinas declared the end of Mexico's one party system.[25] Thus, with the 1988 elections, as Blanca Heredia has put it, "Conflict among political elites overflowed the bounds of party and state and spilled into the electoral sphere."[26]

Under the Salinas administration, three subsequent electoral reforms would take place. But since they are an integral part of the political environment in which the international monitoring of the 1994 electoral process took place, I will incorporate them into the narrative of the state of Mexico's domestic structure during the Salinas administration, in the next section. Before doing that, though, a brief note is in order about a fifth distinguishing feature of Mexico's domestic structure: its foreign policy. But since the Salinas administration effected important changes in this respect too, which bear directly on the 1994 monitoring issue, I will also consider part of it in the next section.

As noted before, Mexico had traditionally been one of the staunchest supporters of the nonintervention principle in the hemisphere. Illustrative in this respect is the already mentioned 1930 Estrada Doctrine, which holds that Mexico does not make any pronouncement regarding the granting or withholding of recognition to other governments, because that practice "hurts the sovereignty of the nations" whose regime is being granted [or denied] recognition. Thus, for instance, Mexico did not break diplomatic relations with Castroist Cuba. Furthermore, since 1988 the nonintervention principle in the conduct of Mexican foreign policy is enshrined in Mexico's Constitution.[27] It is the centrality of foreign policy in the identity of the post revolutionary regime, acting as an emblem of the country's collective self-esteem, that warrants its consideration as an element of Mexico's domestic structure.[28]

The autonomy of Mexico's foreign policy (vis-à-vis the United States) has of course always been relative. Mexico reached a tacit agreement with its northern neighbor about its right to disagree on secondary issues. As Bernardo Mabire has noted, "For a long time Mexico's government feigned in its rhetoric certain leftist radicalism, and the U.S. kindly pretended to believe it."[29] Thus, Mexican President Gustavo Díaz Ordaz told Lyndon B. Johnson in 1964 that "there will be a considerable advantage [for both nations] if Mexico is able to continue demonstrating its political independence, disagreeing with the United States on relatively minor affairs."[30] Thus, during the 1962 missile crisis, Mexico decisively sided with the Kennedy administrations actions, arguing that the presence of Soviet missiles in Cuba constituted "a threat to the peace and security of the hemisphere."[31]

Consequently, Luis Echeverría's Third-Worldism during the 1970s, and López Portillo's activist policy toward Central America in the late 1970s and early 1980s were tolerated by Washington. This independence was a treasured asset that served to legitimize the post-revolutionary regime domestically. As Jorge G. Castañeda, a stern critic of the post-revolutionary regime, recognized: "modern Mexico possesses one redeeming virtue: a foreign policy of its own."[32] The bilateral bargain also implied that Mexico would be relatively isolated from US pressures on human rights and democracy issues.[33] As Pastor has put it, "there is no country in the world which is more sensitive to U.S. efforts to influence it than Mexico, and no country as successful in resisting American influence."[34]

The United States' main concern regarding its southern neighbor was stability—and that, the PRI and its ancestors proved very adept at providing. As Meyer has put it, "historically, the non-democratic nature of the Mexican political system has not been a significant factor in Mexican-U.S. relations."[35] The bilateral arrangement, indeed, was very much alive in 1988, when the murky elections took place. As Lawrence Whitehead has noted, "The breadth of the apparent US consensus in favor of Salinas was startling to those who had grown accustomed to the polarized rhetoric of the Reagan years; it was even more striking in the light of Washington's strictures of the purity of suffrage in Chile and Nicaragua. But the record is clear."[36]

MEXICO DURING THE SALINAS ADMINISTRATION

Mexico's foreign policy tradition began to change with the advent of the Salinas administration. Allegedly convinced by a 1990 trip to Europe that the end of the Cold War dictated that Mexico should pursue closer integration with the remaining super power, lest financial resources started to flow massively to Central and Eastern Europe, Salinas embarked on one of the most adventurous foreign policy decisions of a Mexican president ever: the establishment of a trade agreement with the United States.[37] Thus, in June 1990 George Bush and Carlos Salinas announced their intention to pursue closer economic integration through the North American Free Trade Agreement (NAFTA), which also came to include Canada. The protracted NAFTA negotiations (which formally started in June 1991, and ended in the Summer of 1993, under the Clinton presidency) signaled an unprecedented shift in Mexico's foreign policy.

Thus, during the Salinas administration the intent of Mexico's foreign policy was to establish ever-closer links with the United States.[38] Gone were the country's aims of the early 1980 to act as an independent middle-sized power. As Humberto Garza Elizondo has noted, "Few things changed more during Salinas' *sexenio* [six-year term] than foreign policy."[39] Economic issues came to occupy center stage in Mexico's relation with its northern neighbor, as made clear by the replacement of the Foreign Relations Ministry by the Commerce Ministry in the conduct of bilateral relations.[40] Establishing closer links to the United States was part of the two-fold domestic strategy Salinas had for Mexico: accelerated economic restructuring and restrained political opening. The former reform had precedence for Salinas. As he put it: "They are linked, but we ought to consider the priority that economic reform has, without excluding political reform."[41] Mexico seemed to be undergoing a *perestroika* without *glasnost*.[42]

But before Salinas was inaugurated, in the five-month hiatus between the July elections and his swearing in on 1 December, the volatile political environment did not stabilize. Thus, he acted swiftly upon taking office: at his inaugural speech, Salinas proposed a *National Accord for the Enhancement of our Democratic Life*. Its stated objectives were "to improve the electoral processes, bring up to date the party system, and modernize the practices of the political actors, beginning with the government itself." Another electoral reform was thus negotiated. Significantly, the Party of the Democratic Revolution (PRD), the party formed by Cárdenas, played a marginal role in the 1990 electoral reform. This was due largely to the open animosity between the PRI and the PRD. The PAN had become the privileged interlocutor with the government and its party. Hence, in an unprecedented political gesture, in 1989 the government recognized the PAN's victory in the gubernatorial elections in the northern state of Baja California—while allowing, the same day, wholesale fraud in the PRD's stronghold, Michoacán.

As a result of the new legislation approved by the PRI and the PAN in 1990, the Federal Electoral Institute (IFE) was born as a formally autonomous entity in charge of organizing the elections. Six magistrate counselors, proposed by the president and approved by qualified majority in Congress, became members of its governing body, the General Council. In addition to the counselors, the IFE was composed of the Interior Minister, two representatives from each house, and a variable number of representatives per party, depending on the percentage of votes obtained in the previous election. This was a significant improvement over the previous composition of the electoral body, in which the government and its party had an overwhelming majority—although the government still remained in control. Furthermore, the composition of the lower house was partially improved by establishing a floor of 35 percent before the governability clause could go into effect. Nevertheless, this clause still guaranteed a large overrepresentation for the largest party—in that context, the PRI. Moreover, the electoral rules were changed so that parties could not propose common candidates—as had occurred in 1988 with Cárdenas' challenge.

Thus, the 1990 reform did not cool off the heated political environment. The 1991 midterm elections, conducted according to the new electoral law, produced not fully reliable results. In them, the PRI experienced a remarkable comeback: it obtained 320 seats in the lower chamber, as opposed to 89 of the PAN, and 41 of the PRD.[43] Furthermore, the PRI won 31 out of 32 Senate seats, and all six governorships being contested that day—a feat achieved not without resorting to questionable electoral practices. As Roderic Ai Camp put it at the time, "The group that is currently in power has not evolved to the point at which it would be willing to respect the results of the elections, which is the definitional point of a true democracy."[44]

Shortly after the electoral process, the PAN denounced Salinas' "nonfulfillment" of the above-mentioned offer of a national accord for the enhancement of the democratic life. Its fallout with the Salinas administration notwithstanding, the PAN emerged from the 1991 elections as a more consolidated party, and retained its condition of being the main interlocutor of the government.[45] Thus, when state elections held during the summer of 1992 in the states of Chihuahua, a traditional PAN stronghold, and Michoacán, a PRD's bastion, the differentiated treatment given to the two parties was clear again. While the government recognized the PAN victory in the northern state, the PRI and the government resorted to their traditional electoral machinery, probably stealing the election from the PRD.[46]

Subsequently, in his 1992 state of the union address, Salinas accepted that new electoral legislation would be necessary. The government's alleged intention was to end the symbiotic relationship between the PRI and the government. Accordingly, in March 1993 Salinas declared: "The PRI will continue to be the great party of Mexico, not of the government anymore, but still the best choice for the nation."[47] The outcome was the 1993 electoral reform—but it was a disappointing one. One of the crucial issues, the independence of the electoral body, the IFE, did not significantly improve. As a CC's report on the 1993 reform put it: "The perception of partiality by IFE, in our judgment, has some validity. The new reforms have reduced the PRI's control of IFE, but the reforms don't eliminate the ability of the government/PRI to shape the outcome if the need arises. Progress was made, but much remains to be done."[48] Furthermore, the 1993 reform reinforced the governability clause, by taking the percentage of votes obtained in the districts as the basis upon which to assign the number of representatives under the principle of proportionality, up to 60 percent. Thus, with 50.2 percent of the votes, the PRI would get 60 percent of the seats in the lower house in the next national elections.

On the other hand, the term "elector observer" was introduced in the electoral legislation for the first time in 1993. Article 5 of the law was amended with a clause stating that "it is the exclusive right of Mexican citizens to take part as observers of the electoral activities during election day." But the restrictions attached to the new legislation were so profuse that they apparently violated constitutional guarantees.[49] In any case, as soon as they were passed the new regulations became "irrelevant," according to Sergio Aguayo of Alianza Cívica, the largest Mexican observation group.[50] Furthermore, observation was limited to election day, to the exclusion of the campaign leading to it. Nevertheless, the fact that the practice was recognized at all was telling.

THE ORIGINS OF ELECTION MONITORING AND THE 1994 ELECTORAL REFORM

Election monitoring got to a rough start in 1991. That year, the PRD invited four members of Canada's New Democracy Party to observe the February 1991 elections in the southern state of Morelos. But the experience was hardly a success. The observers did not speak Spanish, their arrival to Morelos took place two days before the elections, and they did not even visit the polling sites. Nonetheless, the observers' presence caused strong adverse reactions. Alfonso Martínez Domínguez, a PRI Senator and former leader of the party said the observers were "unacceptable;" Antonio de Icaza, who had just left his position as Mexico's representative at the OAS declared: "we do not have anything to hide, but we are not going to submit to anybody nor do we accept any kind of tutelage." IFE's magistrate counselor Manuel Barquín went further, arguing that "their [the observers'] presence can even be dangerous for the political processes."[51] After that first experience, the PRD—as well as other opposition parties—forgot about inviting foreign observers. But Mexican NGOs did not.

Later that year, a group of NGOs started election monitoring in a more consistent fashion. The Democratic Assembly for Effective Suffrage, the National Accord for Democracy, the Study Center for a National Project, and the Mexican Academy of Human Rights (AMDH), observed the 1991 electoral processes.[52] Some of these organizations were inspired by the civic undertaking the Chileans had conducted three years earlier. As two leaders of the Mexican monitoring efforts put it: "The success achieved by the Chilean civil society [in the 1988 plebiscite] contrasted with the experience of Mexican society, which in 1988 was subjected to the most incredible and huge vacuum of information decreed by the government . . . Following the steps of the Chilean effort, several not-party affiliated citizen groups started to organize monitoring efforts" in 1991.[53]

Of the organizations just mentioned, the AMDH would constitute itself into one of the leading actors in the 1994 monitoring exercise within the umbrella organization Alianza Cívica, having observed 15 local elections between 1991 and 1993.[54] In its foundational experience as an election-watch organization in the state of San Luis Potosí, the AMDH joined forces with a local NGO, the Potosino Center for Human Rights. Three were the main reasons behind the first election monitoring experience of the human rights organization, according to Aguayo, then president of the AMDH. As he recalls

> One [reason] had to do with the electoral fraud of 1988, I was really impressed by the fact that the [computing] system [on election night, at the electoral body] went down and there were no alternative mechanisms of information. Indeed during all the 1980s, I was already involved in development and human rights NGOs, and the idea of elections was not taken into account. . . . Second, the creation [by the Salinas administration] of the National Human Rights Commission which, for me, allowed the broadening of the NGOs' agenda . . . and then a merely contingent factor . . . the invitation I received [from the CC] to go to Haiti to observe the 1990 elections.[55]

As Aguayo has put it, "Monitoring by outside observers seemed to me an effective way to promote fair elections, but I found that exercise expensive, and not enough in any case to consolidate a culture of democracy. The logical alternative for Mexico was electoral observation by the country's own citizens."[56] Thus, more than 300 domestic observers monitored the San Luis Potosí gubernatorial elections the next year. Interestingly, part of the funding for the 1991 drive came from the Canadian International Centre for Human Rights and Democratic Development, in which Elizabeth Spehar, later head of the OAS' UPD, was involved.[57] But perhaps more significant is the way the human rights agenda was expanded so as to include the electoral aspect. As Aguayo recollects,

> I had been candidate to the presidency [of the AMDH] with a platform in which I had spell out very clearly that I wanted to be president to

> include the issue of civil rights, electoral rights, political rights. And that is the way I won. So I arrived [to the presidency] with the clarity that I was going to do something. Now, I did not have any idea of how I was going to push the agenda.[58]

Then came the Carter Center's invitation to go to Haiti. By then, the main rationale for election monitoring had settled in: "the idea that elections could be an instrument for change."[59] And in the process of recognizing the importance of elections as a means for change, according to Aguayo, the experiences of other countries were fundamental.[60]

Thus, the following year Aguayo, on behalf of eight Mexican observer groups, invited the CC, through Robert Pastor, to accompany them in observing the state elections in the states of Chihuahua and Michoacán.[61] But the CC also wanted a government invitation. Pastor tried to convince Salinas, whom he had met in Harvard when both were graduate students, to extend them one, but Salinas wouldn't accept foreign observers in a Mexican electoral process. Pastor suggested a compromise: the CC's group would simply "witness the observation of the elections in Michoacán and Chihuahua" in July 1992, but it would not comment on the elections.[62] By that time, the Mexican government was well aware that IEM was hovering around Mexico. In February 1990, President Salinas had declared that "[A] Country that leaves the organization and sanction of its internal political processes to foreign forces is giving away its sovereignty."[63] More to the point, the day after Salinas' declaration appeared, the head of the IFE (the electoral body) asserted that "nobody certifies Mexicans."[64] It was, as Jorge Chabat put it at the time "as though the Mexican states's [sic] traditional concept of sovereignty has found its last refuge in the ballot box."[65] Still, in October 1990 Foreign Minister Fernando Solana declared that the country's problems regarding democracy would need to be solved by Mexicans "and not by importing specialized observers from Atlanta or Milwaukee who tell us how to do things."[66]

Nevertheless, people from Atlanta were present in Chihuahua and Michoacán two years later. Trying to persuade his former graduate fellow to let foreign observers in for future occasions, Pastor went back to Mexico City after the elections, and told Salinas that although in his judgment the elections had gone reasonably well, "I can't say anything about the elections because you told me [not to comment on them], so all we can do is talk about the election observers, and that's what we are going to do."[67] Salinas was not moved. His government continued to refuse foreign observers in Mexico. That's why the 1993 electoral reform did not even mention foreign observers.

But it wasn't just the government that wasn't interested in receiving foreign observers. In a pioneering study, "International Observers: The Citizenry's Perception," José Antonio Crespo found that 63 percent of those polled (in November 1990) rejected the presence of foreign observers in Mexican elections.[68] In this sense, as Crespo observes, "the official [i.e., governmental] justification for rejecting foreign supervisors [sic] has fell in fertile soil."[69] As political analyst René Delgado put it in the early 1990s, "promoting the presence of foreign observers in elections, at the moment, is not completely advisable . . . the practice of election observing, for the moment, should be carried out by national groups."[70]

Furthermore, the international environment was relatively benign vis-à-vis the Mexican government's position. As Crespo points out, "the international pressure so that transparent electoral process in our country take place, without being nonexistent, shows a much lower intensity than the one registered in other cases, such as that of Chile during the Pinochet dictatorship or that of Sandinista Nicaragua."[71] Thus, in the dawn of the Salinas administration, as Crespo surmised, "neither are the pressures on the government to invite international observers so strong, nor is the internal political situation so chaotic, nor is the PRI's confidence in winning over its competitors in a completely clean manner sufficient."[72]

As a matter of fact, in the early 1990s not even opposition forces were convinced about the advantages of inviting foreign observers to domestic elections. After the timid 1991 precedent in the state of Morelos, the PRD pretty much dropped the matter; hence, it did not invite foreign observers to that year's mid-term elections. Still, in May 1992 Cárdenas traveled to Atlanta, where he talked to Carter about international observers. Nevertheless, inviting foreign observers was not popular in the PRD. Cárdenas did not pursue the issue further.[73]

Similarly, the PAN had an ambiguous position vis-à-vis foreign observers—although in a way it was this party that introduced the issue, if indirectly.[74] After considering that it had been the victim of electoral fraud in the 1986 gubernatorial elections in the state of Chihuahua, and in the municipal elections in the capital city of the state of Durango, the PAN decided to take an unprecedented action: to take its case to the Inter-American Human Rights Commission (IAHRC), as mentioned above. The government's reaction was fierce, practically accusing the PAN of treason.

The PAN argued that the Mexican government had violated the American Convention on Human Rights. More precisely, the opposition party claimed that there had been legal anomalies both in the pre-election period as well as in the vote counting process. Furthermore, it contended that its post-electoral legal appeals had been disregarded by the electoral body, since it was controlled by the PRI. The Mexican government, on its part, claimed that the IAHRC lacked competence to pronounce itself on electoral matters for reasons of national sovereignty. Nonetheless, the IAHRC accepted the PAN's request, and issued a preliminary report in 1989. In its reply to it, the Mexican government argued that if a state "were to pact to subject itself to an international body on issues concerning the election of its political organs, it would cease being both sovereign and a state," and it further reiterated that "any pronouncement on the part of the Commission on the 'authenticity' of an electoral process . . . would constitute an act of intervention."[75]

In May 1990, the IAHRC issued its ruling, in which it noted that since the popular will is the basis of public authority, as recognized by both the Universal Declaration on Human Rights, and the American Declaration on the Rights and Duties of Man and that, consequently, the right to elect popular representatives should be "authentic," as established in the American Convention. It also pointed out that the IAHRC was competent to make pronouncements on the issue, and that since the Mexican state had signed and ratified the Convention, it had accepted that some domestic matters could be the object of pronouncements on the part of the established organs for the protection of the rights recognized by the Convention.[76] Mexico, of course, rejected the Commission's report.

By that time, although the PAN was not openly pursuing the external support for its electoral battles, it was still sympathetic to it. In fact, the same month the Commission issued its final report, the PAN's 1988 presidential candidate, Manuel Clouthier, took part in the CC's mission to observe the Panamanian elections.[77] But by the early 1990s the PAN seemed to have decided not to emphasize the issue of foreign assistance anymore. Bringing electoral matters to an international forum had caused strife within the party. In 1991, Luis H. Alvarez, its national leader and one of the key figures in the 1986 Chihuahua protest movement, declared that the PAN had no official position regarding the presence of foreign observers in Mexico. He noted, however: "The issue is being amply debated by different groups, and it is understandable that it be that way, since the presence of observers in electoral processes is already a universal practice. Only very few countries are still reluctant to such vigilance."[78] The PAN's ambivalence was in part due to the fact that, as a co-architect of the 1990 electoral reform, its resorting to external observers could somehow be taken as a recognition that the reform was flawed—as the PRD maintained.

In any case, Mexican NGOs continued their relationship with the CC. After Mexican observers pointed out to CC's delegates during their 1992 visit to Mexico that although they roamed the world observing election and giving advice to others, they had never invited foreigners to do the same in their country, the CC decided to invite a Mexican delegation to observe that year's US presidential election.[79] The CC intended the mission to be plural, so in addition to representatives from observers groups and an independent political analyst, it also invited representatives from Mexico's three main parties, PAN, PRD, and PRI. Significantly, the latter declined to send delegates.[80]

But even for the Mexicans who agreed to participate in the observation, it was not an easy decision to make. As they noted in their report, "Accepting this invitation in a country like Mexico is not exempt from complications."[81] That was not an overstatement. One of them was advised by a high Mexican government official not to take part in the monitoring effort because his presence in the mission was "contrary to the [Mexican] national interest."[82] Similarly, the government-owned newspaper *El Nacional* ran an article criticizing what "our naïve observers" whose "protagonic aim will not contribute at all to improve the quality of the electoral process in that country [the United States]."[83] It was clear that the government didn't want the delegation to be used as a stepping stone by their hosts to make inroads in Mexico.

And that exactly had been the CC's intention. As Pastor recalls, inviting the Mexicans to observe elections in the United States was the second step in a strategy he had devised to be able to observe elections in Mexico. The first step had been to invite them to observe elections somewhere else (e.g., Sergio Aguayo to Haiti 1990, Manuel Clouthier to Panama 1990), in order to get an invitation to go to Mexico.[84] At least some of the Mexican observers were well aware of the way their visit could be construed. Thus, for instance, before departing for Atlanta, Aguayo told a Mexican newspaper that the AMDH's position was "not to invite international observers to elections, because democracy [in Mexico] is fundamentally a task for Mexicans."[85] And once in Atlanta, he wrote an op-ed for another Mexican newspaper in which he asked rhetorically: "Could this observation trip be used in the future by the Americans for interfering in our electoral affairs? The answer is negative, because one of the criteria to carry out electoral observation in other countries is that there has to exist an invitation from the parties and the government."[86] And in a later article Aguayo openly stated his opposition to having foreign observers in Mexican elections.[87]

In any case, when the time came to make an official pronouncement on the US presidential elections, at the end of their brief (2–4 November) monitoring exercise, the Mexican observers were rather reluctant to express their opinion. Pastor had to insist, telling them that the CC would feel insulted if they didn't present a report on the US election.[88] In their report, the observers were careful to point out that "We have no interest in interfering in the American political system. We offer these criticisms and suggestions in the same spirit of friendship and openness with which we were invited and with a strong belief that all sides benefit from the free flow of ideas and information."[89]

A few months later, there was a failed attempt by a group of academics and politicians to organize an international forum on international electoral assistance in Mexico. In February 1993, PRI's Senator Silvia Hernández, who at the time was the president of Parliamentarians for Global Action, attended a meeting in Stockholm on IEM organized by the Swedish government. Senator Hernández then proposed holding another meeting on the same matter in Mexico. Back home, she contacted the Study Center for a National Project (one of the NGOs which monitored the 1991 elections), as well as some cabinet members. The reactions were varied. Luis Donaldo Colosio, secretary of Social Development and later the PRI's presidential candidate, was sympathetic to the idea. Interior Minister Patrocinio González refused to even emit an opinion, deferring to the Foreign Minister. And Foreign Minister Fernando Solana rejected the idea. According to Jorge Alcocer, then head of the Study Center and later former senator Hernández's husband, the Foreign Minister "clearly said no. 'This can't be, it is a violation of national sovereignty, we are not going to accept foreign observers in our elections' [Alcocer said paraphrasing the Foreign Minister], and that was the opinion Salinas finally settled on."[90] The international electoral assistance meeting did take place in the end—but in Caracas, Venezuela.

The government was adamant in its position regarding foreign observers. In October 1993, on the eve of the formal start of the 1994 presidential race, Foreign Minister Solana declared: "the Mexican government will not allow foreign observers in the electoral processes, only Mexican ones. The most fundamental exercise of sovereignty are the elections, which should always be in the hands of the citizens of Mexico."[91] But the momentum gained by IEM since the Nicaraguan 1990 elections was palpable. Thus, Rosario Green, a Mexican career diplomat at the UN at the time, recognized: "Even though Mexico has always been opposed to international organisms having the capacity to intervene on issues that are of the exclusive domain of states, it is a fact that the recent evolution of these fora tends to consolidate such tendency."[92]

International pressure on the Mexican government was thus increasing. NAFTA, on which Salinas had staked out his presidency, was going to be voted on in the US Congress in November. Moreover, by that time the bifurcated political economy of the Salinas administration (in which economic openness went hand in hand with political closeness) was flagrant, thus creating problems for the Mexican government. As the IFE's director for international affairs remarked, around 1994 "we seemed very open in the economic aspect, very open in trade matters, but a dike in political-electoral matters."[93] Nevertheless, as Monica Serrano has noted, "In spite of Salinas' efforts to administer and control political change, the opening and internationalization of domestic politics undermined the capacity of the system to respond, simultaneously, both to the demands by new actors as well as those of the *priista* family who had been affected by the new dynamics."[94]

On the internal front, Salinas faced pressures to designate the PRI's candidate. But he did not want to do so before the fate of NAFTA was decided in the United States. The president's heir apparent was traditionally announced during September or October before the election year (presidential elections take place during the Summer). But Salinas wanted to wait for Congress to vote on NAFTA. It was widely rumored in high political circles that the name of the candidate depended on NAFTA's fate: if it was approved, Luis Donaldo Colosio, Salinas' Social Development Minister, would be the chosen one; but if the proposed agreement didn't pass, then the more politically skilled and conciliatory Manuel Camacho, who had served as the appointed Mayor of Mexico City since Salinas' inauguration, would be the PRI's candidate.[95]

The House of Representatives voted in favor of NAFTA on 17 November. 10 days later, Salinas invited Colosio to the presidential house and told him that "the party was decisively inclined in his favor." The next day, Colosio's nomination was announced.[96] Everything was going well for Salinas: with NAFTA scheduled to go into effect on 1 January 1994, and Colosio as his very likely successor, the permanence of the political system—and of Salinas' legacy—seemed secured. The international and domestic environment seemed again under control. On 20 December 1993 Mexico expressed its opposition to foreign electoral assistance in UN resolution 48/124.[97]

THE 1994 ELECTIONS

Mexico's political environment was totally altered as election year opened. On January first 1994, the same day NAFTA went into effect, an armed uprising broke out in the southern state of Chiapas. As the Zapatista National Liberation Army, named after 1910 revolutionary leader Emiliano Zapata, gained popular sympathy throughout the country, the Salinas administration was led not only to initiate peace talks with the guerrillas, but also to restructure his cabinet and eventually to offer a new electoral reform. Thus, on 10 January Salinas removed Interior Minister Patrocinio González, a hard-liner, and replaced him with Jorge Carpizo, a widely respected lawyer and human rights advocate who had no party affiliation. At the same time, Salinas brought Camacho, whom after being passed for the PRI's presidential candidacy had been appointed as Foreign Minister, and designated him commissioner for peace negotiations with the rebels. In his place at the foreign ministry he appointed a career diplomat, Manuel Tello. Along with the cabinet reshuffle, Salinas also declared a unilateral cease-fire.

That same month, the main political forces and the government signed what came to be known as the Barcelona Agreements, in which they agreed to change the structure of the electoral bodies at the federal, state, and district level. Another electoral reform was coming up. Since the political campaigns had already started, this meant that the rules would be changed in the middle of the game.

The rationale for such an extemporaneous initiative was clear: the government wanted to restore the legitimacy of non-violent means for political contestation. As Jorge Alcocer, then adviser to Interior Minister Carpizo, put it: "If the PRD, in its most radical wing, moved to positions openly supporting the Zapatistas, the August 1994 election could get enormously complicated. In those conditions . . . one of the first issues that Dr. Carpizo brings up is how to achieve an accord with the PRD and with the PAN without the PRI opposing it."[98] The electoral process needed to be presented as the only viable and acceptable way of gaining power. Hence, in the next four months a constitutional amendment and 41 changes to the electoral law were passed. Thanks to the former, the IFE was to be formed by six "citizens counselors" (approved by consensus among the PRI, PAN, and PRD), two representatives from each house of Congress, and the Interior Minister. Neither the government nor his party controlled the electoral body anymore. Furthermore, the Interior Minister could not use his vote to break a tie. The electoral institution had thus become a different body, one in which independent citizens played a cardinal role. As a WOLA-AMDH joint report on the 1994 Mexican elections put it, "The 'citizenization' of the IFE is the most important reform of all."[99]

But the changes introduced to the electoral law were significant, too. It improved the status of national observers and allowed the presence of accepted foreign observers under the semantic guise of "international visitors." The rarefied political environment had made the potential validation of the August electoral process provided by observers a highly valued item for the government. Thus, for instance, Salinas, through an intermediary, sought the leadership of AC in order to make sure that their organization was going to monitor the elections. According to Aguayo, "it is not that they [high governmental officials] were pleased with us, but they said, 'well, there they are.'"[100] Furthermore, in order to insure that domestic monitoring actually took place, the government set up public funding for it (more on this below), and allowed foreign financing of Mexican NGOs. As Aguayo recalls, "in 94 the issue of foreign financing changes completely because the government stops worrying about it. There is a fundamental turn because of the Zapatista rebellion . . . and because of the appointment of Carpizo as Interior Minister."[101] Thus, in February the IFE approved the "Guidelines for the Accreditation and development of the Activities of the Mexican Citizens who will act as Observers during the Electoral Process of 1994," and in May Article 5 of the electoral law was amended, thus extending the observing period from election day to the electoral campaign.[102]

Regarding "international visitors," the issue was more complicated. Although the change in the government's position seemed unavoidable, there was no consensus among high government officials and PRI leaders. Salinas' cabinet indeed debated the issue several times.[103] The eventual acceptance of foreign observers was not immediate. Thus, for instance, in January Santiago Oñate, secretary of international affairs of the PRI, was approached by US government officials regarding the possibility of Mexico accepting OAS electoral monitors, but he refused.[104] "Sovereignty" remained a principled issue for most of the Mexican political class. As Pastor notes, "the Mexicans had always constructed an elaborate philosophical and legalistic basis" for national sovereignty; "only the Mexicans do this kind of thing."[105]

But the topic of foreign observers got in the agenda right from the start of the new negotiations. According to Alcocer, "what triggers the need for international observation is the EZ [Zapatista Army]. That is what triggers it."[106] As a matter of fact, the issue of foreign observers was on the front burner of Carpizo's agenda—even though he personally was reluctant to it. As Alcocer recalls, it was

> one of the issues to which he devoted more attention . . . he knew that there was a strong resistance in government circles, not only in government circles, but also among the public opinion and political parties, to allow the presence of international observers, due to the [prevailing] notion of national sovereignty, and in particular the rigidity of constitutional article 33, which explicitly prohibits the intervention of foreigners in political matters . . . it was a vision of national sovereignty widely shared by the population and the political class.[107]

But there were segments both within the opposition parties, particularly the PRD, and the government, which favored the IEM of Mexican elections. Interestingly, the single PRD member who most strongly pushed for international observers, and indeed the one who came up with the idea of calling them "international visitors" in order to get around constitutional article 33, was Porfirio Muñoz Ledo, a former PRI president who had left the party with Cárdenas back in 1987. As Alcocer, who actively participated in the 1994 negotiations acknowledges, "the one who most insisted on the topic, and it needs to be said in recognition of his tenacity, was Porfirio Muñoz Ledo. He is the one who brings the issue to the table . . . toward the end of January."[108]

Concurrently, there was a team within the IFE that had been advocating a change of policy regarding IEM since late 1993. Nevertheless, as Manuel Carrillo, head of IFE's international affairs office and a member of that team put it, Carpizo's predecessor, Patrocinio González Garrido, on whose ministry the IFE still depended, "had a vision, let's say strict, orthodox, of sovereignty."[109] But with the 1994 electoral reforms things begin to change for this group of people, headed by IFE's director Arturo Nuñez. During the IFE's internal debate in late January, still in the midst of the political upheaval brought about by the Zapatistas, recalls Carrillo, "somebody comes and says: 'look at this video, from El Salvador. Can you see that [foreign] observers are substituting the people at the [voting] tables. They say that is observation.' The reasoning was devastating."[110]

But by that time it was not really up to Salinas, i.e. to the government, to decide on the issue.[111] Alcocer, who was also a friend of and advisor to Colosio recalls: "the decision wasn't Salinas' anymore, Salinas was operating under the presidential logic: once the candidate is designated, it was he who made the decisions regarding the electoral process . . . and the logic was this: 'this is your election, not mine; if you want observers, I am not opposed.'"[112] As Alcocer has written, "Knowing that the eyes of the international community would continue to be focused on Mexico, and that the August elections had provided the impetus for the EZLN [the Zapatista Army] rebellion, Colosio recognized that it would be foolish to employ Mexico's traditional attitude of rejecting international election observers."[113]

Colosio had already sent some signals that he was more open to electoral observation than Salinas had been, at least regarding domestic observers. Thus, for instance, on 8 December Colosio said: "I am in favor of a plural group of impartial and prestigious national observers, made up by citizens proposed by all parties."[114] Nevertheless, international observers were not even mentioned. But with the political environment brought by the new year, Colosio (and Salinas) perceived the need to count on international observers. Furthermore, by inviting observers rather late in the electoral process, as Jennifer McCoy, who headed the CC's team for the 1994 elections has noted, the government "had the positive thing of getting international legitimacy, having observers coming to election day, and saying, 'well, election day looked very good.' I think . . . there was a emerging norm, and recognizing the practice. . . . it was a recalculation of interests, of national interests."[115]

Colosio seemed to have made up his mind on the issue around February. Interestingly, during the negotiations held during that month between the PAN, PRD, and PRD with the Interior Minister, only the second, through its representative Muñoz Ledo, openly favored the presence of international observers in the August elections. The PAN had no official position yet, whereas the PRI was still against it.[116] Toward the end of February or early March, though, Colosio went to Washington, where he met with NDI leaders. As Patrick Merloe, who succeeded Garber at NDI as Director of NDI Programs on Election and Political Processes, and who participated in the meeting with Colosio recalls, "he told us, please come, be involved, we want you in Mexico, we want you to help the Civic Alliance, we want you to come as international observers . . . he reiterated that it was his view that there should be international observers in Mexico's elections."[117]

Around that time, on 6 March, Colosio said in a campaign rally:

> [The elections'] transparency demands the participation of observers, and it does not exclude the possibility that anybody give an extensive testimony about it, not only on the part of our citizens but also on the part of international visitors. By no means should we regard with fear those who wish to learn about the nature of our democratic processes. Our elections, and I say this with full conviction, will have no shame to conceal.[118]

From then on, there was a noticeable change in the government's position on foreign observers. A week after Colosio's speech, Mexico's ambassador to the UN declared that accepting foreign observers "does not mean abandonment of sovereignty, but declaring that there is nothing to hide and that electoral processes in Mexico can be observed freely."[119] Nevertheless, not everybody within the government was equally convinced. Foreign Minister Tello declared in early April: "I have yet to be persuaded about the necessity of having people from abroad coming to observe the [electoral] process."[120] In the end, the Foreign Minister did not need to be convinced. As he told me, he was not involved in negotiating the issue of foreign observers, his role being limited to issuing the invitations. As Tello put it, "The one who negotiated everything was Carpizo."[121] The Interior Minister certainly played a key role in bringing about the acceptance of foreign observers—although he acquiesced to their presence "not without sadness."[122] But even Carpizo's pragmatic position could not have materialized had Colosio not agreed to it. For Alcocer: "If the PRI candidate had said no, not even Carpizo would have been able to pull off the [international] observers issue."[123]

By March, the political environment started to acquire a relative sense of restfulness again. During the first week, Peace Commissioner Camacho signed a preliminary peace agreement with the Zapatistas, and on the 23rd the constitutional reforms that came out of the negotiations among the main three parties and the government were approved by Congress. But just then Mexico entered again in a state of commotion, as Colosio was assassinated that same day. This was a most extraordinary event in Mexico, where the last time something equivalent had happened was about seven decades before. As a result of the rarefied political environment, the rebels suspended peace talks. Furthermore, in the midst of internal strife, Salinas had to hurriedly designate a second PRI candidate: Ernesto Zedillo, a former cabinet member who had quit to become Colosio's campaign manager.

Nevertheless, the agreements regarding foreign observers remained untouched. Furthermore, in April the Mexican government officially approached the UN, inviting it to play a role in the forthcoming electoral process (more on this below). Regarding the broader issue of foreign observers, the reformed IFE decided to leave the drafting of the official invitation to the six citizen counselors, who took their seats on 3 June. Twenty days later, and only two months before election day, the IFE issued the guidelines for "international visitors." As José Woldenberg, then one of the six citizen counselors and later counselor president of the IFE recalls, the counselors decided to issue a "generic" invitation (i.e., not to make a list or invited organizations) so as not to offend any one; political parties and NGOs could then issue particular invitations.[124] The guidelines of course kept the term "international visitor," which for Woldenberg was "an intermediate formulation" between the closeness mandated by constitutional article 33 and a complete opening. Nevertheless, Woldenberg recognizes that "once groups or individuals from abroad come to follow the elections, what are they? Observers. They are international observers, there is no way around it."[125]

Interestingly, although it was the PRD the party which, as noted, pushed the most to include foreign observers in the agenda, this was not a pervasive position within it. Thus, for instance, in mid-March Amalia

García, the PRD's secretary for international affairs, downplayed the importance of international observers. She declared that in the negotiations to the electoral law then underway, "We do not consider this change [allowing foreign observers] a priority. We only stressed electoral impartiality, which is what really matters."[126] It seemed that, as Aguayo has argued, "opposition parties never finished digesting the presence . . . of electoral observers. They saw [electoral observation] as an intrusion."[127]

In the remaining of this section I focus on the three most prominent organizations in the monitoring of the 1994 Mexican elections: AC, the UN, and the CC.

Alianza Cívica

AC was established in April 1994 as an umbrella organization formed by more than 300 NGOs. But the decision to embark on an observation project had been taken months before, in November 1993, when the AMDH and other six organizations (Citizen Movement for Democracy, Convergence of Civil Organizations for Democracy, National Accord for Democracy, Council for Democracy, and the Arturo Rosenblueth Foundation) first had the idea to launch a monitoring effort for the August 1994 elections.[128] As Aguayo recalls,

> we decided to monitor the 1994 elections in Yucatan. We were observing the [state] elections . . . it was the day Colosio was *destapado* [unveiled, i.e., nominated] . . . those of us who would later form Alianza Cívica were talking and decided to do the observation of the presidential election. Knowing that we would not have money, we said, 'we have to do it, even if it is symbolic, even if Colosio is going to win, even if . . . it doesn't matter, let's do it anyway.'[129]

The founding NGOs were still trying to reach a consensus on a myriad of issues, such as whether or not to accept foreign funding, when the Zapatista rebellion broke out. Everything changed for the nascent monitoring project from then on. As noted earlier, President Salinas decided to get in touch with its leaders to make sure that they would carry out their monitoring project, to set up public funding for observation efforts, and to relax restrictions on foreign financing. Furthermore, the amendments to the electoral laws enhanced both the legitimacy and the opportunities to carry out observation activities. Suddenly, the long neglected and despised observer organizations seemed to have become the government's darlings. Whereas counting with an enhanced legal status and more open access to external sources made the work of the still nascent AC and other monitoring organizations easier, the sudden change in the government's attitude toward them also entailed risks. Governmental attempts at interfering in what had been conceived of as an independent citizen effort was the most obvious danger.

But the leaders of the seven organizations continued to work on their own, building a consensus plan for the August elections. By the end of February 1994, the preliminary project was concluded, and then presented for discussion in several states. AC's legal establishment and a national meeting in Mexico City to approve the final scheme took place subsequently, in April 1994.

In the meantime, AC's project was also taken to Washington D.C., in order to request funds from sympathetic foundations and NGOs.[130] Thus, AC and NGOs within it received a $820,000 grant from indirect public funding, including NDI.[131] That NDI gave financial aid to AC was rather unusual, since NDI usually provided technical assistance, not cash. But the case of AC was different. As Aguayo recalls his organization's dealing with NDI: "I told them: 'we need support in cash, not in kind, we don't need training nor technical assistance, nor that you tell us how to observe elections. We know how to do that. What we need is that you support us financially.' . . . NDI understood that [and] they even provided us with resources without providing technical assistance. I don't know how they managed [to do this] with their board of directors."[132] The decision to provide funds to AC through NDI seems to actually had come from higher up, from the State Department.[133]

AC's relationship with NDI was completely different from the one it had with the UN. For Enrique Calderón and Daniel Cazés, two of AC's leaders, the UN envoys "thought they could manipulate" AC. Calderón and Cazés charge the UN with trying to make AC "g[ive] up on any serious observation effort."[134] Similarly, according to Aguayo, "the relationship with the UN was my nightmare, our nightmare. Only that I had a good deal of the burden in the relationship with them. It was a nightmare. . . . [this kind of problem] did not happen even with the *gringos* [people from the U.S.], nor with anybody else; it was only with the UN. That indeed was a nightmare."[135] The root cause of the problem, according to Aguayo, was that the world organization "wanted to have a place under the universe of Mexico's democratization, and that we [AC] had taken that place that they, in a natural manner, should have had."[136] The difficulties arose because the assistance the government had requested the UN to provide put the international organization in a position of power vis-à-vis domestic NGOs (more on this below). AC resented this. Aguayo recollects there was

> a terrible struggle over the methodology [AC wanted to use for its monitoring efforts], and in a meeting we [AC] had [with UN personnel],

> there was a moment in which I told them, 'listen,' or we told them, it is not important who said it but it was said, on the part of Alianza Cívica, 'listen, at this table–they were five or six, we were six—four of us hold Ph. D.'s from various foreign universities' . . . the installed capacity at the table sitting in front of them was impressive.[137]

Nguyen Huu-Dong, who coordinated the 1994 UN mission, recognizes the problems his team had with AC. According to him, two factors underlay the heated discussions over methodological issues: the "lack of communication and lack of trust" between AC and the UN mission, and the fact that national observers tend to be, inherently, more aggressive or suspicious of the government's intention in the electoral process than international observers are.[138] For Huu-Dong,

> it is a normal difference, between national and foreign observers. Regarding the code of conduct, for instance, speaking about foreigners, I do not have the same responsibility, I have a different responsibility, from the national observer. The national observer has more pronounced the reaction of someone who can fix the mistakes [of the electoral process], and the foreign observer does not have such a capacity; he has a much more passive role . . . [if this difference] is not well presented, it can generate a certain difference in conception between the two [kinds of observers]. That was, I would say, the problem in 94 with Alianza Cívica.[139]

Nevertheless, working with the UN was important for AC, for two reasons. The most obvious one was the financial support it would receive from the international organization. As noted, the government had set up a fund to be distributed among monitoring organizations—and the UN was in charge of managing the resources (more on this below). But arguably more important than the fund was the legitimacy the UN could invest AC with. The neutrality of AC had become an issue from early on; it was constantly accused of being partial to the PRD. This kind of criticism made Aguayo realize that the legitimacy of the organization was at stake. As he put it, "I said [to his fellow activists]: 'this is the battle for legitimacy. Therefore we are going to fight for international legitimacy' . . . when the internal discussion [within AC] comes about why we had to accept someone from the UN . . . [I] used to tell them, 'that is the way it is, tough luck. We have no option; that is the game, there has to be someone from the UN.'" It was clear for Aguayo that the UN could provide them, more than with anything else, with "the political legitimacy."[140]

Thus, AC focused its effort on putting together a comprehensive monitoring effort of the whole electoral project, which included the establishment of a media-watchdog project, opinion polls, a study of Mexican electoral laws, as well as a program to denounce illegal electoral activities (such as the use of government funds in political campaigns). AC actually mounted the largest organized, independent citizen effort in Mexico's history. The consolidation of Mexico's civil society since the late 1980s was crucial in this respect. It was the firmness of Mexican civil society which made the monitoring effort in Mexico different from those carried previously, such as the Nicaraguan experience in 1990. As Aguayo put it, "Insofar as Mexico had a stronger civil society [than countries such as Haiti], foreign monitoring was less aggressive."[141] Without a doubt. As McCoy, the CC's mission chief to Mexico in 1994 put it, "the international observers didn't play a crucial role, it was domestic observers . . . Alianza Cívica."[142] Similarly, Pastor notes that in the 1994 electoral process, "what was critical was civil society."[143]

The fact that Mexicans had the leading role in the monitoring effort was important for AC. As Aguayo explains, "we had it very clear that as long as we had the support of the [Mexican] community of NGOs, and of the citizenship we worked with, the international observation was complementary. That was the thesis. Right from the start: [foreign observers] are going to complement our work, and they are going to do what we decide. Period. Or they can come on their own."[144] This is not to say that AC was closed to foreign observers—only that it wanted to coordinate the activities of foreign NGOs which had offered to work with it, such as WOLA. In fact, AC invited about half of the 777 foreign observers present on election day. The profusion of invitations issued by AC was not fortuitous. It had to do with the work many of the NGOs which composed it had been doing to establish links with sister organizations abroad. Absent this previous relationship, AC would not have invited foreigners to monitor the elections. "If the 94 observation had taken place in 82, we would never had invited foreigners . . . it was unthinkable," notes Aguayo.[145]

On 21 August, AC had 18,280 Mexican observers, and 450 "foreign visitors" distributed throughout the country.[146] Based on a 2168-polling places sample, before midnight AC put out its first report, which questioned the cleanliness of the election. An hour after midnight, and based on a smaller sample, AC released the results of its quick count: Ernesto Zedillo, the PRI's candidate, was well ahead in the electoral race, with a 20-point difference from his closest competitor, the PAN's candidate. Although the election was certainly far from being a model one, it was the cleanest Mexico had ever had. Tellingly, there was no widespread post-election mobilization, as had happened six years before. Furthermore, on this occasion the irregularities did not seem to have affected the outcome of the presidential election. The results for the presidential election were: 48.7 percent for Zedillo (PRI), 25.9 percent for Fernández de Cevallos (PAN), and 16.6 percent for Cárdenas (PRD). As AC's report put it: "The quantitative impact of [the documented irregularities] cannot be calculated with certainty and precision. It is likely that they did not alter the outcome of the presidential election. Nevertheless, they did alter the correlation of the national forces at the national, regional, and local levels, the composition of the Chamber of Deputies, and possibly that of the Senate, generating an overall impression of governing-party predominance."[147] Even though Aguayo recognizes that he "would've liked a different outcome" of the electoral process, he thinks that with the 1994 monitoring effort "we, collectively, delivered a hard blow to the authoritarian regime that year."[148] They certainly did—and Aguayo received NED's "Democracy Award" the following year.

The United Nations

Around February 1994, the Mexican government, through the IFE, furtively approached the United Nations with something in view for the August general elections. As Manuel Carrillo, since that time head of IFE's international affairs office recalls, "We got in touch with the United Nations around February 94, in order to have a first approach . . . [in which] we arranged a visit by a UN team to Mexico . . . we were having meetings. Imagine, in February and March [1994] I was having breakfast with somebody at the United Nations in order to talk about the monitoring issue; I mean, I was not going to do it just like that. I had to have important [political] support."[149] Nguyen Huu-Dong, then director of the UN Electoral Assistance Division, subsequently visited Mexico. As he remembers, "I talked with the authorities at the Interior Ministry . . . because at that time IFE's president was the Interior Minister."[150]

According to Carrillo, by mid-March negotiations with the UN were going well, if slowly. The UN's reaction when the Mexican government first approached it was one of caution, if not reluctance. As the PRI's foreign affairs secretary would say in a forum in Washington two months before the elections, the UN had advised Mexico not to present a formal request for electoral support, citing bureaucratic reasons.[151] The world organization, to be sure, stated that it would not consider sending an observation delegation to Mexico because it was too late, because the country was too big, and because it was not clear that Mexico met the criteria required by the UN for countries to receive observer missions.[152]

Similarly, according to Alcocer, who along with Interior Minister Carpizo wrote the letter asking for the world organization's assistance in the electoral process, when the Mexican ambassador to the United Nations presented the letter to Secretary-General Boutros Boutros-Ghali, he asked: "Are you sure you want to do this? We don't really want to be in Mexico."[153] Huu-Dong confirms this account:

> Jorge Alcocer is right: that is, finally when the request for an observation [sic] was presented, the first reaction is: hey, why does the current situation justify an observation in Mexico, since it is a constitutional election, it is a country without a major problem. There is the problem of distrust, but that is not a problem the UN can solve. So, the first reaction was that, and we know the nationalistic sensitivities of all countries, Mexico included, then the reaction was not one of rejection, but one of caution.[154]

Nevertheless, the assassination on 23 March of the PRI's candidate hastened the negotiating process. According to Carrillo, it "initiate[d] a process of acceleration . . . by that time [Interior Minister] Carpizo was much more flexible."[155] In a preliminary visit to Mexico, Horacio Boneo, from the UN's Electoral Assistance Office, had pointed out to Carrillo that UN observation of the Mexican elections was out of the question, since the country was very large. "So I asked him, then what do we do with so many NGOs and national observers, here they are, what do we do with them? And what do we do with the international ones."[156] Thus, in its 10 May letter to the UN Secretary-General, Carpizo requested the UN 1) "to send a mission of experts in electoral matters so that it can know the Mexican electoral system, and it can put out a technical report" on the matter, and 2) "to collaborate by providing technical assistance to the groups of national observers that request it. . . . in order to ensure their professionalism, independence, and impartiality."[157] Thus, Mexico ended up not requesting the UN to send a monitoring mission to the Mexican elections. Nevertheless, the mere act of contacting the world organization in order to request its assistance in an electoral matter was a turning point in Mexico's foreign policy.[158] Manuel Tello, Foreign Minister at the time, accepts that inviting the UN was a qualitative change for Mexico.[159] Without approval from the General Assembly, the UN accepted Mexico's request.[160]

Interestingly, the OAS was not invited by the Mexican government. This did not go unnoticed by the regional organization. For Santiago Murray, of the OAS' UPD, this non-invitation was not surprising, since Mexico had traditionally been against electoral observation, "always defending the nonintervention principle by all means"[161] Similarly, UPD's head Spehar thinks that Mexico did not invite the inter-American organization in 1994 "because I think they [Mexican diplomats] still see the OAS as an American instrument. Therefore, they don't want the OAS to get involved in democracy issues in their country. . . . It is not even a matter of preferring the UN over the OAS [like Nicaragua]; it is that they [Mexican diplomats] see the OAS differently."[162] There is certainly something to that. As IFE's Carrillo put it, "With the OAS [unlike with the UN] more than a relationship there have been elements of friction."[163] Nevertheless, Carrillo claims that Mexico did invite the OAS and that although it initially showed interest, in the end it decided not to attend—something Spehar categorically denies and of which I found no evidence at the OAS archives.[164]

In any case, the UN's five-member technical mission started its activities on 28 June, and concluded them on 9 July. In its report, it stated that "Mexico has lived in a permanent reform on electoral matters" since the late 1970s, and noted that only the last electoral reform—the one carried out as a result of the Zapatista uprising—"has been the only one of the three [during the Salinas administration] approved with the support of the [political] forces with the greatest electoral power."[165] The evaluation of the Mexican electoral system, in which the latest electoral reform weighed heavily, was positive. Thus, the technical mission concluded that "the structure of the electoral system is able to carry out free and fair elections" in August 1994.[166] This view obviously irritated opposition parties and some observer groups. But as Boneo, co-leader of the UN mission noted before the elections, there was no way of preventing the Mexican government from using the report to legitimize the electoral process.[167] Nevertheless, the UN technical mission was careful to point out that although the Mexican electoral system possessed a rather complex and well articulated legal structure, "it has to be taken into account that the norm, by itself, does not presuppose that the situation which it aims to regulate and the objective it pursues will take place by the established and desired means."[168]

More conspicuous than the UN's technical team, though, was ETONU-MEX, the intergovernmental organization's team set up in early June to provide assistance to domestic observers. With a staff of about 50, ETONU-MEX provided assistance to 16 organizations—the most important of which was AC. Other monitoring groups included Coparmex, an umbrella business organization, the Teachers' National Organization for Electoral Observation, of the Education Workers' National Union, an organization closely associated with the PRI, and the Institute for Democratic Transition Studies, an independent think tank. As noted, the government entrusted a fund it created to assist monitoring groups to the UN mission. Thus, ETONU-MEX managed about $3 million, of which AC received half.[169] The world organization sent an expert to each state of Mexico in order to serve as a representative of the organization with local and electoral authorities, and as a liaison with local NGOs—the expert whose presence caused irritation among AC activists, as Aguayo noted. On election day, UN representatives did not visit the polling places; instead they visited the offices of the domestic observers.

With the exception of AC, the relationship between the UN mission and Mexican monitoring NGOs was smooth. The performance of the UN mission was generally considered a success, with many people within and without the organization talking about the birth of a "Mexican model." Thus, ETONU-MEX co-leader Huu-Dong recognizes that "this was a new experience" for the world organization, and its partner Boneo pointed out that the UN's Electoral Assistance Unit would be able "to use [the kind of tasks assigned to it in Mexico] in the future as one of our tools."[170] Similarly, Alcocer notes that after the 1994 electoral process in Mexico, "a new model emerges [for the UN]. . . . I think it was a very successful experience for everybody, and it allowed the United Nations . . . to reevaluate its concept of observation and monitoring."[171] Paradoxically, though, the success of the UN effort was directly related to the success of the organization it had more trouble with: AC. Talking about the effectiveness and legitimacy of AC, Vikram Chand notes: "Had Mexican civil society not been as developed, it is unlikely that [the UN] mission would have been as successful."[172]

As a matter of fact, thanks to the existence of AC and other domestic monitoring groups, ETONU-MEX became a prominent actor in the Mexican electoral process. That is, by putting the intergovernmental organization between the state and civil society, the Mexican government turned the by 1994 customary role of the UN as an external judge into one of being one more player in the elections. This is not to suggest that the organization's mission played a leading role in the electoral process—far from it. But it ended up being an actor alongside the government, the political parties, and civil society. The center that held the relationship among the domestic actors in 1994 was, of course, the deep suspicion of the fairness of the electoral process. And it was that center which pulled the UN into Mexico. As Huu-Dong said at the time: "The fraud hypothesis is the basic reason for electoral observation."[173]

The UN was in Mexico to vouch for the fairness of the electoral process. That is why it became another political actor, although of a peculiar nature, in the electoral process. This was certainly not an easy job for ETONU-MEX. On the one hand, it had to deal with leaders of NGOs such as AC claiming that it had an ignoble pact with the government, or that the fairness of the election was not its main concern, and on the other it had to be ever careful so as not to offend the Mexican government.[174] As Huu-Dong later commented, "The relationship with each of the governments represents . . . a problem: how to convince them that we work for them."[175] In the final analysis, according to Huu-Dong, "I would say that our contribution [was] not to improve the Mexican system at all, but to shed a little bit of light into the system."[176] That "little bit of light," regardless of how much agreement and discord might it have created in the Mexican actors, ended up nevertheless lighting Mexico's dim conception of its sovereignty.

The Carter Center

The CC's involvement in the 1994 Mexican electoral process was very different from other experiences the semi-official organization had had, or at least from that one could have expected at the time. On the one hand, the prestige and international authority of its head, Jimmy Carter, as well as the impressive record it had built by 1994 in the field of election monitoring, suggested the organization would play an important role in Mexico during that momentous year. Furthermore, the personal relationship between Carter's chief aide on election monitoring matters, Robert Pastor, and Mexico's President Carlos Salinas, as well as the vast network of contacts Pastor had with academics, activists, and political leaders from the opposition parties, reinforced the expectation of a leading role for the CC in the monitoring of the 1994 elections.

But, on the other hand, the CC had an indelible mark that made its playing of a visible role in any Mexican elections extremely unlikely: Carter himself. When he was president, he had a few unfortunate experiences, and a series of disputes on a number of issues with his Mexican counterpart, that made the bilateral relationship with López Portillo rather sour.[177] From then on, as Aguayo, a specialist on US-Mexican relations, put it, Carter "produced urticaria" in the ruling party. Furthermore, Aguayo notes that Pastor was part of the problem as well: he was not particularly appreciated by many in the NGO community, perhaps because of his closeness to Salinas: "He caused animadversion in some people; I knew him and I know the kind of character he is, so he did not cause me problems, but he did indeed generate tensions."[178]

Immersed in this contradictory environment, the CC ended up playing a relatively discreet role in the Mexican 1994 elections. As Vikram Chand, a member of the CC delegation to Mexico that year, has put it, "[The CC's] council's approach was low-key . . . [it] chose not to bring Carter to Mexico at all. . . . Of all the three major political parties, only the PRD was willing to consider inviting Carter . . . Mexican political actors

. . . were simply unwilling to turn to an ex-US President to sort out their differences. What was possible in Nicaragua was impossible in Mexico; and the Council had to adjust its strategy accordingly."[179]

The CC started its involvement in light of the August 1994 elections almost a year in advance. In September 1993, a four-person team visited Mexico in order to analyze the electoral reforms being discussed at the time. Two months later, it published a report, "Electoral Reform in Mexico." The document included specific recommendations, some of which were later enacted. By the end of 1993, the CC was thus already involved, if more as a bona fide consulting firm or a think tank than as a monitoring organization, in the Mexican electoral process. But then came the Zapatista uprising in January 1994, which pulled the CC closer to the action. Salinas himself contacted his former graduate fellow to request the presence of the CC in the electoral process. As Pastor recollects, about March or April Salinas called him up and, repeating by heart an argument Pastor had used (unsuccessfully) in the past to convince him to invite foreign observers to Mexican elections, told him: "I think you have a point, but you know we can't invite international observers because the Mexican people won't accept it, you know it will offend their nationality [sic], but what we'll do is that we'll permit international visitors." With that decision, as Pastor notes, Salinas had "obviously crossed the threshold." [180]

At that time, though, it was too late for the CC to form a large monitoring team, as the Mexican case would have required, so it did not properly monitor the elections—at least not to the extent the organization had grown used to. Instead, it sent "study missions," produced four reports on "Elections in Mexico," and carried out a reduced monitoring effort. For this, the CC joined forces with NDI and IRI, "because we knew we would be too small for a big country like Mexico to have the same effect that we had in Nicaragua or Panama," recalls Jennifer McCoy, who headed the CC's team during the whole 11-month process.[181] Part of the strategy of the combined mission was to work in tandem with Mexican observers. As NDI's Merloe, a 1994 delegation-member, puts it:

> if you were concerned about promoting democracy in the world, you had somehow to have some role in helping Mexican reformers. And at that point we had learned a very good lesson from Chile . . . we knew that if we were going to be involved in a country, that international observers to be effective had to connect with the domestic political reformers . . . When we engage in a country like Chile or a country like Mexico . . . where civil society is extraordinarily well organized [NDI just offers its assistance] on any terms, whatever the terms.[182]

The joint CC/NDI/IRI delegation totaled 80 members from 17 countries. Interestingly, although the IFE was supposed to issue only a "generic" invitation and not individual ones, NDI was specifically invited by the electoral organization to attend the general elections. As Merloe recalls, Carrillo called them up to tell them the IFE would appreciate their presence in Mexico, and then faxed the invitation.[183] The CC team was composed of 11 members, among whom were former Costa Rican President Rodrigo Carazo, former Guatemalan President Vinicio Cerezo, former Canadian Prime Minister Joseph Clark, and Harry Barnes, the former ambassador to Chile at the time of the 1988 plebiscite. It arrived in Mexico City four days before the election, and then joined with NDI/IRI mission-members to travel, in pairs, to 25 states (and some stayed in the Federal District). In total, the combined delegation visited about 500 polling places, and witnessed the vote count in 34 polling sites.[184] Two days later, it issued a favorable preliminary report, noting: "This election represents a significant step forward for the Mexican democratic process."[185]

Five months later, the CC issued its own detailed report on the Mexican elections.[186] Although mostly approving of the way the electoral process had been conducted, the CC's report was guarded in its endorsement of the Mexican political system. Referring to AC's electoral report on the election, the CC's one notes that, "a number of irregularities were observed which may have had an effect on congressional or local races, and which continue to raise questions about the legitimacy of the outcome." Nevertheless, and also in keeping with the tone of AC's report, the CC's account recognizes that "Our delegation received no evidence that irregularities were sufficiently serious or widespread to have affected the outcome of the presidential race." The report states that "further reforms were needed to raise credibility and address the inordinately unequal campaign conditions in the future," and it underscores "the active and effective role played by civic groups in election-monitoring."[187] Regardless of the specific weight of the CC or any other foreign mission in Mexico, the important part was that they were involved in the monitoring effort at all. As McCoy notices, "For Mexico [the electoral process of] 94 was landmark . . . in terms of Mexico inviting observers. . . . the international observers didn't play a crucial role . . . but for Mexico, one of the most nationalistic states, to allow what they call visitors, to witness the election" was what made it a milestone.[188]

CONCLUSIONS

The 1994 Mexican elections epitomize the nature of IEM. State and non-state actors, both at the domestic and international level interacted intensively to make the monitoring of the electoral process possible. The most interesting part of their interaction, though, was the novel normative structure in which it was inscribed. Only six years before, this structure was not present—and no interaction leading to a monitoring effort took place. There was no UN Electoral Assistance Office for the de la Madrid administration to resort to, for instance. Furthermore, the Mexican experience is interesting not only because domestic observers took the leading role in the monitoring of the electoral process, but precisely because, despite their late entrance into electoral monitoring, they were able to play such a prominent role. But again: it was the international structure that made the entrance of Mexican NGOs into monitoring activities possible in the first place.

The Chiapas rebellion was certainly what triggered the monitoring of the electoral process, but the issue was already floating in the environment—and even without the uprising some independent groups would undoubtedly have monitored the process (it should be remembered that the organizations that eventually formed AC decided to watch the election in November 1993, and that the CC initiated its involvement in the 1994 electoral process in September 1993). Certainly, though, the UN would not have been present in Mexico. But my point is precisely that it was the institutionalization of IEM at the international level that allowed the government to respond to the challenge posed by the rebels. So the trigger itself was a contingent factor.

The case could be made that by compelling the government to accept the international monitoring of the elections, the Chiapas rebellion validates realist propositions. After all, the government was practically forced to concede on this issue only after the rebels appeared on the scene. But even allowing for the "perceptions" factor in at the bottom materially-based neoclassical realist approach, was not the government's response to the insurgency threat mediated by something more than the perception of the relative (material) position of Mexico in the international system? Might the response have had something to do with the legitimacy—both in the domestic and in the international realms—of the incoming government? If the latter is the case, I would argue that conceding on this point to realist approaches is giving them too much rope (because the argument really rests on intersubjective, not material, premises).

The Mexican 1994 experience also shows again that if the interaction of domestic and systemic factors had not taken place, IEM would not have emerged. Both governmental and non-governmental actors were constantly involved in a two-level game. The Mexican case is paradigmatic as well in the redefinition of interests the acceptance of IEM implied. The international monitoring of the 1994 electoral process marked a breakthrough in

Mexico's history; after that year, the Mexican state not only started to see this practice differently, but also came to conceive of its sovereignty, identity, and interests as being partially defined by the international community (more on this in the general conclusions chapter).[189]

This chapter has thus illustrated the extent to which the understanding of sovereignty enshrined in the WHI had permeated the international system in its entirety by the early 1990s. The Mexican case shows that by 1994 the complex structure of IEM was fully institutionalized—and state sovereignty redefined. An IEM TAN was already active, bringing the WHI closer to its realization through the instantiation of its dialectical understanding of state sovereignty. Furthermore, this chapter highlights the importance of domestic structures when it comes to the diffusion of international norms. Mexico had been a dissenter in the inter-American system in its opposition to foreign "intervention" on issues such as human rights and electoral matters. Nevertheless, as the noun used implies, it was not an isolated actor, but part of a system of communicative action—that is why Mexico ended up adopting the hemispheric-wide understanding of sovereignty. It is in this way that the narrative presented in these pages traces the process by which an international practice shaped a state's interests and identity. In making sense of these developments, theoretical approaches matter. Among other things, IEM is about state sovereignty—an essentially normative attribute. Self-interest and material factors do not take us very far in understanding it; the evolving international normative structure does.

Chapter Six

Peru's 2000 Elections: Domestic Politics as an International Affair

The Peruvian 2000 elections were monitored practically by only three missions, one domestic and two international: *Transparencia* (Transparency), National Democratic Institute/Carter Center (NDI/CC), and OAS. Nevertheless, the limited number of monitoring organizations was compensated by the depth of their work—which was made possible by the existence of an IEM TAN. Unlike the previous three monitoring experiences analyzed in this work, the Peruvian electoral process was disapproved by poll watchers. But what is more relevant for my purposes here is the extent to which the Peruvian government accepted the activist role played by the monitoring organizations.

The attitude of the Fujimori regime might be related to two features that distinguish the Peruvian case from the other three analyzed before. On the one hand, the framing of the international monitoring of the 2000 elections of the Andean country was different from the other ones, comprising features that previously would have been thought of as antinomic. Thus, if the monitoring of the 1988 Chilean plebiscite was seen mainly as a human rights issue, the international observation of the 1990 Nicaraguan elections was framed in the context of a regional peace process, and the monitoring of the 1994 electoral process in Mexico brought to the forefront state sovereignty issues, the work done by international observers in Peru in 2000 was framed squarely within the country's democratic transition. Notably, though, as the Peruvian case makes clear, by the end of the twentieth century a democratic transition was no longer seen as a "domestic" affair. Domestic elections had become international events.[1] The normative structure of the Western Hemisphere was indeed still operating towards the beginning of the twentieth-first century.

On the other hand, the regime that emerged in the Andean country in the 1990s was distinctive in its own manner. It was not exceptional in the way the Pinochet regime was in Chile, nor did it feature the continuity in political practice the Sandinista government did in Nicaragua, nor did it have the sophistication of a well-institutionalized political regime, like the Mexican one in the 1990s. In a sense, the Peruvian regime of the 1990s presented a mixture of the three situations, but it was characterized by a rather cyclical pattern.[2] Let's consider this issue briefly.

In 1925 Stanford political scientist Graham Stuart noted: "Peru at present time presents the curious picture of a South American republic without political parties."[3] At the time Stuart wrote, Peru's incipient party system had collapsed; under the authoritarian *oncenio* (eleven-year rule) of President Augusto B. Leguía, Peru's traditional political parties had actually ceased to exist—and with them what was known as the Aristocratic Republic.[4] Ironically, though, what would become the most important political force in Peru during the twentieth century, the American Popular Revolutionary Alliance (APRA), emerged during the Leguía administration. Formed in 1924 in Mexico City by intellectual Víctor Raúl Haya de la Torre, APRA advocated a planned economy, the nationalization of foreign companies, the unity of American indigenous peoples, and the end of US imperialism. Although its nationalist and anti-imperialist stance gained APRA a large following among Indians, the lower classes, and intellectuals, it was to remain in the opposition for 61 years.

Thus, 43 years after Stuart wrote, a period during which democratic and dictatorial regimes alternated, the military once more deposed an elected government, this time the one headed by Fernando Belaúnde Terry. Although the regime did not ban political parties, the party system obviously did not fare well under the military government. Nevertheless, a decade later and after protracted negotiations, it ended up negotiating its exit—and Belaúnde returned to the presidency. Nevertheless, after both his administration (1980–1985) and that of his Aprista successor Alan García, (1985–1990) showed a dismal performance, the political system was again in disarray. By the end of ten years of democratic life, what Stuart wrote in 1925 was valid again: "[I]n the case of Peru to-day, both critic and apologist agree that the old political parties are bankrupt."[5] Hence, *Cambio 90* (Change 90), a hurriedly formed organization, took outsider Alberto Fujimori to the presidency in 1990. Two years later, Fujimori dissolved congress, intervened in the judiciary, and suspended the 1979 Constitution.

As the previous sketch suggests, Peru's political life during the twentieth century indeed had a cyclical pattern to it. As Belaúnde himself would write in 2000: "The [twentieth] century has passed and in half of it constitutional order was respected and in the other it was interrupted. Such is the drama we have lived."[6] But the cyclical pattern was not reduced to military regimes alternating with civilian ones; it was also related to the ups and downs of the generally weak party system. This combination, of course, constituted fertile soil for an authoritarian tradition, a tradition which reached its culmination with Fujimori's decade-long rule.[7]

In order to show how these two distinguishing features (the framing of the monitoring exercise, and the recurrent character of the country's political life) impacted upon the Peruvian 2000 electoral process, I proceed in the following manner in this chapter. In the first section I briefly outline one cycle of Peru's domestic structure: the one that started when the constitutional order was interrupted by the military, and ended with the ascent of Alberto Fujimori to the Presidency. In the second I deal with the advent of Fujimorism, emphasizing its "anti-politics" discourse. In the third section, I review the construction of a "competitive authoritarian" regime under Fujimori. Finally, in the fourth I consider in detail the monitoring of the 2000 presidential elections, paying particular attention to the coordinated work of the three main monitoring missions. As in previous chapters, the character of the Peruvian political regime, and the impact international observers might have had on it are secondary to my argument. To reiterate: this work is not about democracy; it is about how the regional discourse on human rights and representative government, as instantiated in the monitoring practice, partially altered traditional conceptions of state sovereignty—a process that, I claim, culminated in the Peruvian 2000 elections.

This chapter then shows the extent to which the WHI had contributed to a new understanding of sovereignty in the Americas at the dusk of the twentieth century. But as the continental constitutional structure entails, state sovereignty is a Janus-faced property. That is why its redefinition was accompanied by the consolidation of the right to democratic governance. The Peruvian case thus shows that both the rights of a state in the international system, and the political regime it adopts, had in fact become thoroughly intertwined by 2000. This of course does not mean that the democratic entitlement has been effectively enacted (that "truly democratic" regimes have been established as a result of this norm), as this and many other instances make clear. What is relevant for my argument here, though, is that what used to be considered a domestic affair is not anymore.

Furthermore, this chapter also drives home the point that sovereignty had become increasingly "destatized" in the last years of the last century; as will become clear below, IEM TAN activists were considered legitimate players in what used to be a states-only game. Peru's domestic structure was of course an important intervening variable in the consolidation of

IEM, in what this practice implied in terms of the two-fold meaning of state sovereignty, and in the process by which non-state actors gained recognition as valid players in the sovereignty game. Without the well developed and internationally-minded civil society the Andean country possessed by the mid-1990s, the 2000 international monitoring experience would not have shown so clearly the changes operated in the international system.

PERU'S DOMESTIC STRUCTURE BEFORE FUJIMORI: THE LAST CYCLE

On 3 October 1968, army general Juan Velasco Alvarado led a coup, ousting President Belaúnde. The plotters then constituted themselves into the Revolutionary Government of the Armed Forces (GRFA), which, for the standards of the time and the region, became an atypical dictatorship. In the first place, it had a relatively benign character. The GRFA, as noted, did not suppress political parties, nor did it repress workers' unions, or engage in widespread human rights violations. Furthermore, the military adopted many of the progressive and statist positions advanced by Haya de la Torre's APRA, and developed a nationalist ideology centered on national integration.[8] Thus, one of its first actions was to expropriate the assets of the US-based International Petroleum Company. Moreover, the military regime undertook a series of radical and populist measures, such as the recognition of the equality of women, land reform, the imposition of price controls, and the seizure of foreign-owned landed estates. The military regime also attempted to organize civil society along corporatist lines.[9] Furthermore, the Peruvian junta pursued an active policy toward the Soviet bloc.

Nevertheless, the military regime failed both at garnering popular support and at reactivating the economy. Instead, by the early 1970s Peru was undergoing an unprecedented economic crisis. Thus, in August 1975 another coup took place. Commanders of the military regions toppled General Velasco, replacing him with Army Commander and War Minister General Francisco Morales Bermúdez. The new leader immediately announced the initiation of a "second phase" in the "Peruvian Revolution." It was during this second phase of the military regime that the return to a civilian government was devised and negotiated (though not pacted). Along with a pronounced shift to the right in its economic policy, the government initiated a process of political opening.[10] It also attempted to start a dialogue with APRA, and with Acción Popular, Belaúnde's party. Belaúnde himself was allowed to return from his exile in the United States, which he did in 1976.

The formal statement of the return to a democratic regime took place in 1977. In February, General Morales announced the government's intention to hold elections for a Constituent Assembly, which would draft a new constitution. After Belaúnde rejected the government's rapprochement, calling instead for the immediate restoration of the civilian regime, APRA became the government's privileged interlocutor—as well as the military's first choice as successor.

But APRA was not the only actor the military regime had to negotiate with during its sometimes equivocal withdrawal process. Peru's active popular sector, and some of the historically well-organized leftist groups, were in no mood to simply accept the timetable and conditions advanced by the discredited military government.[11] Similarly, the Carter administration, through its embassy in Lima, sent clear messages to the military government opposing any derailment of the democratization process.[12] Thus, in July 1977 the popular sectors, with the backing of both APRA and Acción Popular, organized a highly successful national strike, forcing the government to speed up the transition process. Ten days later, the government announced that the elections to the Constituent Assembly would take place in June 1978.[13] True to its oppositional stand, Acción Popular refused to participate. APRA, on the other hand, was the main beneficiary of the limited electoral process. It won the largest share of votes, 35.4 percent, followed by the various leftist groups, which together received about another third of the total vote.[14]

With the biggest block in the Constituent Assembly, and Haya de la Torre as its president, the nationalist party and its leader became critical actors in the transition process. Haya de la Torre would have likely become the next president had he not died shortly after the Constituent assembly concluded its task. The new constitution was signed in July 1979, and elections were held in May 1980. Due in part to the internal strife that engulfed APRA after the death of its historic leader, and despite the open governmental support APRA's candidate received, Belaúnde was returned to the presidency with 45 percent of the vote.[15] Thus, being a process initiated by the military, but under strong societal pressure, the Peruvian process falls somewhere in between what Alfred Stepan calls redemocratization led by "Military-as-Institution," and "Society-led Regime Termination."[16]

Belaúnde's second government was inaugurated on 29 July 1980. Soon after taking office, he moved to distance his administration from the preceding one. Thus, he returned to their previous owners some newspapers that had been confiscated by the military, and adopted a still more liberal economic policy. Unfortunately, the new Belaúnde administration was soon immersed in a most unfavorable international and domestic context. On the external front, and due in part to the free-market policies his government had implemented, Peru's imports increased substantially, thus negatively impacting the trade account. Aggravating the external environment, the prices of Peru's major export commodities experienced a major drop. Moreover, the higher interest rate associated with the international debt crisis of the early 1980s made the Peruvian external economic situation untenable. On the domestic front, along with the domestic economic crisis came the consolidation of the recently formed terrorist organization *Sendero Luminoso* (Shining Path) as the chief threat to the state. This last development not only constituted itself as a menace to the social stability, but also as a drain of scarce state resources and, more importantly, as a hazard to the permanence of the democratic regime.

Nevertheless, Belaúnde was able to keep the military from taking power once more, and managed to make a democratic transfer of power—the first time this had happened at least since 1912. The transfer was remarkable also because Belaúnde's successor belonged to APRA, being the first time the party founded in the time of Leguía's *oncenio* came to hold power. Led by the young and charismatic Alan García, APRA had been able to survive the internal strife that engulfed it in the aftermath of its founder's death six years earlier. Appealing mainly to the unorganized poor, García obtained an impressive electoral victory—and embarked on a project that in many aspects seemed a replay of the Alvarado regime. Thus, he imposed price controls, implemented protectionist measures in Peru's foreign trade, and adopted a redistributionist rhetoric.[17] Furthermore, García announced that his government would not devote more than 10 percent of its export earnings to service its debt, and later nationalized the banking system.

Although García's heterodox policies initially seemed to have worked, they ended up being a failure. Real wages suffered greatly as a hyperinflationary spiral (reaching 7,650 percent annually) set on towards the end of García's administration, and the Peruvian economy contracted by 25 percent between 1988 and 1990. Furthermore, *Sendero Luminoso* and other terrorist organizations such as the Movimiento Revolucionario Tupac Amaru (MRTA) ran rampant during the first-ever Aprista administration, exposing the frailness of the country's political system. Toward the end of his mandate, García was repudiated even by his own party. Thus, as Steven Levitsky has noted, "By the late 1980s, all of Peru's political parties, including the United Left and APRA, had lost the capacity to attract broad-based support in a society that remained highly stratified along racial and sociocultural lines."[18] In this political environment, García resorted to a desperate political tactic: he supported outsider Alberto Kenya Fujimori to succeed him.[19]

THE ADVENT OF FUJIMORISM, OR THE DECADE OF "ANTI-POLITICS"

Fujimori, an agricultural engineer who had been president of La Molina Agrarian University, was mostly unknown in the Peruvian political scene before 1990. The son of Japanese immigrants, he decided to run for the presidency in 1990 by forming a loose organization called *Cambio 90,* which he made up of friends from academic and business circles.[20] Fujimori built his public image by differentiating himself both from the discredited political class, and from his main rival in the electoral process, writer Mario Vargas Llosa, who ran as the candidate of the also newly formed *Frente Democrático* (Democratic Front). Fujimori campaigned against ideological programs, traditional politicians, and the *partidocracia* (partidocracy) they had erected. His discourse was thus built around the idea of "anti-politics," arguing that what Peru needed was simply "honesty, technology, and hard work"—as his campaign slogan read. Capitalizing on his Japanese ancestry, he also portrayed himself as a hard-working underdog, alien to the white elite that Vargas Llosa and the traditional political class represented. In this Fujimori meant what he said, as his founding political allies indeed came from a variety of provinces (in contrast to the Lima-based elite who had traditionally ruled Peru), and from diverse racial and cultural backgrounds.[21] Furthermore, in contrast to the not very popular "shock therapy" that Vargas Llosa was advocating to rid the country of its economic crisis, Fujimori offered a more gradual way out of the crisis, one based on honesty, hard work, and efficiency.[22]

Fujimori gave the first surprise when he made it to the runoff by capturing 24.6 of the vote in the first-round of the elections, with Vargas Llosa coming in first with 27.6 percent but without surpassing the necessary 50 percent to become president-elect. In the second-round he received only 33.9 percent of the votes, while Fujimori, who had managed to exploit the Aprista and leftist voters' distrust of conservative Vargas Llosa, received 56.6 percent of the votes.[23] Despite his impressive personal victory, Fujimori's coalition lacked a majority in Congress. He was actually the first civilian president since the first Belaúnde administration who lacked a legislative majority.[24] This adverse situation only increased the resentment of the maverick president against the political establishment. Fujimori embarked then on a campaign to discredit Peru's political institutions such as Congress and the Judiciary.[25] Simultaneously, the president initiated a covert alliance with the army and the intelligence sectors, thanks to his main advisor and intelligence chief: Vladimiro Montesinos (more on this later).[26]

In the meantime, Fujimori launched a personal crusade against the political class, presenting it as the chief obstacle for the changes the country needed. In taking on this task, Fujimori was building on the strong presidentialist and centralist Peruvian tradition. Thus, the domestic structure in which the 2000 monitoring experience would take place comes close, again following Risse-Kappen, to "state-controlled" ones. In this type, as noted in previous chapters, political institutions are highly centralized and the executive power is patently strong, whereas intermediate organizations are generally weak.[27]

Fujimori's transformative project, though, went beyond exploiting his country's customary practice of concentrating power in Lima. His political project was based on the twin pillars of personalism and lack of institutionalization, which to some extent was facilitated by the weakness of the Peruvian party system.[28] Although flawed, the political regime he inherited after a decade of the country's return to democracy at least met the minimum procedural requirements to be considered a democracy. But the regime Fujimori ended up building quickly deteriorated into what Steven Levitsky and Lucan Way call "competitive authoritarian regimes." In these regimes, "formal democratic institutions are widely viewed as the principal means of obtaining and exercising political authority [but nevertheless] Incumbents violate those rules so often and to such an extent . . . that the regime fails to meet conventional minimum standards of democracy."[29]

Fujimori's Peru would then be an instance of "competitive authoritarianism." As the narrative below will show, Peru in the 1990s met the four requirements of this kind of regime: 1) allowing foreign observers; 2) closing down legislatures; 3) subordinating of the judiciary to the executive; and 4) attempting to control the media.[30] Fujimori's path to build a competitive authoritarian regime was simple: a self-coup.

FUJIMORI'S COMPETITIVE AUTHORITARIANISM

Claiming to intend to improve Peru's democratic system by making it more direct and efficient, on 5 April 1992 Fujimori dissolved Congress, intervened the judiciary, and assumed dictatorial powers.[31] With the coup, as Carlos Iván Degregori has noted, "Fujimori delivered the second great surprise in less than two years. But most surprising was the massive support of public opinion, which according to surveys bordered 80 percent in all socio-economic levels all over the country."[32] Domestic support for the suspension of the constitutional order contrasted with the unanimous condemnation Fujimori's desperate measure elicited abroad. Thus, for instance, resorting to Resolution 1080, the day after the self-coup the OAS

Permanent Council called for an ad hoc ministerial meeting. The meeting took place on 13 April 1992, and in it the ministers unanimously condemned the political maneuver and called for the "urgent reestablishment" of democratic constitutional order in Peru.[33]

Faced with these contradictory responses, Fujimori immediately embarked on a campaign to persuade both fronts that the measures just taken were necessary to fight Peru's two most pressing predicaments: terrorism and hyperinflation. Beneath this logic, of course, lay the claim that Peru's traditional political class was the real obstacle to solving Peru's problems—a logic that the country's erratic political life made sound plausible to the general public. Fujimori thus presented his actions as the only way to maintain political stability.[34] Nevertheless, the ascending right to democratic governance in the hemisphere was not fertile ground for Fujimori's reasoning. The history of the continent was full with supposedly well-meaning presidents who had seized more than their fair share of power early on, only to end up becoming dictators. Thus, international pressure did not recede, and Fujimori was forced to attend an OAS meeting the following month in Bahamas, where he promised to restore the constitutional order.[35] Later in 1992, Fujimori called for elections for a "Democratic Constituent Congress."

After his self-coup, Fujimori put together a new organization in order to contend in the legislative elections: *Nueva Mayoría* (New Majority). As in *Cambio 90,* Fujimori was the undisputed leader of the new movement, thus guaranteeing that should its candidates make it to congress, they would unconditionally support his proposals.[36] Right after the coup Fujimori also set out on a radical restructuring of the executive power. The most significant one was the creation of the Ministry of the Presidency, which became a veritable mammoth in the Peruvian public administration. By 1998, this ministry—which became the hub from which the president launched a series of populist programs—controlled over 20 percent of the country's national budget.[37] Not as conspicuous as the Ministry of the Presidency, the National Intelligence Service (SIN) acquired unknown powers in Peru's history. Headed by Fujimori's top aide Vladimiro Montesinos, a former member of the military who had been convicted in 1976 for selling Peruvian military secrets to the United States, in his role as "legal adviser" to the president, the SIN became a massive governmental operation, with thousands of agents and a myriad of targets.[38]

The elections for the Constituent Congress were set for November 1992, with the whole country taken as an electoral district with 80 representatives. Two months before the elections, Abimael Guzmán, *Sendero Luminoso*'s leader, was arrested. The seizure of the terrorist leader was an immense victory for Fujimori; for most Peruvians, it validated the president's extraordinary moves five months earlier. Not surprisingly, Fujimori's *Nueva Mayoría/Cambio 90* came out victorious at the November elections, obtaining 44 out of the 80 seats in the new legislative body. As a result of the commitments Fujimori had acquired with the OAS in Bahamas, his government asked the regional organization to send an observer mission to the first post-coup electoral process. The OAS accepted, sending a large, 228-member mission under the direction of Secretary-General Baena Soares himself.

The OAS role in this utmost delicate situation was not regarded favorably by Fujimori's opponents. It was not that they were against the presence of foreign observers on sovereignty grounds. As Rafael Roncagliolo, Secretary General of *Transparencia,* an election-monitoring NGO put it, "the opposition always asked for international monitoring of the elections [and the government] was not opposed either . . . because Fujimori went to Bahamas to give satisfactions to the OAS, so he made commitments which he needed to be blessed by the OAS."[39] The point for the critics of the regime was that the OAS was perceived as being complicit with the Fujimori administration. As César Landa, a law scholar at Peru's Catholic University and a Director of *Transparencia* explains:

> For many people outside the government Baena Soares played a rather distant role, in the sense of not wanting to receive or see many complaints being made. Of course, after the 92 coup, power was completely concentrated, so having enough evidence so as to properly make the formal complaint, which the OAS mission was practically requesting . . . [was very hard, and in addition] precisely that was the investigative task they [OAS observers] were supposed to have in the first place.[40]

According to Landa, the presence in 1992 of Baena Soares constituted, if not an explicit backing for the regime, at least "a way out" for Fujimori's legitimacy crisis.[41] The OAS report noted that "In general terms, the electoral process for the CCD [Constituent Democratic Congress] was accomplished in a satisfactory manner. . . . [and that] consequently it constituted an important step in the process of completely reestablishing the democratic institutions in Peru."[42]

The 1979 constitution was reestablished in January 1993, and Fujimori declared the constitutional head of state by the CCD. Beyond this back-to-normal move, the elected legislators set out to write a new constitutional text, which they finished in July 1993. The new fundamental law abolished one of the two chambers of congress, rendered the whole country an at-large 120-seat district, introduced the death sentence to convicted terrorists, and increased the president's powers. Furthermore, the 1993 Constitution featured what seemed to be an *ad hominem* amendment: it allowed for immediate reelection of the incumbent president for one additional term; the first electoral process to which this change applied was to take place in 1995.

Interestingly, despite what looked like Fujimori's unfettered control of the political initiative, when the new Constitution was put to a referendum on 31 October 1993, it was approved by a slim margin: only 52 percent of the electorate voted favorably. Once again, the OAS was present to observe the development of the voting process, once again Baena Soares was the mission's director—and once again the opposition was deeply dissatisfied with the regional organization's role.

This was in fact the third time since the self-coup that the OAS was present in Peru to observe an electoral process, the second one being the January 1993 municipal elections; in this short period, the opposition had come to be highly skeptical of the regional organization's contribution to the redemocratization process of the Andean country. This time, though, Baena Soares' team had at least raised some critical observations concerning the referendum.[43] The final report concluded that while

> The referendum has been carried out in an acceptable fashion and, in general, there were enough guarantees for the free expression of the political will of the citizens. . . . it is worth mentioning the necessary concern because of the occurrence of these restrictions [to individual and electoral guarantees] which had not taken place in the same number during the previous two electoral processes which the Organization observed in Peru.[44]

Despite the narrow margin by which the new constitution was approved, four years after his election Fujimori had achieved the ostensible objective of his "anti-politics" campaign: to spread the sense of deep distrust toward the country's political institutions. By 1994, 86 percent of the population asserted that they were politically independent. Not surprisingly, the 9 April 1995 presidential elections showed the electorate's strong preference for "independent" candidates—including the incumbent, of course—who received over 90 percent of the votes. Fujimori came first with 64 percent of the votes—the highest vote obtained by any president since 1950—thus obviating the need of a runoff.[45] Tellingly, the opposition chose a non-traditional politician to face Fujimori: former U.N. Secretary-General Javier Pérez de Cuellar. The diplomat ran for the

Unión por el Perú (UPP) coalition, and received 22.8 of the votes. UPP managed to elect 17 representatives; this bloc, however, being a diverse set of personalities lacking a party or program to coalesce around, soon disbanded.[46] More dramatic was the situation of APRA, Acción Popular, and the United Left coalition, which failed to obtain five percent of the vote and therefore lost their legal status.[47] The success of Fujimori's "anti-politics" crusade was unmistakable.[48]

Furthermore, Fujimori's electoral organization, *New Majority,* obtained 67 out of the 120 seats in the unicameral congress—which would subsequently become the president's rubber stamp.[49] Fujimori's frontal battle against terrorist groups, his successful anti-inflationary policies (which had brought inflation down to about 10 percent by 1994), and the 12.5 percent GDP growth rate in 1994—the highest in the world that year—undoubtedly contributed to Fujimori's and his allies' victory.[50]

As was to be expected, Peru's 1995 elections were again observed by the OAS. This time the regional organization's mission arrived in Peru farther in advance: two months before the elections (in contrast with about one month lead time on the previous three occasions). The mission started its activities with a small team, and on election day it had 70 observers present. In addition, 46 domestic observers from local NGOs such as *Transparencia* worked in tandem with the OAS mission. NDI also coordinated its activities with the OAS team.[51] Not surprisingly, given the OAS previous monitoring experiences in Peru since the self-coup, most of the opposition (APRA, Acción Popular, UPP) did not welcome the OAS intervention in the Peruvian electoral process. The reason, again, had to do with lack of trust in the regional organization. The opposition's misgivings about the OAS were such that a few days before the elections its leading candidates asked Fujimori to have the OAS mission leave the country (which did not happen).[52] The opposition perceived that the regional body had not been an unbiased actor on the previous occasions, particularly for not issuing explicit pronouncements indicating what had gone wrong in each of the electoral processes.[53]

The 1995 experience turned out to be somewhat different—but only to a point. Headed by Santiago Murray, an OAS official, the mission did an acceptable job in the opinion of independent observers. According to *Transparencia*'s Landa, Murray's position in 1995 was less complacent than those of Baena Soares in 1992 and 1993.[54] He notes, however, that in 1995 the Fujimori regime was stronger in terms of its domestic legitimacy, and that for that reason "Murray's task might have been more successful." Furthermore, Landa remarks that Murray's presence "allowed, thanks to the more consolidated domestic scenario, the electoral process to suffer no major incident, other than the complaints raised [by the opposition], which in any case did not alter the results."[55] Similarly, Roncagliolo notes that "there was great discontent with Murray among the opposition. We were also discontent, but with the difference that we did not blame that on Murray's person, but in the way OAS missions work." He explains:

> we were not unhappy with Murray, I personally am not unhappy with Murray, I am unhappy with the OAS, because Murray's reports had to go through the Secretary General [César Gaviria], who corrected them, and he had to discuss them with Beatriz Ramacciotti [Peru's representative in the OAS] . . . our quarrel was that if [the head of the mission] was a [Secretary General's office] bureaucrat, he had no autonomy.[56]

In the end, Roncagliolo points out, "the OAS played a traditional role: it did not issue communiqués; it just wrote a report at the end [of the process]."[57]

In contrast to previous reports, though, the one corresponding to the 1995 electoral process is more circumspect. Although it notes that the electoral process took place in an "atmosphere of tranquility," it does not refer to it as a great exercise in democratic practice or anything close to it. Moreover, the report records several minor problems during the campaign as well as on election day, such as the use of state resources in Fujimori's campaign and the distribution of electoral material.[58] But as the report notes, the difficulties present on election day "did not constitute a generalized factor that could have compromised the final development of the [electoral] process."[59] Especially important in this respect, as the report points out, was the role played by the National Electoral Jury (JNE), the highest electoral authority. By 1995, as the Latin American Studies Association observer mission noted, there still was "confidence in the autonomy and integrity" of the JNE.[60]

The 1995 elections, as noted, were also observed by Peruvians. In 1994, responding to the collapse of the Peruvian party system, a group of personalities created *Transparencia*.[61] Its purposes, as Roncagliolo recalls, were two: "first, to observe the 1995 elections . . . and second, which was very important for us, to develop a democratic culture, which is a permanent task . . . In 1994 there was a kind of . . . [collective] conscience that something like this needed to be done."[62] *Transparencia* agreed with the OAS mission in that the 1995 electoral process had been clean, and in that the JNE had played a decent role.[63] In the final analysis, as Peruvian Studies Institute's Martin Tanaka notes, "the 1995 elections gave Fujimori such an overwhelming triumph, that there was not much [to fight about] although certainly there were some problems."[64]

Fujimori's second term in office was nothing like the first one. Five years of anti-politics, shock-therapy, and mostly authoritarian government had transformed the Peruvian political economy. One feature, though, seemed to remain. On the economic front, the radical policies of Fujimori seemed to have ceased operating the wonders they had in the first years. Thus, if in the 1993–1995 period GDP growth averaged almost 8 percent, in the 1996–2000 period it went down to 3 percent. In 1996 only, GDP grew at 2.4 percent.[65] The economic problem thus seemed to be of a recurrent nature. In contrast, in the aftermath of the 1995 elections the predicament posed by terrorist organizations seemed to have been taken care of. Paradoxically, though, the effectiveness of Fujimori's heavy-handedness in this respect seemed to undermine the avowed indispensability of his rule. Not surprisingly, the president's approval rate drastically dropped during his second term. Whereas in the 1991–1996 period the average presidential approval was around 65 percent, between 1996–1998 it went down to 38 percent.[66]

In an ironic twist, the reemergence of the supposedly solved terrorist threat served as a boost to Fujimori's popularity. On 17 December 1996, a command of the MRTA took the Japanese Ambassador's house during a reception. Immediately after the incident, presidential popularity went up—and security climbed again to the top of the list of public concerns.[67] The terrorist group, as Maxwell Cameron has noted, "handed Fujimori a golden opportunity."[68] Four months later, on 22 April 1997, the army broke into the Ambassador's house, rescuing the hostages. The president's popularity gained between six and 12 percentage points as a result of the hostage crisis.[69]

By that time, Fujimori's scheme to run for a third term was well under way. On 23 August 1996, Congress had approved the "Authentic Interpretation" Law of Article 112 of the 1993 constitution, which in fact opened the way to Fujimori for a third term.[70] The new law proclaimed that since Fujimori's first presidential term was not regulated by the 1993 constitution, he was eligible to run for another five-year term. The seven-member Constitutional Tribunal, with three members signing and four abstaining, subsequently issued an opinion asserting that the new law was "not applicable" to Fujimori. But then Congress removed the three dissenting magistrates from the bench.

What was more remarkable about this process was that, for the first time since Fujimori's arrival to power, the governmental maneuvers elicited massive popular protests by students, workers and political parties.[71] Furthermore, by late 1996, a civic organization called *Foro Democrático* (Democratic Forum) decided to confront Fujimori on his own territory: it gathered over one and a half million signatures (more than the required 10 percent of registered voters) in order to put the issue to a national referendum. Once again, Congress intervened in order to uphold its pro-incumbent law. This time, the legislature passed a law stipulating that in addition to the percentage of signatures established by the 1993 constitution, the referendum initiative needed to count on the support of 48 members of Congress. Obviously, the government made sure that the initiative didn't get enough votes in Congress.[72]

It had thus become evident that the civil and political rights of the Peruvian people were being curtailed by the Fujimori regime. In addition to the ever-increasing presence of the government's intelligence services, it had come to exercise an excessive control over the mass media, particularly electronic ones. Thus, for instance, in September 1997 the government decided to go after one of the very few independent TV outlets: *Frecuencia Latina.* After stripping its Israeli-born owner, Baruch Ivcher, of his Peruvian nationality, the government, through the courts, managed to transfer the station to minority holders with close ties to intelligence chief Montesinos.[73] Similarly, the government created or co-opted eight tabloids (*prensa chicha*), which consistently not only supported governmental measures, but also maligned the opposition.

In the context of this deteriorating situation, municipal elections were held on 11 October 1998. Faithful to his practice of creating "disposable parties" (Steven Levitsky *dixit*), in March of that year Fujimori established *Vamos Vecino* (Let's Go, Neighbor). Within a few months of its establishment, the new organization's committees had emerged around the country. As Degregori notes: "Never had a Peruvian political party covered so rapidly the national territory, nor had it had so many resources to do it."[74] Making widespread use of state resources, *Vamos Vecino* performed reasonably well nationwide: it obtained 25.2 percent of the votes, coming second after the also recently formed electoral front *Somos Perú* (We Are Peru), which received 29.2 of the suffrage.[75]

As had become customary in the Fujimori regime, the OAS observed—for the fifth time—the 1998 electoral process. Its mission was headed again by Santiago Murray. In addition to a September 22–25 preliminary trip to Lima, the mission properly worked in Peru from October 1 to 13. It was a medium-sized mission, composed of 30 observers from 18 member states.[76] As on the previous occasions, the OAS delegation's assessment was fairly positive. As an election day press statement by Murray put it: "These elections constitute a political instance of unique importance . . . [because of] the strict fulfillment of duties and responsibilities of civic, political and public nature that correspond, respectively, to the various actors in the whole electoral process."[77] More to the point, the Mission's final report stated that "Bearing in mind the complexity of the elections, held simultaneously in 194 provinces and 1,618 districts, the electoral process generally obeyed the provisions governing its organization and conduct."[78] Nevertheless, the report once again noted some minor problems. As Murray put it, "The Peruvian electoral process has clearly been evolving favorably, and it is therefore important to consider the possibility of taking steps to avoid some of the problems observed in the October 11, 1998, elections."[79] Among these problems were the training of poll workers, education programs for citizen participation, and the training of party monitors in order to "strengthen the role of the parties as channels of society's demands."[80] By this time, the constant presence of the regional body in the Andean country had increased the sensitivity toward its monitoring activities and had produced a tight relationship between some of its members and electoral observers both in Peru and in Washington.

Interestingly, the OAS final report of the 1998 elections mentions that the Peruvian NGO *Transparencia* had over 10,000 observers in the 1998 elections, and notes that "the domestic observation by the civil association *Transparencia* was very significant."[81] By 1998, both groups had indeed established a close relationship. As Roncagliolo observes, in 1998 "we [*Transparencia*] had a sort of idyll with the OAS. I remember that in '98 Murray and I, at his request, spent all day together, covering the voting places, always the OAS appearing with *Transparencia,* in public statements, in everything. And there were irregularities—and we pointed them out."[82] It was clear that a IEM TAN was consolidated by 1998.

TOWARD THE 2000 ELECTIONS

With the "Authentic Interpretation" law, and the OAS-certified 1998 municipal elections behind, Fujimori's drive to a third presidential term started. To boast the democratic commitment of his regime, that same year Fujimori signed with his neighbors the "Andean's Community Commitment to Democracy," by means of which the four Andean presidents committed their countries to a democratic form of government, and instructed their foreign ministers to write a protocol modeled after OAS Resolution 1080. But that high-minded act was accompanied by more prosaic ones. Thus, in 1999 Fujimori substantially increased public spending, surpassing both the "fiscal prudence" spending limits congress had set, as well as the expenditure levels agreed on with the International Monetary Fund.[83]

On 27 December 1999, Fujimori officially presented his candidacy, backed by an alliance of four electoral movements: *Cambio 90, Nueva Mayoría, Vamos Vecino,* and *Frente Independiente Nacional Perú 2000.*

The alliance was called *Perú 2000.*[84] Interestingly, after 10 years in office Fujimori had not established a more permanent political organization. His "anti-politics" discourse might have been part of the reason why he did not attempt to create a stable political party of his own, but perhaps more important in this respect was the autocratic control he was able to exert on his "disposable parties." Thus, for instance, Fujimori used to rely on focus groups to decide who the candidates of his support groups should be.[85] Furthermore, as Levitsky notes, he relied "on personalistic appeals and periodic spending projects" to boost his popularity.[86] Not surprisingly, the mammoth Ministry of the Presidency, created only a few years before, became his chief electoral machinery.

Indeed, the use of state resources to back Fujimori's candidacy only increased in 2000.[87] But it was not just spending and clientelist measures that Fujimori resorted to. By the time of his third presidential campaign, Fujimori had also managed to have almost complete control over the media and the judiciary. Thus, according to a *Transparencia* survey, TV stations gave the president-candidate 112 minutes of air time weekly, whereas the other eight presidential candidates combined got 49 minutes during the same period.[88] Similarly, many judges—up to the Supreme Court—were caught in the corruption scheme developed by Fujimori and his top adviser and intelligence chief Montesinos.[89] Thus, for instance, after the daily *El Comercio* broke the news that about one million signatures had been forged in order to register Fujimori's candidacy, the JNE ruled, without conducting a rigorous investigation, that the issue did not affect his nomination.[90] Furthermore, the president's contempt for civil liberties was not limited to his country. In July 1999 his government announced that it would no longer recognize the jurisdiction of the Inter-American Court of Human Rights.[91]

It was in this context that the 2000 Peruvian elections were to take place—and that its monitoring by domestic and international observers acquired unprecedented salience.

As noted, *Transparencia* had been established six years earlier to observe the 1995 elections. Interestingly, though, the IEM TAN played an important role in the emergence of the first national monitoring organization in Peru. As Rafael Roncagliolo, its Secretary General, puts it, "we knew about the Philippine experience, about the great front [the Command for the *No*] in Chile . . . about Mexico, Alianza Cívica."[92] *Transparencia* also established contacts with NDI and other US organizations. As Roncagliolo recalls, at first "we didn't even know NDI existed. We wanted to bring people from *Alianza Cívica,* from *Participa* [from Chile]," but then *Transparencia*'s founders got in touch with NDI, and this organization ended up playing an instrumental role in helping them bring activists from other countries to Peru.[93]

Five years later, *Transparencia* would become a major player in the electoral process. For the monitoring organization, what was at stake in the 2000 presidential elections was nothing less than the country's return to a democratic regime.[94] Consequently, it started its work early on. In August 1999, *Transparencia* announced that it would undertake a survey of the widely questioned electoral registry. Four months later, it signed an agreement with *El Comercio* in order to carry out the project jointly. The report was presented on 1 March 2000.[95] As expected, the auditing project discovered several deficiencies in the electoral registry, such as dead people still appearing in it, as well as outdated information. The report found the registry to be "obsolete," and suggested several measures in order to correct its shortcomings.[96] This and other critical positions quickly turned *Transparencia* into an organization *non grata* for the regime. As Landa notes, Fujimori was willing to make concessions to foreign observers, "but not to domestic ones, only to international ones, because, in the final analysis, domestic observers were for him an internal problem, a conflict [which he perceived to exist] between the government and the opposition . . . even though the observation task is not in favor of one side or the other."[97] Not surprisingly, the *prensa chicha* included the civic organization among its targets. Thus, for instance, on 11 April the daily *Expreso* claimed that "Transparencia, in a biased manner, blew up its denouncements in order to tarnish an absolutely clean [electoral] process."[98]

Nevertheless, *Transparencia*'s close association with the two most important organizations monitoring the Peruvian 2000 electoral process, NDI/CC and OAS, provided it with some cover from governmental attacks. At *Transparencia*'s request, the government agreed to send out an invitation to the CC—which on the other hand had announced that it was going to Peru even without an invitation.[99] Thus, by the time the joint NDI/CC mission arrived in Peru for a pre-electoral assessment, *Transparencia* had already started to make unfavorable remarks concerning the fairness of the electoral process. Soon afterwards, though, the NDI/CC mission joined *Transparencia* in issuing critical reports. Thus, for instance, in its first report, dated 3 December 1999, the NDI/CC mission noted that both the institutional framework and the pre-election environment suffered from shortcomings that required "concerted and sustained efforts" in order for the April 2000 electoral process to meet international standards. The report also made critical observations on the lack of equitable access to the media, and media bias; on the harassment of candidates and domestic observers; on the misuse of state resources; on the Peruvian Judiciary, and on the administration of the elections.[100]

The Fujimori administration paid close attention to the joint mission's remarks. As Patrick Merloe, NDI's Senior Associate and Director of Programs on Election and Political Processes, and member of the first delegation, recalls, "we were completely embraced, by the government and the electoral authorities; there was no question about our being welcome in the country . . . the government decided to engage, and so they came to us, they had discussions here in Washington, they took our recommendations, issued a response, recommendation by recommendation."[101] The governmental cooperation with NDI/CC contrasted with its attitude toward domestic observers, and toward *Transparencia* in particular. According to Roncagliolo, the government's strategy was to "isolate" *Transparencia* from the foreign observers, since in the government's view "we were the bad guys of the movie."[102] Roncagliolo's account seems to be on target. As Merloe puts it: "I remember [prime minister] Bustamante coming to visit in December, shortly after the delegation, and engaging in a conversation . . . attacking the credibility of *Transparencia*." And in actual fact, Merloe agrees in that the government tried to keep the joint mission apart from *Transparencia:* "it was a strong tactic that they took."[103]

Thus, the joint mission returned to Peru in February, and noted that the pre-electoral environment not only had not improved, but had actually gotten worse. The Fujimori administration nevertheless continued to heed, at least formally, the delegation's advice. After the second report noted that "the electoral process is still marred by serious problems, and it is this delegation's assessment that in many respects conditions have worsened since the first delegation issued its report in early December 1999," and issued seven specific recommendations, the Peruvian government established a "hotline" for election complaints, and named prosecutors for each electoral region.[104]

The joint mission's clout undoubtedly had a lot to do with its semi-official nature. Thus, for instance, on 11 February, the State Department issued a press statement entitled "Findings of NDI/Carter Center on Peruvian Electoral Process." The communiqué established: "The United States Government welcomes and essentially concurs with the recommendations issued today by the National Democratic Institute and the Carter Center on pre-election conditions in Peru."[105] Eleven days later, Peru's Prime Minister Alberto Bustamante sent a letter to NDI's president Kenneth Wollack thanking him for having met him on his recent trip to Washington, and noting that "I and the government welcomed the recent recommendations from the NDI/Carter Center on ways to improve the process." Furthermore, the prime minister committed himself to "act quickly to address the matters raised" in the last delegation's report.[106] And a week later, Peru's ambassador in Washington Alfonso Rivero sent another letter to Wollack remarking that "Following the report from the first NDI/Carter Center delegation, the government acted quickly" to attend its recommendations.[107]

But the measures the Fujimori regime was taking were marginal and did not fundamentally improve the pre-electoral conditions and environment. Thus, on 9 March the Clinton administration issued another press statement, in which it called on the Peruvian government to "Continue cooperation with the NDI/Carter Center, OAS" and other international and domestic observer organizations.[108] But the influence of the NDI/CC mission was not limited to the US government. As Merloe recalls, the mission's critical comments on the Peruvian electoral process "helped to shape the attitude of a number of governments, not just the United States' . . . The Canadian government also made some statements that were quite similar, and we worked very closely with the delegation of European ambassadors . . . the decision of the European Union to send a delegation was based upon our recommendation that they should do so."[109]

Despite the close attention the international community was paying to the Peruvian electoral process, the Andean government failed to act decisively to improve the situation. Consequently, in its 14 March report, the NDI/CC mission noted that "Irreparable damage to the integrity of the election process has already been done." But it also noted that "improvements can and should be made," and offered 11 recommendations. This third highly critical report seemed to have been too much for the Fujimori regime's patience. Thus, on 18 March Francisco Tudela, Fujimori's former Foreign Minister, and his running mate in the 2000 electoral contest, exploded, declaring to the press: "The Carter Center does not represent the government of the United States, nor its citizens, nor the OAS nor the UN . . . So, tell me, who the heck does it represent!."[110] The government began to distance itself from the joint mission. Thus, for instance, when in late March NDI's Wollack visited Lima, several government officials refused to meet with him. As the weekly *Caretas* put it, "It seems that the government realized that its efforts to convince international observers have no chance of succeeding . . . The new tactic consists of . . . keeping only the minimum indispensable of formalities . . . That is why Prime Minister Alberto Bustamante received on Monday the NDI-CC mission. That is the minimum indispensable."[111] And after the Clinton administration once more endorsed the NGOs report, the Peruvian ambassador in Washington expressed his disagreement with the US government's backing statement.[112]

The US support of the NDI/CC mission also provided cover for *Transparencia,* which had been working closely with the joint delegation. As the North American organizations' final report notes, "NDI and The

Carter Center are particularly grateful for *Transparencia's* commitment to serving as an informal coordinator between Peruvian and international election monitors."[113] The report also notes that "The sustained level of cooperation between Peruvian and international observers in Peru represented a model of the type of election observation that NDI and TCC advocate worldwide. Throughout the election process, the NDI/TCC mission and *Transparencia* provided each other with mutual support."[114] But *Transparencia* also counted on another important political cover: the one provided by the OAS mission. The three missions came to form a solid triangle the Peruvian government was unable to break. But it was more than that. The very character of the involvement of the OAS in Peru in 2000 was heavily influenced both by *Transparencia* and by the NDI/CC mission.

Since around mid-1999, *Transparencia* began to lobby the government and the JNE to invite foreign observers for the 2000 general elections. The monitoring group provided the government with a list of about 50 foreign monitoring organizations.[115] But the case of the OAS was special. Fujimori wanted the regional organization to send a mission, probably thinking, as a CC-member of the joint NDI/CC 2000 mission who asked to remain unnamed put it, "that the OAS was a do-nothing organization." But precisely for this reason there was widespread opposition both in Lima and in Washington to the OAS sending another mission to Peru.[116] As Roncagliolo recollects, "In Washington there was a lot of controversy around the issue of whether an OAS mission should come to Peru or not . . . the pressure to have a mission came from the government, not from the opposition. Because the opposition did not trust the OAS."[117]

Thus, both NDI and *Transparencia* became involved in negotiating the presence of an OAS mission in Peru. According to Merloe, "NDI was put in a rather awkward situation with a number of decision makers, policy makers turning to us and asking, 'should the OAS be there? Should the OAS not be there?' And our opinion was that the OAS should be there, it should be forceful, and credible and so on, and so on. So . . . we lobbied for their presence."[118] After the intervention of the US ambassador to the OAS, Luis Lauredo, and of Roger Noriega, the chief international staff person for Senator Jesse Helms, there was an agreement that the United States would support the sending of a OAS mission if it had certain characteristics, foremost among which was that its chief be a high-level leader from outside the intergovernmental organization. Other requirements included that it arrive in Peru well in advance of election day, that it issue reports during the process, and that it coordinate its work with domestic observers such as *Transparencia*.[119]

The list of requirements established by the US government was consulted both with NDI and *Transparencia.* As Roncagliolo recalls,

> there were two negotiations with the OAS . . . an official negotiation, and an informal, parallel negotiation we had with them . . . Sometimes, we dealt directly with Gaviria, but mainly we dealt with the ambassadors, with [Luis] Lauredo [U.S. ambassador to the OAS], with the Canadians, there was a very intense negotiation, and then with the Peruvian opposition. But the Peruvian opposition doesn't get involved in negotiating the coming of the [OAS] mission; we did participate in negotiations, all informal, also with people from the OAS' UPD, and in addition we had a very fluid relationship with Santiago Murray.[120]

Thus, NDI's Program Officer Linda Frey recalls an early February 2000 visit by Roncagliolo and other *Transparencia* members in which "they came up here [Washington] and we actually kind of hosted them and set up a series of meetings . . . we went jointly to these meetings with Roger Noriega and with Luis Lauredo, and basically, some of the ideas about how the OAS mission should be structured also came from *Transparencia,* ideas that Rafael had."[121]

Although UPD's Executive Coordinator Elizabeth Spehar does not accept that the OAS negotiated the characteristics of the OAS mission with *Transparencia,* recognizing only that the "extremely difficult electoral process" led the OAS to name an independent person as head of the mission, she does acknowledge that "many organizations, even many governments, many people thought that the OAS should not go to Peru to observe."[122] Furthermore, Spehar agrees with Roncagliolo and Merloe in that the widespread distrust among the Peruvian opposition and the rarefied pre-electoral environment "made clear that it was going to be a very visible and very critical electoral observation . . . and therefore what was needed was a person from outside the organization, with a lot of prestige and political recognition in the hemisphere to carry out this mission."[123]

Eduardo Stein, a former foreign minister of Guatemala, and more importantly, not an OAS bureaucrat, was chosen by OAS Secretary General César Gaviria to head the organization's Electoral Observation Mission (EOM). The day Stein accepted the OAS Secretary General's offer, he went to the NDI headquarters in Washington to discuss the state of affairs in the Peruvian electoral process. By that time, the joint mission had issued several reports and was well aware of the difficult task that Stein was about to embark on. NDI pledged to collaborate closely with the OAS mission.[124]

Transparencia, on its part, once it knew that Stein had accepted, started a lobbying campaign with the Peruvian opposition parties. As Roncagliolo recalls, the organization objective was not only that the opposition come to accept Stein, "but our argument was: if this mission has certain characteristics, it is to our advantage that this mission come, it is better to have a mission here and then have it leave . . . than not having any mission at all."[125] Transparencia's effort was only marginally successful. To make matters worse, soon after his arrival in Lima on 2 March, Stein went to see Fujimori, and afterwards made a statement which the opposition considered to be too lenient to the regime. The morning after the statement, Roncagliolo recalls, he went to Stein's hotel and told him: "Eduardo, you have achieved what nobody had done: the total unity of the opposition—and not against the OAS's past, but against you."[126] Roncagliolo seemed to be right on that. As Stein would later recognize: "The first two [opposition] candidates I spoke to agreed on one thing: that we should get out of here."[127]

Nevertheless, as Roncagliolo points out, "that statement helped to get Fujimori . . . put all of his confidence on the OAS, because on the media he used to say, 'the people from Transparencia are scoundrel, but [the people from] the OAS are good.'"[128] However, as time went by, the tone of the statements issued by Stein, as well as the mission's frequent reports made clear that his was not a conventional OAS mission. In this way, he started to gain the confidence not only of the opposition parties, but also of the general public.[129] Furthermore, on this occasion the OAS had a large an multidisciplinary team: it counted over 100 members distributed in 12 regions across Peru.[130] The team included a "Technical Mission," in charge of two areas: 1) an analysis of the electoral processes, in order to identify areas where fraud could occur, and therefore make some suggestions, and 2) an evaluation of the computer system to be used for counting the votes.[131] As Stein saw it, the overall mission's purpose was "to find, in the most questioned issues, some emblematic elements with 'demonstrative' weight in order to recover the electorate's confidence in the electoral process." His technical team then focused on one of the most contested issues: the soundness of the computer system the National Office for Electoral Processes (ONPE), the office in charge of organizing and conducting the elections, was going to use to tabulate the votes on election day. In this case, the objective "was to demonstrate, by means of testing software program . . . that there was nothing to hide."[132] Although the electoral office had agreed to collaborate with the OAS mission, it failed to deliver.

By the end of March, the mission's main concerns—in addition to the computer system—were the use of government resources in Fujimori's campaign, and the lack of equitable access to the mass media, specially to open

TV.[133] Hence, on its third report, dated 23 March, Stein noted that two weeks from the end of the electoral campaigns, "unsettling conditions remain for carrying out of general elections which count on sufficient credibility," and called "on the government of Peru and other state organs" to send clear and unequivocal signals that could induce public confidence in the electoral process.[134]

The different disposition of the 2000 OAS mission did not go unnoticed. As the weekly *Caretas* put it in late March: "Contrary to what many feared due to previous experiences, this time the OAS Electoral Observation Mission has turned out to be more independent and sharper than what both the government and the opposition expected. . . . It is true that initially, after a talk with candidate-President Fujimori, Stein issued some very lenient and even complicit comments. But that has changed."[135]

Nevertheless, the stance of the OAS EOM did not always please the opposition. Thus, after it issued its fourth report on 4 April, suggesting that the electoral process might still be viable, *Perú Posible*'s presidential candidate Alejandro Toledo declared: "if the OAS mission intends to legitimize a fraudulent process, it had better leave before April 9."[136] The next day, the OAS mission issued a communiqué stating: "Viability should not be confused with legitimacy. The Electoral Observer Mission has not legitimized beforehand a process which has not concluded."[137] Stein's position was that the OAS would monitor the electoral process as long as the opposition stayed in it.

The OAS mission's unique standing became a most interesting feature of the Peruvian electoral process. Its mostly critical comments, which concurred with those of *Transparencia* and NDI/CC, further reinforced the standing of these organizations. As Merloe notes, "it became more and more clear that there was a deliberate and systematic manipulation" on the government's part.[138] Or as Roncagliolo puts it: "We [*Transparencia*] were the first ones to question the process [then] the first NDI/CC mission arrived, and they were very hard. . . . So that when Stein arrived, this made his work easier, because he counted both on our reports and those of the NDI/CC mission. . . . So you cannot understand Stein if you don't put him side by side with the NDI/CC, who were, along with us, the harsh ones."[139]

Interestingly, though, the government did not change its attitude toward the OAS EOM the way it did toward the NDI/CC one. Thus, for instance, the day after the mission issued its fourth report, a candidate of the officialist *Perú 2000* noted that although Fujimori had accused foreign observer missions of conspiring against him, the OAS one was not included since it respected Peru's autonomy in electoral matters.[140] The government's generous opinion of the OAS mission was all the more remarkable given the unprecedented activist role it was playing. But as UPD's Spehar notes, "In the case of Peru, the situation was such, it was so complex, that the mission had to be more outspoken every time in its appreciations, with its criticisms, with its suggestions, because it considered that perhaps the only way to keep things going was to make them public."[141]

On election day (9 April), the three main monitoring missions, *Transparencia,* NDI/CC and the OAS EOM coordinated their work. The domestic group deployed over 19,000 observers around the country, and carried out a quick count that turned out to be of paramount importance on election night. On election day, NDI/CC had a small "study team," not an observer mission, which coordinated its work with the other main monitoring organizations.[142] The OAS delegation, for its part, observed about 800 voting tables.[143] The strategies employed by the three missions were complementary; thus, as the OAS report notes, "*Transparencia* representatives dispersed to various voting tables, but as they reported to the [OAS] EOM, each of them had to obtain the results of six voting tables, and as a result they did not remain at one voting table continuously, whereas those of the regional organization remain at one table."[144] As the NDI/CC final report put it,

> The most common irregularities in the voting process were: the presence of illegal propaganda in or around polling sites; irregularities in voting materials (including ballots that were pre-marked with votes for *Perú 2000* and/or were missing Alejandro Toledo's *Perú Posible*); attempted intimidation of political party agents (*personeros*) by police and military officials demanding to know *personeros*' names and identification numbers, which the officials then recorded; and the improper participation of government officials in the process.[145]

"The country has lived through an electoral process characterized by unprecedented irregularities and contamination," declared Roncagliolo after the electoral process.[146] Even Peru's last military dictator, Francisco Morales Bermúdez, complained about the quality of the elections, referring to them as "the most fraudulent and aberrant electoral process in our national history."[147]

But the most conspicuous flaw of the 9 April electoral round had to do, not surprisingly, given the OAS pre-electoral reports, with the vote tabulation process. It soon became evident that, in a manner reminiscent of the 1988 Mexican presidential elections, the computer system somehow was not working well. The problem could not be easily solved, because although the OAS mission had requested a computer terminal from which it could monitor the vote tabulation, the ONPE had not complied with its request.[148] Eventually, when the electoral office delivered its results, there was a one-million difference between votes cast and voters who went to the polls in ONPE's final results.

But in the midst of this confusion, and with the official results suggesting that Fujimori would cross the 50 percent threshold required to avoid going to a runoff, *Transparencia*'s quick count became crucial. The JNE had announced that with 56.4 percent of the votes counted, Fujimori had received 49.6 percent, to 40.6 percent for Toledo. *Transparencia,* for its part, released the results of its quick count on election night; it also showed Fujimori ahead, but with only 48.7 percent of the votes—and the NGO noted that this result might still be overestimating Fujimori's strength.[149] The monitoring group was thus suggesting that a runoff would be necessary. The next day, at a press conference at *Transparencia*'s headquarters, OAS mission chief Stein declared that *Transparencia*'s quick count left no doubt that a second-round was required.[150] Not surprisingly, soon afterwards Toledo declared that "The international community has played a critical role in defense of democracy," and that he expected it "to continue monitoring the election," Fujimori's running mate Tudela complained: "We've never had this kind of intervention in our political process before . . . We are not a banana republic. We Peruvians need to defend our national sovereignty."[151] Three days after *Transparencia,* the electoral authorities recognized that a runoff would be necessary; with 97.7 percent of the votes counted, Fujimori's share was 49.8, versus 40.3 for Toledo.[152]

Immediately after the electoral authorities announced that Fujimori and Toledo would face each other in the second-round, the main monitoring groups intensified their efforts in order to ensure that the marred electoral process regain credibility. Thus, for instance, on 12 April the OAS EOM issued a report noting that it would remain monitoring the electoral process "in the understanding that fundamental rectifications will be necessary in the conditions and procedures of this new phase of the electoral process."[153] Two days later, in a meeting with ONPE's head José Portillo, and Prime Minister Alberto Bustamante, Stein asserted that there were three main issues to be solved in order for the runoff to be credible: training of electoral officers at the voting tables, access to the media of the opposition candidate, and the improvement of the software program to be used by the ONPE.[154] On 19 April, Portillo announced that the software program was being improved in order to have a transparent electoral process; he noted that 16 out of the 18 OAS suggestions were being attended.[155]

But international pressure had not receded since the questionable first-round of voting, making the government nervous. Thus, after the ambassadors from Ecuador, France, the United Kingdom, and the United

States had separate interviews with opposition candidate Toledo, Peru's Foreign Relations Minister Fernando De Trazegnies declared that some ambassadors "have exceeded international norms and diplomatic uses and customs by meeting one of the candidates."[156] Similarly, Fujimori went on the defensive, arguing that "On these issues, in spite of globalization, all countries are sovereign. There should not be interventionism."[157] And suggestions by Tudela and by Peru's Foreign Relations Minister de Trazegnies that human rights were not universal, prompted Human Rights Watch Director José Miguel Vivanco to make what to the regime must have been an odious comparison. As Vivanco put it: "In this hemisphere Fidel Castro is the only case, and in the past Pinochet or Somoza, that dares to publicly challenge these principles [political rights], which are an integral part of human rights: representative democracy."[158]

Thus, on 23 April ONPE announced that it was forming three working groups to investigate the deficiencies of the computer system and suggest improvements to the technical aspects of the procedures to be followed in the runoff. The areas to be covered by each group were: training of polling station officials, the computerized vote-tabulation system, and general management of the elections. Each group, in turn, would be formed by two representatives from the ONPE and one representative each from *Perú Posible* and *Perú 2000*, who were both supervised by the OAS and the *Defensoría del Pueblo* (the ombudsman's office). Tellingly, domestic observers were excluded from these groups. On 5 May, the NDI/CC mission held a press conference in which it expressed its agreement with the recommendations put forward by *Transparencia* and the OAS, and then issued 13 specific recommendations.[159] Similarly, the three working groups set up by ONPE made several concrete proposals, but most of them were not implemented.[160]

In the meantime, on 28 April, right after receiving the presidential election's complete results from ONPE, the JNE announced that the runoff would take place on 28 May. In this context, some sectors of the opposition, as well as the three main monitoring missions called on the government to postpone the ballotage, so that the main problems detected in the first round could be adequately dealt with. On 18 May, presidential candidate Toledo announced that he would not take part in the runoff on the date announced by the electoral authorities, and demanded substantial improvements of the electoral environment and the postponement of the second round. That same day, another noteworthy incident arose, with Stein declaring: "we don't understand why they have had us working for weeks in correcting the computing system while they [the ONPE] were developing a completely new system with which they surprised us on 12

May."[161] The OAS mission-ONPE relationship had reached a critical point. Furthermore, to the displeasure of domestic and foreign observers, Fujimori was still using government resources in his campaign.[162] These and other problems were increasingly turning the Fujimori regime into a pariah on the international scene. As analyst Fernando Rospilgiosi noted back then, "No Peruvian government in the last decades had managed to isolate itself so absolutely in the international arena as that of Alberto Fujimori."[163]

But the government remained adamant in its decision to hold the runoff on the date set by the JNE. Not surprisingly, on 23 May *Transparencia* announced that "since the minimum technical conditions for having a free and fair electoral process do not exist, it will abstain from observing the May 28 electoral process." As a gesture of solidarity, members of NDI-CC were present at the Peruvian NGO's press conference.[164] On 25 May, the NDI/CC mission issued a statement noting that since "an election on May 28 will not meet the minimum international standards for a credible, democratic election," it would not observe it.[165] The timing of the withdrawal of the two nongovernmental organizations, according to Merloe, was not explicitly coordinated; it was rather a "convergence." Both organizations were in close contact and knew what the other one was likely to do.[166]

By that time only the OAS mission was left. It had announced on 23 May that it was suspending its monitoring of ONPE's software program, only to back off the next day suggesting that the reason for its rescindment was that it had received signs that the postponement of the second-round could still take place.[167] In reality, as Stein notes in the final report, he had

> learned that in the last hours previous to the issuing of the definitive pronouncement regarding its evaluation of the Peruvian electoral process, efforts were proposed around the possibility of obtaining an extension of the period set for the second-round . . . These responsibilities were initiated on Tuesday the 23 by the Executive, presenting a proposal for the postponement of a few days directly to the Secretary General, Dr. César Gaviria. As of that moment the Government of Peru cut all direct communication with the Chief of the EOM in Lima, and subsequently, all communications were carried out by means of the Secretary General in Washington, D.C.[168]

But on the 25th, without providing an explanation to the Secretary General, the JNE confirmed the 28 May date for the runoff. Immediately following this announcement, Stein noted that the electoral process as a whole was "irregular," pointing out that according to international standards the Peruvian electoral process was far from being free and fair. He also announced that the OAS mission would not observe the ballotage.[169] The Inter-American community had deserted Fujimori at the moment when it became evident that the electoral process was so irregular that it could not be legitimized by the regional organization. In Roncagliolo's opinion, "Stein did an excellent job, because the government could not take authority away from him until the day he left."[170]

That was exactly the case. Peru's ambassador to the OAS, Beatriz Ramacciotti lamented the withdrawal of Stein's mission. Nevertheless, resorting to a rather chauvinist discourse she noted: "These events, far from undermining the democratic calling of the Peruvian people and of its government, reaffirm it as a sovereign government. Peru is a sovereign country that subjects itself only and exclusively to its own norms and to the popular will expressed in the ballot box, as it happened on the electoral process of 9 April and as we are sure it will happen on Sunday [28 May]."[171] But as *Transparencia*'s President Luis Jaime Cisneros observed: "The emphasis countries, both big and small, used to place on their total independence was amusing rhetoric which worked 25 years ago . . . but not anymore."[172]

The second voting round took place as announced. According to ONPE's results, Fujimori got 51.2 percent of the votes, and Toledo 17. 7 (despite his withdrawal).[173] Three days later, at the OAS Permanent Council meeting in Washington, Lauredo, the US ambassador to the OAS, requested the use—like eight years earlier after Fujimori's self-coup—of OAS Resolution 1080.

The US initiative in Washington did not prosper, though. Stein presented a preliminary report on the Peruvian elections to the ambassadors gathered there; Ramacciotti took the opportunity to accuse the Guatemalan diplomat of "amply exceed[ing] its functions by referring on several occasions to supposed attributions to lend or not credibility to the electoral process." She noted that Stein "turned himself into one more political actor in the [electoral] process, setting a serious precedent for the future of the OAS observation missions."[174] When Lauredo's turn came, he presented the proposal to invoke Resolution 1080, but the representatives of Mexico and Venezuela, among others, suggested instead that the issue be discussed at the 30th OAS General Assembly, which was to take place four days later in Windsor, Canada. The US ambassador then withdrew his proposal, but noted: "This is just the first step, now everything will be taken to Windsor."[175]

At Windsor, OAS Secretary General Gaviria opened the assembly referring to the Peruvian elections. He asserted: "It is our task to ensure the integrity, impartiality and reliability of the electoral processes in order to encourage citizen participation, prevent irregularities, and provide guarantees for the free expression of the popular will." Later, Stein read his over-100-page final report, and the Canadian Foreign Affairs Minister Lloyd Axworthy, who was presiding over the assembly, proposed that the regional organization send to Peru a high-level mission, composed of foreign ministers and the Secretary General, in order to explore options to strengthen democracy in the Andean country with the government and the opposition.[176]

The political situation of Peru had become the focus of the 30th General Assembly. But as the Chilean Foreign Affairs Minister Soledad Alvear put it, "Not only the issue of Peru is at play . . . but the degree of efficiency that the Inter-American system possesses in the defense of democracy in the hemisphere."[177] In the end, Axworthy's proposal was approved, but Stein's highly critical report had not been discarded by the regional organization. As the resolution passed stated: "Taking note of the conclusions presented in the EOM's report. . . . Concerned that the credibility of the process and of the result of these elections has been undermined by persistent reports of irregularities, which have not been satisfactorily examined, including problems in the electoral process itself as well as in existing institutional deficiencies." Furthermore, as Axworthy noted, the Assembly's resolution did not represent a recognition of the Peruvian elections.[178] But the negotiation of the unusual resolution had not been an interstate affair only. As the weekly *Caretas* noted, *Transparencia* and other NGOs had played a role in lobbying for it.[179] For as Roncagliolo had insisted while lobbying in Windsor: "the sending of a high-level OAS mission in order to facilitate the negotiations among the different sectors of Peruvian society would be an important step to defend democracy."[180] For him, the approval of the resolution was positive, "a big step forward," since it meant that "a country accepts a commission that commands it to negotiate a national agenda, with the opposition and with society, in its national territory in order to change state policies, and to change the structure of the state."[181] Indeed, as Peru's Ombudsman Jorge Santiestevan put it: "the OAS resolution [at Windsor] marks the beginning of this kind of international tutoring so that Peru advances in the democratic commitment that is part of the OAS charter."[182]

But it wasn't just Peruvian observers that lobbied, both in Washington and in Windsor, in order to bring about democratic changes in Peru. The NDI/CC team was also involved. Thus, Jimmy Carter and two other personalities sent a letter to the foreign minister meeting in Windsor noting that the flawed electoral process in Peru constituted "a rupture in its democratic development," and suggested that the regional organization "send a mission to Peru with a mandate to explore a consensual solution toward restoring electoral institutions and procedures that meet international standards."[183] Significantly, the idea and drafting of Carter's letter in Washington, came from *Transparencia*'s Roncagliolo, NDI's Merloe, and CC's McCoy.[184] Merloe was pleased with the outcome at Windsor: "What we see here was one state practice, the evolution of the role of international observation, domestic observation, as an accepted part of state practice, whether or not there are treaty obligations and so on."[185]

With the resolution adopted at Windsor, as *El Comercio* noted approvingly, "the OAS has taken the role of supranational comptroller, in order to supervise the political changes Fujimorism is required to make in order to 'redemocratize' the regime."[186] This unprecedented (constructive) "interventionism," though, was widely supported in Peru: by mid June, 68 percent of the population approved of the OAS sending a mission to Peru to help in the democratization of the country.[187]

CONCLUSIONS

By the end of the twentieth century the western hemisphere's regional organization was actively involved in helping Peru leave behind the full circle it had gone through since the redemocratization process initiated in the mid 1970s. This time, though, the eventual end of the authoritarian regime would be a case of "Society-led Regime Termination." [188] But the OAS activist policy in the 2000 electoral process of the Andean country had to do with an obvious fact: the consolidation of the right to democratic governance in the hemisphere. The in-depth scrutiny of the whole electoral process by domestic and international observers was acceptable to the Peruvian government partly for strategic reasons, as the preceding narrative illustrates. It could be argued that the rise of *Sendero Luminoso* allowed Fujimori to be more receptive to international monitors, insofar as they strengthened his rule by delegitimizing the insurgent option, or that he was willing to put up with the OAS and other monitoring organizations as long as he was certain to remain in power. But more relevant than the motives of the Fujimori regime is the fact that "real" (i.e., meaningful) electoral observation had become a requirement of the Inter-American community—that is, that what transpired in national electoral processes had become an international affair (again, whether or not the political system became "truly democratic" is immaterial for my argument). Furthermore, it is noteworthy that the "installed capacity" to fulfill the requirements of the hemisphere's normative structure was an international network in which domestic and international organizations (NGOs, INGOS, and IGOs) all worked in tandem. A truly IEM TAN was thus fully established by the end of the twentieth century.

By 2000, both traditional human rights organizations and the more recent election monitoring ones conceived of the right to democratic governance as a human right. At the Inter-American state system level, the case studied in this chapter also makes clear that the idea of state sovereignty had undergone a profound transformation at the dawn of the twenty-fist century, compared to that of the late nineteenth century, for instance. Thus, being certified by the international community as a democratic state has become a constitutive feature of the units of the international system.

But what was important in the Peruvian case, as this chapter has shown, was not just that the Andean country was perceived as undemocratic, but that this mere fact endowed the international community with the right to advance claims on Fujimori's government, and the Peruvian people with the right to advance claims on the international community. The WHI had thus been actualized at the end of the twentieth century, making clear that both the rights of a state in the international system and the political regime it adopts are not discrete matters. The narrative above has also demonstrated the extent to which nonstate actors—the IEM TAN in particular—had become legitimate sovereignty builders by the late 1990s. Furthermore, the value of looking at domestic structures in some detail is highlighted by the Peruvian component of the TAN. Responding to the collapse of their country's party system, internationally-oriented domestic monitors proved quite accomplished at taking advantage of the enabling properties of the international normative structure—a normative structure they had contributed to build. IEM had become an international norm.

Chapter Seven

IEM in Other Settings and in IR Theory

Back in 1979, after the overthrow of Idi Amin's sanguinary regime, Uganda's President Godfrey L. Binasia observed: "somehow, it is thought to be in bad taste or contrary to diplomatic etiquette to raise matters of violations of human rights by member states within the forums of the United Nations."[1] That is undoubtedly no longer the case. Much has happened in the international normative structure since 1979—including the emergence of the "democratic entitlement" as a human right, and the normalization of IEM. That is why twenty years after Binasia's sardonic remark, the UN Commission on Human Rights unanimously passed (with China and Cuba abstaining) a resolution asserting that "democracy fosters the full realization of all human rights" and listing several "rights of democratic governance"—one of which, free and fair elections, is IEM's *raison d'être*.[2] I begin this concluding chapter by briefly considering IEM's system-wide normalization process. In the second section I revisit my theoretical argument in light of the overall process of emergence and normalization of IEM, considering it as a case of "constructive intervention." In section three I succinctly refer to a literature which, although germane to this work, I only mentioned in passing: democratic peace theory. Finally, in the last section of this chapter I consider both recent approaches to the related issue of "democracy promotion," and the place of IEM in IR theory.

IEM IN OTHER SETTINGS

IEM has become an international norm. As argued above, Latin America served as the springboard for this practice. Thus, as noted, the UN became for the first time involved in it in the 1990 Nicaraguan elections. Telling of the unfamiliar territory the organization was stepping on, at the same time that it was actively involved in the Nicaraguan elections, in January 1990 the UN declined a request by the Romanian government to monitor its first post-communist electoral process; the stated reason: "the United Nations does not monitor internal elections in a country."[3]

The next test for the international community, as anticipated in Chapter Four, came only two weeks after the Nicaraguan elections. On 10 March 1990, shortly before the downfall of his government, Haitian General Prosper Avril requested the UN to supervise the planned elections in his country. It took the General Assembly four months to even consider Haiti's request (which had been renewed by Avril's successor, Pascal Trouillot). The Haitian petition was hotly debated at the world organization. The Haitian provisional Foreign Minister claimed that the presence of a UN observer team in his country would set "a powerful precedent," for the future monitoring of elections by the UN in Third World countries in order "to certify their legitimacy."[4] The main opposition to sending a UN mission, on the grounds that regional peace was not threatened, came from China, Mexico, Cuba, and Colombia; the last two countries argued that it constituted a violation of article 2(7) of the UN Charter.[5] Nevertheless, on 8 October the Security Council asked the Secretary-General to respond "positively" and "on an urgent basis" to the Haitian request.[6] Two days later, the General Assembly approved the petition.[7] Thus, the Secretary-General established the UN Observer Group for the Verification of the Elections in Haiti.[8]

Significantly, the Haitian government also asked the OAS and several non-governmental organizations to participate as electoral observers. Hundreds of foreigners from around the world thus intervened in assisting the Haitian authorities in organizing the elections that took place on 16 December 1990.[9] But what was more consequential about the Haitian case was that, unlike the Nicaraguan experience, it could not be placed in the context of a regional peace process. This had to do only with the establishment of a democratic regime in a member state. As Thomas Franck has put it, "In normative terms, Haiti may be understood as the first instance in which the United Nations, acting at the request of a national government, intervened in the electoral process solely to validate the legitimacy of the outcome."[10]

At the 45th UN General Assembly session in 1990, US President George Bush suggested the creation of a UN electoral commission that would attend member states' requests for electoral observation and other kinds of electoral assistance. During that same session, the world body passed two seemingly contradictory resolutions: 45/150, supporting the democratic form of government and monitoring activities, and 45/151, emphasizing state sovereignty.[11] In 1991, though, the Secretary-General designated the Under-Secretary-General for Political Affairs as the Focal Point for Electoral Assistance Activities. The following year, the UN General Assembly approved the establishment of the Electoral Assistance Unit by 141 votes for, none against, and 20 abstentions.[12] In 1994, the Unit was upgraded to Division, and the next year UN Secretary-General Boutros Boutros-Ghali asserted that "the promotion of democracy is both an end in itself and part of the responsibility of the United Nations to maintain peace and security."[13] There is no doubt about that. The Division has been actively involved providing electoral assistance, attending over 140 requests from member states around the world.[14] By the end of the twentieth century, the world organization had, as a matter of fact, recognized the right to democratic governance as a human right.[15]

As suggested by the previous chapters, the OAS and the UN have not been the only IGOs responsible for IEM's normalization as an international norm. Other IGOs have also been active in this field for a number of years now. Here I refer only to two of the most active ones: the Commonwealth, and the Organization on Security and Cooperation of Europe (OSCE). Although the Commonwealth had been involved in observing elections in British territories, it was not until December 1980 that it observed an electoral process in a sovereign state, Uganda. The next Commonwealth monitoring mission, however, took place almost a decade later, in the Namibian elections mentioned in Chapter One.[16] Since that time, the Commonwealth has observed elections in over a dozen of its member states. As its web page put it "The Commonwealth is deeply committed to a full and all inclusive democratic process for all its members. It helps encourage this through the provision of independent observers at elections, and by publishing reports and documents to assist in a fuller understanding of democracy."[17] The Commonwealth does indeed engage in independent and serious IEM. Thus, for instance, its 61-person mission to the March 2002 electoral process in Zimbabwe concluded: "the conditions in Zimbabwe did not adequately allow for a free expression of will by the electors."[18]

Similarly, the OSCE created an "Office for Free Elections" in July 1991.[19] At that year's meeting of the Conference on the Human Dimension of the OSCE, celebrated three months later in Moscow, the participating states declared "categorically and irrevocably . . . that the commitments undertaken in the field of the human dimension of the CSCE [now OSCE] are matters of direct and legitimate concern to all participating States and do not belong exclusively to the internal affairs of the State concerned."[20] This is a remarkable statement that shows the shifting contours of state sovereignty in the last decade. Furthermore, member-states commit themselves to invite observers, both from NGOs and IGOs, for their national elections.[21] The OSCE has observed elections in more than 27 member countries, including the United States.[22]

As Gregory Flynn and Henry Farrell have noted, "The recognition of democracy as the only legitimate form of governance in Europe had profound implications for the conception of sovereignty."[23] As they observe, an "altered sense of sovereignty" now allows for "constructive intervention" in what used to be considered domestic affairs.[24] For them, the foundational moment of the post-Cold War Europe took place in November 1990, with the signing of the Charter of Paris, by means of which the contracting parties committed themselves "to co-operate and support each other with the aim of making democratic gains irreversible."[25] However, as the narrative explanatory protocol developed in the previous chapters shows, their claim that "The Charter of Paris modified this understanding," is not quite accurate.[26] The WHI had produced that change in the Americas as early as the 1960s, and had made it evident worldwide at least since 1989, when the monitoring effort for the 1990 Nicaraguan elections started. Furthermore, whereas in the early 1990s attention in the new Europe was "focused on how democracy might promote peace between states," this discussion, as noted, had already taken place in the Americas.

Furthermore, in the European milieu of the late twentieth century there was an ideational divide that simply did not exist in the WHI. Thus, for instance, as Flynn and Farrell note, the concluding document of the March-April 1990 CSCE Bonn Conference "saw the former socialist states embracing traditional Western values, including multiparty democracy based on free elections"—a commitment that had already been undertaken by the states of the Americas (even if many of them paid only lip service to it).[27]

But regardless of what region can claim authorship to this "altered sense of sovereignty," by making issues that had been traditionally considered as internal matters an integral part of state sovereignty in its external dimension, the fact remains that, as Flynn and Farrell point out, this broadening has meant an important change for the normative structure of Europe.[28] IEM in the Americas appears to have been just an early instance of constructive intervention—that is why I pointed out in the introductory chapter that the case presented in this book should be of broader interest for IR scholars. The monitoring practice as constructive intervention has subsequently undergone a process of localization.[29]

THE ARGUMENT REVISITED

The brief overview of IEM in other regions presented above should suffice to make the point that this practice has been normalized in world politics. The normalization process was actually a long one, starting with the early OAS missions in the early 1960s. But as argued above, this process moved forward substantially in the 1980s. During the four decades since it first emerged in the Americas, IEM was supported by the continental constitutional structure: the WHI. Nowadays, it can be argued, the identity and interests of the western hemisphere's states are substantially different from what they were in the mid-twentieth century: their sovereignty has been redefined.

The reconstruction of the meaning of state sovereignty, as the third chapter showed, received impetus from the Chilean 1988 monitoring effort, which was carried out by non-state actors. But as that chapter evinced, the human rights activists who made this effort possible were discursively relying on the WHI—while acting in a domestic structure that was highly receptive to their work. In this way, the Chilean experience showed the extent to which the domestic structure can serve as a second image intervening variable, linking domestic and international politics. The monitoring of the 1988 plebiscite was thus an important stepping stone for the redefinition of sovereignty.

Similarly, the Nicaraguan 1990 elections were a watershed in IEM. As described in Chapter Four, it was in this case where for the first time INGOs and IGOs worked in tandem. That sole experience made clear that national elections were no longer a domestic affair—and that sovereignty had been redefined in the process. By emphasizing the role of non-state actors, the narrative drove home the point that states should not be conceived of as totally self-organizing actors in the international arena. It was in this way, I argued, that IEM then contributed to making explicit the understanding of sovereignty enshrined in the WHI.

Four years later, IEM had already become an institutionalized practice worldwide. The significance of the 1994 Mexican elections then lies in the nature of the country in which the monitoring took place. As described in the fifth chapter, Mexico had been one of the fiercest opponents of this practice on nonintervention grounds. This was thus a critical case for IEM. In Mexico the sovereignty-related component of IEM was laid bare: the discussion about the presence of foreign observes centered squarely on the issue of sovereignty. More fundamentally, though, the Mexican experience evinces the enabling character of the international normative structure. As noted, when the state found itself in desperate need of external legitimation, it was possible for it to resort to the world organization and to a myriad of NGOs in order to lend legitimacy to the upcoming electoral process. Chapter Five also contributed to illustrate my larger argument that domestic structure matters in the diffusion of international norms. As I pointed out, had the ideology on nonintervention not been so pervasive in Mexico's domestic structure, IEM would not have figured so prominently in the 1994 electoral process.

The chronicle of the Mexican elections highlights as well the consolidation of the monitoring TAN, which was largely responsible for actualizing the WHI in the hemisphere. That is, after this initiation experience, the Mexican state not only stopped opposing IEM but also came to conceive of its identity and interests as being partially defined in more cosmopolitan—and less nationalistic—terms than it used to. That is why the Mexican electoral body started an intense international activity after 1994, and why there was no major governmental opposition to the international monitoring of the two subsequent electoral processes (in 1997 and 2000).[30] As a matter of fact, Mexico has gone as far in the last years as to make of democracy assistance one of its chief foreign policy objectives.[31]

Finally, the thorough monitoring of the 2000 Peruvian electoral process, described in Chapter Six, shows the extent to which elections had become international events by the end of the twentieth century—and also the extent to which one of the ordering principles of the international system had been altered. Furthermore, the new understanding of state sovereignty had been developed concomitantly with the emerging right to democratic governance, thus bringing to light the dual nature of sovereignty. That is, the monitoring of the Peruvian elections showed how the international community was advancing claims on the Andean state just as the Peruvian people were advancing their demands on the international system. Sovereignty had thus expressly become a two-way street.[32]

But besides making explicit the recursive nature of state sovereignty, the Peruvian case also shows the extent to which it had stopped being a states-only affair. The IEM TAN was widely recognized in the international arena as a legitimate interlocutor. We have thus come full circle: the Peruvian case is the mirror image of the Chilean case, in which non-state actors, being the only monitors of the plebiscite, were in a sense ghetto-ized; in contrast, twelve years later independent observers were openly acting as partners (and opponents) of state actors. Monitoring activists were fully embraced by the state system.

I do not intend to suggest that the four cases I cover here (plus the early IEM instances reviewed in ChapterTwo) tell the whole IEM story. Of course the universe of cases is much larger—and all of them might be considered relevant in the emergence and consolidation of this practice.[33] Nevertheless, since the four "observational units" covered in this work are significant in the development of this process, they suffice—from a genealogical standpoint—to summarize a more complex story. Moreover, the fact that a story can be sketched by connecting four dots of practice is by itself indicative of a deeper theoretical claim advanced here: that these apparently unconnected events took place in a milieu which makes their linking intelligible. The milieu is, of course, the normative structure of the Americas. The four cases could of course be told independently—and going deeper into the domestic politics of each of them would have certainly turned up some interesting findings. But my point here is that if the four cases could be put together and produce a plausible narrative at all, it is because they were interwoven into a larger a fabric. That is why my overall argument is systemic.

As I suggested in the introductory chapter, my claim is that IEM has transformed a structural element of the international system: sovereignty. In Chapter Two I further argued that by the end of the twentieth century not only had the international system's normative structure partially changed by virtue of attaching a representative-government factor to the notion of sovereignty, but also that the main component elements of that system—the states—had been transformed since they had partially redefined both their identity and interests, thanks to the normalization of IEM. Accordingly, the four empirical cases intended to show how international practices shape state identities and interests.

I claimed as well that in the western hemisphere, this process had been the result of a state interaction that was *not* predicated upon actors with completely formed pre-social interests—as the historical sketch presented in the second chapter showed. Furthermore, during the period I covered changes in material capabilities in the Americas were far from being a meaningful explanatory factor. That is why I held that it was an ideationist and social structure, not a material and individualist one, that explains the presence of IEM in current international politics.

I developed my argument from a moderate constructivist stance. I took the WHI as the constitutional structure that made the emergence of IEM in the Americas possible in the first place. I also traced the development of the IEM TAN, conceiving of it as the actor that, by helping bring about the emergence and consolidation of this practice, partially actualized the WHI. The network's discursive reliance on the continental constitutional structure thus showed the importance of the logic of argumentative rationality in the cases covered. I now do it considering the IEM story as a whole.

As the previous chapters suggest, if the WHI had not been in place, IEM would not have emerged in the Americas in the early 1960s. It was the state discourse that existed by the mid-twentieth century which enabled hemispheric states, through their regional organization, to launch IEM in its incipient form. But by the same token, if the state discourse that allowed for symbolic IEM had not existed, "real" (or at least nonstate-lead) IEM would not have emerged. Non-state actors used the legitimacy bestowed by the regional state system on this practice to initiate their monitoring activities; hence, their undertaking could not be constructed as an alien or subversive endeavor.

In the end, though, it was not an either/or approach that advanced IEM. Both state and non-state actors worked in tandem. Thus, if the interaction between human rights activists and state officials had not taken place, IEM would not have been normalized. It was the synergy created by their interplay that pushed IEM center stage by the late twentieth-century. But similarly, if the interaction of domestic and systemic factors had not taken place, IEM would not have emerged. The boomerang effect constantly at play in each of its instantiations was thus fundamental in the emergence and consolidation of this practice. Furthermore, the consolidation of IEM in the Americas not only contributed to bringing forward this distinctive understanding of sovereignty, but also contributed to its dissemination worldwide. That is, by making explicit what had remained implicit in the hemisphere, IEM has contributed to the conception of sovereignty that has emerged in the post-Cold War normative structure.

The new understanding, however, has not only affected the international structure; the units of the system have also been affected by it. Rules have constitutive effects. That is why if a transitional state becomes the target of third phase-IEM, it partially redefines its identity and national interests. This, of course, need not be a major redefinition; in some cases it might be quite inconspicuous, but as long as democracy- and (external) legitimacy-related factors come to inform the target state's ulterior discourse, a case can be made that a (partial) redefinition of identity (and therefore of interests) has taken place.

IEM's story also seems plausible looking at it through NLI's lenses, though. As I noted in the first chapter, my analysis is problem-driven; the empirical puzzle drives the analysis.[34] Thus, one could argue that if a state perceives a potential benefit in allowing the IEM of its elections, it engages on it. The question is then: what drives this perception? Self-interest, as this approach suggests, is of course the answer. But self-interest driven by what? For as Joseph Nye has argued, "To say that states act in their self-interests is merely tautological . . . unless we have a reasonable account of how such interests are perceived and redefined."[35] Furthermore, what made the rationality underlying the perception of self-interest change?

Similarly, it sounds plausible to expect that if a state is going through a democratic transition, it is more likely to allow IEM, as a liberal approach would have it. This would be due in part to the arguably undefined nature of interests in the transition process since one could make a NLI-inspired case that in these periods state interests are up for grabs. What a NLI explanation lacks, though, is causal depth—what Miller calls "depth as priority."[36] In this case, WHI's composite understanding of sovereignty is prior to the statesmen's decision to allow IEM—that is why they can resort to it. Notwithstanding these shortcomings, I would argue that the reason why an individualist approach such as NLI fares reasonably well in this subject matter is because, like the constructivist one, it focuses on process and leaves the possibility of learning open. Although I would not go as far as Jennifer Sterling-Folker, who argues that constructivism and NLI are "birds of the same feather," I would maintain that they are not necessarily incompatible.[37] Joseph Nye's "sociological liberalism," which emphasizes "the transformative effect of transnational contacts and coalitions on national attitudes and definitions of interests," is an appropriate instance of their common ground.[38]

In contrast, NCR fares least well when reconstructing IEM's story. Material factors as such did not figure prominently in the emergence and consolidation of this practice. Even making room for perceptions, the relative distribution of material factors does not seem relevant in explaining IEM. On the contrary, a domestic structure-based factor, the democratic character of a regime, is in fact significant—and it incidentally has little to do with material capabilities. But taken as a whole, with its overtly materialistic conception of power, NCR proves of scant utility when considering normative issues such as IEM.[39]

DEMOCRATIC PEACE THEORY AND IEM

The issue put forward in the NCR-based statement on democracy is also significant because, paradoxically, it is reminiscent of a definitely liberal approach: Democratic Peace Theory (DPT). As neoclassical realist Randall Schweller has granted "Inasmuch as the spread of liberal democracy creates shared values, common interests, and, most important, greater transparency of state motivations, it should lower threat perceptions and increase cooperation among such states. As a realist, I have no problem supporting these claims."[40] And as I noted in the first chapter, DPT is germane to the issues raised by the emergence of IEM as an international norm. Although I pointed out that its assumption about a democratic zone being created by democratic states—which has not been historically the case in the Americas—made it less useful as an alternative explanation than NLI, which simply assumes a rational self-interested actor, I think it is nevertheless relevant to the problematique I am concerned with—at least for a certain period of it. I therefore shall consider it briefly.[41]

Tracing its lineage to Immanuel Kant, DPT contends that the republican kind of government is conducive to international peace. For Kant, chief among the republican attributes that lead to international peace are representative government, constitutional arrangement, separation of powers, and the encouragement of commerce.[42] It is important to note, however, that Kant was talking about "republics," not about "democracies." For Kant, "*Democracy* is necessarily *despotism,* as it establishes an executive power contrary to the general will; all being able to decide against one whose opinion may differ."[43]

Interestingly, as Ido Oren has noted, US elites of the nineteenth century preferred to identify their country with republican than with democratic principles.[44] Furthermore, Kant's republicanism is not synonymous with liberalism. Kant's understanding of republicanism emphasizes community—an emphasis that fits uncomfortably with classical liberal thought. As Nicholas Onuf has noted, Kant anticipated liberalism but was not a liberal himself.[45] Democratic or not, liberal or not, Kant's republics were to maintain peace with each other. They would be able to form a separate peace. That is, republics could continue engaging in bloody conflicts with nonrepublican states, but not with each other. Although the debate on definitional and methodological issues remains,[46] in general terms the evidence gathered so far supports Kant's insight. Democracies seem in truth to have created a separate, peaceful subsystem. The "absence of war between democratic states," Jack Levy has observed, "comes as close as anything we have to an empirical law in international relations."[47]

As Kant's seminal proposition evolved into what we now know as democratic peace theory, the terms used and the arguments based on it have broadened. Thus, for instance, some claim that liberal democracies are more pacific in general (i.e. that they are less likely to engage in war, either with democratic or nondemocratic states). As Samuel Huntington put it, "Liberalism does not understand and is hostile to military institutions and the military function."[48] Underlying the previous arguments are the assumed reasons for the behavior of democratic regimes.[49] Some authors claim that democracies are less conflict-prone for institutional reasons: that the very nature of the domestic institutions and the social compact on which they are founded make it harder for democratic regimes to actually engage in war. Other authors assert that the peacefulness of liberal democracies is better explained by normative factors: democratic regimes simply extrapolate to their international interactions the norms on which they operate domestically.[50] In either case, the central claim of the democratic peace theory remains that a domestic regime type is central for explaining the international behavior of a state.[51] As Waltz put it recently, "The democratic peace thesis will hold only if all of the causes of war lie inside of states."[52]

From the arguments advanced by DPT, and extrapolating this approach to my subject matter, one could venture that by requesting electoral observers, leaders of democratic states have indeed attempted to create a democratic zone in the Americas. This proposition is of course of limited application, as I noted above, since it has been only after the "third wave" engulfed the hemisphere in the 1980s that (most) democratic states started requesting—or at least allowing—the presence of foreign observers. The clause in dashes is crucial: what is important now is *not* the presence of foreign observers per se, but just the possibility that they might be present if they so desire. That is, in democratic states—as DPT would expect it to be the case in a zone of peace—foreign observes become superfluous as guarantors of the a free and fair political process. Like Minerva's owl, international observers fly out when democracy appears to have settled in a state. But, more importantly for my argument here, their work has already been done: by making IEM an international norm, sovereignty has been partially redefined.

RECENT APPROACHES TO "DEMOCRACY PROMOTION" AND THE PLACE OF IEM IN IR THEORY

The last point is important: IEM as such should be treated as a structural variable, not simply as a foreign policy matter. As noted in the introductory chapter, there have been some recent publications on a topic that in many respects overlaps with the one I cover here: "democracy promotion." Nevertheless, as I anticipated, these contributions tend to regard it as a foreign policy issue. Thus, for instance, Carothers, who is among the foremost experts on the subject, rightly notes in his *Aiding Democracy Abroad* that "Academic specialists—whether in international relations, comparative politics, or development studies—have not devoted much attention to the subject."[53] And then he complains that "The most basic questions about the field, such as, 'Does it work?' and 'Do we know what we are doing?' are left unanswered for most observers."[54]Those are certainly fine and important questions, but not ones that address the issue structurally.

Similarly, Michael Cox, John Ikenberry, and Takashi Inoguchi in their jointly edited *American Democracy Promotion: Impulses, Strategies, and Impacts* have regretted the fact that "the exponential growth in democracy studies has not been matched by an equally significant body of work by students of international relations or American foreign policy."[55]But they then announce in the introduction that their volume "seeks to untangle the theoretical and historical issues that are at stake in the American pursuit of democracy worldwide."[56]Their quest is indeed to explain (among other things) where this practice "fits within the larger foreign policy tradition" of the United States, and to problematize "the particular—and increasingly important—part played by democracy promotion in US international affairs"—again, not exactly a third-image approach to the subject[57]

This is not so say that the works just mentioned do not "belong" in IR—it could not be farther from my intention to attempt to prescribe what should be and what shouldn't be part of the field.[58] My only point here is that their focus is on (the effectiveness of US) foreign policy. Works of this nature are undeniably very useful in analyzing and improving the cottage industry "democracy assistance" has spawned, as well as the effects of U.S.' political endeavors abroad. But IR still faces the task of addressing the theoretical challenges posed by practices such as "democracy promotion" and IEM from a systemic perspective—a task to which this work aims to contribute.

Furthermore, the research agenda opened by the consideration of IEM from a systemic perspective should also be useful in bringing DPT and Comparative Politics closer. The development of IEM in the Americas makes clear that the democratic ideal has been a systemic attribute in the hemisphere—which in turn suggests a third image reading of the Kantian foundation of the democratic peace literature. This, of course, does not mean that harmonic consensus would be the normal state of affairs should perpetual peace be achieved, for as Kant put it:

> The means which nature employs to accomplish the development of all faculties is the antagonism of men in society, since this antagonism becomes, in the end, the cause of a lawful order of this society. I mean by antagonism *the asocial sociability of man;* i.e., the propensity of men to enter into a society, which propensity is, however, linked to a constant mutual resistance which threatens to dissolve this society.[59]

The "asocial sociability of man," however, should not be seen by democratic peace theorists as applying only to interstate relations. It also applies to the political process within states. That is why Kant did not consider the international and national spheres as completely discernible realms.[60] As Latin Americanists know all too well, domestic politics has oftentimes not been a sphere of peace, law, and order in the subcontinent. The Peruvian case reviewed in this work, and the recent political situation in Venezuela, show that even when the trappings of a democratic government are installed in a country—sometimes with the assistance of foreign observers—there is no guarantee that a democratic regime will develop.[61] It takes more than free elections and foreign monitors to harness the asocial sociablity of man and consolidate a truly democratic regime, as comparativists have demonstrated. Comparative Politics should then shed some light on the types of democracy that are most conducive to actualizing the DPT's zone of peace, both within the states and throughout the western hemisphere.

Notes

NOTES TO THE INTRODUCTION

1. Following common practice, I will use the terms "election monitoring," "election observing," and "election watching" interchangeably. Robert Pastor (Pastor1998) differentiates between the first and second terms in reference to the duration and comprehensiveness of the task undertaken. Although this is an important distinction when considering the effect of the activities carried out in particular cases, it is largely irrelevant for my purposes here.
2. Quoted in Stoelting 1992, 372.
3. Krasner 1999, 22.
4. Váli 1958.
5. Interestingly, even the few International Relations scholars who have recently dealt with IEM (although focusing on the broader concept of "democracy promotion") treat it as a foreign policy issue.
6. Ruggie 1998, 861.
7. Beigbeder 1994, 78.
8. Wambaugh 1933, 15.
9. Padilla and Houppert 1993, 94–95.
10. Wambaugh 1933, 20.
11. Ibid., 25.
12. Farley 1986, 34; Wambaugh 1933, 40.
13. The system of Mandates established after World War I had been superseded by the International Trusteeship System established in Chapter XII of the UN Charter.
14. Fox 2000, 72.
15. Beigbeder 1994, 98.
16. Ibid., 149–151.
17. Ibid., 161.
18. Both Angola and South Africa, where the two super-powers had clashing interests, were deeply involved in Namibia.
19. Fox 2000, 73.

20. Franck 2000, 32. The difference is analogous to that between general restrictions of territorial sovereignty and that implied by the legal concept of international servitude. See Váli 1958.
21. O'Gorman 2003, 156.
22. Quoted in Callcott 1968, 14. My italics.
23. Whitaker 1954, 29.
24. Ibid., 1.
25. Quoted in Corrales and Feinberg 1999, 2.
26. Whitaker 1954, 5.
27. Wendt 1999, 251.
28. That is why this work is *not* about democracy (contrary to what the emphasis on the electoral nature of the practice studied, and the representative government component of the WHI suggest), but about state sovereignty.
29. Santa-Cruz 2000, 132–3.
30. Zehfuss 2001, 318.
31. Hurd 1999, 381.
32. As Hedley Bull put it: "rules are not infinitely malleable and do circumscribe the range of choice of states which seek to give pretexts in terms of them (Bull 1977, 45)."
33. Weber 1995, 2.
34. Quoted in Inter-American Dialogue 1992, 31.

NOTES TO CHAPTER ONE

1. Quoted in Waltz 1997, 913.
2. Krasner 1999. I focus on this work because it is here where Krasner has more fully elaborated his view of sovereignty.
3. Katzenstein, Keohane, and Krasner 1998.
4. March and Olsen 1998, 949.
5. Ibid., 951. It is important to note, however, that March and Olsen are more subtle in their differentiation of the two logics, noting that they are "not mutually exclusive" (Ibid., 952). Furthermore, there might be a methodological problem in trying to juxtapose explanations based on each of two logics, as they might stand not on a "rivalry" position, but in one that involves emdeddedness. See Wendt 2000, 1020–1021.
6. Interestingly, "anarchy" does not appear in the book's index. Instead, the pervasiveness of the logic of consequences in international system serves as a proxy for anarchy in Krasner's book. The closest he gets to mentioning anarchy is when he writes that "Given the absence of international authority structures, the asymmetries of power among states, and the diversity of norms espoused by rulers and their constituents, it is impossible for any institutional arrangement at the international level to become embedded (220)." But given that there is no problematization of the anarchical nature of international relations, or of the logic of consequences in the

international realm, for that matter, one is left wondering if Krasner is not selling old wine in new bottles.

7. Interestingly, Krasner is now taking the "utilitarian" approach he criticized in a 1988 article on sovereignty, in which he took an "institutional" perspective. He wrote then: "It is exactly this taken-for-granted quality that distinguishes institutional analysis from even those utilitarian perspectives that recognize the importance of institutions but regard that as being constantly under challenge, constantly subject to the rational maximizing calculations of their members (Krasner 1988, 77)."
8. Unfortunately, the constructivism Krasner portrays is a straw man. To begin with, he misunderstands the nature of norms in constructivist arguments. As Alexander Wendt has noted, "Shared knowledge and its various manifestations—norms, rules, etc.—are analytically neutral with respect to cooperation and conflict (Wendt 1999, 253)." But for Krasner norm-talk is synonymous with *morally* appropriate behavior. Thus, for instance, having noted that the logic of consequences is dominant in the international system, he goes on to contrast the effectiveness of "norms" vs. that of "guns," finding the latter are superior, since "a bullet through the head has the same effect regardless of the cognitive perspective of the target." He thus concludes that "Norms, though not irrelevant, do not have the weight that Constructivism has attributed to them (51)." Krasner is of course equating "norms" with "good" norms, and consequently misconstruing what the logic of appropriateness means. He is thus missing the point that, as Finnemore and Sikkink have noted, "norm conformance can often be self-interested (Finnemore and Sikkink 1998, 912)."

    Furthermore, Krasner also misconstrues the role of norms in constructivism. He interprets the constructivist claim about norms being taken for granted, or embedded, to mean that they are not contested. Thus, for him when sociological approaches, such as Constructivism, "suggest that there are more or less taken-for-granted norms," they mean "that there are some aspects of international relations that are so deeply embedded in the world views of political leaders that they are not questioned (51)." Krasner thus misses the point that most constructivist research, as Martha Finnemore and Kathryn Sikkink have noted, "emphasizes the highly contingent and contested nature of normative change and normative influence (Ibid., 912)."

    Krasner is willing to concede that actors could internalize norms—but this would happen at the domestic, not at the international level: "If rulers are socialized into normative structures at all . . . these are most likely to be associated with domestic environments whose principles may, or may not, be consistent with those prevailing with the international system. The Westphalian model has never been taken for granted (69)." In his reading, institutions become embedded when they "dictate actual behavior (226)." The alleged constructivist claim of international norms being taken for granted is clearly an excess for Krasner; as he points out: "The international system is complex . . . Logics of consequences can trump logics of appropriateness (25)." And indeed, he claims, "Logics of consequences have trumped Westphalian logics of appropriateness (41)."

Nevertheless, Krasner accepts that there might be exceptions, as when a ruler is willing to sign a convention (thus violating his own state's Westphalian sovereignty) not out of self-interest. This might happen, he argues following John Meyer and the World Culture school, when rulers simply follow the "script of modernity." However, this anomalous behavior can be explained in terms of Krasner's preferred logic, the logic of consequences—even if a contrario sensu. That is, for Krasner the explanation that rulers might follow cultural norms and willingly compromise the sovereignty of their states has to do with them "not hav[ing] an autonomous conception of appropriate behavior (33)"—appropriate behavior in this case being conforming to the individualist logic of consequences. His view of the logics of appropriateness and consequences as being inherently in conflict leads Krasner to ignore the fact that, as constructivists emphasize, "choices take place on at least two levels—the decisional and the cultural (Wildavsky 1994, 154.)" It is perhaps because of his failure to understand the dual character of social action that the constructivism Krasner depicts is no more than a straw man.

9. Quoted in Elster 1991, 117–118.
10. Quoted in Kratochwil 1978, 52.
11. Risse-Kappen 2000, 6.
12. Ibid., 6.
13. For instance, in the figure he uses to illustrate the three logics of social action, in which each of them is equidistant from the other two.
14. Risse-Kappen 2000, 7.
15. Alker 1990.
16. Kratochwil 1978, 80. Forrestal's quote in there too.
17. Cited in Alker 1990, 174.
18. Kratochwil 1987, 304.
19. Risse-Kappen 2000, 7.
20. Ibid., 9.
21. Habermas 1989, 124.
22. The cultural component is thus pervasive. As Neta Crawford has noted, "The fact that actors consciously employ culture, perhaps even cynically or disingenuously, as part of their rhetorical menu does not mean that we should discount cultural framing. Rather, this use underscores the importance of culture's role in argumentation and the grounding of particular beliefs (Crawford, 2002, 73)."
23. Ibid., 138.
24. Wiley 1990, 376. See also Murase 1976; Santa Cruz 2000, 181–218.
25. Outhwaite 1994, 40. As Kratochwil has noted, a system of communicative action in the international system might be said to exist in so far as state actors use rules by "making demands as well as proposals for the settlement of disputes. . . . and by justifying action through their invocation." Kratochwil 1984, 350.

26. Cf. Wendt 1999, 317.
27. Krasner 1999, 226.
28. Kratochwil 1987, 159.
29. Bull 1977.
30. Risse-Kappen 2000, 16.
31. Reus-Smit 1997.
32. Ibid., 556.
33. Ibid., 556.
34. Kratochwil 1995, 21.
35. As Michael Barnett has observed, states "care about their legitimacy because they are part of an international community from which they derive their rights, obligations, and authority to act in legitimately sanctioned ways (Barnett 1997, 543)." And as Kratochwil notes, authority means "an assurance that comes with amplification (*auctoritas* is based on *augere,* to increase, amplify), that is based on accepted ways of dealing with life's choices (Kratochwil 1996, 221)."
36. Wight 2004, 280.
37. Thomson 1995, 219.
38. Arendt 1990, 31.
39. Reus-Smit 1997, 565.
40. Carozza 2003.
41. Larsen 1997, 203.
42. On societal collective identity see Hall 1999.
43. Reus-Smit 1997, 568.
44. Kratochwil 1996, 216.
45. Cited in Clinton 1986, 504.
46. Risse-Kappen 2000, 29.
47. Ibid., 34.
48. Hurd 1999, 397.
49. Keck and Sikkink 1998, 2.
50. Risse-Kappen 2000, 20.
51. Wendt 1999, 244–245.
52. Ibid., 95.
53. McSweeney 1999, 162.
54. Keck and Sikkink 1998, 216.
55. Ibid., 3.
56. Ibid., 20.
57. Ibid., 12.
58. Murphy 1996, 91.
59. Sikkink 1993, 414–415.
60. McSweeney 1999, 165.
61. Waltz 1979.
62. Risse-Kappen and Sikkink 1999, 5.
63. O'Donnell and Schmitter 1986. For an article linking constructivist IR to the literature on democratic transitions see Peceny 1999.
64. Finnemore 1996, 339.

65. Risse-Kappen and Sikkink 1999, 6.
66. Kaufmann and Pape 1999.
67. Finnemore and Sikkink 1998, 900.
68. Ibid., 901.
69. Ibid., 906.
70. For an elaboration on this point see Legro 2000.
71. Walker 2000, 28.
72. Keck and Sikkink 1998, 205. Or as Hegel put it, "The buds have the tree within them and contain its entire strength, although they are not yet the tree itself" (Hegel 1996, 25)."
73. Although several of the statements are presented here as counterfactuals, this should not be a problem, since counterfactuals are sometimes helpful devices to clarify an explanation. As Stephen Van Evera has noted, "Counterfactual analysis helps us recognize theories." In this case, one of the elements in the "conjectured relationship between two phenomena" is assumed to be absent in order to elucidate how the story would have developed (Van Evera 1997, 26, 9). On the utility of counterfactuals in explanation in the social sciences see Hawthorn 1993. On the use of the butterfly effect in IR see Gaddis 1993, 28.
74. Arguably, Democratic Peace Theory would also have something to say in this respect. However, the sporadic actualization of the democratic ideal in the Americas makes it less fitting to my story than NLI and NCR. I will briefly come back to DPT in the concluding chapter.
75. Since, as Hans Morgenthau noted, "Rationalism misunderstands the nature of man, the nature of the world, and the nature of reason itself (Morgenthau 1946, 204)." Classical realism and constructivism thus seem to share at least some ontological presuppositions. See Ashley 1981; Ashley 1984; Johnston 1995. On approach-, and problem-driven style of analysis see Hemmer and Katzenstein 2002.
76. Wendt 1999, 258.
77. Moravcsik 1997, 523.
78. For a related argument see McSweeney 1999, 161.
79. Elman 1996; Rose 1998, 145.
80. Kapstein 1995, 757.
81. Fearon and Wendt, 68.
82. I am thus heeding Jeffrey Legro's call for a "wider application in norm scholarship [of the] relative assessment of alternative explanations for the same effects (Legro 1997, 58)."
83. Hasenclever, Mayer, and Rittberger 1997, 4.
84. Schweller and Priess 1997, 3.
85. Keohane 1984, 12.
86. Keohane 1989, 11.
87. Katzenstein 1996, 11.
88. Keohane 1989, 3.
89. Ibid., 2.
90. Keohane 1988, 392.

91. Keohane 1989, 4.
92. Keohane 1984, 246.
93. Caporaso 1992, 610.
94. Keohane 1984, 45.
95. See Krasner 1983.
96. Hurd 1999, 386.
97. Keohane 1984, 74–75.
98. Guzzini 2000, 164.
99. Wildavsky 1994, 136.
100. Keohane 1989, 16.
101. Keohane 1983, 171.
102. Keohane 1993, 285.
103. Haggard and Simmons 1987, 506.
104. Although they are *not* coterminous with it. Wallander 1999, 5, 16.
105. Moravcsik 1997, 517.
106. Johnston 2001, 488.
107. Rose 1998, 181.
108. Wohlforth 1994/5, 109.
109. Gunther Hellman in Feaver et al. 2000, 177. My italics. Randall identifies himself as a neoclassical realist in Schweller 2000.
110. Brooks and Wohlforth 2000/01, 12.
111. Hellman in Feaver et al. 2000, 177.
112. Jeffrey Taliaferro in Ibid., 178. For a discussion of the viability of constructing neo-realist theories of foreign policy see Elman 1996.
113. Rose 1998, 145.
114. Legro and Moravcsik 1999, 28; Rose 1998, 152.
115. Rose 1998, 146.
116. Wohlforth 1994/5, 109.
117. Taliaferro in Feaver et al. 2000, 181.
118. Kapstein 1995, 769.
119. Wohlforth 1994/5, 98.
120. An important exception in this respect is the recent work of Stephen Brook and William Wohlforth, who point out that "there is no reason to think that material incentives in the environment cannot at least sometimes help explain shifts in actors' fundamental interests and/or in their very identities." Brooks and Wohlforth 2000/01, 52–53.
121. Peter Feaver in Feaver et al. 2000, 169.
122. Rose 1998, 170–171.
123. Brooks and Wohlforth 2000/01, 8.
124. Wildavsky 1994, 150.
125. Kornai 1992, 367.
126. Cf. Mitchell 1991.
127. I am not suggesting with this that constitutive processes should always be placed above causal influences, but only that causality (as usually understood) does not go all the way down. On the constitution of states at both levels see McSweeney 1999, 161.

128. Because in order to have a conception of self-interest the actor needs to have an identity—which is socially constructed. As Henry Nau has put it, "Identity is an inherently collective act. It is not something that stands outside a system of relationships, that is, something achieved in isolation; it is part of the system. Thus the identity of states is not a unit-level characteristic; it is a system characteristic (Nau 1993, 24)." See also Klotz 1995, 167–168.
129. Waltz 2000, 29.
130. This embeddedness is analogous to the one of the economy in society, as put forward by Karl Polanyi 1944 (Polanyi 1944).

NOTES TO CHAPTER TWO

1. We can thus think of the WHI as the continent's culture, which, like any culture, "makes some things possible, some things desirable, and some things unimaginable (Kier 1997, 165)."
2. Quoted in Dessler 1999, 136.
3. Atkins 1977, 10.
4. Davis 1977, 67.
5. Burr 1973, xxi.
6. Peck 1977, 166.
7. Wilson 1989, 477.
8. Burr 1973, xxii. Note that the European threat (as the "relevant other") is still pertinent as a justification for action.
9. Corrales and Feinberg 1999, 6. On "dominant powers" see Triska 1986.
10. Ibid., 21.
11. Burr 1973, xxiv-xxv.
12. www.yale.edu/lawweb/avalon/intdip/interam/intam07.htm. Accessed 27 May 2002.
13. Burr 1973, xxvi; Corrales and Feinberg 1999, 7.
14. Burr 1973, xxviii.
15. Hale 1986, 369. There are interesting parallels between republicanism as I treat it here and nationalism, as described by Rodney Bruce Hall. Thus, for instance, he claims that "nationalism is not just a unit level factor, or a 'property' of the units which may be assumed to foster self-seeking of [sic] self-interested behavior. National identity is a relatively new form of collective identity whose development is contingent upon both domestic and international sources (Hall 1999, 11-12)." Italics original.
16. Onuf 1998, 4.
17. Ibid., 232.
18. Ball 1969, 491.
19. Quoted in Reisman 1990, 868.
20. Quoted in Hartz 1983, 290.
21. Peck 1977, 173.
22. Weber 1992, 320.
23. Quoted in Sikkink 1997, 708.

24. Quoted in Ronning 1963, 68.
25. Smith 1994; Carothers 1991.
26. Atkins 1977,12.
27. Farer 1993, 339.
28. Interestingly, Brazil was not originally invited either. See Davis 1977, 72. I am not suggesting that Latin America has (or had at the time) an "essential" identity. See O'Gorman 1988.
29. Hale 1986, 367.
30. Ibid., 414, 416.
31. Corrales and Feinberg 1999, 6.
32. Peck 1977, 179. My italics.
33. Slater 1967, 244.
34. Sikkink 1997, 720-1.
35. Cited in Reus-Smit 2001, 532 .
36. Thérien, Fortman, and Gosselin 1996, 221.
37. Farer 1988, 25.
38. Ibid., 27.
39. Wilson and Dent 1995, 27. My italics.
40. Cited in Sikkink 1997, 727. My italics.
41. See Muñoz 1990, 28.
42. Using an analogy, it could be said that material interests are not independent of ideational factors just like rational thought is not independent of feeling. Cf. Adolphs et al. 1996. To put it another way: as Diedre McCloskey (McCloskey 1998) has noted, economists since Bentham (and I would argue that by extension rationalist scholars in IR) have tried to explain behavior in terms of a single variable, P (which stands for the bourgeois virtue of prudence and refers to categories such as prices, property and preferences), disregarding anything that has to do with another explanatory variable S (which stands for solidarity, and includes issues such as society, sociology and speech). McCloskey argues that in terms of an econometric equation, economists dump anything that is related with S into the quasi error term. The problem is that the quasi-error term, where the construction of social reality operates, will be correlated with the included variable, P. Consequently, the coefficient will be biased.
43. Cf. Andrews 1994, 196-197.
44. This was thus a very different structure from a Waltzian one.
45. Cited in Ball 1969, 493.
46. Cox 1989, 42.
47. Cited in Wilson and Dent 1995, 27.
48. Whitaker 1954, 177. My italics.
49. Onuf 1998, 8.
50. That is, Latin American statesmen were aware of the structural inequality in the system, candidly recognized by a senior Reagan administration official decades later when he said: "[the administration] debated whether we had the right to dictate the form of another country's government. The bottom line was yes, that some rights are more fundamental that the right of

nations to nonintervention. . . . We don't have the right to subvert a democracy, but we do have the right against an undemocratic one." Quoted in Waltz 2000, 27.

51. Cf. Johnston 1996.
52. Ruggie 1997, 93.
53. Ikenberry 2000, 104.
54. Ikenberry 1996.
55. Wilson and Dent 1995, 27.
56. Quoted in Waltz 2000, 11.
57. See also Kryzanek 1995, 398-399; Van Evera 1990, 27.
58. Quoted in Waltz 2000, 8.
59. Sikkink 1993, 143.
60. Ibid., 143.
61. Pastor 1987, 368.
62. Carothers 1991, 242.
63. Carothers 1995, 23.
64. See also Herman and Brodhead 1984; Smith 2000, 73-74.
65. Cited in Jason 1992, 1827.
66. Pastor 1987, 377.
67. Carothers 1991, 244.
68. Smith 1994.
69. OAS 2000. My translation.
70. Canada did not become a member of the OAS until 1990.
71. Wilson 1989.
72. See March and Olsen 1998; Risse-Kappen 2000.
73. Wildavsky 1994, 154.
74. Cited in Pastor 1989, 149.
75. Cited Pastor 1989, 150.
76. Inter-American Institute of International Legal Studies 1966, 58.
77. Cited Ball 1969, 488.
78. Comité Jurídico Interamericano 1965.
79. Ball 1969, 494. My italics.
80. OAS 1962b, 5.
81. Ibid., 13. The report does not specify how many polling places were visited.
82. Ibid., 15.
83. Ibid., 11.
84. Ibid., 15.
85. Ibid., 16-7.
86. Cited in Slater 1967, 213.
87. Beigbeder 1994, 232-233. According to an internal OAS document on early monitoring missions (on file with author), the team was composed of 36 observers. Perhaps some of the "distinguished individuals" of the OAS mission included in Beigbeder's account were not observers strictly speaking. In any case, the number of observers was significant.
88. Slater 1967, 209.
89. OAS 1962a, 80.

90. OAS 1963, vii.
91. OAS 1963, vii.
92. Ibid., 19-21.
93. Ibid., viii, 5.
94. Farer 1993, 337.
95. Baena Soares 1994, 184. The OAS monitoring missions, though, were generally quite small. Thus, for instance, in 1968 the Ecuadorian government requested the Secretary General to designate "three high ranking figures of the American continent" to serve as observers. Not surprisingly, the mission's report points out that "it was not possible to cover the national territory in its entirety, as in the case of several similar missions that have serve [sic] as a precedent for this one." OAS 1968, 2.
96. OAS 1965.
97. OAS 1978.
98. OAS 1980.
99. OAS 1984a.
100. OAS 1984b.
101. For a discussion of the human rights regime see Donnelly 1986. Unfortunately, Donnelly does not consider the role of NGOs in it. On this issue see Sikkink 1997.
102. Jason 1992, 1802 .
103. International Human Rights Law Group and Washington Office on Latin America 1985.
104. Carter Center 1996.
105. Ibid, 7.
106. Pastor 1990, 18-19.
107. Jason 1992, 1817.
108. Ibid., 1841.
109. Keck and Sikkink 1998, 24. See also Sikkink 1993.
110. Interview with Robert Pastor, Atlanta, Georgia, 5 September 2000, and with Sergio Aguayo, Mexico City, 8 May 2002.
111. Interview with Sergio Aguayo, former head of Alianza Cívica, Mexico City, August 16, 2000.
112. Jason 1992, 1843 .
113. AG/RES. 993, XIX-0/89.
114. AG/RES. 1063, XX-0/90.
115. AG/RES. 1080, XXI-0/91.
116. Acevedo 1993, 141. Emphasizing this trend, in December 1992 the OAS General Assembly approved the "Protocol of Washington," an amendment to the OAS Charter. The Protocol provides that a state "whose democratically constituted government has been overthrown by force may be suspended" from participation in the regional organization by a two-thirds votes of the member States. It entered into force in October 1997 (Schnably 2000, 163). Similarly, four years later, at the third Summit of the Americas in Quebec City, state leaders adopted a "Democratic Clause" which stated that "any unconstitutional alteration or interruption of the democratic

order in a state of the Hemisphere constitutes an insurmountable obstacle to the participation of that state's government in the Summit of the Americas process." Out of this meeting also came the Inter-American Democratic Charter, which practically replaces Resolution 108. It was adopted on 11 September 2001 in Lima, Peru. As Heraldo Muñoz has put it: "The great merit of the Inter-American Democratic Charter is that is has brought the resolutions, declarations and modifications of the OAS Charter that constituted the democratic foundations and raison d'etre of the Organization into a single text. It thus institutionalized the political and juridical commitment of the member States for the maintenance and defense of democratic regimes ('The Right to Democracy in the Americas: From the Commitment of Santiago to the Democratic Charter,' 2002 www.upd.oas.org)." Accordingly, Article 1 states: "The peoples of the Americas have a right to democracy and their governments have an obligation to promote and defend it." Furthermore, in Article three the Charter defines what the main elements of a democratic regime are: "Essential elements of representative democracy include, inter alia, respect for human rights and fundamental freedoms, access to and the exercise of power in accordance with the rule of law, the holding of periodic, free, and fair elections based on secret balloting and universal suffrage as an expression of the sovereignty of the people, the pluralistic system of political parties and organizations, and the separation of powers and independence of the branches of government." Significantly, the initial proposal for the new document came from the transitional government that was installed in Peru in the aftermath of the collapse of the Fujimori regime in late 2000.

117. Degregori 2001, 47.
118. Público 8 June 2000, 32.
119. Acevedo 1993, 121.
120. Sikkink 1993, 170.
121. Quoted in Guzzini 1993, 474.
122. Although some date its end to 1985 (with the ascent of Mikhail Gorbachev to power), the Cold War had definitively ended by 1990 (Wohlforth 1994/5, 101).
123. Hobson 2000, 11.
124. Audi 1995, 158.
125. Interestingly, Johnston's view of culture seems limited to the logic of appropriateness: "Cultural patterns and behavioral patterns are not the same thing. Insofar as culture affects behavior, it does so by presenting limited options and by affecting how members of these cultures learn from interaction with the environment (Johnston 1995, 35); I assume . . . that strategic culture . . . is, like culture, an ideational milieu that limits behavioral choices (Ibid., 36) . . . at the very least we have to show that strategic culture first limits in some way the options considered (Ibid., 37)." Johnston thus does not consider the positive, generative effects of culture.
126. Risse-Kappen 1995, 23-4.

127. Although the boundaries between these two disciplines are becoming increasingly blurred. Cf. Green 2002.
128. Evangelista 1997, 210-ff.
129. State sovereignty, after all, is what happens while statesmen and activists are busy making other plans, as John Lennon and other theorists of path dependence (i.e., history) would say. Cf. Evans in Kohli 1995, 7.
130. Evangelista 1997, 223. See also Checkel 1997; Checkel 1999; Cortell and Davis 2000.
131. Ruggie 1998, 861.
132. Bartelson 1995, 7-8.
133. Ibid.: 8.
134. Eckstein 1975.
135. Alexander and McKeown 1985.
136. Ragin 1987, 8-9.
137. Wendt 1998, 105.
138. Miller 1987, 61-64; Searle 1995, 127-147.
139. See Dessler 1999.
140. Buss 1999.
141. Hollis and Smith 1990; Lapid 1989; Price and Reus Smit 1998.
142. Where, for instance, dependent variable refers simply to the issue to be explained-without making any further ontological claims.
143. See Hopf 1998.
144. Edwards, Ashmore, and Potter 1995, 42.
145. The crucial point here has to do with the nature and role of constitutive rules. While most practitioners of "normal science" deny them any explanatory role, some post-positivists see them as being inherently at odds with causal explanations. My argument here is that constitutive rules do entail causal explanation—although the causality at issue is not of the conventional kind. It is worth remembering that, at least since Hume, there is more than one view of causality.

NOTES TO CHAPTER THREE

1. Fernández 1997, 268.
2. Interview with Juan Ignacio García, Santiago, Chile, 7 August 2001.
3. Tellingly, passing over its cherished Estrada Doctrine, which establishes Mexico's practice of nonrecognition of foreign governments (because passing judgment on the legitimacy of a national government is considered as a form of undue interventionism in the domestic affairs of other states), Mexico broke diplomatic relations with Chile.
4. Cavallo, Salazar, and Sepúlveda 2001, 383.
5. Lagos 1995, 59.
6. Trying to induce the vote in a not so subtle way, the box for checking "Yes" featured the Chilean flag, whereas the one for the "No" was just a square in black. Aylwin Azócar 1998, 142. The consultation's official

results were: 75% yes, 23 % no, and the remaining null and blank. Americas Watch Report 1988, 19.

7. Interview with Carlos Huneeus, Santiago, Chile, 3 August 2001.
8. Hawkins 2002.
9. Forsythe 1991, 76 .
10. Interview with Genaro Arriagada, Speaker of the Technical Secretariat for the "No," Santiago, Chile 9 August 2001.
11. Ropp and Sikkink 1999, 181.
12. Interview with Arriagada, Santiago, Chile 9 August 2001.
13. Ibid.
14. Portales 1991, 258–259.
15. Ropp and Sikkink 1999, 175.
16. Hawkins 1997, 409.
17. Wilson 1989, 496.
18. Wilson and Dent 1995, 34.
19. Thérien, Fortman, and Gosselin 1996, 215.
20. Interview with Thomas Carothers, Washington, D.C. 7 December 2001. As Allen Weinstein, now President of the Center for Democracy and the person in charge of launching NED noted: "There used to be a huge argument between the Carter people and the Reagan people. The Carter people would say, you are not being faithful to the human rights initiative, the Reagan people would say, no we are in favor of democratic institutions, not just human rights, the Carter people would say, no, you're against human rights; they went back and forth." Interview with Allen Weinstein, Washington, D.C. 5 December 2001.
21. Kirkpatrick 1981, 31.
22. United States Department of State 1987, 7.
23. Carothers 1991, 3.
24. Loveman 1994, 105. This is not to say that these countries were at that time consolidated democracies; many of them would end up with "protected democracies (Loveman 1994)," "delegative democracies (O'Donnell 1994)," or some other distortion of (liberal) democracy.
25. Fernández 1997, 247.
26. Interview with Carothers, Washington, D.C. 7 December 2001.
27. Lutz and Sikkink 2000, 657.
28. Ibid., 659.
29. For the two components of the containment policy see Van Evera 1990, 3. I say "ostensibly more ideological component" because the geopolitical one was, at bottom, ideological as well.
30. Bunce 1985.
31. Lebow 1994, 259. The fact that, as William Wohlforth (Wohlforth 1994/5, 101) has observed, structural realism attempted "to explain the Cold War by reference to bipolarity," serves to illustrate the insufficiency of approaches that privilege material factors per se.
32. Pastor 1987, 363.
33. Quoted in Karl and Fagen 1986, 232.

34. Quoted in Van Evera 1990, 44.
35. Pastor 1987, 382; Muñoz 1986, 149.
36. Wilson 1989, 484.
37. Bloomfield and Lowenthal 1990, 870; Wesson 1986.
38. Aylwin Azócar 1998, 9 .
39. Portales 1991, 252, 254.
40. Tironi 1998, 44.
41. Garreton 1986, 97.
42. Oxhorn 1995, 3.
43. Tironi 1998, 52.
44. Valenzuela 1990, 135.
45. Garreton 1986, 96.
46. Kacowicz 1998, 123.
47. Chalmers 1977.
48. Barros 2002, 221; Godoy Arcaya 1990.
49. Oxhorn 1995, 37–39.
50. Tironi 1998, 56.
51. Schamis 1991, 214; Tironi 1998, 55.
52. Risse-Kappen 1995, 22.
53. Stepan 1978, 107.
54. Risse-Kappen 1995, 24.
55. Cited in Godoy Arcaya 1990, 22.
56. Tironi 1998, 58.
57. Arriagada 1998, 32.
58. Godoy Arcaya 1990, 12.
59. Garreton 1986, 106; Garreton 1989, 204.
60. Cited in Aylwin Azócar 1998, 137.
61. The government had burned the electoral record in July 1974 (Arriagada 1998, 110; Aylwin Azócar 1998, 75). Indeed, two Junta members would later recognize that neither the 1978 or the 1980 plebiscite complied with traditional Chilean standards. Americas Watch Report 1988, 15.
62. Garreton 1986, 111.
63. Barros 2002, 217.
64. Aylwin Azócar 1998, 184–186; Garreton 1990, 212.
65. Arriagada 1998, 116.
66. Ibid., 119.
67. Significantly, even in the adverse circumstances they were immersed, the opposition forces managed to obtain 30 percent of the votes for the "No" option. Aylwin Azócar 1998, 183.
68. Risse-Kappen 1995, 23.
69. Oxhorn 1995, 246.
70. Tironi 1998, 93.
71. Aylwin Azócar 1995, 71.
72. Tironi 1998, 73.
73. Schamis 1991.
74. Cited in Arriagada 1998, 103.

75. Huneeus 2000, 135.
76. Arriagada 1998, 45; Huneeus 2000, 38.
77. Tironi 1998, 77.
78. This is the more accepted figure now. See Hawkins 2002, 2. According to the Rettig Report, prepared by the National Commission on Truth and Reconciliation, and presented by President Patricio Aylwin in March 1991, the figure is 2025, of which 957 correspond to *desaparecidos* (people who have disappeared). For a summary see http://www.derechoschile.com/espanol/rettig.htm
79. Cited in Arriagada 1998, 67.
80. Americas Watch Report 1988, 1.
81. Valenzuela and Constable 1989, 130.
82. Aylwin Azócar 1998, 121; Ensalaco 2000, 117.
83. Portales 1991, 262.
84. Arriagada 1998, 220.
85. Ropp and Sikkink 1999, 176. See also Ensalaco 2000, 99, and Hawkins 2002.
86. Huneeus 2000, 256.
87. Oxhorn 1995, 11.
88. Quoted in Lowden 1996, 118. For the role of the Church as opposition to the military regime see Lowden 1996.
89. Garreton 1990, 213.
90. Interview with Monsignor Sergio Valech, from the Vicaría de la Solidaridad, Santiago, Chile, 7 August 2001.
91. Aylwin Azócar 1998, 234.
92. Oxhorn 1995, 78.
93. Portales 1991, 255.
94. The other two being the already mentioned 1978 National Consultation and the 1980 Constitutional plebiscite.
95. Huneeus 2000, 560.
96. Cavallo, Salazar, and Sepúlveda 2001, 756.
97. Arriagada 1998, 232.
98. Aylwin Azócar 1998, 334.
99. Cited in International Human Rights Law Group et al. 1989, 34.
100. Washington Office on Latin America 1989, 28.
101. International Human Rights Law Group et al. 1989, 112.
102. Interview with Jeffrey Puryear, Washington, D.C., 7 December 2001. Puryear was sent to Chile by the Ford Foundation shortly after the 1973 coup.
103. ECO Taller de Análisis, December 1988, Santiago, p. 4 Oxhorn 1995, 248.
104. Tironi 1998, 135.
105. National Democratic Institute for International Affairs 1988, 28.
106. Mónica Jiménez, E-mail communication, 13 September 2001.
107. Aylwin Azócar 1998, 334.
108. Arriagada 1998, 242; Huneeus 2000, 585.

109. Thus, for instance, from 1985 to 1987, the economy had grown at a rate of 3.5, 5.6, and 6.6 percent, respectively. In 1988 it would expand by 7.3 percent. Arriagada 1998, 289 (based on data from Chile's Central Bank).
110. Aylwin Azócar 1998, 266.
111. Huneeus 2000, 584.
112. Garreton 1988, 17. The *Command for the No* would eventually agglutinate 16 parties.
113. Lagos 1995, 49.
114. Nef and Bensabat 1989, 19; Valenzuela and Constable 1989, 129.
115. Cavallo, Salazar, and Sepúlveda 2001, 765.
116. Cited in Aylwin Azócar 1998, 346.
117. National Democratic Institute for International Affairs 1988, 22.
118. Huneeus 2000, 556.
119. Ibid, 559.
120. Tironi 1998, 90.
121. Interview with Juan Ignacio García, Santiago, Chile, 7 August 2001; Barros 2002, 294.
122. Aylwin Azócar 1998, 354.
123. Ibid., 357.
124. Valenzuela and Constable 1989, 130.
125. Interview with Carlos Portales, Santiago, Chile, 7 August 2001.
126. Interview with Arriagada, Santiago, Chile 9 August 2001. See also Barbara Gamarekian, "Foreign Affairs: How U.S. Political Pros Get out the Vote in Chile," *New York Times,* 18 November 1988, p. B6.
127. Huneeus 1989, 171.
128. Aylwin Azócar 1998, 358–359.
129. Ibid., 359.
130. Arriagada 1998, 220.
131. Muñoz and Portales 1991, 95.
132. *New York Times,* 11 December 1987, "Chile's Leader Takes to Task Foreign Foes."
133. Fernández 1997, 262. Cf. Americas Watch Report 1988, 203. See also WOLA July/August 1988 Update. "A growing bipartisan consensus with respect to Chile is emerging on Capitol Hill."
134. Fernández 1997, 271; Valenzuela and Constable 1989, 130.
135. Arriagada 1998, 253.
136. Arriagada 1995, 23.
137. Puryear 1994, 131.
138. Ibid., 153.
139. Ibid., 165.
140. Puryear 1991, 7.
141. Ibid., 31.
142. Ibid., 12.
143. Ibid., 14.
144. Puryear 1994, 139.

145. Ibid., 140.
146. Tironi 1998, 108.
147. Valenzuela and Constable 1989, 131.
148. Interview with Wollack, Washington, D.C., 7 December 2001.
149. Jarpa 1995, 64.
150. Puryear 1994, 142.
151. Cited in Puryear 1991, 1.
152. Interview with García, Santiago, Chile, 7 August 2001. See also Shirley Christian, "Foreigners to Observe Plebiscite in Chile," *New York Times,* 18 September 1988, A6.
153. Statement by Senator Edward M. Kennedy at press conference announcing the formation of *U.S. Committee for Free Election in Chile,* 4 August 1988 (From the Office of Senator Edward M. Kennedy of Massachusetts). On file with the author.
154. Letter dated 15 July 1988. On file with the author.
155. "Plebiscito: cita para más de 300 parlamentarios del mundo," in *Fortín Mapocho* 09/28/88, p. 4.
156. Interview with Monsignor Valech, Santiago, Chile, 7 August 2001.
157. Juan Ignacio García; Santiago, Chile, 7 August 2001.
158. Washington Office on Latin America 1988, 24.
159. Interview with Wollack, Washington, D.C., 7 December 2001. NDI nevertheless split into two teams: one supporting the "No" campaign, and the other in the monitoring mission. Still, as Wollack recognized in the interview, there probably was a "conflict of interests."
160. National Democratic Institute for International Affairs 1988, 39. See also Americas Watch Report 1988, 203.
161. Aylwin Azócar 1998, 332. My italics.
162. E-mail communication, 13 September 2001.
163. Interview with Portales, Santiago, Chile, 7 August 2001.
164. Interview with Arriagada, Santiago, Chile 9 August 2001. See also Christian, "Foreigners," note 152.
165. National Democratic Institute for International Affairs 1988, v.
166. Interview with Arriagada, Santiago, Chile 9 August 2001.
167. Interview with Monsignor Valech, Santiago, Chile, 7 August 2001.
168. E-mail communication, 15 November 2001.
169. International Human Rights Law Group 1988, 1; National Democratic Institute for International Affairs 1988, 4.
170. E-mail communication, 13 September 2001.
171. Interview with Puryear, Washington, D.C., 7 December 2001.
172. Interview with Oscar Godoy, Santiago, Chile, 9 August 2001.
173. International Human Rights Law Group et al. 1989, ii.
174. Interview with Hernán Felipe Errázuriz, Santiago, Chile, 8 August 2001. As noted, this is confirmed by a Law Group report, which states that "the Embassy of Chile in Washington has been quite cooperative (International Human Rights Law Group et al. 1989, 76)."
175. Juan Ignacio García; interview, Santiago, Chile, 7 August 2001.

176. Fernández 1997, 263–264.
177. Interview with Arriagada, Santiago, Chile 9 August 2001.
178. *El Mercurio,* 10/02/88, pp. A1 and C9. Former Spanish President Suárez replied to the Foreign Minister saying that observing elections "is not an intrusion, but a common practice in many democracies around the world." "Le responden destacados observadores que vienen a Chile: 'El Canciller García está totalmente equivocado,'" *Fortín Mapocho,* 3 October 1988, p. 20.
179. See, for instance, Christian, "Foreigners," note 152; "Observadores y Plebiscito" (unsigned editorial) *Fortín Mapocho,* 09/15/88, p. 9; "Cariñosa acogida para los 'humanoides,'" *Análisis,* October 10–16 1988.
180. Drake 1994, 29.
181. Interview with Godoy, Santiago, Chile, 9 August 2001.
182. According to Arriagada, "they [government leaders] were worried that we would not recognize the election." And he tells an anecdote about "the day I had an interview with the general in charge of the place and I tell him, look, the truth is that we cannot not recognize the election, because we are going to have information down to the voting tables. Consequently, if you want to know if I am lying, you just call me and tell me: 'give me the information at the voting table level.' If I say I don't have it, I am lying—and the guy was very impressed with that." Interview with Arriagada, Santiago, Chile 9 August 2001.
183. Interview with Godoy, Santiago, Chile, 9 August 2001. Pinochet actually told an interviewer after the plebiscite: "Of course I expected a different result [in the plebiscite]!." See Vázquez 1989, 21.
184. Ibid.
185. International Human Rights Law Group 1987, back cover.
186. Garber 1984, 1.
187. International Human Rights Law Group et al. 1989, 1.
188. E-mail communication, 15 November 2001.
189. Carothers, interview, Washington, D.C. 7 December 2001.
190. International Human Rights Law Group 1988, 3.
191. International Human Rights Law Group 1987, 47.
192. International Human Rights Law Group et al. 1989, iii.
193. Ibid., 2.
194. Ibid., 3. The Law Group sent this delegation in cooperation with three other organizations: the Danish Center for Human Rights, the Netherlands Institute of Human Rights, and the Robert F. Kennedy Memorial Center for Human Rights.
195. IHRLG News Release 08/04/88; International Human Rights Law Group et al. 1989, 24–25.
196. International Human Rights Law Group 1987, 15.
197. International Human Rights Law Group 1988, 20.
198. International Human Rights Law Group 1987, i.
199. International Human Rights Law Group et al. 1989, 76.
200. Ibid., 3–4.

201. Ibid., 55–56.
202. National Democratic Institute for International Affairs 1988, 5.
203. Interview with Wollack, Washington, D.C., 7 December 2001.
204. National Democratic Institute for International Affairs 1988, 6.
205. Interview with Wollack, Washington, D.C., 7 December 2001.
206. Interview with Arriagada, Santiago, Chile 9 August 2001.
207. National Democratic Institute for International Affairs 1988, 7.
208. Ibid., 7.
209. Ibid., 71.
210. Interview with Wollack, Washington, D.C., 7 December 2001.
211. National Democratic Institute for International Affairs 1988, 70.
212. According to Wollack, Arriagada told him that if violence erupted, it would get on the way of the long term political struggle the democratic forces were undertaking. Interview with Wollack, Washington, D.C., 7 December 2001.
213. Interview with Wollack, Washington, D.C., 7 December 2001.
214. Arriagada 1998, 259; Puryear 1991, 11; Washington Office on Latin America 1990, 22.
215. Interview with Wollack, Washington, D.C., 7 December 2001.
216. National Democratic Institute for International Affairs 1988, 1.
217. Ibid., 4.
218. Ibid., 88.
219. Ibid., v.
220. E-mail communication, 15 November 2001.
221. National Democratic Institute for International Affairs 1988, 67.
222. On November 1985 Philippine President Ferdinand Marcos announced that the next presidential election, scheduled for 1987, would be held one year early. The National Movement for Free Elections (NAMFREL), a diverse group of business, civic, professional, and religious leaders organized a massive domestic electoral effort. On election day, 7 February 1986, 500,000 NAMFREL volunteers watched the voting booths.

    Although NAMFREL was a Philippine-made achievement, foreign support was important here too. Thus, for instance, at the request of Senators Richard Lugar and Claiborne Pell, the Center for Democracy sent a preliminary delegation to the Philippines. The delegation, headed by the Center's President Allen Weinstein, who—as noted—had been director of the project that gave birth to NED, kept in contact with NAMFREL during its stay in Manila. He has noted that the Marcos regime did not quite appreciate the delegation's presence there and, furthermore, it "made it very clear that from their point of view, we should be looking at the opposition (interview with Allen Weinstein, President and CEO, Center for Democracy, Washington, 5 December 2001)." In its report, the Center established a set of requirements they considered critical in evaluating the February electoral process. Among these, was the accreditation of NAMFREL as a poll watching organization (National Democratic Institute for International Affairs 1991, 8).

But the main foreign actor in the Philippine electoral process was NDI. Its mission was organized jointly with the NRIIA, but the final report was written by NDI's Larry Garber, and published by NDI. The 44-member delegation, headed by British parliamentarian John Hume and Colombian former President Misael Pastrana, arrived in Philippines 12 days before the election (National Democratic Institute for International Affairs 1991, 11). NAMFREL not only welcomed foreign observers; it enthusiastically supported their presence, and eventually got 800 of them accredited (Byington 1988,189). NAMFREL also received financial support, approximately $1 million, from foreign donors. Among them were the United States Agency for International Development, and the NED (Hedman 2001, 183).

The interaction between domestic and foreign observers in the Philippine elections was quite a success, magnifying the opposition's denunciation of the electoral fraud perpetrated by the Marcos administration, and contributing to its eventual downfall in late February. This success made the international monitoring of elections acquire certain modularity (i.e., that it was susceptible to be replicated elsewhere following its same basic features). As the NDI-NRII report notes, "As a result of the Philippine experience, there has been increased attention on the role of the international community in supporting democratic development in different countries (National Democratic Institute for International Affairs 1991, 2)." Thus, after its involvement in the Asian archipelago, as David Stoelting has noted, "the National Democratic Institute has emerged as the most prominent NGO in the election observation field (Stoelting 1992, 423)." For NDI, "NAMFREL serve[d] as a model for organizing individuals who are not politically active and sensitizing them to political issues in a manner that will not arouse their fears (National Democratic Institute for International Affairs 1991, 75)." As its involvement with Chile evinced, NDI indeed drew on Philippine activists in order to build an international prodemocracy network.

223. Cited in National Democratic Institute for International Affairs 1991, 81.
224. Garber 2001, 373–374.
225. Ibid., 374.
226. Ropp and Sikkink 1999, 190.

NOTES TO CHAPTER FOUR

1. The figure was provided by Rosa Marina Zelaya, member of Nicaragua's Supreme Electoral Council at the time of the elections. Interview, Managua, 3 October 2001.
2. Pastor 2002, 231.
3. There was a brief period (August 1925-January 1927) when the marines actually left Nicaragua.
4. Dodd 1992, 4–5.
5. McClellan 1933, 37.

6. United States Department of State 1931, 3.
7. Dodd 1992.
8. Mares 1988, 95.
9. United States Department of State 1931, 2.
10. United States Department of State 1931, 4.
11. McClellan 1933, 33.
12. Carter Center 1990, 13; Pastor 2002, 22.
13. Herrera Zúñiga 1991, 91.
14. Ibid., 95.
15. Ibid., 96.
16. Ibid., 102–3.
17. Ibid., 116.
18. The mission, though, consisted of only three observers. OAS Electoral Observation Missions 1962–1989, internal document. On file with author.
19. Ramírez 1999, 88.
20. Herrera Zúñiga 1991, 132; Pastor 2002, 30.
21. Herrera Zúñiga 1991, 131–3. Interestingly, OAS observers (12 of them) were present at the National Constituent Assembly elections, held on 6 February 1972, but not for the presidential elections which took place the on 1 September 1974. OAS Electoral Observation Missions 1962–1989, internal document on file with author.
22. Pastor 2002, 59.
23. Herrera Zúñiga 1991, 137.
24. Ibid., 145.
25. Herrera Zúñiga 1994, 106.
26. Herrera Zúñiga 1991, 146–7.
27. Ramírez 1999, 185–6.
28. Castañeda 1985, 80.
29. Thus, for instance, the party's first contribution amounted to $50,000 (dollars). Ramírez 1999, 73.
30. Castañeda 1985, 81.
31. Pastor 2002, 44.
32. Cited in ibid., 45.
33. Cited in Washington Office on Latin America and International Human Rights Law Group 1984, 9–10.
34. Pastor 2002, 122. The passage of this resolution represented a defeat for the US government, which had called the OAS meeting in order to ask for the military intervention of a peace keeping force in Nicaragua.
35. Cited in ibid., 321.
36. Risse-Kappen 1995, 23.
37. Pérez 1992, 117; Ramírez 1999, 245.
38. Williams 1989, 80.
39. Ramírez 1999, 95.
40. Ibid., 109; Pastor 2002, 116–7.
41. Vanden and Prevost 1989, 89.
42. Gilbert 1988, 177.

43. Pérez 1992, 111. Similarly, another FSLN founder, Carlos Fonseca cherished "The Marxism of Lenin, Fidel, Che, Ho Chi Minh. . . . acquired by the Sandinista Liberation Front." Cited in Pastor 2002, 29–30.
44. Vanden and Prevost 1989, 90.
45. "In order to achieve a 20 percent growth in GDP," and advisor to the Minister of Planning of the Sandinista government would say, "it is enough to expropriate 20 percent of the private companies." Cited in Ramírez 1999, 231.
46. Robinson and Norsworthy 1985, 87.
47. Hoyt 1997, 27.
48. Ramírez 1999, 138.
49. Vanden and Prevost 1989, 90–2.
50. Cited in Pastor 2002, 140.
51. Pérez 1992, 133; Ramírez 1999, 148.
52. Ibid., 106.
53. Williams 1994, 177.
54. Bunce 1999, 151.
55. Washington Office on Latin America and International Human Rights Law Group 1984, 16.
56. Robinson and Norsworthy 1985, 88.
57. Washington Office on Latin America and International Human Rights Law Group 1984, 23.
58. McConnell 1997, 46.
59. Nicaraguan President Ortega told Costa Rican President Oscar Arias in 1986: "our democracy is different." Cited in Pastor 2002, 208–9. Vice-President Ramírez declared in 1984: "There is a dominant party here—the FSLN." LASA 1984, 23.
60. International Human Rights Law Group 1990, 14–15.
61. Williams 1994, 174.
62. International Human Rights Law Group 1990, 8–9.
63. Williams 1994, 177.
64. Williams 1989, 81.
65. Ibid., 83–88.
66. Herrera Zúñiga 1994, 101–2; Pérez 1992, 119.
67. Gilbert 1988, 177–9.
68. LASA 1984, 29.
69. Washington Office on Latin America and International Human Rights Law Group 1984, 41.
70. Interview with Miguel D'Escoto, Managua, 9 October 2001.
71. Ramírez 1999, 150.
72. LASA 1984, 18.
73. Ibid., 13.
74. Martínez Cuenca 1992, 128; Williams 1990, 19 .
75. Cornelius 1986, 67; Washington Office on Latin America and International Human Rights Law Group 1984, 1–2.
76. Williams 1994, 178.

77. Washington Office on Latin America and International Human Rights Law Group 1984, 51.
78. Robinson and Norsworthy 1985, 100–104.
79. For Antionio Lacayo, who would later become Minister of the Presidency in the Chamorro government, "those elections [of 1984] for us in the opposition practically did not exist . . . once Dr. Cruz was out, the process was over, since we already knew what was going to happen. . . . Those elections were really very similar to those that Somoza used to make." Interview with Lacayo, Managua, 6 October 2001.
80. Vanden and Prevost 1989, 103.
81. McConnell 1997, 46.
82. Pérez 1992, 121.
83. Ibid., 121 .
84. Kryzanek 1995, 413.
85. Kirkpatrick 1981, 36. Italics in original.
86. Kirkpatrick 1981, 40.
87. Kirkpatrick 1979. Roosevelt allegedly said about the first Somoza: "He is a son of a bitch, but he is *our* son of a bitch." The statement, though, seems to be apocryphal; see Pastor 2002, 3.
88. Carothers 1991.
89. Forsythe 1990, 40.
90. Tesón 1987, 173 and 180.
91. Brodhead 1987; Herman and Brodhead 1984; Pastor 1987, 371; Zak 1987, 177–178.
92. Karl 1986.
93. United States Department of State 1987, 28.
94. Karl 1986, 21.
95. Carothers 1991.
96. *New York Times,* 20 July 1984.
97. Reagan quoted in LASA 1984, 70; Robinson and Norsworthy 1985, 106.
98. Brodhead 1987, 35.
99. Cited in LASA 1984, 32.
100. Pastor 2002, 210.
101. Quoted in ibid. 2002, 210 .
102. Wilson 1989, 478.
103. Hey and Kuzma 1993, 39.
104. Castañeda 1985, 84.
105. Interview with D'Escoto, Managua, 9 October 2001.
106. Rico 1990, 94.
107. Wilson 1989, 482.
108. Comisión Internacional de Apoyo y Verificación 1998, 17.
109. Pastor 2002, 208–9; Rico 1990.
110. Pastor 2002, 208–9; Wilson 1989, 482.
111. Herrera Zúñiga 1994, 72.
112. Leogrande 1998, 508.
113. Ibid., 515.

114. Stoelting 1992, 378.
115. LASA 1990, 6.
116. Quoted in Leogrande 1998, 515.
117. Ibid., 514.
118. Ibid., 516–7.
119. McCoy, Garber, and Pastor 1991, 103.
120. Wilson 1989, 479; Wilson and Dent 1995, 35.
121. Leogrande 1998, 528.
122. Ibid., 529.
123. Ibid., 537; Pastor 2002, 223–4.
124. Ramírez 1999, 273.
125. Comisión Internacional de Apoyo y Verificación 1998, 20; Leogrande 1998, 555–6. Carter Center 1990, 14.
126. Leogrande 1998, 556.
127. Williams 1994, 179.
128. Interview with Mariano Fiallos, León, 5 October 2001.
129. Quoted in Leogrande 1998, 554.
130. Quoted in Pastor 2002, 224.
131. Carter Center 1990, 14.
132. Ramírez 1999, 162.
133. Leogrande 1998, 558.
134. Ibid., 562.
135. Ibid., 528.
136. Interview with Fiallos, León, 5 October 2001.
137. Interview with Lacayo, Managua, 6 October 2001.
138. Interview with Zelaya, Managua, 3 October 2001.
139. Interview with Lacayo, Managua, 6 October 2001.
140. OAS 1990, 2.
141. Interview with Zelaya, Managua, 3 October 2001.
142. Interview with Fiallos, León, 5 October 2001.
143. Interview with Lacayo, Managua, 6 October 2001.
144. Interview with Zelaya, Managua, 3 October 2001.
145. Interview with D'Escoto, Managua, 9 October 2001.
146. Hemisphere Initiatives (HI) was an organization formed mainly by academic in the United States in 1989 "to observe the elections and counteract what they thought would be a repeat of the disqualifying of the 1984 elections." Interview with IH member Judy Butler, Managua, 6 October 2001.
147. Interview with Zelaya, Managua, 3 October 2001. International Human Rights Law Group 1990, 67.
148. International Human Rights Law Group 1990, 15.
149. López Pintor 1998, 41–2.
150. International Human Rights Law Group 1990, 58; Williams 1990, 21.
151. Leogrande 1998, 561.
152. McCoy 1998, 59.
153. Pastor 2002, 251.
154. Carter Center 1990, 32; Pastor 2002, 238, 245, 252, 256 .

155. Mark A. Uhlig, "Nicaragua Vote Monitors Confident," *New York Times,* 23 February 1990, A3.
156. Strictly speaking, the mission was the CFEHG's. As noted in Chapter Two, the Council was established in 1986 in Atlanta, after a conference on democracy in the Americas held at the Carter Center. Jimmy Carter was chosen as its President, and Robert Pastor, Executive Director of the Center's Latin American Program, was named its Executive Secretary. For practical purposes, the Council is part of the Carter Center. Pastor 2002, 230. Thus, I refer to the Council's mission as the Carter's mission.
157. Ibid., 230.
158. Interview with Robert Pastor, Atlanta, 5 September 2000.
159. Pastor 2002, 231.
160. *New York Tiimes,* 9 August 1989, "Carter to Monitor Elections Next February in Nicaragua."
161. Carter Center 1990, 15.
162. Pastor 2002, 234.
163. Carter Center 1990, 10.
164. Pastor 2002, 237–8. Italics original.
165. Interview with Jennifer McCoy, Atlanta, 8 September 2000.
166. Carter Center 1990, 16.
167. Ibid., 17.
168. InternationalHuman Rights Law Group 1990, 39. www.centerfordemocracy.org/elect_monitor.nicaragua.html
169. Carter Center 1990, 18.
170. Ibid., 20.
171. Ibid., 20.
172. Pastor 2002, 256.
173. Ibid., 250.
174. Ibid., 252.
175. Carter Center 1990, 21.
176. Ibid., 21.
177. Ibid., 22.
178. Ibid., 22.
179. Williams 1990, 23.
180. Carter Center 1990, 22–3.
181. Babbitt 1990, 17.
182. Arriagada had already been to Nicaragua four or five times during the electoral process invited by NDI, to serve as a consultant to UNO. Interview with Arriagada, Santiago, 9 August 2001.
183. Carter Center 1990, 25–6.
184. Ramírez 1999, 144.
185. Interview with Fiallos, León, 5 October 2001.
186. Ramírez 1999, 144.
187. Interview with Lacayo, Managua, 6 October 2001. The prominence achieved by Carter was not well seen by the two IGOs. According to Pastor: "The only feeling shared by officials in the OAS and UN was the

professional's disdain for the politician's ability to grab the world's attention, even though that politician, Carter, was a different breed." Pastor 2002, 251.

188. Carter Center 1990, 31.
189. A/44/927 (30 March 1990) p. 5.
190. Interview with Elizabeth Spehar, Washington, 6 December 2001.
191. Murray 1999, 245.
192. Interview with Spehar, Washington, 6 December 2001.
193. Interview with Fiallos, León, 5 October 2001.
194. OAS 1989a, 27.
195. Ibid., 2.
196. Ibid., 1.
197. OAS 1989b, 25.
198. OAS 1990, 3.
199. OAS 1989b.
200. OAS 1990, 3.
201. OAS 1989b, 2.
202. Pastor 2002, 251.
203. Interview with D'Escoto, Managua, 9 October 2001.
204. Interview with Pastor, Atlanta, 5 September 2000.
205. Murray 1999, 67.
206. OAS 1990, 3.
207. Ibid., 3, 5.
208. Ibid., 11, 34.
209. Ibid., 15.
210. Ibid., 22.
211. Ibid., 25.
212. Ibid., 29–30.
213. Ibid., 29. Tellingly, Mexico's ambassador, Antonio de Icaza, did not make any pronouncement at the session in which the previous opinions were expressed.
214. Quoted in Pastor 2002, 250.
215. Quoted in Nolte 1998, 683.
216. United Nations A/46/609, 19 November 1991, par. 28.
217. Ibid. As the UN Mission's co-leader Nguyen Huu Dong put it: "There is a rule that in order for the UN to observe elections, they have to have an international impact, which is the UN's mandate. . . . Nicaragua entered in this category, since the elections in Nicaragua were part of Esquipulas II, and so they were going to open the way to negotiation for Central America. In that sense, the monitoring mission was completely justified." Interview with Nguyen Huu-Dong, Mexico City, 22 November 2001.
218. United Nations A/44/642, 20 October 89, 5.
219. Quoted in Stoelting 1992, 379.
220. Interview with UN mission member Shelly McConnell, Atlanta, 4 December 2001.
221. United Nations A/46/609, 19 November 1991, par. 34.

222. United Nations A/44/927, 30 March 1990, 7.
223. United Nations A/46/609, 19 November 1991, par. 32.
224. Quoted in United Nations A/44/927, 30 March 1990, 5.
225. Ibid., 3.
226. Interview with Butler, Managua, 6 October 2001.
227. Interview with Zelaya, Managua, 3 October 2001.
228. Interview with McCoy, Atlanta, 8 September 2000.
229. Interview with McConnell, Atlanta, 4 December 2001. Although no US or Soviet citizen was supposed to be a member of ONUVEN, McConnell was hired because she was working in Costa Rica at the time and could somehow be considered a "local hire." Additionally, although she performed as an observer, she was technically hired as a "research assistant." Nevertheless, a Soviet counterpart was soon hired to make up for their presence in ONUVEN.
230. Quoted in International Human Rights Law Group 1990, 71.
231. Interview with Fiallos, León, 5 October 2001.
232. United Nations A/44/927, 30 March 1990, 1.
233. Ibid., 12.
234. Ibid., 9.
235. United Nations A/46/609, 19 November 1991, par. 35.
236. Ibid, par. 35
237. United Nations A/44/927, 30 March 1990, 3.
238. Of course the case could be made that material factors would be involved down the road, since the international recognition of the legitimacy of the new Nicaraguan regime would bring increased financial assistance to it, but I would argue that this factor was not decisive—and in any case it would have rested on intersubjective factors (as suggested by the fact that the expected trigger of more resources is the "legitimacy" of the new regime).

NOTES TO CHAPTER FIVE

1. Instituto Federal Electoral 1995, 259 and 278.
2. *New York Times,* 25 November 1990, 3.
3. In Delgado 1994, 131.
4. In this section I draw on Santa Cruz 2002.
5. Garrido 1986, 238.
6. The president cannot be reelected. The rallying cry of the Mexican revolutionaries, fighting against the over thirty-year old dictatorship of Porfirio Díaz, was "Effective suffrage, no reelection."
7. Garrido 1989, 423.
8. Eisenstadt 1998, 11; Serrano Carreto 1996, 460.
9. Meyer 1996, 23.
10. In *Proceso,* 15 March 1993, No. 854, 10.
11. Aguilar Camín and Meyer 1993, 23.
12. Bizberg 1996, 94; Levy and Bruhn 1999, 527; Schmitter 1974.

13. Casar 1989.
14. Gibson 1997; Stevens 1977.
15. Bizberg 1996, 101; Gibson 1997.
16. Risse-Kappen 1995, 24.
17. It is relevant to point out that although the military sector was a central element in the first stages of the post-revolutionary domestic structure, it had been subordinated to civilian power by the late 1940s. See Diamond, Hartlyn, and Linz 1999, 19.
18. Aguilar Camín 1999.
19. Sartori 1976, 230.
20. The Communist Party also nominated a contender, but the party was proscribed.
21. The 1963 electoral reform had already prefigured some of these changes by introducing what were called "party representatives." These were elected to the lower house based on the percentage of votes obtained by their party (which needed to be at least 2.5 points).
22. The Federal Electoral Commission included the Interior Minister as its president, one representative from each house of Congress (controlled by the PRI), one from each registered party, and a notary public, appointed by the government.
23. Aguilar Camín and Meyer 1993, 239.
24. Lindau 1993, 96–97.
25. Aguayo Quezada 1998, 233.
26. Heredia 1994, 280.
27. In Article 89.
28. Wendt 1999, 235–237.
29. Mabire 1994, 545.
30. Quoted in Aguayo Quezada 1998, 110.
31. Ibid., 111.
32. Castañeda 1990, 407.
33. Serrano Carreto 1996, 446.
34. Pastor and Castañeda 1989, 10.
35. Meyer 1991, 228.
36. Mazza 2001, 55.
37. Chabat 1991, 19.
38. Mabire 1994, 545.
39. Garza Elizondo 1994, 536.
40. Chabat 1991, 2–5.
41. Dresser 1994, 6 .
42. Sánchez Susarrey 1993.
43. Significantly, the PRI-dominated LV Congress was one of the most active in Mexico's history. It amended more than 34 constitutional articles (out of 136), which covered areas ranging from the privatization of the banking system and the autonomy of the central bank, to land tenure, the establishment of the Human Rights Commission, and the relationship between the state and the churches—in addition, of course, to electoral legislation.

Francisco Gil Villegas argues that this congress, turned itself "de facto into a constituent assembly." Gil Villegas 1996, 159.

44. *Este País,* 25 April 1993, p. 10.
45. Serrano Carreto 1996, 451.
46. Dresser 1994, 64; Pastor in Eisenstadt 1998, 3.
47. *Proceso,* 8 March 1993, 853, p. 12. Apparently, behind this move was a sort of "privatization" of the PRI. Two weeks before his statement, Salinas had presided over a confidential dinner with 30 of the most powerful businessmen of Mexico, where they were asked to give 25 million dollars each for the 1994 PRI's electoral campaign. *New York Times,* 10 March 1993.
48. Carter Center 1993, 32.
49. Alcocer 1997, 693.
50. Aguayo Quezada 1993, 12.
51. All cited in *Proceso,* 23 March 1991, No. 751.
52. Delgado 1994, 136–139.
53. Calderon Alzati and Cazés 1996, 145.
54. Aguayo Quezada 1995, 159.
55. Interview with Sergio Aguayo, Mexico City, 8 May 2002. The mission was organized jointly by the CC's Council of Freely-Elected Heads of Government and NDI. Interestingly, Gregorio Atienza, former Secretary General of the Philippine election monitoring group NAMFREL (mentioned in chapter three) was a mission-member. See Council of Freely-Elected Heads of Government and National Democratic Institute for International Affairs 1991.
56. Aguayo Quezada 1995, 158.
57. Interview with Aguayo, Mexico City, 8 May 2002; Aguayo Quezada 1995, 159.
58. Interview with Aguayo, Mexico City, 8 May 2002.
59. Ibid.
60. Interview with Sergio Aguayo, Mexico City, 16 August 2000.
61. Interestingly, Genaro Arriagada, who—as noted—played a crucial role both in the 1988 Chilean plebiscite in general and in its international monitoring in particular, was a mission-member. As he recalls, "there were op-eds in the newspapers asking that we be expelled . . . Salinas' advisors met with us [but] it was a drag, with people following us, with guards at the hotel." Interview with Arriagada, Santiago, 9 August 2001.
62. In Eisenstadt 1998, 4.
63. Quoted in Vera 1994, 11.
64. Quoted in Delgado 1994,130.
65. Chabat 1991, 17.
66. Quoted in Chabat 1991, 14.
67. Interview with Robert Pastor, Atlanta, 5 September 2000.
68. Crespo 1992, 9.
69. Ibid., 10.
70. Delgado 1994, 140.
71. Crespo 1992, 8.

72. Ibid., 8.
73. Castañeda 1994, 53.
74. Morales 1995, 145.
75. Quoted in Acosta Romero and Castañeda 1997, 111 and 113.
76. Acosta Romero and Castañeda 1997, 113–128.
77. Castañeda 1994, 54–55.
78. Quoted in Delgado 1994, 132.
79. Interview with Aguayo, Mexico City, 8 May 2002.
80. Carter Center 1992, 7.
81. Ibid., 31.
82. Ibid., 55.
83. Ibid., 48.
84. Interview with Pastor, Atlanta, 5 September 2000.
85. Aguayo declared this to *El Universal;* reproduced in Carter Center 1992, 46.
86. Carter Center 1992, 49.
87. Ibid., 50.
88. Interview with Pastor, Atlanta 4 December 2001. Interestingly, Pastor notes that the observations the Mexicans made "presage all the problems that occurred in 2000," in the US presidential elections.
89. Carter Center 1992, 33.
90. Interview with Jorge Alcocer, Mexico City, 12 November 2001.
91. Quoted in Benitez Manaut 1996, 539.
92. Green 1994, 101.
93. Interview with Manuel Carrillo, Mexico City, 30 October 2001.
94. Serrano Carreto 1996, 453.
95. Castañeda 1994, 21.
96. Salinas in Castañeda 1999, 288.
97. Benitez Manaut 1996, 541.
98. Interview with Alcocer, Mexico City, 12 November 2001.
99. Washington Office on Latin America and Academia Mexicana de Derechos Humanos 1994, 19.
100. Interview with Aguayo, Mexico City, 8 May 2002.
101. Ibid.
102. Olguín Salgado 1998, 453.
103. Interview with Pastor, who debriefed several cabinet members on the issue. Atlanta, 5 September 2000.
104. Mazza 2001, 108.
105. Interview with Pastor, Atlanta, 4 December 2001.
106. Interview with Alcocer, Mexico City, 12 November 2001.
107. Ibid.
108. Ibid.
109. Interview with Manuel Carrillo, Mexico City, 30 October 2001.
110. Ibid.
111. According to Jorge Castañeda, Mexican writer Carlos Fuentes convinced Salinas to accept foreign observers on 23 December 1993. But

subsequently, when Fuentes tried to arrange a meeting between Cárdenas and Colosio to talk about the issue, Cárdenas showed some resistance to meet with his counterpart, and the issue fell apart. Salinas did not pursue it further. Castañeda 1994, 30–35.

112. Interview with Alcocer, Mexico City, 12 November 2001.
113. Alcocer 1997, 696.
114. Ibid., 696.
115. Interview with Jennifer McCoy, Atlanta, 8 September 2000.
116. Alcocer 1997, 699.
117. Interview with Patrick Merloe, Washington, 7 December 2001.
118. Quoted in Benitez Manaut 1996, 547.
119. Benitez Manaut 1996, 547.
120. *La Jornada,* 10 April 1994
121. Interview with Manuel Tello, Mexico City, 12 November 2001.
122. Carpizo 1995, 30.
123. Interview with Alcocer, Mexico City, 12 November 2001.
124. The IFE was reformed again in the 1996, as a result of a further electoral reform that falls out of the scope of this work. Quote from interview with José Woldenberg, Mexico City, 30 October 2001.
125. Interview with Woldenberg, Mexico City, 30 October 2001.
126. Quoted in *Proceso,* 14 March 1994, No. 906, p. 13.
127. Interview with Aguayo, Mexico City, 8 May 2001.
128. Calderon Alzati and Cazés 1996, 146.
129. Interview with Aguayo, Mexico City, 8 May 2001.
130. Calderon Alzati and Cazés 1996, 147.
131. Washington Office on Latin America and Academia Mexicana de Derechos Humanos 1994, 34 . Total foreign funding to AC reached $2 million Aguayo Quezada 1995, 162.
132. Interview with Aguayo, Mexico City, 8 May 2002. The sum was modest, though: $8,941. Aguayo, email communication, 31 March 2005.
133. Mazza 2001, 113. This of course doesn't mean that AC was an instrument of the US government, as some interested commentators suggested at the time.
134. Calderon Alzati and Cazés 1996, 157.
135. Interview with Aguayo, Mexico City, 8 May 2002.
136. Ibid.
137. Ibid.
138. Interview with Nguyen Huu-Dong, Mexico City, 22 November 2001.
139. Ibid.
140. Interview with Aguayo, Mexico City, 8 May 2002.
141. Interview with Aguayo, Mexico City, 16 August 2000.
142. Interview with McCoy, Atlanta, 8 September 2000.
143. Interview with Pastor, Atlanta, 5 September 2000.
144. Interview with Aguayo, Mexico City, 8 May 2002.
145. Ibid.
146. Aguayo Quezada 1995, 165.

147. Ibid., 166.
148. Interview with Aguayo, Mexico City, 8 May 2002. For a description of the environment that transpired at AC's headquarters on election night see Armendares 1994.
149. Interview with Carrillo, Mexico City, 30 October 2001.
150. Interview with Nguyen, Mexico City, 22 November 2001.
151. Castañeda 1994, 53.
152. Carter Center 1994, 32.
153. Interview with Alcocer, Mexico City, 12 November 2001.
154. Interview with Nguyen, Mexico City, 22 November 2001.
155. Interview with Carrillo, Mexico City, 30 October 2001.
156. Ibid.
157. "Carta de Jorge Carpizo, secretario de Gobernación, a Boutros Ghali," *La Jornada,* 12 May 1994, 3. Cited in Benitez Manaut 1996, 551.
158. As Tim Golden put it in the *New York Times:* "Trampling an ancient political taboo in pursuit of new legitimacy, for Mexico's coming presidential vote, the Government has invited the United Nations to evaluate its electoral system and help organize independent groups of election observers." "Mexico Invites U.N. to Attend Election to Observe the Observers," 13 May 1994, A9.
159. Interview with Manuel Tello, Mexico City, 12 November 2001.
160. No General Assembly authorization was required because no electoral observers were being sent.
161. Interview with Santiago Murray, Managua, 4 October 2001.
162. Interview with Elizabeth Spehar, Washington, 6 December 2001.
163. Interview with Carrillo, Mexico City, 30 October 2001.
164. As Spehar put it, "In the case of Mexico the great problem is that we have never been invited." Interview with Elizabeth Spehar, Washington, 6 December 2001.
165. United Nations 1994, 38.
166. Ibid., 60.
167. Benitez Manaut 1996, 559.
168. United Nations 1994, 59.
169. Benitez Manaut 1996, 559; Chand 1997, 553.
170. Interview with Nguyen, Mexico City, 22 November 2001. Armendares 1994, 52.
171. Interview with Alcocer, Mexico City, 12 November 2001.
172. Chand 1997, 553.
173. In *Proceso,* 15 August 1994, No. 928, p. 7.
174. Cf. Informe Alianza Cívica-Observación 94. La elección presidencial; entre el escepticismo y la esperanza. *La Jornada*, 21 August 1994 (Perfil).Aguayo Quezada 1995, 162 ; Armendares 1993, 166–167 .
175. No author 2000, 9.
176. Interview with Nguyen, Mexico City, 22 November 2001.
177. See Aguayo Quezada 1998.
178. Interview with Aguayo, Mexico City, 8 May 2002.

179. Chand 1997, 555.
180. Interview with Pastor, Atlanta, 5 September 2000.
181. Interview with McCoy, Atlanta, 8 September 2000.
182. Interview with Merloe, Washington, 7 December 2001.
183. Ibid.
184. Carter Center 1995, 8.
185. Preliminary report reproduced in Carter Center 1995, 31.
186. The NDI-IRI delegation, on the other hand, did not deliver its final report. Mazza 2001, 122.
187. Carter Center 1995, 11–12.
188. Interview with McCoy, Atlanta, 8 September 2000.
189. Salinas (Salinas 2000, 1058) would later boast about the UN's positive assessment of the electoral process, referring to it as an "objective endorsement" of the cleanness of the electoral process, and noting that "the participation of almost 82,000 Mexican observers and 777 foreign observers contributed in a fundamental way to provide the electoral process with credibility." This is consistent with NLI. Nevertheless, the issue here is that this approach under-theorizes how the international system can become an endower of legitimacy. This is an eminently intersubjective process, which NLI, with its focus on the self-interested individual [state] does not satisfactorily address.

NOTES TO CHAPTER SIX

1. Rosenau 1997.
2. Kenney 2003.
3. Quoted in Atwood 2001, 158.
4. Ibid, 158.
5. Quoted in ibid. 2001, 158.
6. Letter to *El Comercio,* 8 April 2000, A6.
7. Atwood 2001, 156.
8. Cotler 1989, 151–4.
9. Stepan 1978; Wise 1997, 95.
10. Conaghan, Malloy, and Abugattas 1990, 14.
11. O'Donnell and Schmitter 1986, 45.
12. Cotler 1989, 165–166.
13. Bermeo 1997, 312; Cotler 1989, 163.
14. Ibid., 166.
15. Ibid., 170.
16. Stepan 1988, 76–79.
17. Wise 1997, 75.
18. Levitsky 1999, 81.
19. Kenney 2003, 1234.
20. Roberts 1995, 95.
21. Levitsky 1999, 82.
22. Roberts 1995, 93.

23. Degregori 2001, 30.
24. Wise 1997, 84.
25. Roberts 1995, 97.
26. Cameron 1998, 127.
27. Risse-Kappen 1995, 23.
28. Diamond, Hartlyn, and Linz 1999, 25, 27–28; Mainwaring 1998, 69; Weyland 1996.
29. Levitsky and Way 2002, 52.
30. Ibid., 55–58.
31. Cameron 1998, 124.
32. Degregori 2001, 42.
33. MRE/RES. 1/92; in Unidad para la Promoción de la Democracia 1996, Annex 1.
34. García Calderón 2001, 48; Levitsky 1999, 81.
35. Degregori 2001, 47.
36. Roberts 1995, 100.
37. Atwood 2001, 167; Weyland 1996.
38. Atwood 2001, 171; García Calderón 2001, 48.
39. Interview with Rafael Roncagliolo, Lima, 14 October 2001.
40. Interview with César Landa, Lima, 16 October 2001.
41. Ibid.
42. Unidad para la Promoción de la Democracia 1996, 36–37.
43. Baena Soares had also led the mission to observe the municipal elections.
44. Unidad para la Promoción de la Democracia 1996, 71.
45. Degregori 2001, 80.
46. Ibid., 55.
47. Roberts 1995, 101.
48. Degregori 2001, 35.
49. Cameron 1998, 129.
50. Inflation rate in Roberts 1995, 97.
51. Unit for the Promotion of Democracy 1997, xi and 28 .
52. Interview with Santiago Murray, Washington, 6 December 2001.
53. Unit for the Promotion of Democracy 1997, 14.
54. Interview with Landa, Lima, 16 October 2001.
55. Ibid.
56. Interview with Roncagliolo, Lima, 14 October 2001.
57. Ibid.
58. Unit for the Promotion of Democracy 1997, 28–29.
59. Ibid. 28.
60. Cited in Youngers 2000, 54.
61. Washington Office on Latin America and George Washington University 2000, 15.
62. Interview with Roncagliolo, Lima, 14 October 2001.
63. Ibid.
64. Interview with Martín Tanaka, Lima, 17 October 2001.
65. Cotler and Grompone 2000, 44–45.

66. Ibid, 47–48.
67. Degregori 2001, 86.
68. Cameron 1998, 128.
69. Degregori 2001, 86.
70. Degregori 2001, 82.
71. Ibid., 89.
72. Ibid., 89.
73. García Calderón 2001, 50.
74. Degregori 2001, 95.
75. Ibid 95.
76. Unit for the Promotion of Democracy 1999, ix, 11.
77. Ibid: Appendix IV, n. pag.
78. Unit for the Promotion of Democracy 1999, 46.
79. Ibid., 48.
80. Ibid., 48.
81. Ibid., x, 47.
82. Interview with Roncagliolo, Lima, 14 October 2001.
83. Cotler and Grompone 2000, 50.
84. The *Frente Independiente* would later be decertified as a member of *Peru 2000,* because of a falsification of signatures scandal (more on this below).
85. Mainwaring 1998, 78.
86. Levitsky 1999, 82.
87. Cotler and Grompone 2000, 125–137.
88. García Calderón 2001, 52.
89. Levitsky and Way 2002, 56.
90. Cotler and Grompone 2000, 54.
91. Fujimori took this step when the Court was about to rule on the confiscation of the TV channel 2 (*Frecuencia Latina*), and after it had ruled that some Chilean citizens who had been charged with treason to the country, should be tried by civil tribunals. Cotler and Grompone 2000, 55–6.
92. Interview with Roncagliolo, Lima, 14 October 2001.
93. Ibid.
94. Interview with Landa, Lima, 16 October 2001.
95. Transparencia 2000.
96. Ibid., 63.
97. Interview with Landa, Lima, 16 October 2001.
98. From *Expreso,* 18 May, cited in *Caretas,* 1621, 2 June 2000, 52.
99. Interview with Roncagliolo, Lima, 14 October 2001.
100. National Democratic Institute for International Affairs and Carter Center 2000, 11–12.
101. Interview with Patrick Merloe, Washington, 7 December 2001.
102. Interview with Roncagliolo, Lima, 14 October 2001.
103. Interview with Merloe, Washington, 7 December 2001.
104. National Democratic Institute for International Affairs and Carter Center 2000, 19.
105. Ibid.

106. Ibid.
107. Ibid: Appendix 3 .
108. Ibid.: Appendix 2 .
109. Interview with Merloe, Washington, 7 December 2001.
110. Quoted in Degregori 2001, 321.
111. *Caretas,* 1611, 24 March 2000, 12.
112. *Caretas,* 1613, 7 April 2000, 31.
113. National Democratic Institute for International Affairs and Carter Center 2000, n. pag.
114. Ibid., 2.
115. Interview with Roncagliolo, Lima, 14 October 2001.
116. Interestingly, the government does not seem to have invited the UN to observe the elections, despite the explicit request by the JNE that it be invited. Interview with Ramiro Valdivia Cano, JNE Magistrate, Lima, 15 October 2001.
117. Interview with Roncagliolo, Lima, 14 October 2001.
118. Interview with Merloe, Washington, 7 December 2001.
119. Interviews with Merloe, Washington, 7 December 2001, and with Roncagliolo, Lima, 14 October 2001. See also *El Comercio,* 1 June 2000, A4.
120. Interview with Roncagliolo, Lima, 14 October 2001.
121. Interview with Linda Frey, Washington, 7 December 2001.
122. Interview with Elizabeth Spehar, Washington, 6 December 2001.
123. Ibid.
124. Interview with Merloe, Washington, 7 December 2001.
125. Interview with Roncagliolo, Lima, 14 October 2001.
126. Ibid.
127. *El Comercio,* 7 April 2000: A5.
128. Interview with Roncagliolo, Lima, 14 October 2001.
129. Interview with Valdivia Cano, JNE Magistrate, Lima, 15 October 2001.
130. OAS 2001, 3.
131. Ibid., 35.
132. Ibid., 25.
133. Ibid., 21.
134. Ibid., 28–29.
135. *Caretas,* 1611, 24 March 2000, 14.
136. *El Comercio,* 5 April 2000, A4.
137. *El Comercio,* 6 April 2000, A1.
138. Interview with Merloe, Washington, 7 December 2001.
139. Interview with Roncagliolo, Lima, 14 October 2001.
140. *El Comercio,* 5 April 2000, A4.
141. Interview with Spehar, Washington, 6 December 2001.
142. Interview with Shelly McConnell, Carter Center's Associate Director, Atlanta, 4 December 2001.
143. OAS 2001, 30.
144. Ibid., 32–33.

145. National Democratic Institute for International Affairs and Carter Center 2000, 21.
146. *EL Comercio,* 10 April 2000, A4. See also Clifford Krauss, "Peruvian's Lead in Vote Prompts Charge of Fraud," *New York Times,* 11 April 2000, A2.
147. Clifford Krauss, "Charging Fraud, Peruvian Challenger Demands Runoff," *New York Times,* 12 April 2000, A6. The Congressional election results were also widely questioned. See National Democratic Institute for International Affairs and Carter Center 2000, 22.
148. Ibid., 21.
149. Krauss, "Peruvian's," A1.
150. *El Comercio,* 10 April 2000, A2.
151. Clifford Krauss, "Peru's President, Short of Majority; Now Faces Runoff," *New York Times,* 13 April 2000, A4.
152. Ibid. A1.
153. Misión de Observación Electoral, Elecciones Generales República del Perú, Año 2000, Boletín No. 8.
154. *El Comercio,* 15 April 2000, A4.
155. *El Comercio,* 20 April 2000, A2.
156. *El Comercio,* 19 April 2000, A4.
157. *El Comercio,* 20 April 2000, A4.
158. *Caretas* 1619, 18 May 2000, 23.
159. *El Comercio,* 6 May 2000, A4.
160. National Democratic Institute for International Affairs and Carter Center 2000, 23; OAS 2001, 75.
161. *El Comercio,* 19May 2000, A4.
162. *Caretas*1619, 18 May 2000, 21.
163. *Caretas* 1619, 18 May 2000, 17.
164. *El Comercio,* 24 May 2000, A4.
165. National Democratic Institute for International Affairs and Carter Center 2000, Appendix 1.
166. Interview with Merloe, Washington, 7 December 2001.
167. *El Comercio,* 24 May 2000, A2.
168. OAS 2001, 121.
169. *El Comercio,* 26 May 2000, A2.
170. Interview with Roncagliolo, Lima, 14 October 2001.
171. *El Comercio,* 27 May 2000, A2. See also *Caretas,* 1621, 2 June 2000, 18.
172. *Caretas* 1621, 2 June 2000, p. 53.
173. Tellingly, 29.9 percent of the voters spoiled their ballots, and 1.2 percent left them blank. National Democratic Institute for International Affairs and Carter Center 2000, 25.
174. *El Comercio,* 1 June 2000, A2.
175. Ibid., A2.
176. *El Comercio,* 5 June 2000, A2.
177. *Caretas* 1622, June 8 2000, 16.
178. *El Comercio,* 7 June 2000, A5.

179. *Caretas,* 1622, June 8 2000, 18.
180. *El Comercio,* 6 June 2000, A2.
181. Interview with Roncagliolo, Lima, 14 October 2001.
182. *Caretas,* 1623, 15 June 2000, 31.
183. Reproduced in National Democratic Institute for International Affairs and Carter Center 2000, Appendix 1. The other two personalities were former Costa Rican President Rodrigo Carazo Odio, and former prime minister of Barbados L. Erskine Sandiford.
184. Interviews with Roncagliolo, Lima, 14 October 2001, and with Merloe, Washington, 7 December 2001.
185. Interview with Merloe, Washington, 7 December 2001.
186. *El Comercio,* 8 June 2000, A15.
187. *El Comercio,* 15 June 2000, A5.
188. Stepan 1988, 79.

NOTES TO CHAPTER SEVEN

1. Cited in Franck 2000, 45.
2. Fox and Roth 2000, 3.
3. Fox 1995, 1661.
4. Quoted in Reisman 1990, 874.
5. Franck 1992, 81.
6. Cited in Beigbeder 1994, 173.
7. UN Resolution 45/2.
8. Tellingly, Mexico denied that the authorization of the Haiti Mission set any precedent. Franck 1992, 81.
9. Carey 1998, 147.
10. Franck 1992, 72–73 .
11. Resolution 45/150 was called "Enhancing the effectiveness of the principle of periodic and genuine elections," and Resolution 45/151 "Respect for the principles of national sovereignty and non-interference in the internal affairs of States in their electoral processes." The passage of the two resolutions became a tradition in subsequent sessions of the General Assembly.
12. Beigbeder 1994, 104. This does not mean that the approval of the Unit's creation had no opposition. Mexico, for instance, initially opposed its creation because it considered the new office would undermine Article 2 (7). Cf. Pellicer 1995, 494.
13. Boutros-Ghali 1995, 3.
14. Rich 2001, 26.
15. Fox and Roth 2000, 3. Furthermore, the 2004 Report of the Secretary-General's High-level Panel on Threats, Challenges and Change notes that nowadays state sovereignty "carries with it the obligation of a State to protect the welfare of its own peoples and meet its obligations to the wider international community (United Nations 2004, 17). This echoes the 2001 Report of the International Commission on Intervention and State Sovereignty (ICISS) to the Secretary-General, whose central theme is "the idea

that sovereign states have a responsibility to protect their own citizens from avoidable catastrophe . . . but that when they are unwilling or unable to do so, that responsibility must be borne by the broader community of states." It also notes that "Sovereignty as responsibility has become the minimum content of good international citizenship (ICISS 2001, VIII and 8)."

16. Beigbeder 1994, 242–243.
17. www.thecommonwealth.org
18. "Preliminary Report of the Commonwealth Observer Group to the Presidential Election in Zimbabwe 9—10 March 2002" (Publication date: 14/03/2002, on file with author). The European Union (EU), which also sent an observer mission, withdrew after the Zimbabwean government expelled the mission's head, and later voted to imposed sanctions against President Robert Mugabe (*New York Times,* "Europe Places Penalties on Zimbabwe's Chief," 19 February 2002). The EU and the United States later condemned the electoral process, considering it illegitimate. Interestingly, the Organization of African Unity's observer mission found the Zimbabwean elections "transparent and credible" (*New York Times,* "An Election, Yes. But Free and Fair?, 17 March 2002). The regional organization was thus paying lip service to its 2001 launched "New Partnership for African Development," whose chart demands its leaders "to respect the global standards of democracy, the core components of which include . . . fair, open, free, and democratic elections."
19. The office was renamed "Office for Democratic Institutions and Human Rights" in January 1992. Back then the OSCE was known as the Conference for Security and Cooperation in Europe. The change to Organization became effective January 1995.
20. http://www.csce.gov/csce_human.cfm.
21. Ibid.
22. www.osce.org/odhir For the United States see *United States of America General Elections 5 November 2002: OSCE/ODIHR ELECTION ASSESSMENT MISSION REPORT* (15 January 2003, Warsaw), at http://www.osce.org/odihr/documents/reports/election_reports/us/us_5nov 2002_fr.php3
23. Flynn and Farell 1999, 524. It is worth noting that the 1975 CSCE's Helsinki Final Act does not even mention the word "democracy." Rich 2001, 27.
24. Ibid., 528.
25. Ibid., 516.
26. Ibid., 524.
27. Ibid., 515. Tellingly, during the negotiations to establish the European Convention on Human Rights and Fundamental Freedoms, the issue of including "free elections" as a human right came up, but it was not accepted. See Moravcsik 2000, 241.
28. Ibid., 512.
29. Acharya 2004.
30. Thus, for instance, the IFE participated in 33 electoral observation missions around the world from 1996 to 2001, and in July 1996 it became a member

of the Inter-American Union of Electoral Organisms. Documents on file with author. The IFE also played an important role in the 2004 Iraqi elections, even though Mexico had opposed the US-led invasion of that country.

31. Although the change of party in power in 2000 is certainly a stronger explanatory factor for this change. As Jorge G. Castañeda, Mexico's first Foreign Minister in the Fox administration, declared a few days before taking office: "Mexico didn't engage the issue of fair, free, and competitive elections abroad because it didn't hold them at home. Now Mexico is going to give a greater importance to this topic because to a certain extent it has been solved inside." *Reforma,* "La política exterior, con autoridad moral," 27 November 2000. Four years later, a document posted on the OAS web page by the Mexican government notes: "When democracy was strengthened in Mexico with the alternation of political parties, its vision of the OAS became more similar to that of the rest of the countries on the continent (www.oas.org). An analogous change of state identity arguably took place in Chile in 1990, when the austral country recognized the compulsory jurisdiction of the Inter-American Court of Human Rights. Ropp and Sikkink 1999, 190.
32. This would become much clearer a few months after my narrative ends, when the OAS High Level Mission arrived in Lima. What transpired after the arrival of the mission, though, falls outside my central concern in this work.
33. The 1990 Haitian experience mentioned above would be an important case in point.
34. Hemmer and Katzenstein 2002. On analytical eclecticism and epistemological agnosticism see Katzenstein and Okawara 2001/02.
35. Nye 1988, 239.
36. Miller 1987, 102–104.
37. Sterling-Folker 2000.
38. Nye 1988, 246.
39. In contrast, a cultural realist approach is better equipped to deal with normative issues. Nevertheless, its "realist" component draws quite a bit on constructivist arguments. Cf. Johnston 1995; Johnston 1996. I base my rejection of NCR for inquiring into eminently normative issues merely on question-driven grounds. I do not deny that its analysis might be useful for other questions. The superior performance of the constructivist approach also has to do with the fact that, as I noted before, mine is an eminently normative topic.
40. Schweller 2000, 43. Nevertheless, Schweller immediately qualifies his agreement with DPT by noting that "extending the democratic zone will not lead to a perpetual peace among nations."
41. I did not develop the post-structuralist approach either. Although, to my knowledge, authors within that perspective have not addressed my subject matter directly either, they would certainly make some valuable contributions if they engaged the matter. My treatment of the issue should not be

completely alien to them. Der Derian 2000. For a post-structural treatment of a related matter see Debrix 1999.

42. Doyle 1983, 212; Levy 1989, 268; Onuf 1998, 222.
43. Cited in Oren 1995, 151.
44. Ibid., 151.
45. Onuf 1998, 16. As a matter of fact, the debate between liberal and republican understandings of politics is still alive. Cf. Habermas 1998.
46. For an overview of these issues see Elman 1997.
47. Levy 1989, 271.
48. Quoted in Schweller 1992, 244.
49. Oren 1995, 149.
50. Russett 1993, 35.
51. Elman 1997, 10. Perhaps carrying DPT too far, the US Department of State claimed in May 2000: "Democratically governed nations are more likely to secure peace, deter aggression, expand open markets, promote economic development, protect American citizens, combat international terrorism and crime, uphold human and worker rights, avoid humanitarian crises and refugee flows, improve the global environment, and protect human health." *Mission Statement for the Office of Democracy,* cited in Fox 2001, 304.
52. Waltz 2000, 8. But compare with Huntley 1996.
53. Carothers 1999, 9.
54. Ibid., 10.
55. Cox, Ikenberry, and Inoguchi 2000, 4–5.
56. Ibid., 7.
57. Ibid., 17.
58. Thus, Gregory Fox and Brad Roth's edited *Democratic Governance and International Law,* although framed explicitly within a jurisprudential approach, contains many useful insights for IR (and for Comparative Politics as well). Fox and Roth 2000, 22. Indeed, the editors point in the direction of blurring disciplinary borders. As they put it: "The [democratic] entitlement is not simply law *affected by* politics. It is law that penetrates and regulates the very essence of political life, both domestically and internationally." Emphasis original Ibid., 18. See also Fox 2001.
59. Cited in Huntley 1996, 54 (emphasis in Huntley).
60. Ibid., 63.
61. The Venezuelan case is indicative both of this and of the extent to which IEM has become a norm in the hemisphere. On 11April 2002, a disparate coalition drove Venezuelan President Hugo Chávez from office. General Chavez was elected to the presidency by a landslide in 1998, six years after heading a failed coup attempt against President Carlos Andrés Pérez. The electoral process was observed by several international organizations, and it was deemed to be fair. Two years later, Chavez was reelected in an electoral process the Carter Center characterized as "flawed," although it pointed out that the irregularities would have not changed the outcome of the presidential election (http://www.cartercenter.org/activities/printdoc.asp?countryID=87).

After what at first appeared a successful coup, the OAS condemned the "alteration of the constitutional order" in that country. Within four days, though, Chávez was back in office. The day the failed coup took place, the Group of Rio issued a statement invoking the Inter-American Democratic Charter (IDC) and condemning "the interruption of the constitutional order in Venezuela (OAS, *Declaración del Grupo de Río sobre la situación en Venezuela,* 12 April 2002)." Shortly thereafter, the Permanent Council issued Resolution 811, *Situation in Venezuela,* also invoking the IDC and condemning the break of the democratic regime in the South American country. Furthermore, the foreign ministers instructed the Secretary General to carry out a fact finding mission in the troubled state and, citing Article 20 of the IDC, called for a special session of the General Assembly for 18 April (OAS, CP/RES. 811 (1315/02), *Situation in Venezuela*). But by that time, as noted, Chavez was back in office. At the special session, Gaviria presented his report. In it he assessed the Venezuelan political situation in light of the IDC, and summarized the active role he played in trying to mediate between the opposition and the government during his visit to the Andean country. From that moment on to the present, the OAS has played a very active role in stabilizing the political situation in Venezuela.

Thus, on 25 March 2002 the OAS delivered the document establishing the terms and conditions for an eventual recall referendum on Chavez's government, which could eventually solve the political impasse.

When the document was signed on 29 May, OAS Secretary General Gaviria noted "For the OAS it is particularly important the acknowledgment that both government and opposition make of the hemispheric commitment entitled Democratic Charter." In the agreement, both government and opposition "express [their] adherence to the principles enshrined in the Inter-American Democratic Charter," "invoke the principles of the Charter of the American States," and "recognize the support and facilitation provided . . . by the OAS . . . by the Carter Center, and by the UNDP (OAS, *Acuerdo entre la representación del Gobierno de la República Bolivariana de Venezuela y los factores políticos y sociales que lo apoyan y la Coordinadora Democrática y las organizaciones políticas y de la sociedad civil que la conforman*)."

The electoral exercise took place according to the rules established with the help of international mediators such as the OAS and the CC. Beyond their important mediating role, their monitoring function was carried out very thoroughly. According to the joint OAS-Carter Center mission, "the process was completed peacefully and without major obstacles that would have impeded the free exercise of constitutional rights ("Signature Collection in Venezuela: Joint OAS-Carter Center Statement," 1 December 2003, at www.oas.org/OASpage/eng/latestnews/latestnews.asp)." 8.5 million of 14 million registered voters voted. Whereas the 27-party opposition *Coordinadora* received 3.6 million votes, Chávez got almost 5 million; the president had thus received the support of 59 percent of the voters (*New York Times,* 17 August 2004; Ibid., 22 August 2004).

In its resolution on the results of the Venezuelan referendum, issued on 26 August, the OAS Permanent Council notes: "the Chavez government has fulfilled the commitments acquired with the hemispheric community. . . . Contributing to the strengthening of democracy in the Americas(CP/RES 869 (1436/04))." Thus, Chávez's staying in power was ultimately decided by constitutional means, something on which the regional organization played an instrumental role—even if it would be hard to argue that a liberal democratic regime prevails in Venezuela.

Bibliography

Acharya, Amitav. 2004. How Ideas Spread: Whose Norms Matter? Norm Localization and Institutional Change in Asian Regionalism. *International Organization* 58 (2): 239–275

Acevedo, Domingo E. 1993. The Haitian Crisis and the OAS Response: A Test of Effectiveness in Protecting Democracy. In *Enforcing Restraint: Collective Intervention in Internal Conflicts,* edited by L. F. Damrosch. New York: Council on Foreign Relations.

Acosta Romero, Miguel, and Jorge A. Castañeda. 1997. *La observación de elecciones.* Mexico: Porrúa.

Adolphs, R., D. Tranel, H. Bechara, H. Damasio, and A. R. Damasio. 1996. Neuropsychological Approaches to Reasoning and Decision-Making. In *Neurobiology of Decision,* edited by A. R. Damasio, Y. Christen and H. Damasio. New York: Springer.

Aguayo Quezada, Sergio. 1993. Los mirones son de palo. *Voz y Voto* (November): 12–13.

———. 1995. A Mexican Milestone. *Journal of Democracy* 6 (2): 157–167.

———. 1998. *Myths and [Mis] Perceptions.* Translated by J. Brody. San Diego: University of California, San Diego-El Colegio de Mexico.

Aguilar Camín, Héctor. 1999. La muerte del tapado. *Nexos* (263): 36–38.

———, and Lorenzo Meyer. 1993. *In the Shadow of the Mexican Revolution: Contemporary Mexican History, 1910–1989.* Translated by L. A. Fierro. Austin: University of Texas Press.

Alcocer, Jorge. 1997. The International Observation of Electoral Processes: The Mexican Experience in 1994. *Houston Journal of International Law* 19 (3): 689–703.

———. 1997. Observadores Internacionales. *Voz y Voto* (May 1997): 61–62.

Alexander, George, and Timothy J. McKeown. 1985. Case Studies and Theories of Organizational Decision Making. In *Advances in Information Processing in Organizations: A Research Annual,* edited by L. S. Sproull and et al. Greenwich: JAI Press.

Alker, Hayward R. 1990. Rescuing 'Reason' from the 'Rationalists': Reading Vico, Marx and Weber as Reflective Institutionalists. *Millennium* 19 (2): 161–184.

Americas Watch Report. 1988. Chile: Human Rights and the Plebiscite. New York.

Andrews, David M. 1994. Capital Mobility and State Autonomy: Toward a Structural Theory of International Monetary Relations. *International Studies Quarterly* 38 (2): 193–218.

Arendt, Hannah. 1990. *On Revolution.* New York: Penguin.

Armendares, Pedro Enrique. 1993. Sergio Aguayo ¿Alianza para qué? *Voz y Voto,* November 1993, 54–55.

———. 1994. Alianza: sus dilemas. *Voz y Voto,* September 1994, 22–23.

———. 1994. Horacio Borneo: Mirones de Palo. *Voz y Voto,* August 1994, 52–53.

Arriagada, Genaro. 1995. Tres lecciones del 5 de Octubre. In *El Plebiscito del 5 de Octubre de 1988,* edited by M. Tagle. Santiago: Corporación Justicia y Democracia.

———. 1998. *Por la razón o la fuerza: Chile bajo Pinochet.* Santaigo: Editorial Sudamericana.

Ashley, Richard. 1981. Political Realism and Human Interest. *International Studies Quarterly* 25 (2): 204–237.

———. 1984. The Poverty of Neorealism. *International Organization* 38 (2): 225–286.

Atkins, G. Pope. 1977. *Latin America in the International Political System.* New York: Free Press.

Atwood, Roger. 2001. Democratic Dictators: Authoritarian Politics in Peru from Leguía to Fujimori. *SAIS Review* 21 (2): 155–176.

Audi, Robert, ed. 1995. *The Cambridge Dictionary of Philosophy.* Cambridge: Cambridge University Press.

Aylwin Azócar, Patricio. 1995. El plebiscito: Un hito en la historia de la patria. In *El plebiscito del 5 de Octubre de 1988,* edited by M. Tagle. Santiago: Corporación Justicia y Democracia.

———. 1998. *El Reencuentro de los Demócratas: Del Golpe al Triunfo del No.* Santiago: Ediciones B.

Babbitt, Bruce. 1990. Poll Position. *New Republic,* March 19, 1990, 17–19.

Baena Soares, João Clemente. 1994. *Profile of a Mandate: Ten Years at the OAS.* Washington: OAS.

Ball, Margaret M. 1969. *The OAS in Transition.* Durham, N. C.: Duke University Press.

Barnett, Michael N. 1997. Bringing in the New World Order: Liberalism, Legitimacy, and the United Nations. *World Politics* 49: 526–51.

Barros, Robert. 2002. *Constitutionalism and Dictatorsip: Pinochet, the Junta, and the 1980 Constitution.* Cambridge: Cambridge University Press.

Bartelson, Jens. 1995. *A Genealogy of Sovereignty.* Cambridge: Cambridge University Press.

Beigbeder, Yves. 1994. *International Monitoring of Plebiscites, Referenda and National Elections: Self-Determination and Transition to Democracy.* Dordrecht: Martinus Nijhoff Publishers.

Benitez Manaut, Raúl. 1996. La ONU en México. Elecciones presidenciales de 1994. *Foro Internacional* 36 (3): 533–565.

Bermeo, Nancy. 1997. Myths of Moderation: Confrontation and Conflict during Democratic Transitions. *Comparative Politics:* 305–322.

Bizberg, Ilán. 1996. La transformación del régimen político mexicano: entre el pluralismo y el neocorporativismo. In *México: una agenda para fin de siglo,* edited by A. Aziz Nassif. Mexico City: La Jornada Ediciones-UNAM.

Bloomfield, Richard J., and Abraham F. Lowenthal. 1990. Inter-American Institutions in a Time of Change. *International Journal* 45: 867–888.

Boutros-Ghali, Boutros. 1995. Democracy: A Newly Recognized Imperative. *Global Governance* 1 (1): 3–11.

Brodhead, Frank. 1987. Demonstration Elections as Counterinsurgency. In *Intervention on Trial: The New York War Crimes Tribubal on Central American and the Caribbean,* edited by P. Ramshaw and T. Steers. New York: Praeger.

Brooks, Stephen G., and William C. Wohlforth. 2000/01. Power, Globalization, and the End of the Cold War: Reevaluating a Landmark Case for Ideas. *International Security* 25 (3): 5–53.

Bull, Hedley. 1977. *The Anarchical Society.* New York: Columbia Unversity Press.

Bunce, Valerie. 1985. The Empire Strikes Back: The Evolution of the Eastern Bloc from a Soviet Asset to a Soviet Liability. *International Organization* 39: 1–46.

———. The Return of the Left and the Future of Democracy in Central and Eastern Europe. In *Comparative Political Parties and Party Elites,* edited by B. A. Yesilada. Ann Arbor: University of Michigan Press.

Burr, Robert. 1973. United States Latin American Policy 1945–1972: Introduction. In *The Dynamics of World Power: A Documentary History of United States Foreign Policy 1945–1973,* edited by A. M. J. Schlesinger. New York: Chelsea.

Buss, Andreas. 1999. The Concept of Adequate Causation and Max Weber's Comparative Sociology of Religion. *British Journal of Sociology* 50 (2): 317–329.

Byington, Kaa. 1988. *Bantay ng Bayan: Stories from the NAMFREL Crusade (1984–1986).* Manila: Bookmark.

Calderón Alzati, Enrique, and Daniel Cazés. 1996. La observacion ciudadana del proceso electoral. In *Las elecciones presidenciales de 1994,* edited by E. Calderon Alzati and D. Cazes. Mexico City: La Jornada Ediciones-UNAM.

Callcott, Wilfrid Hardy. 1968. *The Western Hemisphere: Its Influence on United States Policies to the End of World War II.* Austin: University of Texas Press.

Cameron, Maxwell. 1998. Self-Coups: Peru, Guatemala, and Russia. *Journal of Democracy* 9 (1): 125–139.

Caporaso, James A. 1992. International Relations Theory and Multilateralism: The Search for Foundations. *International Organization* 46 (3): 599–632.

Carey, Henry F. 1998. Electoral Observation and Democratization in Haiti. In *Electoral Observation and Democratic Transitions in Latin America,* edited by K. J. Middlebrook. San Diego: University of California Press.

Carothers, Thomas. 1991. *In the Name of Democracy: U. S. Policy Toward Latin American in the Reagan Years.* Berkeley: University of California Press.

———. 1995. Democracy Promotion Under Clinton. *Washington Quarterly* 18 (4): 13–28.

———. 1999. *Aiding Democracy Abroad: The Learning Curve*. Washington: Carnegie Endowment for International Peace.

Carozza, Paolo G. 2003. *From Conquest to Constitutions: Retrieving a Latin American Tradition of the Idea of Human Rights*. Human Rights Quarterly 25: 281–313.

Carpizo, Jorge. 1995. La reforma federal electoral de 1994. In *Eleccions, diálogo y reforma: Mexico 1994 / I,* edited by J. Alcocer. Mexico City: Nuevo Horizonte.

Carter Center. 1990. Observing Nicaragua's Elections, 1989–1990. Atlanta.

———. 1992. The International Observation of U. S. Elections. Atlanta.

———. 1993. Electoral Reform in Mexico. Atlanta.

———. 1994. Elections in Mexico: Third Report. Atlanta.

———. 1995. The August 21, 1994 Mexican National Elections: Fourth Report. Atlanta.

———. 1996. The Journey to Democracy: 1986–1996. Atlanta.

Casar, María Amparo. 1989. Corporativismo y transición. *Nexos,* 55–59.

Castañeda, Jorge. G. 1994. *Sorpresas te da la vida: México 1994*. Mexico City: Aguilar.

———. 1999. *La herencia: Arqueología de la sucesión presidencial en México*. Mexico City: Alfaguara.

———. 1985. Don't Corner Mexico! *Foregin Policy* 60:75–90.

———. 1990. Salinas's International Relations Gamble. *Journal of International Affairs* 43 (2): 407–422.

Cavallo, Ascanio, Manuel Salazar, and Oscar Sepúlveda. 2001. *La historia oculta del régimen militar.* Santiago: Grijalbo-Mondaori.

Chabat, Jorge. 1991. Mexico's Foreign Policy in 1990: Electoral Sovereignity and Integration with the United States. *Journal or Interamerican Studies and World Affairs* 33 (1): 1–25.

Chalmers, Douglas A. 1977. The Politicized State in Latin America. In *Authoritarianism and Corporatism in Latin America,* edited by J. Malloy. Pittsburgh: University of Pittsburgh Press.

Chand, Vikram K. 1997. Democratisation from the Outside in: NGO and International Efforts to Promote Open Elections. *Third World Quarterly* 18 (3): 543–561.

Checkel, Jeffrey. 1997. International Norms and Domestic Politics: Bridging the Rationalist-Constructivist Divide. *European Journal of International Relations* 3 (4): 473–495.

———. 1999. Norms, Institutions, and National Identity in Contemporary Europe. *International Studies Quarterly* 43: 83–114.

Clinton, W. David. 1986. The National Interest: Normative Foundations. *The Review of Politics* 48 (4): 495–519.

Comisión Internacional de Apoyo y Verificación. 1998. *La Desmovilización y Reinserción de la Resistencia Nicaragüense*. Washington: OAS.

Comité Jurídico Interamericano. 1965. Estudio sobre la relación jurídica entre el respeto de los derechos humanos y el ejercicio de la democracia. Washington: OAS.

Conaghan, Catherine, James Malloy, and Luis Abugattas. 1990. Business and the "Boys": The Politics of Neoliberalism in the Central Andes. *Latin American Research Review* 25 (2): 3–30.

Cornelius, Wayne A. 1986. The Nicaraguan Elections of 1984: A Reassessment of Their Domestic and International Sgnificance. In *Elections and Democratization in Latin America, 1980–1985,* edited by P. W. Drake and E. Silva: Center for Iberian and Latin American Studies, University California Press.

Corrales, Javier, and Richard E. Feinberg. 1999. Regimes of Cooperation in the Western Hemisphere: Power, Interests, and Intellectual Traditions. *International Studies Quarterly* 43: 1–36.

Cortell, Andrew P., and James W. Jr. Davis. 2000. Understanding the Domestic Impact of International Norms: A Research Agenda. *International Studies Review* 2 (1): 65–87.

Cotler, Julio. 1989. Military Interventions and "Transfer of Power to Civilians" in Peru. In *Transitions from Authoritarian Rule: Latin America,* edited by G. O'Donnell, P. Schmitter and L. Whitehead. Baltimore: Johns Hopkins University Press.

———, and Romeo Grompone. 2000. *El fujimorismo: ascenso y caída de un régimen autoritario.* Lima: Instituto de Estudios Peruanos.

Council of Freeely-Elected Heads of Government, and National Democratic Institute for International Affairs. 1991. The 1990 General Elections in Haiti. Washington.

Cox, Michael, G. John Ikenberry, and Takashi Inoguchi. 2000. Introduction. In *American Democracy Promotion: Impulses, Strategies, and Impacts,* edited by M. Cox, G. J. Ikenberry and T. Inoguchi. Oxford: Oxford University Press.

Cox, Robert W. 1989. Production, the State, and Change in World Order. In *Global Changes and Theoretical Challenges: Approaches to World Politics for the 1990s,* edited by E.-O. Czempiel and J. N. Rosenau. Lexington: Lexington Books.

Crawford, Neta C. 2002. *Argument and Change in World Politics: Ethics, Decolonization and Humanitarian Intervention.* Cambridge: Cambridge University Press.

Crespo, José Antonio. 1992. *Observadores internacionales: la percepción ciudadana, Documento de trabajo 3.* Mexico City: CIDE.

Davis, Harold Eugene. 1977. Relations During the Times of Troubles, 1825–1860. In *Latin American Diplomatic History: An Introduction,* edited by H. E. Davis, J. J. Finan and F. T. Peck. Baton Rouge: Louisiana State University Press.

Debrix, Francois. 1999. Space Quest: Surveillance, Governance, and the Panoptic Eye of the United Nations. *Alternatives* 24: 269–294.

Degregori, Carlos Iván. 2001. *La década de la antipolítica: auge y huida de Alberto Fujimori y Vladimiro Montesinos.* Lima: Instituto de Estudios Peruanos.

Delgado, René. 1994. Observando a los observadores. In *La organización de las elecciones. Problemas y proyectos de solución,* edited by J. Alcocer and R. Morales. México: Porrúa.

Der Derian, James. 2000. Virtuous war/virutal theory. *International Affairs* 76 (4): 771–788.

Dessler, David. 1999. Constructivism within a Positivist Social Science. *Review of International Studies* 25: 123–137.

Diamond, Larry, Jonathan Hartlyn, and Juan J. Linz. 1999. Introduction: Politics, Society, and Democracy in Latin America. In *Democracy in Developing Countries: Latin America,* edited by L. Diamond, J. Hartlyn, J. J. Linz and S. M. Lipset. Boulder: Lynne Rienner.

Dodd, Thomas J. 1992. *Managing Democracy: A Case Study: United States Election Supervision in Nicaragua, 1927–1933.* New Brunswick: Transaction Books.

Donnelly, Jack. 1986. International Human Rights: A Regime Analysis. *International Organization* 40 (3): 599–642.

Doyle, Michael W. 1983. Kant, Liberal Legacies, and Foreign Affairs. *Philosophy and Public Affairs* 12 (3 & 4): 205–35; 323–53.

Drake, Paul W. 1994. International Factors in Democratization. Madrid: Estudio/Working Paper 1994/61.

Dresser, Denise. 1994. Five Scenarios for Mexico. *Journal of Democracy* 5 (3): 57–71.

Eckstein, Harry. 1975. Case Study and Theory in Political Science. In *Handbook of Political Science,* edited by F. I. Greenstein and a. N. W. Poslby. Reading: Addison-Wesley.

Edwards, Derek, Malcolm Ashmore, and Jonathan Potter. 1995. Death and Furniture: The Rhetoric, Politics and Theology of Bottom Line Arguments against Relativism. *History of the Human Sciences* 8 (2): 25–49.

Eisenstadt, Todd A. 1998. Electoral Justice in Mexico: From Oxymoron to Legal Norm in Less Than a Decade: A Case-Based Analysis of theEvolution of Mexico's Federal Electoral Courts (1988–1997).

Elman, Colin. 1996. Horses for Courses: Why *Not* Neorealist Theories of Foreign Policy. *Security Studies* 6 (1): 7–53.

Elman, Miriam Fendius, ed. 1997. *Paths to Peace: Is Democracy the Answer?* Cambridge: MIT Press.

Elster, Jon. 1991. Rationality and Social Norms. *Archives Europeennes de Sociologie* 32 (1): 109–129.

Ensalaco, Mark. 2000. *Chile under Pinochet: Recovering the Truth.* Philadelphia: University of Pennsylvania Press.

Evangelista, Matthew A. 1997. Domestic Structure and International Change. In *New Thinking in International Relations Theory,* edited by M. W. Doyle and G. J. Ikenberry. Boulder: Westview Press.

Farer, Tom J. 1988. *The Grand Strategy of the United States in Latin America.* New Brunswick: Transaction Books.

———. 1993. A Paradigm of Legitimate Intervention. In *Enforcing Restraint: Collective Intervention in Internal Conflicts,* edited by L. F. Damrosch. New York: Council on Foreign Relations.

Farley, Lawrence. 1986. *Plebiscites and Sovereignty: The Crisis of Political Illegitimacy.* Boulder: Westview Press.

Fearon, James D., and Alexander Wendt. 2002. Rationalism v. Constructivism: A Skeptical View. In *Handbook of International Relations,* edited by W. Carlsnaes, T. Risse and B. A. Simmons. London: Sage Publications.

Feaver, Peter D., Gunther Hellman, Randall L. Schweller, Jeffrey W. Taliaferro, William C. Wohlforrth, Jeffrey W. Legro, and Andrew Moravcsik. 2000. Brother, Can You Spare a Paradigm? (Or Was Anybody Ever a Realist?). *International Security* 25 (1): 165–193.

Fernández, Sergio. 1997. *Mi lucha por la democracia.* Santiago: Editorial Los Andes.

Finnemore, Martha. 1996. Norms, Culture,and World Politics: Insights from Sociology's Institutionalism. *International Organization* 50 (2): 325–347.

———, and Kathryn Sikkink. 1998. International Norm Dynamics and Political Change. *International Organization* 52 (4): 887–917.

Flynn, Gregory, and Henry Farrell. 1999. Piecing Together the Democratic Peace: The CSCE, Norms, and the "Construction" of Security in Post-Cold War Europe. *International Organization* 53 (3): 505–535.

Forsythe, David P. 1990. *The Politics of International Law: U.S. Foreign Policy Reconsidered.* Boulder: Lynne Rienner.

———. 1991. Human Rights, The United States and The Organization of American States. *Human Rights Quarterly* 13 (1): 66–98.

Fox, Gregory H. 1995. Multinational Election Monitoring. Advanced International Law on the High Wire. *Fordham International Law Journal* 18 (5): 1657–1667.

———. 2000. The Right to Political Participation in International Law. In *Democratic Governance and International Law,* edited by G. H. Fox and B. R. Roth. Cambridge: Cambridge University Press.

———. Election Monitoring: The International Legal Setting. *Wisconsin International Law Journal* 19 (3): 295–319.

———, and Brad R. Roth. 2000. Introduction: The Spread of Liberal Democracy and Its Implications for International Law. In *Democratic Governance and International Law,* edited by G. H. Fox and B. R. Roth. Cambridge: Cambride University Press.

Franck, Thomas M. 1992. The Emerging Rigth to Democratic Governance. *American Journal of International Law* 86 (1): 16–91.

———. 2000. Legitimacy and the Democratic Entitlement. In *Democratic Governance and International Law,* edited by G. H. Fox and B. R. Roth. Cambridge: Cambridge University Press.

Garber, Larry. 1984. *Guidelines for Intertnational Election Observing.* Washington: The International Human Rigths Group.

———. 2001. Book Review: Democratic Governance and Interational Law. *Wisconsin International Law Journal* 19 (3): 369–377.

García Calderón, Ernesto. 2001. Peru's Decade of Living Dangerously. *Journal of Democracy* 12 (2): 46–58.

Garretón, Manuel Antonio. 1986. The Political Evolution of the Chilean Military Regime and Problems in the Transition to Democracy. In *Transitions from Authoritarian Rule: Latin America,* edited by G. O'Donnell, P. C. Schmitter and L. Whitehead. Baltimore: Johns Hopkins University Press.

———. 1988. *El plebiscito de 1988 y la transición a la democracia.* Cuadernos de Difusion. Santiago: FLACSO.

———. 1989. *The Chilean Political Process.* Translated by S. Kellum. Boston: Unwin Hyman.

———. 1990. The Political Oppostition and the Party Sytem under the Military Regime. In *The Struggle for Democracy in Chile, 1982–1990,* edited by P. W. Drake and I. Jaksic. Lincoln: University of Nebraska Press.

Garrido, Luis Javier. 1986. *El partido de la Revolución institucionalizada.* Mexico City: SEP.

———. 1989. The Crisis of Presidencialismo. In *Mexico's Alternative Political Futures,* edited by W. A. Cornelius, J. Genelman and P. H. Smith. San Diego: Universtity of California Press.

Garza Elizondo, Humberto. 1994. Los cambios de la política exterior de México. *Foro Internacional* 34 (4): 534–575.

Gibson, Edward. 1997. The Populist Road to Market Reform: Policy and Electoral Coalitions in Mexico and Argentina. *World Politics* 49:339–370.

Gil Villegas, Francisco. 1996. Cambio constitucional en México durante el sexenio de Carlos Salinas de Gortari. *Foro Internacional* 36 (1–2): 159–87.

Gilbert, Dennis. 1988. *Sandinistas: The Party and the Revolution.* New York: Basil Blackwell.

Godoy Arcaya, Oscar, ed. 1990. *Hacia una democracia moderna: La opción parlamentaria.* Santiago: Universidad Católica de Chile.

Green, Daniel M., ed. 2002. *Constructivism and Comparative Politics.* Armonk: M.E. Sharpe.

Green, Rosario. 1994. El debate ONU-OEA: Nuevas competencias en el ámbito de la paz y la seguridad nacionales? In *Las Naciones Unidas hoy: visión de México,* edited by O. Pellicer. Mexico City: Fondo de Cultura Económica.

Guzzini, Stefano. 1993. Structural Power: The Limits of Neorealist Power Analysis. *International Organization* 47 (3): 443–478.

———. 2000. A Reconstruction of Construtivism in International Relations. *European Journal of International Relations* 6 (2): 147–182.

Habermas, Jürgen. 1989. *The Theory of Communicative Action. Volume Two: Lifeworld and System: A Critique of Functionalist Reason.* Translated by T. McCarthy. Boston: Beacon Press.

———. 1998. Three Normative Models of Democracy. In *The Inclusion of the Other: Studies in Political Theory,* edited by C. Cronin and P. De Greiff. Cambridge: MIT Press.

Haggard, Stephan, and Beth Simmons. 1987. Theories of International Regimes. *International Organization* 41 (3): 491–516.

Hale, Charles A. 1986. Political and Social Ideas in Latin America, 1870–1930. In *The Cambridge History of Latin America,* edited by L. Bethell. Cambridge: Cambridge University Press.

Hall, Rodney Bruce. 1999. *National Collective Identity: Social Constructs and International Systems.* New York: Columbia University Press.

Hartz, Louis. 1983. *The Liberal Tradition in America.* San Diego: Harvest/HBJ.

Hasenclever, Andreas, Peter Mayer and Volker Rittberger. 1997. *Theories of International Regimes*. Cambridge: Cambridge University Press.

Hawkins, Darren G. 1997. Domestic Responses to International Pressure: Human Rights in Authoritarian Chile. *European Journal of International Relations* 3 (4): 403–434.

———. 2002. *International Human Rights and Authoritarian Rule in Chile*. Lincoln & London: University of Nebraska Press.

Hawthorn, Geoffrey. 1993. *Plausible Worlds: Possibility and Understanding in History and the Social Sciences*. Cambridge: Cambridge University Press.

Hedman, Eva-Lotta E. 2001. *In the Name of Society: From Free Election Movements to People Power in the Philippines*. Book ms.

Hegel, Georg W. F. 1996. *Elements of the Philosophy of Right*. Cambridge: Cambridge University Press.

Hemmer, Christopher, and Peter Katzenstein. 2002. Why is There No NATO in Asia? Collective Identity, Regionalism, and the Origins of Multilateralism. *International Organization* 56 (3): 575–607.

Heredia, Blanca. 1994. Making Economic Reform Politically Viable: The Mexican Experience. In *Democracy, Markets, and Structural Reform in Latin America*, edited by W. Smith, C. Acuña and E. Gamarra. New Brunswick: Transaction Books.

Herman, Edward S., and Frank Brodhead. 1984. *Demonstration Elections: U.S.-Staged Elections in the Dominican Republic, Vietnam, and El Salvador*. Boston: South End Press.

Herrera Zúñiga, René. 1991. *Relaciones internacionales y poder político en Nicaragua*. Mexico City: El Colegio de México.

———. 1994. *Nicaragua: El derrumbe negociado*. Mexico City: El Colegio de México.

Hey, Jeanne A. K., and Lynn M. Kuzma. 1993. Anti-U.S. Foreign Policy of Dependent States: Mexican and Costa Rican Participation in Central American Peace Plans. *Comparative Political Studies* 26 (1): 30–62.

Hobson, John M. 2000. *The State and International Relations*. Cambridge: Cambrdige Unviverstity Press.

Hollis, Martin, and Steve Smith. 1990. *Explaining and Understanding in International Relations*. Oxford: Clarendon Press.

Hopf, Ted. 1998. The Promise of Constructivism in International Relations Theory. *International Security* 23 (1): 171–200.

Hoyt, Katherine. 1997. *The Many Faces of Sandinista Democracy:* Ohio University Press.

Huneeus, Carlos. 1989. La derrota del general Pinochet. *Opciones* 15: 155–173.

———. 2000. *El régimen de Pinochet*. Santiago: Editorial Sudamericana.

Huntley. 1996. Kant's Third Image: Systemic Sources of the Liberal Peace. *International Studies Quarterly* 40: 45–76.

Hurd, Ian. 1999. Legitimacy and Authority in International Politics. *International Organization* 53 (2): 379–408.

Ikenberry, G. John. 1996. The Myth of Post-Cold War Chaos. *Foreign Affairs* 75 (3): 79–91.

———. 2000. America's Liberal Grand Strategy: Democracy and National Security in the Post-war Era. In *American Democracy Promotion: Impluses, Strategy, and Impacts,* edited by M. Cox, G. J. Ikenberry and T. Inoguchi. Oxford: Oxford University Press.

Instituto Federal Electoral. 1995. *Memoria del Proceso Electoral Federal.* Mexico City: IFE.

Inter-American Dialogue. 1992. Convergence and Community: The Americas in 1993. Washington.

Inter-American Institute of International Legal Studies. 1966. *The Inter-American System: Its Development and Strengthening.* Dobbs Ferry, NY: Oceana Publications.

International Commission on Intervention and State Sovereignty. 2001. *The Responsibility to Protect.* Ottawa: International Development Research Centre.

International Human Rights Law Group. 1987. Report on the Chilean Electoral Process. Washington, D. C.

———. 1988. Supplemental Report on the Chilean Electoral Process. Washington, D. C.

———. 1990. Preliminary Report on the Upcoming Nicaraguan Elections. Washington, D. C.

———, Danish Center of Human Rights, Netherlands Institute of Human Rights, and Robert F. Kennedy Memorial Center for Human Rights. 1989. Chile: The Plebiscite and Beyond. Washington, D. C.

———, and Washington Office on Latin America. 1985. From Shadow into Sunlight: A Report on the 1984 Uruguayan Electoral Process. Washington, D. C.: Internatinal Human Rights Law Group and Washington Office on Latin America.

Jarpa, Sergio. 1995. Proyecciones del plebiscito de 1988. In *El Plebiscito del 5 de Octubre de 1988,* edited by M. Tagle. Santiago: Corporación Justicia y Democracia.

Jason, Karen J. 1992. The Role of Non-Governmental Organizations in International Election Observing. *International Law and Politics* 24: 1795–1843.

Johnston, Alastair. 1995. *Cultural Realism: Strategic Culture and Grand Strategy in Chinese History.* Princeton: Princeton University Press.

———. 1996. Cultural Realism and Strategy in Maoist China. In *The Culture of National Security: Norms and Identity in World Politics,* edited by P. J. Katzenstein. New York: Columbia University Press.

———. 2001. Treating Internatioanl Institutions as Social Environments. *International Studies Quarterly* 45: 487–515.

Kacowicz, Arie M. 1998. *Zones of Peace in the Third World: South America and West Africa in Comparative Perspective.* New York: State University of New York Press.

Kapstein, Ethan B. 1995. Is Realism Dead? The Domestic Sources of International Politics. *International Organization* 49 (4): 751–74.

Karl, Terry. 1986. Imposing Consent? Electionalism vs. Democratization in El Salvador. In *Elections and Democratization in Latin America, 1980–1985,* edited by P. W. Drake and E. Silva. San Diego: University of California.

———, and R. R. Fagen. 1986. The Logics of Hegemony: The United States as a Superpower in Central America. In *Dominant Powers and Subordinate States: The United States in Latin America and the Soviet Union in Eastern Europe,* edited by J. F. Triska. Durham, Duke University Press.

Katzenstein, Peter J. 1996. Introduction: Alternative Perspectives on National Security. In *The Culture of National Security: Norms and Identity in World Politics,* edited by P. J. Katzenstein. New York: Columbia University Press.

———, Robert O. Keohane, and Stephen D. Krasner. 1998. *International Organization* and the Study of World Politics. *International Organization* 54 (4).

———, and Nobuo Okawara. 2001/2. Japan, Asia-Pacific Security, and the Case for Analytical Eclecticism. *International Security* 26 (3): 153–185.

Kaufmann, Chaim D., and Robert A. Pape. 1999. Explaining Costly International Moral Action: Britain's Sixty-year Campaign Against the Atlantic Slave Trade. *International Organization* 53 (4): 631–668.

Keck, Margaret, and Kathryn Sikkink. 1998. *Activists Beyond Borders: Advocacy Networks in International Politics.* Ithaca: Cornell University Press.

Kenney, Charles D. 2003. The Death and Rebirth of a Party System, Peru 1978–2001. *Comparative Political Studies* 36 (10): 1210–1239.

Keohane, Robert O. 1983. The Demand for International Regimes. In *International Regimes,* edited by S. D. Krasner. Ithaca: Cornell University Press.

———. 1984. *After Hegemony: Cooperation and Discord in the World Political Economy.* Princeton: Princeton University Press.

———. 1988. International Institutions: Two Approaches. *International Studies Quarterly* 32: 379–396.

———. 1989. *International Institutions and State Power: Essays in International Relations Theory.*

———. 1993. Institutional Theory and the Realist Challenge after the Cold War. In *Neorealism and Neoliberalism: The Contemporary Debate,* edited by D. A. Baldwin. New York: Columbia University Press.

Kier, Elizabeth. 1997. *Imaginining War: French and British Military Doctrine Between the Wars.* Princeton: Princeton University Press.

Kirkpatrick, Jeane. 1979. Dictatorsphips and Double Standards. *Commentary* 68 (5): 34–45.

———. 1981. U. S. Security & Latin America. *Commentary* 71 (1): 29–40.

Klotz, Audie. 1995. *Norms in International Relations: The Struggle against Apartheid.* Ithaca: Cornell University Press.

Kohli, Atul, et al. 1995. The Role of Theory in Comparative Politics: A Symposium. *World Politics* 48: 1–49.

Kornai, János. 1992. *The Socialist System.* Princeton: Princeton University Press.

Krasner, Stephen D. 1983. Regimes and the Limits of Realism: Regimes as Autonomous Variables. In *International Regimes,* edited by S. D. Krasner. Ithaca: Cornell University Press.

———. 1988. Sovereignty: An Institutional Perspective. *Comparative Political Studies* 21 (1): 66–94.

———. 1999. *Sovereignty: Organized Hypocrisy.* Princeton: Princeton University Press.

Kratochwil, Friedrich. 1987. Rules, Norms, Values, and the Limits of "Rationality." *Archiv Fur Rechts-Und Sozialphilosophie ARSP* 73 (3): 301–329.

———. 1978. *International Order and Foreign Policy.* Boulder: Westview Press.

———. 1984. Thrasymmachos Revisited: On the Relevance of Norms and the Study of Law for International Relations. *Journal of International Affairs* 37 (2): 343–356.

———. Norms and Values: Rethinking the Domestic Analogy. *Ethics and International Affairs* 1: 135–159.

———. 1995. Sovereignty as *Dominium:* Is There a Right of Humanitarian Intervention? In *Beyond Westphalia? State Sovereignty and International Intervention,* edited by G. M. Lyons and M. Mastanduno. Baltimore: Johns Hopkins University Press.

———. 1996. Is the Ship of Culture at Sea or Returning? In *The Return of Culture and Identity in IR Theory,* edited by Y. Lapid and F. Kratochwil. Boulder: Lynne Rienner Publishers.

Kryzanek, Michael J. 1995. Intervention and Interventionism. In *U. S.—Latin American Policymaking: A Reference Handbook,* edited by D. W. Dent. Wesport: Greenwood Press.

Lagos, Ricardo. 1995. El plebiscito de 1988: Una jornada inconclusa. In *El plebiscito del 5 de Octubre de 1988,* edited by M. Tagle. Santiago: Corporación Justicia y Democracia.

Lapid, Yosef. 1989. The Third Debate: On the Prospects of International Theory in a Post-Positivist Era. *International Studies Quarterly* 33: 235–254.

Larsen, Henrik. 1997. *Foreign Policy and Discourse Analysis: France, Britain, and Europe.* London: Routledge.

LASA (Latin American Studies Association). 1984. The Electoral Process in Nicaragua: Domestic and International Influences.

———. 1990. Electoral Democracy Under International Pressure. Pittsburgh: Latin American Studies Asociation.

Lebow, Richard Ned. 1994. The Long Peace, the End of the Cold War, and the Failure of Realism. *International Organization* 48 (2): 249–277.

Legro, Jeffrey W. 1997. Which Norms Matter? Revisiting the "Failure" of Internationalism. *International Organization* 51 (1): 31–63.

———. 2000. The Transformation of Policy Ideas. *American Journal of Political Science* 44 (3): 419–432.

———, and Andrew Moravcsik. 1999. Is Anybody Still a Realist? *International Security* 24 (2): 5–55.

Leogrande, William M. 1998. *Our Own Backyard: The United States in Central America, 1977–1992.* Chapel Hill: University of North Carolina Press.

Levitsky, Steven. 1999. Fujimori and Post-Party Politics in Peru. *Journal of Democracy* 10 (3): 78–92.

———, and Lucan A. Way. 2002. The Rise of Competitive Authoritarianism. *Journal of Democracy* 13 (2): 51–65.

Levy, Daniel C., and Kathleen Bruhn. 1999. Mexico: Sustained Civilian Rule and the Question of Democracy. In *Democracy in Developing Countries: Latin*

America, edited by L. Diamond, J. Hartlyn, J. J. Linz and S. M. Lipset. Boulder: Lynne Rienner.

Levy, Jack S. 1989. The Causes of War: A Review of Theories and Evidence. In Behavior, Society and Nuclear War. In *Behavior, Society, and Nuclear War,* edited by T. P. E., J. L. Husbands, R. Jervis, P. C. Stern and C. Tilly. New York: Oxford University Press.

Lindau, Juan D. 1993. *Los tecnócratas y la élite gobernante mexicana.* Mexico City: Joaquín Mortiz.

López Pintor, Rafael. 1998. Nicaragua´s Measured Move to Democracy. In *Post-conflict Elections, Democratization and International Assistance,* edited by K. Kumar. Boulder: Lynne Rienner.

Loveman, Brian. 1994. "Protected Democracies" and Military Guardanship: Political Transitions in Latin America, 1978–1993. *Journal of Interamerican Studies and World Affairs* 36 (2): 105–189.

Lowden, Pamela. 1996. *Moral Opposition to Authoritarian Rule in Chile, 1973–90.* Oxford: Macmillan.

Lutz, Ellen L., and Kathryn Sikkink. 2000. International Human Rights Law and Practice in Latin America. *International Organization* 54 (3): 633–659.

Mabire, Bernardo. 1994. El fantasma de la antigua ideología y su resistencia al cambio de la política exterior en el sexenio de Salinas de Gortari. *Foro Internacional* 34 (4): 545–71.

Mainwaring, Scott. 1998. Party Systems in the Third Wave. *Journal of Democracy* 9 (3): 67–81.

March, James G., and Johan P. Olsen. 1998. The Institutional Dynamics of International Political Orders. *International Organization* 52 (4): 943–969.

Mares, David R. 1988. Mexico's Foreign Policy as a Middle Power: The Nicaragua Connection, 1884–1986. *Latin American Research Review* 23 (3): 81–107.

Martínez Cuenca, Alejandro. 1992. *Sandinista Economics in Practice.* Boston: South End Press.

Mazza, Jaqueline. 2001. *Don't Disturb the Neighbors: The United States and Democracy in Mexico, 1980–1995.* New York: Routledge.

McClellan, Edwin North. 1933. Supervising Nicaraguan Elections, 1928. *United States Naval Institute Proceedings* 59 (1).

McCloskey, Deidre N. 1998. Burgeois Virtue and the History of *P* and *S*. *Journal of Economic History* 58 (2): 297–317.

McConnell, Shelley A. 1997. Institutional Development. In *Nicaragua without Illusions: Regime Transition and Structural Adjustment in the 1990's,* edited by T. W. Walker. Wilmington: SR Books.

McCoy, Jennifer, Larry Garber, and Robert Pastor. 1991. Pollwatching and Peacemaking. *Journal of Democracy* 2 (4): 102–114.

———. 1998. Monitoring and Mediating Elections During Latin American Democratization. In *Electoral Observation and Democratic Transitions in Latin America,* edited by K. J. Middlebrook. San Diego: University of California.

McSweeney, Bill. 1999. *Security, Identity, and Interests: A Sociology of International Relations.* Cambridge: Cambridge University Press.

Meyer, Lorenzo. 1991. Mexico: The Exception and the Rule. In *Exporting Democracy: The United States and Latin America,* edited by A. F. Lowenthal. Baltimore: Johns Hopkins University Press.

———. 1996. La crisis del presidencialismo mexicano. Recuperación espectacular y recaída estructural, 1982–1996. *Foro Internacional* 36 (1–2): 11–30.

Miller, Richard W. 1987. *Fact and Method: Explanation, Confirmation and Reality in the Natural and the Social Sciences.* Princeton: Princeton University Press.

Mitchell, Timothy. 1991. The Limits of the State: Beyond Statist Approaches and Their Critics. *American Political Science Review* 85 (1): 77–96.

Morales, Rodrigo. 1995. Observadores electorales, una evaluación. In *Elecciones, diálogo y reforma,* edited by J. Alcocer. México: Nuevo Horizonte-CEPNA.

Moravcsik, Andrew. 1997. Taking Preferences Seriously: A Liberal Theory of International Politics. *International Organization* 51 (4): 513–53.

———. 2000. The Origins of Human Rights Regimes: Democratic Delegation in Postwar Europe. *International Organization* 54 (2): 217–252.

Morgenthau, Hans J. 1946. *Scientific Man vs. Power Politics.* Phoenix Books-University of Chicago Press ed. Chicago.

Muñoz, Heraldo. 1986. The Latin American Policy of the Reagan Administration. In *Latin American Views of U. S. Policy.* New York: Praeger.

———. 1990. The Rise and Decline of the Inter-American System: A Latin American View. In *Alternative to Intervention: A New U.S.-Latin American Security Relationship,* edited by R. J. Bloomfield and G. F. Treverton. Boulder: Lynne Rienner.

———, and Carlos Portales. 1991. *Elusive Friendship: A Survey of U.S.-Chilean Relations.* Translated by O. Garcia Vlaverde. Bolder: Lynne Rienner.

Murase, Shinya. 1976. The Most-Favored-Nation Treatment in Japan's Treaty Practice During the Period 1854–1905,. *The American Journal of International Law* 70: 273–297.

Murphy, Alexander B. 1996. The Sovereign State System as Political-Territorial Ideal: Historical and Contemporary Considerations. In *State Sovereignty as Social Construct,* edited by T. J. Biersteker and C. Weber. Cambridge: Cambridge University Press.

Murray, Santiago. 1999. La OEA y la observación electoral. Paper read at Seminario Internacional sobre Legislación y Organización Observación Electoral: Una Visión Comparativa, at Lima, Peru.

National Democratic Institute for International Affairs. 1988. Chile's Transition to Democracy: The 1988 Presidential Plebiscite: National Democratic Institute for International Affairs.

———. 1991. Reforming the Philippine Electoral Process: Developments 1986–88. Washington, D. C.

———, and Carter Center. 2000. Peru Elections 2000. Washington and Atlanta: National Democratic Institute for International Affairs and Carter Center.

Nau, Henry R. 1993. Identity and International Politics: An Alternative to Neorealism. Paper read at 1993 Annual Meeting of teh American Political Science Association, September 2–5, at The Washington Hilton.

Nef, J., and Remonda Bensabat. 1989. Chilean Plebiscite: Exit Pinochet? *International Perspectives* 18 (1): 18–21.

No author. 2000. Nguyen Huu Dong. *Voz y Voto,* July-August 2000, 7–9.

Nolte, Detlef. 1998. La observación internacional de elecciones. In *Tratado de derecho electoral comparado de América Latina,* edited by D. Nohlen, S. Picad and D. Zovatto. Mexico City: Fondo de Cultura Económica.

Nye, Joseph S. 1988. Neorealism and Neoliberalism. *World Politics* 40 (3): 235–251.

OAS (Organization of American States). 1962a. Annual Report of the Secretary General. Washington.

———. 1962b. Informe de la misión de asistencia técnica de la Organización de los Estados Americanos sobre las elecciones presidenciales en la República de Costa Rica. Washington: Organization of American States.

———. 1963. Informe de la Misión de Asistencia Técnica de la Organización de los Estados Americanos a la República de Honduras en Materia Electoral. Washington.

———. 1965. Informe de la Comisión Preparatoria de la Reunión de Consulta de Ministros de Relaciones Exteriores sobre Democracia Representativa sometido al Consejo de la Organización de los Estados Americanos el 26 de febrero de 1965. Washington.

———. 1968. Report Presented by the Mission of Observers to the President of the Republic of Ecuador. Washington.

———. 1978. Note Dated January 24, 1978, from the Chairman of the Committee on Juridical and Political Affairs Regarding the Topic of the Appointment of Election Observers. Washington.

———. 1980. Note from the Permanent Mission of Guatemala Requesting Dispatch of a Mission of Observers Designated by the Organization of American States to Witness the Municipal Elections to be Held in that Country on April 20, 1980. Washington.

———. 1984a. Request by the Government of Guatemala that Observers be Sent to Witness the Election that will be Held on July 1, 1984. Washington.

———. 1984b. Request from the Government of El Salvador for Observers to be Sent to Witness the Elections to be Held on March 25, 1984. Washington.

———. 1989a. Report of the Secretary General on Observation of the Passage of the Electoral and Mass Media Laws of Nicaragua and the Agreement on the Privileges and Immunities of Observers of the Nicaraguan Election Process. Washington.

———. 1989b. Second Report on the Observation of the Nicaraguan Electoral Process (July 13 to November 3, 1989). Washington.

———. 1990. Informe del Secretario General de la Organización sobre su observación del proceso electoral en Nicaragua. Washington.

———. 2000. Manual para la Organización de Misiones de Observación Electoral. Washington: Organization of Ameircan States

———. 2001. Observación Electoral en Perú: Elecciones Generales 9 de abril de 2000. Washington, D.C.: OAS.

O'Donnell, Guillermo. 1994. Delegative Democracy. *Journal of Democracy* 5 (1): 55–69.

———, and Philippe C. Schmitter. 1986. *Tentative Conclusions about Uncertain Democracies.* Edited by G. O'Donnell, P. C. Schmitter and L. Whitehead. John Hopkins University Press ed, *Transitions from Authoritarian Rule.* Baltimore.

O'Gorman, Edmundo. 1988. Latinoamérica: Así no. *Nexos* 123: 13–14.

———. 2003 [1958]. *La Invención de América: Investigación acerca de la estructura histórica del nuevo mundo y del sentido de su devenir.* Third ed. Mexico City: Fondo de Cultura Económica.

Olguín Salgado, Eduardo. 1998. La observación electoral durante los comicios presidenciales de 1994. In *Elecciones y partidos políticos en Mexico, 1994,* edited by M. Larrosa and L. Valdés. México: UAM-Iztapalapa.

Onuf, Nicholas G. 1998. *The Republican Legacy in International Thought.* Cambridge: Cambridge University Press.

Oren, Ido. 1995. The Subjectivity of the 'Democratic' Peace. *International Security* 20 (2): 147–184.

Outhwaite, William. 1994. *Habermas: A Critical Introduction.* Stanford: Stanford University Press.

Oxhorn, Philip. 1995. *Organizing Civil Society: The Popular Sectors and the Struggle for Democracy in Chile.* University Park: Pensylvania State University Press.

Padilla, David, and Elizabeth Houppert. 1993. International Election Observing: Enhancing the Principle of Free and Fair Elections. *Emory International Law Review* 7 (4): 73–132.

Pastor, Robert. 1987. The Reagan Administration and Latin America: Eagle Insurgent. In *Eagle Resurgent? The Reagan Era in American Foreign Policy,* edited by K. A. Oye, R. J. Lieber and D. Rothchild. Boston: Little, Brown, and Co.

———, ed. 1989. *Democracy in the Americas.* New York: Holmes and Meier.

———. 1990. Nicaragua's Choice: The Making of a Free Election. *Journal of Democracy* 1 (3): 13–25.

———. 2002. *Not Condemned to Repetition: The United States and Nicaragua.* Second Edition ed. Boulder: Westview Press.

———, and Jorge G. Castañeda. 1989. *Limits to Friendship: The United States and Mexico.* New York: Vintage Books.

Peceny, Mark. 1999. The Social Construction of Democracy. *Review of International Studies* 1 (1): 95–102.

Peck, F. Taylor. 1977. Latin America Enters the World Scene, 1900–1930. In *Latin American Diplomatic History: An Introduction,* edited by H. E. Davis, J. J. Finan and F. T. Peck. Baton Rouge: Louisiana State University Press.

Pellicer, Olga. 1995. Nuevas avenidas para la acción de la ONU: el debate sobre la intervención en asuntos internos de los estados. *Foro Internacional* 35 (4): 182–502.

Pérez, Andrés. 1992. The FSLN After the Debacle: The Struggle For The Definition of Sandinismo. *Journal of Interamerican Studies and World Affairs* 34 (1): 111–139.

Polanyi, Karl. 1944. *The Great Transformation: The Political and Economic Origins of Our Time*. Boston: Beacon Press.

Portales, Carlos. 1991. External Factors and the Authoritarian Regime. In *The Struggle for Democracy in Chile, 1982–1990,* edited by P. W. Drake and I. Jaksic. Lincoln: University of Nebraska Press.

———. 1991. The Transition to Democraty and US-Chilean Relations. In *From Dictatorship to Democracy: Rebuilding Political Consensus in Chile,* edited by J. S. Tulchin and A. Varas. Boulder: Lynne Rienner.

Price, George, and Christian Reus Smit. 1998. Dangerous Liasons? Critical International Theory and Constructivism. *European Journal of International Relations* 4 (3): 259–294.

Puryear, Jeffrey M. 1991. Building Democracy: Foreign Donors and Chile. New York.

———. 1994. *Thinking Politics: Intellectuals and Democracy in Chile, 1973–1988.* Baltimore: Johns Hopkins University Press.

Ragin, Charles C. 1987. *The Comparative Method.* Berkeley: University of California Press.

Ramírez, Sergio. 1999. *Adiós muchachos: Una memoria de la revolución sandiista.* Bogotá: Aguilar.

Reisman, Michael W. 1990. Sovereignty and Human Rights in Contemporary International Law. *American Journal of International Law* 84 (4): 866–876.

Reus-Smit, Christian. 1997. The Constitutional Structure of International Society and the Nature of Fundamental Institutions. *International Organization* 51 (4): 555–89.

———. Human Rights and the Social Construction of Sovereignty. *Review of International Studies* 27: 519–538.

Rich, Roland. 2001. Bringing Democracy into International Law. *Journal of Democracy* 12 (3): 20–34.

Rico, Carlos F. 1990. The Contadora Experience and the Future of Collective Security. In *Alternative to Intervention: A New U.S.-Latin American Security Relationship,* edited by R. J. Bloomfield and G. F. Treverton. Boulder: Lynne Rienner.

Risse-Kappen, Thomas. 1995. Bringing Transnational Relations Back-In: Introduction. In *Bringing Transnational Relations Back-In,* edited by T. Risse-Kappen. Cambridge: Cambridge University Press.

———. 2000. 'Let's Argue!': Communicative Action in World Politics. *International Organization* 54 (1): 1–39.

———, and Kathryn Sikkink. 1999. The Socialization of International Human Rights Norms into Domestic Practices: Introduction. In *The Power of Human Rights: International Norms and Domestic Change,* edited by T. Risse, S. C. Ropp and K. Sikkink. Cambridge: Cambridge University Press.

Roberts, Kenneth M. 1995. Neoliberalism and the Transformation of Populism in Latin America: The Peruvian Case. *World Politics* 48: 82–116.

Robinson, William I., and Kent Norsworthy. 1985. Elections and U. S. Intervention in Nicaragua. *Latin American Perspectives* 12 (2): 83–110.

Ronning, C. Neale. 1963. *Law and Politics in Inter-American Diplomacy.* New York: John Wiley & Sons.

Ropp, Stephen C., and Kathryn Sikkink. 1999. International Norms and Domestic Politics in Chile and Guatemala. In *The Power of Human Rights: International Norms and Domestic Change,* edited by T. Risse, S. C. Ropp and K. Sikkink. Cambridge: Cambridge University Press.

Rose, Gideon. 1998. Neoclassical Realism and Theories of Foreign Policy. *World Politics* 51: 144–72.

Rosenau, James N. 1997. *Along the Domestic-Foreign Frontier: Exploring Governance in a Turbulent World.* Cambridge: Cambridge University Press.

Ruggie, John Gerard. 1997. The Past as Prologue? Interests, Identity, and American Foreign Policy. *International Security* 21 (4): 89–125.

———. 1998. What Makes the World Hang Together? Neo-utilitarianism and the Social Constuctivis Challenge. *International Organization* 52 (4): 855–885.

Russett, Bruce. 1993. *Grasping the Democratic Peace: Principles for a Post-Cold War World.* Princeton: Princeton University Press.

Salinas de Gortari, Carlos. 2000. *México: un paso difícil a la modernidad.* Mexico City: Plaza & Janés.

Sánchez Susarrey, Jaime. 1993. México: perestroika sin glasnost? *Vuelta* (176): 47–51.

Santa Cruz, Arturo. 2000. *Un debate teórico empíricamente ilustrado: la construcción de la soberanía japonesa, 1853–1902.* Guadalajara: University of Guadalajara Press.

———. From Transition to Consolidation: Mexico's Long Road to Democracy. *Revista de Ciencia Política* 22 (1): 90–111.

Sartori, Giovanni. 1976. *Parties and Party Systems: A Framework for Analysis.* Cambridge: Cambridge University Press.

Schamis, Héctor E. 1991. Reconceptualizing Latin American Authoritarianism in the 1970s: From Bureaucratic-Authoritarianism to Neoconservatism. *Comparative Politics* 23 (2): 201–220.

Schmitter, Philippe. 1974. *Still the Century of Corporatism?* Edited by F. B. Pike and T. Stritch. University of Notre Dame Press ed, *The New Corporatism.* Notre Dame.

Schnably, Stephen J. 2000. Constitutionalism and Democratic Government in the Inter-American System. In *Democratic Governance and International Law,* edited by G. H. Fox and B. R. Roth. Cambridge: Cambrdige University Press.

Schweller, Randall L. 1992. Domestic Structure and Preventive War: Are Democracies More Pacific? *World Politics* 44: 235–269.

———. 2000. US Democracy Promotion: Realist Reflections. In *American Democracy Promotion: Impulses, Strategies, and Impacts,* edited by M. Cox, G. J. Ikenberry and T. Inoguchi. Oxford: Oxford University Press.

———, and David Priess. 1997. A Tale of Two Realisms: Expanding the Institutions Debate. *Mershon International Studies Review* 41: 1–32.

Searle, John R. 1995. *The Construction of Social Reality.* New York: Free Press.

Serrano Carreto, Mónica. 1996. La herencia del cambio gradual. Reglas e instituciones bajo Salinas. *Foro Internacional* 35 (1–2): 440–68.

Sikkink, Kathryn. 1993. The Power of Principled Ideas: Human Rights Policies in the United States and Western Europe. In *Ideas and Foreign Policy: Beliefs,*

Institutions, and Political Change, edited by J. Goldstein and R. O. Keohane. Ithaca: Cornell University Press.

———. 1997. Reconceptualizing Sovereignty in the Americas: Historical Precursors and Current Practices. *Houston Journal of International Law* 19 (3): 705–729.

Slater, Jerome. 1967. *The OAS and United States Foreign Policy:* Ohio State University.

Smith, Steve. 2000. US Democracy Promotion: Critical Questions. In *American Democracy Promotion,* edited by M. Cox, G. J. Ikenberry and T. Inoguchi. Oxford: Oxford University Press.

Smith, Tony. 1994. *America's Mission: The United States and the Worldwide Struggle for Democracy in the Twentieh Century.* Princeton: Pricenton University Press.

Stepan, Alfred. 1978. *The State and Society: Peru in Comparative Perspective.* Princeton: Princeton University Press.

———. 1988. Paths toward Redemocratization: Theoretical and Comparative Considerations. In *Transitions from Authoritarian Rule: Comparative Perspectives,* edited by G. O'Donnell, P. Schmitter and L. Whitehead. Baltimore: Jhons Hopkins University Press.

Sterling-Folker, Jennifer. 2000. Competing Paradigms or Birds of a Feather? Constructivism and Neoliberal Institutionalism. *International Studies Quarterly* 44: 97–119.

Stevens, Evelyn P. 1977. *Mexico's PRI: The Institutionalization of Corporatism?* Edited by J. Malloy. U of Pittsburgh Press ed, *Authoritarianism and Corporatism in Latin America.* Pittsburgh.

Stoelting, David. 1992. The Challenge of UN-Monitored Elections in Independent Nations. *Stanford Journal of International Law* 28: 371–424.

Tesón, Fernando R. 1987. Le Peuple, C'Est Moi! The World Court and Human Rights. *American Journal of International Law* 81 (1): 173–183.

Thérien, Jean-Phlippe, Michel Fortman, and Guy Gosselin. 1996. The Organization of American States: Restructuring Inter-American Multilateralism. *Global Governance* 2: 215–239.

Thomson, Janice E. 1995. State Sovereignty in International Relations: Bridging the Gap Between Theory and Empirical Research. *International Studies Quarterly* 39: 213–233.

Tironi, Eugenio. 1998. *El régimen autoritario: Para una sociología de Pinochet.* Santiago: Dolmen Ediciones.

Transparencia. 2000. Elecciones Generales 2000: Verificación del Padrón Electoral Inicial. Lima: Transparencia.

Triska, Jan F. 1986. Introduction. In *Dominant Powers and Subordinate States: The United States in Latin America and the Soviet Union in Eastern Europe,* edited by J. F. Triska. Durham: Duke University Press.

Unidad para la Promoción de la Democracia. 1996. Observaciones Electorales en Peru 1992–1993. Washington.

Unit for the Promotion of Democracy. 1997. Resumen Ejecutivo: Observacion Electoral Peru 1995. Washington, D.C.

———. 1999. Electoral Observation in Peru 1998. Washington, D.C.

United Nations. 1994. Analisis del Sistema Electoral Mexicano. In *Mision Técnica de la ONU*. New York.

———. 2004. *A More Secure World: Our Shared Responsibility.* Report of the Secreatary-General's High-level Panel on Threats, Challenges, and Change. New York.

United States Department of State. 1931. *Nicaragua*. Washington.

———. 1987. Democracy in Latin America and the Caribbean: The Promise and the Challenge. Washington.

Valenzuela, Arturo. 1990. Partidos políticos y crisis presidencial en Chile: Proposición para un gobierno parlamentario. In *Hacia una democraci moderna: La opción parlamentaria,* edited by O. Godoy Arcaya. Santiago: Universidad Católica de Chile.

———, and Pamela Constable. 1989. The Chilean Plebsicite: Defeat of a Dictator. *Current History* 88 (536): 129–132, 152–3.

Váli, Ferenc A. 1958. *Servitudes of International Law.* London: Sweet & Maxwell (1986 Reprint).

Van Evera, Stephen. 1990. Why Europe Matters, Why the Third World Doesn't: American Grand Strategy After the Cold War. *Journal of Strategic Studies* 13 (2): 1–51.

———. 1997. *Guide to Methods for Students of Political Science.* Ithaca: Cornell University Press.

Vanden, Harry E., and Gary Prevost. 1989. *Democracy and Socialism in Sandinista Nicaragua.* Boulder: Lynne Rienner.

Vázquez Murasa, Luciano. 1989. *Transición a la chilena.* Santiago: Editorial Barcelona.

Vera, Rodrigo. 1994. Ante la presión de Estados Unidos, Colosio anunció lo que rechazaba el presidente: se aceptarán observadores electorales extranjeros. *Proceso,* 3/14/1994, 10–13.

Walker, R. B. J. 2000. Both Globalization and Sovereignty: Re-Imagining the Political. In *Principled World Politics: The Challenge of Normative International Relations,* edited by P. Wapner and L. E. J. Ruiz. Lanham: Rowman & Littlefield.

Wallander, Celeste A. 1999. *Mortal Enemies, Best Friends: German-Russian Cooperation after the Cold War.* Ithaca: Cornell University Press.

Waltz, Kenneth N. 1979. *Theory of International Politics.* New York: McGraw-Hill.

———. 1997. Evaluating Theories. *American Political Science Review* 91 (4): 913–917.

———. 2000. Structural Realism after the Cold War. *International Security* 25 (1): 5–41.

Wambaugh, Sarah. 1933. *Plebiscites Since the World War: With a Collection of Official Documents Vol. 1.* Washington: Carnegie Endowment for International Peace.

Washington Office on Latin America. 1988. General Pinochet: Yes or No. The Chilean Plebiscite-5 October 1988. Washington: Washington Office on Latin America.

———. 1989. Chile's Transition to Democracy. Washington, D. C.

———. 1990. U.S. Electoral Assistance and Democratic Development: Chile, Nicaragua and Panama. Paper read at U.S. Electoral Assistance and Democratic Development: Chile, Nicaragua and Panama, January 19, 1990, at Washington, D. C.

———, and Academia Mexicana de Derechos Humanos. 1994. The 1994 Mexican Election: A Question of Credibility.

———, and George Washington University. 2000. Peace and Democratization in Peru: Advances, Setbacks, and Reflections on the 2000 Elections. Washington.

———, and International Human Rights Law Group. 1984. A Political Opening in Nicaragua. Washington, D. C.

Weber, Cynthia. 1992. Writing Sovereign Identities: Wilson Administration Intervention in the Mexican Revolution. *Alternatives* 17: 313–337.

———. 1995. *Simulating Sovereignty: Intervention, the State, and Symbolic Exchange.* Cambridge University Press ed. Cambridge.

Wendt, Alexander. 1998. On Constitution and Causation in International Relations. *Review of International Studies* 24: 101–117.

———. 1999. *Social Theory of International Politics.* Cambridge: Cambridge University Press.

———. 2000. On the Via Media: A Response to the Critics. *Review of International Studies* 26: 165–180.

———. 2001. Driving with the Rearview Mirror: On the Rational Science of Institutional Design. *International Organization* 55 (4): 1019–1049.

Wesson, Robert. 1986. Summary and Conclusions. In *Latin American Views of U.S. Policy,* edited by R. Wesson and H. Muñoz. New York: Praeger.

Weyland, Kurt. 1996. Neopopulism and Neoliberalism in Latin America: Unexpected Affinities. *Studies in Comparative International Development* 31 (3): 3–31.

Whitaker, Arthur P. 1954. *The Western Hemisphere Idea: Its Rise and Decline.* Ithaca: Cornell University Press.

Wight, Colin. 2004. State Agency: Social Action without Human Activity? *Review of International Studies* 30:269–280.

Wildavsky, Aaron. 1994. Why Self-Interest Means Less Outside of a Social Context: Cultural Contributions to a Theory of Rational Choices. *Journal of Theoretical Politics* 6 (2): 131–159.

Wiley, Peter Booth. 1990. *Yankees in the Land of Gods.* London: Viking.

Williams, Philip J. 1989. *The Catholic Church and Politics in Nicaragua and Costa Rica:* Macmillan.

———. 1990. Elections and Democratization in Nicaragua: The 1990 Elections in Perspective. *Journal of Interamerican Studies and World Affairs* 32 (4): 13–34.

———. 1994. Dual Transitions from Authoritarian Rule: Popular and Electoral Democracy in Nicaragua. *Comparative Politics* 26 (2): 169–185.

Wilson, Larman C. 1989. The OAS and Promoting Democracy and Resolving Disputes: Reactivation in the 1990s? *Revista Interamericana de Bibliografía* 39 (4): 477–499.

———, and David W. Dent. 1995. The United States and the OAS. In *U.S.—Latin American Policymaking: A Reference Handbook,* edited by D. W. Dent. Westport: Greenwood Press.

Wise, Carol. 1997. State Policy and Social Conflict in Peru. In *The Peruvian Labyrinth: Polity, Society, Economy,* edited by M. Cameron and P. Mauceri. University Park: Pennsylvania State University Press.

Wohlforth, William C. 1994/5. Realism and the End of the Cold War. *International Security* 19 (3): 91–129.

Youngers, Coletta A. 2000. Deconstructing Democracy: Peru Under President Alberto Fujimori. Washington: Washington Office on Latin America.

Zak, Marilyn Anne. 1987. Assisting Elections in the Third World. *Washington Quarterly* 10 (4): 175–193.

Zehfuss, Maja. 2001. Constructivism and Identity: A Dangerous Liaison. *European Journal of International Relations* 7 (3): 315–348.

Index

C

For Product Safety Concerns and Information please contact our EU representative GPSR@taylorandfrancis.com
Taylor & Francis Verlag GmbH, Kaufingerstraße 24, 80331 München, Germany

www.ingramcontent.com/pod-product-compliance
Ingram Content Group UK Ltd.
Pitfield, Milton Keynes, MK11 3LW, UK
UKHW040855180926
475701UK00001B/12
* 9 7 8 0 4 1 5 8 0 3 3 5 9 *